THE HOLY ALLIANCE

The Holy Alliance

LIBERALISM AND THE POLITICS OF FEDERATION

Isaac Nakhimovsky

PRINCETON UNIVERSITY PRESS

PRINCETON & OXFORD

Published by Princeton University Press
41 William Street, Princeton, New Jersey 08540
99 Banbury Road, Oxford OX2 6JX

press.princeton.edu

Library of Congress Cataloging-in-Publication Data

Names: Nakhimovsky, Isaac, 1979– author.
Title: The Holy Alliance : liberalism and the politics of federation / Isaac Nakhimovsky.
Description: Princeton ; Oxford : Princeton University Press, [2024] | Includes
    bibliographical references and index.
Identifiers: LCCN 2023038401 (print) | LCCN 2023038402 (ebook) |
    ISBN 9780691195193 (hardback) | ISBN 9780691255491 (ebook)
Subjects: LCSH: Holy Alliance. | Liberalism. | Federal government. |
    Europe—Politics and government. | Europe—History. | BISAC: HISTORY /
    Modern / 19th Century | POLITICAL SCIENCE / History & Theory
Classification: LCC D383 .N35 2024 (print) | LCC D383 (ebook) |
    DDC 320.51—dc23/eng/20230908
LC record available at https://lccn.loc.gov/2023038401
LC ebook record available at https://lccn.loc.gov/2023038402

British Library Cataloging-in-Publication Data is available

Editorial: Rob Tempio and Chloe Coy
Production Editorial: Ali Parrington
Jacket Design: Heather Hansen
Production: Erin Suydam
Publicity: William Pagdatoon

This book has been composed in Miller

Printed on acid-free paper. ∞

Printed in the United States of America

10 9 8 7 6 5 4 3 2 1

For Chitra, Maya, and Ashwin

CONTENTS

ACKNOWLEDGMENTS

THIS BOOK BEGAN to take shape in 2016, as an untimely reflection on systemic problems that had become more conspicuous in Britain and the United States but figure in many other contexts as well. By the time it was finished, writing this book had turned into a way of getting through a great deal else besides. I am grateful to my family, friends, neighbors, colleagues, students—and many others, near and far—who have kept me going through it all.

I have been lucky to learn from many generous and insightful interlocutors while writing this book. I am grateful to Michael Sonenscher for reading absolutely everything, as he has been doing ever since I first walked into his office in 2001. For commenting on earlier drafts, I am also grateful to Lauren Benton, Richard Bourke, Warren Breckman, Paul Bushkovitch, Holly Case, Graham Clure, Sandipto Dasgupta, Noah Dauber, Rohit De, Marcela Echeverri, David Engerman, Hussein Fancy, Bryan Garsten, Adom Getachew, Béla Kapossy, Duncan Kelly, Karuna Mantena, Iain McDaniel, Samuel Moyn, Paul North, Giulia Oskian, Mark Peterson, Eva Piirimäe, Steven Pincus, Michael Printy, Chitra Ramalingam, Sophie Rosenfeld, Lucia Rubinelli, Alexander Schmidt, Marci Shore, Anurag Sinha, Glenda Sluga, Timothy Snyder, Mark Somos, David Sorkin, Daniel Tetlow, Benjamin Tiven, Richard Tuck, Richard Whatmore, Jonathan Wyrtzen, and Nasser Zakariya. For opportunities to present parts of the project as it developed, I am grateful to the organizers of and participants in the following workshops, seminars, and conferences: the Amsterdam-Utrecht Global Intellectual History Seminar; the Quentin Skinner Lecture and Symposium at the University of Cambridge; the panel "Monarchy and Political Thought" at the conference "Monarchy and Modernity since 1500," also at the University at Cambridge; the International History Workshop at Columbia University; the Centre for Intellectual History at the University of Helsinki; the Kandersteg Seminar hosted by the Remarque Institute at New York University; the Research Colloquium in Modern History at the University of Lausanne; the panel "The Political Thought of the Enlightenment: From the Last Saxon King to the Congress of Vienna" at the Fourth International Congress of Polish History; the Triangle Intellectual History Seminar at the National Humanities Center; the Political Theory Workshop and the Global and International History Workshop, both at Yale University; and the conferences "Commercial Republicanism" and "The Invention of Federalism," both hosted by the Yale Center for the Study of Representative Institutions.

Most of this book was written during the two years of research leave afforded by a Morse Fellowship and later an Associate Professor Leave at Yale University; I also benefited from the support of the Frederick W. Hilles Publication Fund of Yale University. I owe special thanks to Rob Tempio and Chloe Coy, together with the rest of the team at Princeton University Press, for patiently smoothing the path to production; to Rene Almeling, Laura Barraclough, Leslie Gross-Wyrtzen, and Daniel HoSang for convening a memorably congenial and productive writing group in 2018; to Sandipto Dasgupta, Adom Getachew, Karuna Mantena, Giulia Oskian, and Anurag Sinha for the remote reading group that kept the lights on in 2020; to Florence Grant for her consummate writerly craft; to Jack Antholis, Grace Bu, Markus Hansen, Ava Hathaway-Hacker, Tanzi Sakib, and Christopher Sung for their research assistance; and to Graham Clure, Gabriel Groz, Alexander Nakhimovsky, Michael Printy, and Radoslaw Szymanski for intrepidly procuring sources that would otherwise have remained inaccessible to me.

My most special thanks of all are too special to enumerate here. They belong to Chitra, Maya, and Ashwin.

THE HOLY ALLIANCE

Introduction

THE HOLY ALLIANCE QUESTION

The masters of the world had united against the future.

—MAZZINI, "TOWARD A HOLY ALLIANCE OF THE PEOPLES"[1]

THE HOLY ALLIANCE was an idea of progress. This idea was linked to an eighteenth-century vision of an end to destructive rivalries among European states and empires: a vision associated with the thought of a celebrated Enlightenment figure, François de Salignac de la Mothe-Fénelon, archbishop of Cambrai. The Holy Alliance was also a label for reaction. In the nineteenth century, this label became a rhetorical weapon aimed against entrenched barriers to the assertion of collective agency: it was used to condemn the obsolete legacies of past conflicts that were no longer capable of meeting present or future needs. The Holy Alliance, finally, was a political intervention. It was a treaty, announced in 1815 by the emperor of Russia, Alexander I, aiming to build a durable new order by transforming a victorious military alliance against an aggressor into a reconciled community of nations. It became an important reference point during later moments of systemic change: "new holy alliances" were frequently identified throughout the twentieth century, from the founding of the League of Nations through the Cold War. The Holy Alliance is still worth revisiting in the twenty-first century because of how it gave rise to both the expectation of progress and the experience of reaction. Asking why it

---

1. Giuseppe Mazzini, "Toward a Holy Alliance of the Peoples," in *A Cosmopolitanism of Nations: Giuseppe Mazzini's Writings on Democracy, Nation Building, and International Relations*, ed. Stefano Recchia and Nadia Urbinati (Princeton: Princeton University Press, 2009), 117.

gave rise to both reveals the complexity of the underlying problems that the political intervention was originally supposed to address. The world of the Holy Alliance is not so distant as it might seem. The persistence of the problems it was supposed to address is a prompt to reconsider the expectations and experiences attached to many other "new holy alliances"—past and present.

At the end of March 1814, just two years after the burning of Moscow and Napoleon's disastrous retreat from Russia, Alexander peacefully entered Paris and proclaimed himself the "friend of the French people." The massive Russian army accompanying him conferred the power as well as the moral authority to herald the resolution of decades of conflict within and among European states following the French Revolution of 1789. A year later, negotiations toward a comprehensive postwar settlement at the Congress of Vienna were interrupted by Napoleon's sudden return from exile. His final defeat at the Battle of Waterloo in June 1815 was followed by a second occupation of Paris, this time spearheaded by a Prussian army, which promptly tried (but failed) to blow up the bridge over the Seine commemorating Napoleon's victory at Jena in 1806. The treaty of the Holy Alliance was a bid to reclaim the role that Alexander had assumed in 1814. It was privately signed in Paris on September 14/26, 1815, shortly before Alexander's return to Russia, by two of his wartime allies—the emperor of Austria and the king of Prussia—who were joined in November by the newly restored king of France. The prince regent of Great Britain did not formally sign it, on constitutional grounds, but instead circulated a private letter declaring his "entire concurrence in the principles" of the treaty.[2] Alexander then published the treaty together with a public manifesto issued in Saint Petersburg on Christmas of 1815. Read together, the texts of the treaty and manifesto jointly announced the beginning of a new era defined by the application of Christian moral principles to politics. According to these principles, the peoples of Europe, together with their governments, were to consider themselves members of "one Christian nation" that had "no other sovereign" but God; all states that accepted these principles were invited to accede to the alliance.[3]

2. "Letter of the Prince Regent to the Emperor of Russia, the Emperor of Austria and the King of Prussia," October 6, 1815, in Werner Näf, *Zur Geschichte der Heiligen Allianz* (Bern: Paul Haupt, 1928), 41.

3. "Sainte Alliance entre LL.MM. l'Empereur de toutes les Russies, l'Empereur d'Autriche et le Roi de Prusse, signé à Paris le 14/26 septembre 1815," in Näf, *Zur Geschichte der Heiligen Allianz*, 31–34.

When it first appeared, a British political dictionary of the 1840s recalled, "many liberal politicians throughout Europe, especially in Germany, looked to the Holy Alliance with most sanguine expectations of its happy results."[4] In 1816, and again in 1823, the Holy Alliance was declared to be "the most liberal of all ideas" by a former professor of logic and metaphysics at the University of Königsberg: not Immanuel Kant, the renowned philosopher who had died in 1804, but his immediate successor, the self-proclaimed liberal Wilhelm Traugott Krug.[5] Krug was joined by a wide variety of others—not only in Germany but also in Britain, France, the Netherlands, Denmark, Switzerland, and even New England—who saw the Holy Alliance as the dawning of a peaceful and prosperous age of progress. From their perspective, the purpose of the Holy Alliance was to avert the dismal specter of modern Europe's decline and fall, of national hatred, class warfare, financial collapse, and demographic catastrophe. The Holy Alliance would supply a definitive resolution to the Anglo-French imperial rivalry whose effects had been felt around the world. It would stabilize the European balance of power and inaugurate a more robust legal order that provided for collective security as well as national autonomy. It would give rise to representative institutions throughout Europe, together with a federal constitution: structures within which atavistic fetters on social and economic progress could gradually be eliminated, placing political authority under the guidance of public opinion without repeatedly unleashing the volatile dynamics of revolution and reaction. The ecumenical form of Christianity espoused by the Holy Alliance would foster the formation of a robust pan-European civic culture, marked by religious toleration, the peaceful coexistence of diverse nationalities, and the responsible exercise of expanding liberties. Finally, the Holy Alliance would advance the cause of liberty globally: not only by emancipating Greece from Ottoman rule but also by transforming the economy of the Atlantic world. There, in addition to universalizing the abolition of the slave trade and guaranteeing the independence of Haiti, it would help reverse the global expansion of extractive systems powered by unfree labor.

4. "Holy Alliance," in *Political Dictionary: Forming a Work of Universal Reference, Both Constitutional and Legal: And Embracing the Terms of Civil Administration, of Political Economy and Social Relations, and of All the More Important Statistical Departments of Finance and Commerce* (London: Charles Knight and Co., 1845), 2:92.

5. In 1816, it was "die liberalste aller Ideen," in 1823, "die allerliberalste." Wilhelm Traugott Krug, *La sainte alliance: Oder Denkmal des von Oestreich, Preußen und Rußland geschloßnen heiligen Bundes* (Leipzig: H. A. Koechly, 1816), 42–43; Wilhelm Traugott Krug, *Geschichtliche Darstellung des Liberalismus alter und neuer Zeit: Ein historischer Versuch* (Leipzig: F. A. Brockhaus, 1823), 149.

The pathologies that had given rise to these systems would be displaced by a new collective imperial project. Under the aegis of the Holy Alliance, Europe would take its place in a new global economy, freed from the distortions caused by the militarism of Europe's feudal past and anchored in the continental expanses of the Russian Empire as well as the Americas.

These expectations have long been overwritten by subsequent developments. In the 1820s, the Holy Alliance came to be associated with the Carlsbad Decrees of 1819, which cracked down on the press and universities throughout Germany. The Holy Alliance also came to be associated with the expansive right to international intervention asserted by Russia, Austria, and Prussia in 1820. In 1821, Austria invaded Naples to suppress the liberal constitution that the king had granted there under pressure; in 1823, France invaded Spain in similar circumstances. Many liberals feared further interventions against the independence of Spain's former American colonies; these did not occur, but neither did the intervention many liberals did want, in support of the Greek Revolution of 1821. Looking back after the revolutions of 1848, the exiled Italian patriot Giuseppe Mazzini declared that "the masters of the world had united against the future." According to Mazzini, the Holy Alliance had come to encompass all who had joined the Russian emperor in his efforts "to prevent progress and protect the oppressors" restored to power after the defeat of Napoleon. Sooner or later, Mazzini promised, this reactionary conspiracy would fall, and the future would belong to the democratic nation-state.[6] Mazzini's words still resonate. The Holy Alliance is still remembered as "inaugurating a period of reaction disastrous for liberal principles," whereas Anglo-American resistance to the Holy Alliance "saved the spirit of republicanism" and "kept the principle of democratic nationalism alive at a time when it was being repressed in Europe itself."[7] Meanwhile, the erosion of the nation-state as a site of political agency, and the persistence of structures less responsive to democratic action, like the European Union, can still be attributed to an "unholy alliance against sovereignty."[8]

In the first instance, this book sets out to render intelligible a set of political judgments that are missing from Mazzini's story and that still

6. Mazzini, "Toward a Holy Alliance of Peoples," 117–18.

7. Helena Rosenblatt, *The Lost History of Liberalism: From Ancient Rome to the Twenty-First Century* (Princeton: Princeton University Press, 2018), 67; Mark Mazower, *Governing the World: The History of an Idea* (New York: Penguin, 2012), 9.

8. Christopher J. Bickerton, Philip Cunliffe, and Alexander Gourevitch, eds., *Politics without Sovereignty: A Critique of Contemporary International Relations* (Abingdon: University College London Press, 2007), 2.

seem wildly implausible in hindsight: why Krug and others initially welcomed the proclamation of the Holy Alliance in 1815 as an emancipatory project. They could do so because the Holy Alliance initially registered as an implementation of eighteenth-century ideas about constitutional reform, prosperity, and peace. Liberal hopes could be invested in the Holy Alliance because of arguments made by a series of eighteenth-century writers, most prominently François Marie Arouet de Voltaire, about the rise of Russia. These writers had identified a historical process that was turning Russia into a force for universal emancipation, capable of fundamentally transforming the behavior of European states and empires. In eighteenth-century terms, they had fashioned Russia into an *ami des hommes* or "friend of mankind": a state capable of assuming responsibility for collective security and prosperity. This role, which went on to become a recurring if indistinctly named fixture of European and indeed global politics, was originally defined in opposition to imperial consolidation on the one hand and an ideal world of self-sufficiently sovereign states on the other. The liberal idea of the Holy Alliance linked this federative strategy for bringing about "perpetual peace" to a version of Christianity that resonated across the Protestant world, including in circles associated with the emerging Anglo-American movements to abolish slavery and war.

The point of reconstructing these ideas here is not to call into question the reactionary outcome of the Holy Alliance. Nor is it to tell a predictably tragic story about how the Holy Alliance ultimately failed to live up to its ideals—or to tell a similarly predictable story about how those ideals might be fulfilled by others.[9] Instead, this book begins by asking how anyone could possibly have formed a liberal idea of the Holy Alliance in the first place. From Mazzini's perspective, the Holy Alliance had always been dedicated to stifling aspirations to democracy and national self-determination throughout Europe, and perhaps in the Americas too. From the opposing perspective, meanwhile, the Holy Alliance was nothing more than an inconsequential diplomatic anomaly: it had briefly surfaced in 1815 due to the influence of the Livonian religious figure Juliane von Krüdener, whom the Russian emperor saw regularly in Paris. According to the British foreign secretary, Lord Castlereagh, the resulting treaty was "a piece of sublime mysticism and nonsense"; according to his Austrian counterpart, Clemens

---

9. On the underlying determinism of such approaches, see Samuel Moyn, "On the Nonglobalization of Ideas," in *Global Intellectual History*, ed. Samuel Moyn and Andrew Sartori (New York: Columbia University Press, 2013), 187–204; Adom Getachew, "Universalism after the Post-Colonial Turn: Interpreting the Haitian Revolution," *Political Theory* 44, no. 6 (2016): 821–45.

von Metternich, it was "a loud-sounding nothing."[10] These pronouncements are still frequently cited out of context when in fact, as we shall see, Castlereagh and Metternich were actively working to redefine Alexander's treaty as an awkward expression of his personal religious sentiments. Rather than reproducing any of these verdicts, this book investigates the liberal idea of the Holy Alliance by setting out from the assessments of Alexander's treaty developed by two less familiar but well-connected figures: Frédéric-César de la Harpe and Adam Jerzy Czartoryski. Both had long-standing ties to Russia as well as revolutionary backgrounds that had integrated them into prominent international networks: La Harpe was a former Swiss revolutionary who had served as Alexander's tutor; Czartoryski was a former Polish revolutionary who had become his foreign minister. Each navigated great power diplomacy with the close attention of those whose countries are especially exposed to its outcomes.

Both La Harpe and Czartoryski were highly critical of the Holy Alliance itself. But at the end of the 1820s, unlike fellow liberals who condemned it as the essence of reactionary politics, both still asserted the emancipatory purpose of what La Harpe called the "initial conception" of the Holy Alliance, as opposed to its "subsequent development."[11] La Harpe and Czartoryski still recognized the Holy Alliance as an unsuccessful version of a familiar process of legal and political change: a process to which both had dedicated themselves following the disappointment of their respective efforts to liberate their own countries through direct revolutionary action and wars of national liberation. Unlike Czartoryski, whose efforts to liberate Poland through Russian intervention came to a calamitous end in 1830, La Harpe continued to regard his parallel efforts to liberate Switzerland as a success: "English diplomacy never intervened in Switzerland except to restore the patricians of the old regime," he wrote. "The Swiss people owes it to Russia alone that the federal pact contains the seeds of liberalism."[12] Behind these divergent outcomes was a widely shared set of expectations. La Harpe's efforts show why the proclamation of the Holy Alliance could be recognized as a performance of Enlighten-

10. Castlereagh to Liverpool, September 28, 1815, in Charles K. Webster, *British Diplomacy, 1813–1815: Select Documents Dealing with the Reconstruction of Europe* (London: G. Bell and Sons, 1921), 383; Clemens Wenzel Lothar Metternich, *Aus Metternich's nachgelassenen papieren*, vol. 1 (Wien: W. Braumüller, 1880), 216.

11. Frédéric-César de la Harpe, "Aux Rédacteurs du Globe," *Le Globe*, August 15, 1829, 517.

12. *Correspondance de Frédéric-César de La Harpe et Alexandre Ier: Suivie de la correspondance de F.-C. de La Harpe avec les membres de la famille impériale de Russie*, ed. Jean Charles Biaudet and Françoise Nicod (Neuchâtel: Éditions de la Baconnière, 1978), 3:409.

ment politics: a politics premised on the communication of private under-standings, which were expected to issue in public actions. And Czarto-ryski's efforts show why the Holy Alliance could be recognized as a stage in a legislative process: as a form of constitutional politics formally theorized by eighteenth-century authorities on the law of nations as well as the pub-lic law of the Holy Roman Empire. The liberal idea of the Holy Alliance articulated by Krug and others represents the merger of these political arguments with a further set of claims about progress and religion.

Considering the Holy Alliance in this way turns a minor diplomatic anomaly into a central episode in a broader picture of the history of political thought. It also shows that an episode usually dismissed as a fleet-ing "retrogression to antiquated forms" in the history of international law actually points toward the construction of new roles for public opinion and constitutional politics in shaping the structure and practice of relations among European states and empires.[13] La Harpe and Czartoryski were deeply embedded in overlapping intellectual networks emanating from Paris and London, which they repeatedly mobilized in support of their respective campaigns to liberate Switzerland and Poland (and by extension, transform European politics and the Atlantic economy) via Russia. Tracing these international networks introduces a whole new cast of characters into the intellectual history of the Holy Alliance: figures such as the English abolitionist Thomas Clarkson, the radical poet Helen Maria Williams, and the legal reformer Jeremy Bentham; the French republican political econo-mist Jean-Baptiste Say; and the American statesman Thomas Jefferson. This approach makes it possible to take advantage of the substantial theo-retical content of the correspondence and journals and treatises that were implicated in the campaigns waged by La Harpe and Czartoryski: sources that can help explain the reasons why these Swiss and Polish revolution-ary patriots, followed by Krug and a variety of other contemporary liber-als, came to think that Russia could play the emancipatory role they had assigned it—and how they thought it might do so—with far greater preci-sion than the diplomatic record can supply on its own.

These reasons turn out not only to be intelligible but to overlap in sig-nificant ways (both historically and conceptually) with other expressions of liberalism, including more familiar ones. This overlap presents a chal-lenge to standard typologies that are often applied not only to the Holy

13. Wilhelm G. Grewe, *The Epochs of International Law*, trans. Michael Byers (Ber-lin: Walter de Gruyter, 2000), 361. On Grewe, see Matthew Specter, *The Atlantic Real-ists: Empire and International Political Thought between Germany and the United States* (Stanford: Stanford University Press, 2022), chap. 4.

Alliance but also to the broader landscape of nineteenth-century political history and intellectual life (such as liberalism and reaction, democracy and monarchy, new and old world). It also opens up a challenging new comparative perspective. The absence of any enduring political identity built around the Holy Alliance as the fulfillment of a liberal ideal helps make it a promising historical site for investigating a revealing disjuncture between expectation and experience. Recovering liberal expectations of what the Holy Alliance was supposed to become is a way of developing a new understanding of what liberals experienced: an approach that avoids either conflating expectations with experience or lapsing into a potentially arbitrary substitution of one retrospective representation of the past for another.[14] The various hopes and fears projected onto Russia after 1815, and aroused by it in turn, may be unedifying as sources of information about Russia itself. But such projections, then as now, can reveal a great deal about the projectors, about what they believe as well as what they prefer to hear: at home as well as abroad. As Friedrich Engels once observed about European views of Russia after 1815, "Once again Europe was befooled in an incredible fashion. To the Princes and the Reactionaries, Tsardom preached Legitimacy and the maintaining of the *status quo*; to the Liberal Philistine, the deliverance of oppressed nations—and both believed it."[15]

There is no reason to suppose that the liberal ideas attached to the Holy Alliance were somehow less liberal than other more familiar versions of liberalism. The first history of liberalism was published by Krug in 1823, and the importance of his inaugural contribution to that genre is still acknowledged—even though Krug's canonization of the Holy Alliance as "the most liberal of all ideas" has gone missing from accounts of the history of liberalism.[16] Yet it would be arbitrary to exclude Krug or his arguments from a canon that recognizes his Swiss contemporary Benjamin Constant—a thinker whom Krug praised and whose ideas were so closely related to Krug's—as the "founding father of modern liberalism."[17] Krug's

14. For an illuminating discussion of such concerns, see Martin Jay, "Intention and Irony: The Missed Encounter between Hayden White and Quentin Skinner," *History and Theory* 52, no. 1 (2013): 32–48.

15. Frederick Engels, "The Foreign Policy of Russian Tsardom," *Time*, May 1890, 526–27.

16. Krug's own endorsement of the Holy Alliance has also gone missing: "Krug's history of liberalism was quite obviously a rejoinder to the pretensions of the so-called Holy Alliance." Rosenblatt, *The Lost History of Liberalism*, 79.

17. Helena Rosenblatt, *Liberal Values: Benjamin Constant and the Politics of Religion* (Cambridge: Cambridge University Press, 2008), 3.

history began with Socrates, celebrated Fénelon, and culminated with the Holy Alliance. It anticipated by a century a development discerned by Duncan Bell in Anglophone writing about liberalism: in the shadow of World War I, and then in tandem with the emergence of the idea of "totalitarianism," "liberalism" was introduced as a concept or tradition serving as a repository for the defining values of Western civilization.[18] The problem with such canonizing efforts is that the strong assumptions they require tend to resolve political complexity into reductively moralized categories. A variety of ideas, including incompatible ones, have become liberal in different ways under different circumstances. The Holy Alliance has been invoked as a threat to national sovereignty by Mazzini and others seeking to define a liberal idea of the state; but it has also been invoked as an ideal by those seeking to define liberalism in opposition to the state. In fact, the liberal ideas of the Holy Alliance discussed in this book were not defined in opposition to the state: they were premised on the emancipatory exercise of state power. Instead of serving to define either a liberal idea of the state or a liberal alternative to the state, the history of the Holy Alliance shows how such efforts to deploy or confine state power rely on a strategy for harmonizing the state's internal and external relations—and on an assessment of the social conditions capable of sustaining this alignment. The history of the Holy Alliance also shows how such political strategies can come to be identified with and redefined by divergent views of progress and religion. The Holy Alliance was seen as a religious barrier to liberal progress; but it was also identified with liberal progress by those who located the moral foundations of liberalism in religion. Some of those who embraced the values enshrined in the "Declaration of the Rights of Man and Citizen" of 1789 recoiled from the religious content of the Holy Alliance; but others welcomed it as the articulation of a new religious consensus around those values. From both perspectives, the Holy Alliance also represented an attempt to revive the emancipatory promise of Enlightenment politics in response to the perceived failures of the French Revolution. "I am still the same," La Harpe complained in 1822, "and will never be diverted from my old path," despite "having been successively designated as sans-culotte, democrat, terrorist, Jacobin, Bonapartist, liberal"; now that he found himself called a "carbonario," he could only surmise that "good sense, justice and reason rank among the elements of carbonarism."[19]

18. Duncan Bell, "What Is Liberalism?" *Political Theory* 42, no. 6 (2014): 682–715.

19. Frédéric-César de la Harpe to Heinrich Zschokke, October 12, 1822, in *Lettres inédites de Frédéric-César de La Harpe à Etienne Dumont et à la famille Duval (1822 à 1831)*, ed. Jean Martin (Lausanne: s.n., 1929), 42–43.

This book is an attempt to capture the complexity of the conceptual resources available for navigating the postrevolutionary ferment of early nineteenth-century Europe: to show how they were incorporated into theories of progress while being deployed for new political purposes via new forms of communication. Approached in this way, the Holy Alliance reveals the kind of disjuncture between expectation and experience extensively analyzed by Reinhart Koselleck, which in his view began to assume a form characteristic of modern politics in the decades around the turn of the nineteenth century.[20] Unlike Koselleck's approach to "conceptual history," however, the story told in this book is not predicated on an effort to deduce "metahistorical" categories of experience and expectation. Instead, it is firmly focused on the immediate questions that the Holy Alliance posed for contemporaries, together with the questions that it was supposed by them to answer: questions in the sense of dense aggregations of interrelated problems to be solved (such as, for example, "The Social Question" or "The Jewish Question"), articulated through public debate in a range of registers, all in the sense that Holly Case has described as characteristic of the "Age of Questions."[21] In short, the history told in this book is a history of what might have been (but was not, at least until now) called "The Holy Alliance Question." Underlying the initial responses to the Holy Alliance was a question about federative politics: to what extent was it possible to legalize the external as well as internal relations of the state, to make international politics constitutional? What sort of European, or global, economy did such a politics presuppose, and what endowed Russia and its emperor with the capacity as well as the commitment to achieve it? In France, as is well known, the restoration of the monarchy after 1814 could be welcomed as the elimination of a revolutionary aberration, or opposed as a regression to a reactionary past; but it could also be perceived as an initial stage in the emergence of a liberal future. The Holy Alliance

20. See Reinhart Koselleck, *Futures Past: On the Semantics of Historical Time*, trans. Keith Tribe (Cambridge, MA: MIT Press, 1985). For a helpful recent discussion, see Sean Franzel and Stefan-Ludwig Hoffmann, "Introduction: Translating Koselleck," in *Sediments of Time: On Possible Histories*, by Reinhart Koselleck (Stanford: Stanford University Press, 2018), ix–xxxi. Liberal expectations of the Holy Alliance can also be described as a variant of the kind of historical analysis and speculation whose history has been told by Catherine Gallagher. See Catherine Gallagher, *Telling It like It Wasn't: The Counterfactual Imagination in History and Fiction* (Chicago: University of Chicago Press, 2018).

21. Holly Case, *The Age of Questions, or, A First Attempt at an Aggregate History of the Eastern, Social, Woman, American, Jewish, Polish, Bullion, Tuberculosis, and Many Other Questions over the Nineteenth Century, and Beyond* (Princeton: Princeton University Press, 2018). For Case's perceptive comments on Koselleck, see 14, 228–29.

projected these possibilities onto a supranational stage and gave them a federal shape. Could federative politics serve as a strategy for liberal progress, or was it a pathway to reaction? Had the postwar settlement merely replaced one form of domination with another? Did it portend the long-awaited decline and fall of European civilization, collapsing through internal divisions only to be overrun by Russian armies? Or did the appearance of the Holy Alliance present an opportunity for emancipation and reconciliation, and perhaps the birth of a federal Europe?

By 1848, for Mazzini and many of his contemporaries, these questions had acquired definitive answers. For Karl Marx and Friedrich Engels, the Holy Alliance represented a broad consensus against revolutionary change. This consensus extended from conservatives like Metternich to liberals like the French historian and politician François Guizot. All were aligned against the "specter" that, in the words of the *Communist Manifesto*, was "haunting Europe": "All the powers of old Europe have entered into a *holy alliance* to exorcise this specter: Pope and Czar, Metternich and Guizot, French Radicals and German police-spies."[22] Understanding why a holy alliance could be seen as both emancipatory and reactionary in the first place calls for a new history of the liberal idea of the Holy Alliance: a history of utilitarians and evangelicals, political economists and abolitionists, French—and English—radicals and German philosophers. This is a history that begins in the Enlightenment and points ahead to the "new holy alliances" identified during the systemic changes of the twentieth century. Its discomfiting but also potentially empowering conclusion is that neither the advocates of emancipatory holy alliances nor the critics of reactionary ones have definitively addressed the kinds of problems that the Holy Alliance was originally supposed to solve. From this perspective, the liberal idea of the nation-state associated with Mazzini does not represent an escape from these problems but their development in a new form. Reopening "The Holy Alliance Question" is a way of exposing some of the strong assumptions that have come to shape perceptions of past and present politics—and may also inhibit the invention of new political possibilities.[23]

22. Karl Marx and Friedrich Engels, *The Communist Manifesto*, ed. Gareth Stedman Jones (London: Penguin, 2002), 218. "Holy alliance" appears in the English translation authorized by Engels; the German original referred to a "heilige Hetzjagd," which the initial English translation had rendered as a "holy crusade." On the original phrase, see Terrell Carver, "Translating Marx," *Alternatives: Global, Local, Political* 22, no. 2 (1997): 195–97.

23. On "inventiveness" in politics, see Raymond Geuss, "What Is Political Judgement?" in *Political Judgement*, ed. Richard Bourke and Raymond Geuss (Cambridge: Cambridge University Press, 2009), 29–46.

The first chapter of this book introduces the Holy Alliance through a survey of contemporary images depicting the Holy Alliance and the consequences of Russian intervention in European politics. The dense, historically specific meanings of these images dispel long entrenched interpretations of the Holy Alliance as either the reactionary foil for the emergence of liberalism or an ephemeral expression of religious romanticism without real political consequence. Unfamiliar contemporary images of the Holy Alliance resist such polarized narratives. They challenge deceptively reductive approaches to questions of progress and reaction by opening up much broader contexts for the religious and political content of the Holy Alliance. They reveal divergences among expectations as well as experiences of the Holy Alliance—and make it possible to explore the legal and economic as well as moral and religious reasons why it generated expectations of liberal progress. From this perspective, the "holy" in the Holy Alliance signaled a form of Christianity embraced by many liberals (some of whom identified it with Fénelon) and closely connected to the Protestant narratives of redemption associated with contemporary Anglo-American efforts to abolish slavery and war; the "alliance" signaled a constitutional transition to a federative form of politics that promised to establish and maintain the material conditions for fulfilling such emancipatory ideals. The four central chapters of the book that follow examine how the Holy Alliance became a site for fusing federative politics with liberal narratives of progress—and demonstrate the complexity of evaluating federative politics more generally.

Chapter 2 shows how the emancipatory role assigned to Russia and associated with the Holy Alliance was forged at the intersection of two prolific Enlightenment debates, which were shaped by Fénelon's moral vision and whose participants included Voltaire. One of these was about "perpetual peace," the subject of a large literature addressing the problem of escalating competition among European states. When the Seven Years War dashed Voltaire's hopes that a stabilized balance of power between Britain and France could become the core of a new federal system, Voltaire helped inaugurate a second debate about the implications of Russia's rapid expansion and development for the progress of what now began to be called "civilization." The confluence of these two debates produced the idea of Russia acting the part of an *ami des hommes* or "friend of mankind." The moral attributes of this eighteenth-century figure have been associated with the emergence of a cosmopolitan sensibility as well as the rise of national citizenship, but it also came to signify a state's capacity to take individual responsibility for collective security and prosperity. Very different understandings of the qualities and course of action that would enable the Russian Empire to assume such a role were advanced by writers on Russia ranging from the Anglican cleric John Brown to the French philosophe Denis Diderot: their contrasting positions on the relationship between the moral and material aspects of the progress of civilization stand behind the later divergence of liberal reactions to the religious content of the Holy Alliance. These eighteenth-century questions about Russia's potential to serve as an *ami des hommes*, solving Europe's problems from the outside, were posed with renewed urgency after the defeat of Napoleon in Russia in 1812, and in light of Alexander's entry into Paris in 1814. To Germaine de Staël and other contemporary liberals, Alexander's association with Krüdener in 1815 and her apparent influence on the religious content of the Holy Alliance looked very different than they did to diplomats like Castlereagh and Metternich. For Staël, the appearance of the Holy Alliance confirmed that Alexander was indeed acting as an agent of universal reconciliation, and that Krüdener had in fact helped him summon a form of Christianity that could serve as the indispensable moral foundation for liberal politics.

The third and fourth chapters of this book connect Enlightenment debates about Russia and perpetual peace to the Holy Alliance by examining the careers of La Harpe and Czartoryski. Following the failure of their respective revolutionary efforts in the 1790s, each set out to channel Russian power into an instrument for transforming European politics. Chapter 3 focuses on La Harpe's efforts, richly documented in his extensive correspondence with Alexander (which he later annotated). La Harpe's campaign had already begun to take shape in the early 1790s, while he was still serving as Alexander's tutor in the court of Catherine II; it resumed after Alexander came to power in 1801, when La Harpe revisited Saint Petersburg, having been ousted as director of the revolutionary Helvetic Republic. Through his correspondence, La Harpe fashioned Alexander into an *ami des hommes*. Following in the footsteps of the eighteenth-century Parisian literary establishment, and using the rhetorical strategies of sentimental literature, La Harpe circulated his testimony of Alexander's private republican sentiments across the international networks he accessed through the Parisian salon of Helen Maria Williams: networks that enabled La Harpe to instigate a private correspondence between Alexander and the newly elected president of the United States, Thomas Jefferson. In a variation on a classic Enlightenment script, La Harpe expected these private understandings to issue in transformative public actions. Alexander's allies would help supply the Russian Empire with the capital, expertise, and population growth it needed in order to assume a course of development similar to the one Jefferson and others envisaged for the United States of America. In enhancing the capacities of the Russian state in this way, Alexander's allies would also be assuming the function of international public opinion: authorizing and guiding him to deploy Russian prestige and power against the recalcitrant political establishments governing European states and empires. In 1814, Alexander transposed his former teacher's script into his own campaign of public diplomacy during his stays in Paris and London; in 1815 he pursued it again in promulgating his treaty of the Holy Alliance. Alexander now deployed a religious idiom that La Harpe (and Jefferson) found distasteful, but was greeted enthusiastically by many others. In place of La Harpe, it was now a different set of actors—not only Krüdener but also leading reformers in London, like Thomas Clarkson—who circulated their testimony of their private understandings with Alexander. As before, such testimony served to authenticate Alexander's capacity to serve as an *ami des hommes*, guiding the projection of Russian power while also enlisting liberals in developing and populating the Russian Empire. Notably, Clarkson's testimony circulated as far as Haiti, where it was recognized and acted upon by King Henri Christophe and his court in a bid to guarantee Haitian independence from the threat of another French invasion.

The fourth chapter of this book links Czartoryski's efforts to secure Poland's future to a series of debates about federal constitutionalism that played out in eighteenth-century literature on the law of nations and public law. As a teenage visitor to Paris and London in the late 1780s, Czartoryski had encountered two influential international networks, one connected to the French philosopher the Marquis de Condorcet and the other to the former British prime minister, the Earl of Shelburne. Both were associated with advocacy for American independence and its benefits for Europe; both were aligned with hopes that the reconciliation of Britain and France could inaugurate a new legal order whose structure would emerge through the promulgation of treaties enshrining free trade. This approach was defined against the idea of consolidating Europe under a supranational authority (as an earlier French writer, the Abbé de Saint-Pierre, had famously proposed in his plan for perpetual peace). It was also defined against the alternative of relying on a system of sovereign states to learn how to align their particular interests (an ideal most closely associated with the Swiss jurist Emer de Vattel). Instead, this approach displaced responsibility for collective security and prosperity onto the internal constitutions and capacities of the state or states legislating the new treaty system. Czartoryski tried twice to revive this approach and initiate it from Russia by reactivating the connections he had made in Paris and London in the 1780s: first in 1803–5, at the outset of Alexander's reign, and again in 1814–15, when he expected Alexander to appoint him to govern Poland as part of the postwar settlement. On the former occasion, Czartoryski's key collaborator was his own former tutor in Paris, Scipione Piattoli: a well-connected Florentine who had played a key role in promulgating the Polish Constitution of 1791, and who is best known as the inspiration for the Abbé Morio (a character in Leo Tolstoy's novel *War and Peace*). In 1814, Czartoryski's collaborator was the English jurist and philosopher Jeremy Bentham: before the English utilitarians of the nineteenth century famously came to regard colonial India as their best opportunity to put their theories into practice, Bentham (together with his entrepreneurial brother Samuel) had looked to the Russian Empire. Though neither of these collaborations achieved its goals, Czartoryski remained committed to the approach he had encountered in the 1780s and reasserted it in a treatise he composed in the 1820s: a treatise that recognized the Holy Alliance as another unsuccessful version of this approach to federalism. This history of Czartoryski's efforts connects the Holy Alliance to a liberal constitutionalism that was defined by its critics as a plot to suppress national sovereignty, but could also be understood as reviving the federal ideals of the 1780s. The persistence of this understanding explains why the French socialist Pierre-Joseph Proudhon—a critic of Mazzini's ideal of the nation-state—could later describe the Holy Alliance as an important stage in the development of a federal Europe.

The fifth chapter of this book shows how, in the early 1820s, the Holy Alliance was integrated into a variety of narratives of progress, including Krug's inaugural history of liberalism. Krug's philosophy of history drew on Kant's approach to the history of religion as well as his theory of the state. The history of liberalism Krug published in 1823 identified the Holy Alliance with Kant's ideal of an ethical community whose universality transcended the necessarily pluralistic world of politics. According to others in the 1820s, however—most importantly, the Danish German banker Conrad Friedrich von Schmidt-Phiseldek, the exiled Danish geographer Conrad Malte-Brun, and the French philosopher Henri de Saint-Simon—the same historical process that had produced the Holy Alliance also pointed ahead to the political unification of the "Christian nation" in a federal state with a liberal constitution and a collective imperial mission. This historical process was theorized in aesthetic, economic, and legal terms that collectively amounted to a new iteration of earlier debates about the moral and material progress of civilization—and that provoked a sharp response from the Catholic writers Joseph de Maistre and Félicité de Lamennais, as well as the philosopher Auguste Comte. Finally, the Holy Alliance was also integrated into theories of progress by prominent Anglo-American reformers, including James Stephen, a member of the "Clapham Sect" of British abolitionists. For Stephen, as for Noah Worcester (the founder of the Massachusetts Peace Society), the Holy Alliance was the product of a providential process leading to the redemption of the Atlantic world from the sins of slavery and war. These expectations were challenged by Alexander Hill Everett, an American man of letters and diplomat stationed in Europe during the 1820s. Everett drew on the thought of the English political economist Thomas Malthus to integrate the Holy Alliance into a history of European unification through a very different kind of providential process. Everett wrote primarily for an American audience but was also translated and debated in Europe. His analysis creates an opportunity to place the liberal idea of the Holy Alliance in a new comparative perspective with schemes to reform the British Empire as well as the two other great federal projects of the 1820s that Everett also wrote about: the United States of America and Gran Colombia. From this perspective, it was no accident that the constitutional challenges confronting the United States of America in the 1820s, such as the crisis provoked by the admission of Missouri to the federal union, prompted some commentators to invoke analogies to the Holy Alliance.

The continuing proliferation of such historical analogies can serve as a map for tracking how some of the problems raised by the Holy Alliance continued to reappear in new forms under new circumstances. This map reveals some less-familiar trails through the twentieth century. From World War I through the end of the Cold War, attempts to assess the possibilities of postwar politics repeatedly appealed to precedents defined by the post-Napoleonic settlement of 1815. In this context, "new holy alliances" were frequently invoked, most often and most colorfully by critics of the League of Nations and of Woodrow Wilson's liberal internationalism. However, they were also invoked by advocates for new systems of international legal arbitration; by those mobilizing collective resistance to fascism; and by those envisaging reconciliation after its defeat, particularly in the form of Christian Democratic politics. It was in a different spirit, however, that the French historian Guillaume Bertier de Sauvigny published an anthology of sources on the Holy Alliance in 1972. Compiled in the wake of the student protests of 1968, Bertier de Sauvigny's anthology was designed to enable students to immerse themselves in contemporary judgments as well as historiographical assessments of the Holy Alliance. Doing so, Bertier de Sauvigny explained, would teach them to draw historical analogies in ways that resisted "hasty conclusions and peremptory judgments," but instead helped cultivate a critical perspective on modern history that would equip them to exercise finer political judgment.[24] Instead of rehearsing old slogans about conspiracies against peoples, Bertier de Sauvigny suggested that his readers connect Alexander's proclamation of the Holy Alliance in 1815 to Woodrow Wilson's rhetoric about the League of Nations in 1919, as well as Harry S. Truman's declaration in 1946 that "we shall establish an enduring peace only if we build it upon Christian principles."[25] In the same fashion, Britain's decision not to accede to the Holy Alliance was to be considered together with the decision of the United States Senate to reject the League of Nations; and the Austrian intervention in Naples in 1821 was to be considered together with the Soviet suppression of the Prague Spring in 1968.

In revisiting the Holy Alliance in the twenty-first century, this book also declines to rehearse old slogans. It is an exercise in critical rather than monumental history. Its aim is not to derive a definitive set of moral or political lessons from the history of the Holy Alliance, but to expose the constricting effects that such derivations can have on political thinking, particularly during moments of potential systemic change.

24. Guillaume de Bertier de Sauvigny, *La Sainte-Alliance*, Collection U2 206 (Paris: Armand Colin, 1972), 7.

25. Ibid., 5–6. Truman's remark had previously been highlighted by a 1948 study of the Holy Alliance under the banner of Christian Democracy: Maurice de La Fuye and Émile Albert Babeau, *La Sainte-Alliance, 1815-1848* (Paris: Denoël, 1948). Reinforcing the analogy: Truman's remark appeared in the context of political and diplomatic maneuvers involving a controversial religious figure, Pope Pius XII. Truman repeated the remark in a correspondence, published in 1947, between the self-described "chosen leader" of "a Christian nation" and the pope. See Harry S. Truman, "Statement by the President upon Reappointing Myron Taylor as His Personal Representative at the Vatican, 3 May 1946," in *Harry S. Truman: Containing the Public Messages, Speeches, and Statements of the President, January 1 to December 31, 1946*, Public Papers of the Presidents of the United States (Washington, DC: Government Printing Office, 1962), 232; "Exchange of Letters between Truman and Pope," *New York Times*, August 29, 1947. On the religious, political, and diplomatic context, see John S. Conway, "Myron C. Taylor's Mission to the Vatican, 1940–1950," *Church History* 44, no. 1 (1975): 85–99.

CHAPTER ONE

The Past against the Future

"Why," he said, "do we delay concluding this holy alliance, of which the gods will be witnesses and guarantees?"

—FÉNELON, *ADVENTURES OF TELEMACHUS*[1]

THE HOLY ALLIANCE initially figured in a variety of attempts to imagine the future of Europe. Some of those futures were apocalyptic, but others were redemptive; some were redemptive through the state, others from the state; some were national in scope, others international, or even universal—and some were liberal. These futures disappear from view when the religious content of the Holy Alliance is reduced to a mere "symbol" of "the conservative, anti-revolutionary restoration and politics of stability," and when its intellectual history is relegated to "a special variant" of romanticism "of limited practical relevance."[2] Dismissed as the dead weight of the past, the Holy Alliance merely supplies the blank backdrop against which the dynamic conflicts making up the real history of liberty can be recounted: from this perspective, its "main goal" was "to restore the prerevolutionary social and political order—in particular its religious and monarchical basis."[3] The redemptive aspirations of the Russian emperor's immediate circle—of Roxandra and Alexander Stourdza as well as the

---

1. François de Salignac de la Mothe-Fénelon, *Telemachus, Son of Ulysses*, ed. Patrick Riley (Cambridge: Cambridge University Press, 1994), 146.

2. Thomas Nipperdey, *Germany from Napoleon to Bismarck, 1800–1866*, trans. Daniel Nolan (Princeton: Princeton University Press, 1996), 83; Jürgen Osterhammel, *The Transformation of the World: A Global History of the Nineteenth Century*, trans. Patrick Camiller (Princeton: Princeton University Press, 2015), 87.

3. Annelien De Dijn, *Freedom: An Unruly History* (Cambridge, MA: Harvard University Press, 2020), 249.

mystical ferment around Juliane von Krüdener—are well established.[4] This introductory chapter reconnects the Holy Alliance to a much wider array of contemporary religious currents by surveying contemporary visual representations of the Holy Alliance. By confounding the categories within which nineteenth-century politics is usually discussed, these images open a new perspective on the politics of the Holy Alliance. They begin to reveal the kinds of claims and judgments upon which the imagined futures of the Holy Alliance rested and the starkly millenarian terms in which its confrontation with the past was often considered. The densely layered and historically specific meanings of these images cannot be accommodated by familiar caricatures of the Holy Alliance as either politically irrelevant or inherently illiberal. Approached in this way, the images serve as a prompt to reconsider the potential of federative politics to issue in progress or reaction; and of appeals to religion to generate universalistic or exclusionary, emancipatory or repressive forms of community.

For Krüdener and others who experienced Alexander's victory over Napoleon as the arrival of a "second savior," the most resonant reference point for a "holy alliance" in 1815 may well have been the Book of Daniel: specifically, its prophecy of a providential intervention involving a holy covenant (*alliance sainte*, in the French edition apparently favored by Alexander).[5] But the vision of moral regeneration associated with the Archbishop Fénelon (which had also been denominated a "holy alliance" [*sainte alliance*] in his enduringly popular *Adventures of Telemachus* of 1699) had a broader appeal, extending even to Protestants like the Kantian philosopher Wilhelm Traugott Krug as well as the Unitarian theologian

4. On the extensive earlier literature examining accounts of the influence exercised by Krüdener and other "mystics" on the Russian emperor, see Andrei Zorin, "'Star of the East': The Holy Alliance and European Mysticism," *Kritika: Explorations in Russian and Eurasian History* 4, no. 2 (2003): 313–42. On the Stourdzas, see Stella Ghervas, *Réinventer la tradition: Alexandre Stourdza et l'Europe de la sainte-alliance* (Paris: Champion, 2008); Stella Ghervas, "A 'Goodwill Ambassador' in the Post-Napoleonic Era: Roxandra Edling-Sturdza on the European Scene," in *Women, Diplomacy and International Politics since 1500*, ed. Glenda Sluga and Carolyn James (Abingdon: Routledge, 2016), 151–66.

5. Daniel 11:30; Nicolas Legros and Louis-Isaac Lemaistre de Sacy, trans., *La Sainte Bible: Traduite sur les textes originaux, avec les différences de la Vulgate* (Cologne: aux dépens de la Compagnie, 1739), 621. On the "second savior," see Philipp Menger, "Die Heilige Allianz: 'La garantie du nouveau système Européen'?" in *Das europäische Mächtekonzert: Friedens- und Sicherheitspolitik vom Wiener Kongress 1815 bis zum Krimkrieg 1853*, ed. Wolfram Pyta and Philipp Menger (Köln: Böhlau Verlag, 2009), 209. On Alexander's edition of the Bible and his reading of the Book of Daniel, see Henri Louis Empaytaz, *Notice sur Alexandre, empereur de Russie* (Genève: Susanne Guers, 1828), 9; Ernest John Knapton, *The Lady of the Holy Alliance: The Life of Julie de Krüdener* (New York: Columbia University Press, 1939), 151.

William Ellery Channing.[6] "Fénelon's liberalism" (as Krug called it) could accommodate those who demanded more systematic understandings of the workings of providence while still identifying with the devotional piety of Krüdener—just as Fénelon himself was identified with the late seventeenth-century mysticism of Madame Guyon.[7] Krüdener's mysticism had appealed not only to Alexander but also to Germaine de Staël, who had both prayed with Krüdener and discussed constitutional reform with Alexander. According to Staël, such mysticism—"the religion of Fénelon"—was the antidote to the materialism that had produced Napoleon; and Krüdener was "a forerunner of a great religious epoch which is arising for the human race."[8] Alexander's association with Krüdener in September 1815, together with his love of "liberal ideas," had positioned him "at the head of the two things nobly perfecting the human race, inward religion and representative government."[9]

As Staël's remark suggests, the Holy Alliance initially figured in the redemptive future of liberalism as well as its apocalypse, and this redemptive future was connected to the political as well as the religious dimension of the Holy Alliance. To many of its liberal admirers, the Holy Alliance announced a constitutional act. When news of Alexander's Christmas proclamation reached Germany in early 1816, Krug and others greeted it as the transformation of the military coalition that had defeated Napoleon into a reconciled community of nations. As Krug put it, the "beautiful" alliance—named after *la belle alliance*, the Belgian inn near Waterloo where the British and Prussian commanders had met after their victory in June 1815—had become "holy."[10] The result was not just the negotia-

---

6. Fénelon, *Telemachus*, 146; Wilhelm Traugott Krug, "Fenelon's Liberalismus," *Literarisches Conversations-Blatt für das Jahr 1823*, no. 53 (March 4, 1823): 209–10; William Ellery Channing, *Remarks on the Character and Writings of Fenelon*, 2nd ed. (London: Edward Rainford, 1830). In Channing's estimation, Fénelon, "though a Catholic," was "essentially free" and could be mistaken for a Quaker (8). It is also worth noting that Channing traveled to Europe in 1822.

7. Hans-Jürgen Schrader, "Madame Guyon, Pietismus und deutschsprachige Literatur," in *Jansenismus, Quietismus, Pietismus*, ed. Hartmut Lehmann, Hans-Jürgen Schrader, and Heinz Schilling (Göttingen: Vandenhoeck & Ruprecht, 2002), 189–225.

8. Helena Rosenblatt, *Liberal Values: Benjamin Constant and the Politics of Religion* (Cambridge: Cambridge University Press, 2008), 140, 147; Staël to Juliette Récamier, October 27, 1814, in Anne-Louise-Germaine de Staël, *Lettres de Madame de Staël à Madame Récamier*, ed. Emmanuel Beau de Loménie (Paris: Domat, 1952), 262.

9. Staël to Madame de Gérando, September 27, 1815, in E. Muhlenbeck, *Étude sur les origines de la Sainte alliance* (Paris: F. Vieweg, 1887), 235–36.

10. Wilhelm Traugott Krug, *La sainte alliance: Oder Denkmal des von Oestreich, Preußen und Rußland geschloßnen heiligen Bundes* (Leipzig: H. A. Koechly, 1816), 21.

tion of another diplomatic "alliance" but the founding of a "federation." This was why Krug and many other German writers referred to the Holy Alliance as the *Heilige Bund* rather than the *Heilige Allianz*, and why the French writer Dominique de Pradt noted that it was initially received as "the apocalypse of diplomacy."[11] The legal, political, and economic ideas underlying these expectations of Europe's constitutional transformation disappear from view when the pronouncements of leading diplomats—the British foreign secretary, Lord Castlereagh, and his Austrian counterpart, Clemens von Metternich—are taken at face value. In fact, as the final part of this chapter will detail, they were part of an effort to change the meaning and even the text of Alexander's treaty, as part of an ongoing struggle to define the settlement that ended the war with France in 1815.

The history of the post-Napoleonic settlement has now become a vast and vibrant subject: one that extends well beyond the confines of the effort, undertaken a century ago by the British historian Harold Temperley, to explain the demise of "that union of three men—Alexander, Metternich, and Castlereagh—which had governed Europe since 1815."[12] In Temperley's account, the system of treaties designed to secure Europe against a recurrence of French aggression (to which the treaty of the Holy Alliance was an awkward appendix) had rested on a consensus that was pulled in opposite directions by Castlereagh and Alexander. Initially, Metternich was able to compromise between "the hard legal practicality of the one and the vague cosmopolitan mysticism of the other," because the "vague and mystic theories of Alexander" could be made to serve his antirevolutionary agenda, whereas Castlereagh, "though an Irishman, had a truly English distrust of all theories." Ultimately, the growing rift between Britain and Russia produced "the closer union of Prussia, Austria, and Russia, the three eastern despotic and military monarchies, against revolution": an arrangement that Temperley distinguished from the original postwar settlement by calling it "the *Neo-Holy* Alliance."[13] Remarkable new insights into the postwar settlement—now addressing its social, cultural, religious, legal, financial, military, and colonial dimensions—still have not clarified the place of the Holy Alliance in it.[14] One recent account

11. Dominique Georges Frederic de Pradt, *L'Europe après le Congrès d'Aix-la-Chapelle, faisant suite au Congrès de Vienne* (Paris: F. Béchet ainé, 1819), 301.

12. Harold Temperley, *The Foreign Policy of Canning, 1822–1827: England, the Neo-Holy Alliance and the New World* (London: G. Bell and Sons, 1925), 16–17.

13. Ibid., 5, 9, 16–17.

14. For some of these new insights, see Brian E. Vick, *The Congress of Vienna: Power and Politics after Napoleon* (Cambridge, MA: Harvard University Press, 2014); Katherine B. Aaslestad, "Serious Work for a New Europe: The Congress of Vienna after Two

identifies the treaty of the Holy Alliance as "the central document of the new European culture of peace."[15] Another, however, describes it as an ephemeral variant of the new European "security culture" epitomized by the "moderate and pragmatic" Duke of Wellington (the hero of Napoleon's final defeat at the Battle of Waterloo, who ultimately oversaw the postwar allied occupation of France). From this perspective, the Holy Alliance was the product of a "Russian approach" that seemed "too megalomaniacal and esoteric at the same time," and whose distinctive discourse "soon retreated into oblivion."[16]

Hundred Years," *Central European History* 48, no. 2 (June 2015): 225–37; Stella Ghervas, "The Long Shadow of the Congress of Vienna: From International Peace to Domestic Disorders," *Journal of Modern European History* 13, no. 4 (2015): 458–63; Jonathan Kwan, "The Congress of Vienna, 1814–1815: Diplomacy, Political Culture, and Sociability," *The Historical Journal* 60, no. 4 (December 2017): 1125–46; Christine Haynes, *Our Friends the Enemies: The Occupation of France after Napoleon* (Cambridge, MA: Harvard University Press, 2018); Beatrice de Graaf, Ido de Haan, and Brian Vick, eds., *Securing Europe after Napoleon: 1815 and the New European Security Culture* (Cambridge: Cambridge University Press, 2019); Beatrice de Graaf, *Fighting Terror after Napoleon: How Europe Became Secure after 1815* (Cambridge: Cambridge University Press, 2020); Glenda Sluga, *The Invention of International Order: Remaking Europe after Napoleon* (Princeton: Princeton University Press, 2021); Elise Kimerling Wirtschafter, *From Victory to Peace: Russian Diplomacy after Napoleon* (Ithaca: Cornell University Press, 2021); Matthijs Lok, *Europe against Revolution: Conservatism, Enlightenment, and the Making of the Past* (Oxford: Oxford University Press, 2023). Among the twentieth-century studies dedicated to the Holy Alliance, the most instructive are Hildegard Schaeder, *Die dritte Koalition und die Heilige Allianz: Nach neuen Quellen* (Königsberg: Ost-Europa-Verlag, 1934); Maurice Bourquin, *Histoire de la Sainte Alliance* (Genève: Georg, 1954); Francis Ley, *Alexandre Ier et sa Sainte-Alliance: 1811–1825, avec des documents inédits* (Paris: Fischbacher, 1975). The most important recent studies of the Holy Alliance are Ghervas, *Réinventer la tradition*; Philipp Menger, *Die Heilige Allianz: Religion und Politik bei Alexander I. (1801–1825)* (Stuttgart: Steiner, 2014); Adrian Brisku, "The Holy Alliance as 'An Order of Things Conformable to the Interests of Europe and to the Laws of Religion and Humanity,'" in *Paradoxes of Peace in Nineteenth Century Europe*, ed. Thomas Hippler and Miloš Vec (Oxford: Oxford University Press, 2015), 153–69; Anselm Schubert and Wolfram Pyta, eds., *Die Heilige Allianz: Entstehung, Wirkung, Rezeption* (Stuttgart: Verlag W. Kohlhammer, 2018); Beatrice de Graaf, "How Conservative Was the Holy Alliance Really? Tsar Alexander's Offer of Radical Redemption to the Western World," in *Cosmopolitan Conservatisms: Countering Revolution in Transnational Networks, Ideas and Movements (c. 1700–1930)*, ed. Matthijs Lok, Friedemann Pestel, and Juliette Reboul (Leiden: Brill, 2021), 241–60.

15. Wolfram Pyta, "Die Heilige Allianz: Ein Versuch zur Etablierung eines neuen Politikstils in den internationalen Beziehungen," in *Die Heilige Allianz: Entstehung, Wirkung, Rezeption*, ed. Anselm Schubert and Wolfram Pyta (Stuttgart: Verlag W. Kohlhammer, 2018), 81. Cf. Matthias Schulz, "The Construction of a Culture of Peace in Post-Napoleonic Europe: Peace through Equilibrium, Law and New Forms of Communicative Interaction," *Journal of Modern European History* 13, no. 4 (2015): 464–74.

16. De Graaf, *Fighting Terror after Napoleon*, 81, 314, 298, 249.

Rather than relying on hypostatized definitions of a wider culture, the rest of this book tells the history of the actual arguments advanced by contemporary actors who recognized the Holy Alliance as a version of a familiar strategy for enacting legal change (whether or not they approved of its religious discourse).[17] This history explains why the Holy Alliance registered as a moment in a political process that was expected to unfold in a particular sequence: the postwar reconciliation enacted by the Holy Alliance, which superseded the military and diplomatic negotiations that had ended the war with France, heralded in turn the legislation of a new legal order. For some, like the American statesman Thomas Jefferson, the defining feature of the new legal regime ushered in through Russian intervention in European politics would be the principle of free trade; for British abolitionists like William Wilberforce and Thomas Clarkson, it was the universal abolition of the slave trade; for liberals like Frédéric-César de la Harpe, Adam Jerzy Czartoryski, and Wilhelm Traugott Krug, it was all of these, but also the introduction of liberal constitutions and representative institutions throughout Europe. The Holy Alliance appeared in these contexts because the treaty's promulgation—its translation of private conviction into public communication—also registered as a variation on a prolific eighteenth-century pattern (associated with Fénelon) for enacting state-driven reform in concert with public opinion.

Apocalypse and Redemption

The Holy Alliance as the apocalypse of liberalism appears in a pair of engravings by the famous illustrator George Cruikshank, accompanying an 1821 pamphlet by the radical satirist William Hone (best known for winning several major trials against censorship), called *The Right Divine of Kings to Govern Wrong* (figure 1). Hone's pamphlet was dedicated "to the visible and invisible members of the Holy Alliance." It took its title from Alexander Pope but was otherwise a reworking of a satirical poem by Daniel Defoe.[18] The pamphlet was occasioned by the Austrian military intervention in Naples in 1821, which had been authorized by Russia and Prussia at the Congress of Laibach. It was also prompted by controversy over

17. Cf. the intervention by Michael Sonenscher in the historiography of the French Revolution in "The Cheese and the Rats: Augustin Cochin and the Bicentenary of the French Revolution," *Economy and Society* 19, no. 2 (May 1990): 266–74.

18. Kyle Grimes, "Daniel Defoe, William Hone, and *The Right Divine of Kings to Govern Wrong!* A New Electronic Edition," *Digital Defoe: Studies in Defoe & His Contemporaries* 4, no. 1 (2012), https://english.illinoisstate.edu/digitaldefoe/features/grimes.html.

George IV's coronation and the Bishop of London's support for his efforts to bring legal charges against his estranged wife Caroline, which many radicals viewed as a reassertion of the divine right of kings. Hone asserted not only an equivalence but outright collusion between the corruption of the British political establishment and the violent suppression of liberty abroad by the Holy Alliance: the captions to Cruikshank's engravings cobbled together various quotations and punning misquotations from Shakespeare, ending with "Iron for Naples, hid with English *gilt*."[19] Cruikshank's title vignette showed a bishop anointing a seething, heavily armed king with "oil of steel" and setting it alight with a flame of "discord"; the illustration at the end showed the Holy Alliance as a "composite caricature," a popular form depicting people as assemblages of the objects they worked with.[20] Conspiring monarchs are composed of instruments of death: the Holy Alliance appears as an automaton of armaments, crowned with a halo of daggers, putting Naples to fire and sword. A detailed description of this apparition was provided by the radical poet and critic Leigh Hunt in *The Examiner*:

> The body is a mortar, the thighs and arms fetters happily linked like bones; the legs have black cannon for boots; and the head, surmounted with a crown, is a cannon-ball or a block,—chuse which you will. The machine is gifted with a monstrous vitality, and is in the act of swinging its sword in a furious manner at the tree of liberty.[21]

"The conspirators at Laybach seem as if they had been sitting for the picture," Hunt wrote. He praised Cruikshank's engravings as "a personification of Royalty in its excess" on the one hand, and on the other as "Spenser's *Iron Man* brought forward in his real character." Hunt referred to the figure of Talus in Edmund Spenser's *The Faerie Queene*, the mythical Greek man of bronze whom Spenser had turned into the squire of the Knight of Justice: a fearsome iron creature ruthlessly meting out justice. Spenser's Talus is often glossed as an allegory for the militarization of Renaissance politics and the Elizabethan conquest of Ireland; he became the stuff of Gothic nightmares, from William Godwin's to Nathaniel

19. William Hone, *The Right Divine of Kings to Govern Wrong! Dedicated to the Holy Alliance*, 3rd ed. (London: Printed for William Hone, 1821), 60.

20. James Secord, "Scrapbook Science: Composite Caricatures in Late Georgian England," in *Figuring It Out: Science, Gender, and Visual Culture* (Hanover, NH: Dartmouth College Press, 2006), 164–91.

21. Leigh Hunt, *The Examiner*, March 18, 1821, 169.

Hawthorne's.[22] Hunt concluded his review by calling for an arms race between liberty and despotism. He invited Hone to produce a sequel to his pamphlet that would bring to life another machine capable of defending the cause of liberty from the technology of despotism:

> Could not Mr. Hone make another of his striking little books out of another machine also gifted with vitality, though to much nobler purpose? We mean the Press,—that new iron creature which contains in itself the mind as well as the force of thousands, and has arisen in these romantic times to put down the brute force that masks itself in human shape.[23]

It was the power of public opinion, communicated ever more efficiently and effectively, that offered the possibility of redemption from the apocalypse unleashed by the Holy Alliance. Hunt encouraged Hone to make this future work a "popular" one by including an account of the recent invention of the cylindrical steam press (famously introduced to print the November 29, 1814, issue of *The Times*).[24]

From another perspective, however, it was the Holy Alliance itself that held out the prospect of redemption from the apocalypse that had been unleashed by the French Revolution. This is the Holy Alliance that appears in an 1815 work by the German artist Heinrich Olivier (figure 2). It shows the three initial signatories of the treaty of the Holy Alliance (the emperor of Russia, the emperor of Austria, and the king of Prussia): three Knights of Justice, as it were, standing in a Gothic cathedral and appealing to God as witness to their vow of brotherhood. However, what Olivier's picture reveals is not a static and monolithic idea of restoration but several competing bids to determine the role of religion in establishing the

22. Lynsey McCulloch, "Antique Myth, Early Modern Mechanism: The Secret History of Spenser's Iron Man," in *The Automaton in English Renaissance Literature*, ed. Wendy Beth Hyman (London: Routledge, 2016), 61–76; Michael Demson, "The Ungovernable Puppets and Biopolitics of Hawthorne's Gothic Satires," *Nathaniel Hawthorne Review* 38, no. 2 (2012): 72–92.

23. Hunt, *The Examiner*, 169. On the "vitality" of "romantic machines," see John Tresch, *The Romantic Machine: Utopian Science and Technology after Napoleon* (Chicago: University of Chicago Press, 2012).

24. Presumably what Hunt had in mind was more like Victor Hugo's "ceci tuera cela" ("this will kill that," referring to the technology of the printing press on the one hand and the edifice of the Gothic cathedral on the other) than Honoré de Balzac's much darker tale of publishing and journalism in *Lost Illusions*. A recent variation on the former: the slogan "this machine kills fascists," which adorned Woody Guthrie's guitar in the 1940s, reappeared on some postboxes during the 2020 elections in the United States (referring to mail-in ballots).

FIGURE 1. *Above* and *overleaf,* William Hone, *The Right Divine of Kings to Govern Wrong! Dedicated to the Holy Alliance,* title vignette and illustration by George Cruikshank. London: William Hone, 1821. Beinecke Rare Book and Manuscript Library, Yale University, New Haven, Conn.

legitimacy of the postrevolutionary state. After volunteering in the war of liberation against Napoleon, Olivier ended up in Vienna in the company of Friedrich Schlegel, the philosopher whose taste for medieval fantasy was bound up with hopes for German unity under Habsburg leadership. The literary precedent for Olivier's *Holy Alliance* was an 1814 work by

FIGURE 1. (*Continued*)

the Tyrolean patriot and Austrian state archivist Joseph von Hormayr, which begins with a poem by Schlegel and goes on to imagine an Austrian cavalry officer dreaming on the eve of the Battle of Leipzig (the "Battle of Nations") in 1813. The dream culminates with the "apotheosis" of "Austria and Germany": Franz I, flanked by the Russian emperor on his right and the Prussian king on his left, appears in the Frankfurt Cathedral, which had long hosted the coronations of Holy Roman Emperors—and

FIGURE 2. Heinrich Olivier, *Die heilige Allianz*, gouache on vellum, 1815. Anhaltische Gemäldegalerie, Dessau.

would now supply the ornate background for Olivier's portrait of the Holy Alliance.[25]

The dream of a unified Germany under a restored imperial constitution was not the only vision of redemption that lay claim to the Holy Alliance. It was not even the only one linked to Olivier. In Prussia, one claim to the Holy Alliance emerged with the union of churches instituted by Friedrich Wilhelm III in 1817. As Christopher Clark has explained, this union "did represent an attempt by the monarch to consolidate the popular legitimacy of the Prussian crown, but it was in no sense a 'restoration.'" On the contrary, it was a program of "modernizing reform," predicated on "an aggressive statism that was arguably unprecedented in Prussian history," which elaborated on the Napoleonic model of state-imposed religious reconciliation.[26] An eclectic new liturgy was personally compiled by Friedrich Wilhelm himself, even incorporating Russian Orthodox and Roman Catholic elements. However, rather than aligning Prussia with the ecumenical Christianity of an alliance comprising an Orthodox emperor, a Catholic emperor, and a Protestant king, this new religious establishment fashioned the Holy Alliance in line with Prussia's identity as a Protestant state: a more restrictive identity that proved hostile to Jewish emancipation as well as expressions of German nationhood independent of the Prussian state.[27] The appearance of the new liturgy prompted the liberal theologian Friedrich Schleiermacher to complain that it did not include a prayer for the German nation, as represented in Frankfurt by the Federal Assembly of the German Federation. The response to Schleiermacher came from Rulemann Eylert: an orthodox Lutheran court chaplain and future bishop who went on to announce the government's crackdown on dissent after 1819 and expanded it into an attack on liberal theology professors (later Eylert also put his own stamp on the Holy Alliance by publishing

25. Joseph von Hormayr, *Oesterreich und Deutschland* (Gotha: In der Beckerschen Buchhandlung, 1814), 107–10, cited in Ludwig Grote, *Die Brüder Olivier und die deutsche Romantik* (Berlin: Rembrandt-Verlag, 1938), 113–14. Hormayr seems to have excised the scene from the revised version he published in 1815 in his journal, the *Archiv für Geographie, Historie, Staats- und Kriegskunst*.

26. Christopher Clark, "Confessional Policy and the Limits of State Action: Frederick William III and the Prussian Church Union, 1817–40," *The Historical Journal* 39, no. 4 (1996): 1004. See also Christopher Clark, "The Napoleonic Moment in Prussian Church Policy," in *Napoleon's Legacy: Problems of Government in Restoration Europe*, ed. David Laven and Lucy Riall (Oxford: Berg, 2000), 217–36.

27. Anselm Schubert, "Preußens Religionspolitik im Rahmen der Heiligen Allianz," in *Die Heilige Allianz: Entstehung, Wirkung, Rezeption*, ed. Anselm Schubert and Wolfram Pyta (Stuttgart: Verlag W. Kohlhammer, 2018), 142–53.

an 1818 interview he conducted with the Russian emperor).[28] According
to Eylert, it would be more "effective and meaningful" to include a prayer
for the Holy Alliance, which had already reconciled Europe by transcending politics: unlike the Federal Assembly in Frankfurt, the Holy Alliance
was "grounded solely in faith in God and the redeemer of the world, and
aims to secure the happiness, prosperity and peace of peoples through this
faith." The king accepted Eylert's suggestion, and a prayer for the Holy
Alliance remained in the Prussian liturgy all the way until 1895.[29]

From yet another perspective, however, the Holy Alliance represented
deliverance from the centralizing power of the state, including its assertion of control over religion. Among the opponents of the Prussian union
of churches were the Gerlachs, childhood friends of Olivier's; among the
Gerlachs were Ludwig (who later became a prominent politician and close
confidant of Friedrich Wilhelm IV) and his brother Leopold (an army
officer).[30] The Gerlachs and other "awakened" members of the aristocracy
initially resisted the Prussian state church. They contested the monarchy's
bid to consolidate popular allegiance by entering into pietistic communion with "Christians of the humblest station, their conventicles and home
prayer groups, their lively opposition to the rationalized and worldly clergy
all around them."[31] The Gerlachs and their circle were great admirers of
the Swiss jurist Karl Ludwig von Haller, who equipped them to reassert

28. Rulemann Friedrich Eylert, *Charakter-Züge und historische Fragmente aus dem
Leben des Königs von Preussen Friedrich Wilhelm III.*, vol. 2 (Madgeburg: Heinrichshofen,
1844), 248–56. On Eylert's subsequent career (he eventually became a counsellor of state),
see Robert M. Bigler, *The Politics of German Protestantism: The Rise of the Protestant
Church Elite in Prussia, 1815–1848* (Berkeley: University of California Press, 1972), 35,
43–44.

29. Schubert, "Preußens Religionspolitik im Rahmen der Heiligen Allianz," 144–46.
See also Anselm Schubert, "Liturgie der Heiligen Allianz: Die liturgischen und politischen
Hintergründe der Preußischen Kirchenagende (1821/22)," *Zeitschrift für Theologie und
Kirche* 110, no. 3 (2013): 291–315. As Schubert describes, the prayer for the Holy Alliance
even outlived the liturgy's memorialization of the victories over Napoleon at Leipzig, Paris,
and Waterloo; after 1829, Schubert notes, it took the "somewhat melancholy form" of a
prayer that the Holy Alliance "endure in the spirit of the monarchs that concluded it."

30. Grote, *Die Brüder Olivier und die deutsche Romantik*, 18. The mothers of the Gerlach and Olivier brothers were childhood friends whose children also became close, particularly Heinrich's brother Friedrich Olivier and Leopold and Ludwig's brother Wilhelm
von Gerlach.

31. Ernst Ludwig von Gerlach, *Aufzeichnungen aus seinem Leben und Wirken
1795–1877*, ed. Jacob von Gerlach, vol. 1 (Schwerin: F. Bahn, 1903), 125, cited in Chris-
topher Clark, "The Politics of Revival: Pietists, Aristocrats and the State Church in Early
Nineteenth-Century Prussia," in *Between Reform, Reaction, and Resistance: Studies in the
History of German Conservatism from 1789 to 1945*, ed. Larry Eugene Jones and James
Retallack (Oxford: Berg, 1993), 44–45.

the patrimonial authority of the landed aristocracy against all the threats it faced: from absolutism in both its royal and revolutionary forms; from the centralizing statist logic of the bureaucratic reformers who served the monarchy—and of the liberal constitutionalists who placed their hopes in it. In fact, as we shall see, one of the most determined liberal opponents of Haller's patrimonialism was Krug, whose identification of the Holy Alliance as "the most liberal of all ideas" was part of his broader defense of the principle that representative institutions and the influence of public opinion could tame the powers of the centralized state. By contrast, after 1848, Leopold von Gerlach came to apply a new label for Haller's alternative to the relentless centralization of state power: the "politics of the Holy Alliance." In this view, the mechanistic power politics of the eighteenth century had sparked the conflagration of the French Revolution, which had in turn compelled the founders of the Holy Alliance to recognize their duty to uphold a community of faith that was greater than their particular political interests: "The kings of the earth noticed the nearness of the Lord, they saw that the old politics no longer sufficed, they concluded the Holy Alliance."[32] Ludwig von Gerlach's commitment to reviving this community of faith famously got him caricatured, in 1849, as "Saint Gerlach": a new Peter the Hermit leading a new People's Crusade, flanked by his protégé Otto von Bismarck and political ally Friedrich Julius Stahl.[33] Later, however, this commitment to the "politics of the Holy Alliance" also led Ludwig von Gerlach to break with Bismarck and oppose his approach to German unification. As Leopold von Gerlach had written in his diary in 1860, "I look at everything now from the standpoint of the Holy Alliance and its restoration."[34]

In Russia, too, the Holy Alliance was initially linked to modernizing state interventions aiming to assert legal authority over religious communities. Even more closely than the Prussian union of churches, these interventions followed the Napoleonic model of a "multi-confessional establishment" aiming to stabilize religious communities without sapping the vitality that could make them a source of social cohesion. The new Russian establishment began to take shape with the consolidation of the Central Directorate for

32. Leopold von Gerlach, *Denkwürdigkeiten aus dem Leben Leopold von Gerlachs*, vol. 2 (Berlin: Wilhelm Hertz, 1892), 724, cited in Werner Näf, "Die Idee der Heiligen Allianz bei Leopold von Gerlach," *Zeitschrift für schweizerische Geschichte* 11, no. 4 (1931): 463.

33. Wilhelm Scholz, "Der neue Peter von Amiens und die Kreuzfahrer," *Kladderadatsch* 2, no. 45 (April 11, 1849): 10.

34. Gerlach, *Denkwürdigkeiten*, 2:755, cited in Näf, "Die Idee der Heiligen Allianz bei Leopold von Gerlach," 470.

the Spiritual Affairs of Foreign Confessions in 1810; in the wake of the French invasion of 1812, it also came to reflect the increasing prevalence of a new religious current that emphasized the cultivation of inward spirituality and intimate communion. In the Russian context, this new current is usually exoticized as "mysticism"—but, as Paul Werth has observed, it "is probably better described as a particular kind of Evangelical Protestantism, substantially inflected by pietist tendencies."[35] The most important institutional manifestation of this new religious current was the Russian Bible Society, which was founded by the emperor's childhood friend Alexander Golitsyn in 1812, on the model of the British and Foreign Bible Society (which established itself in Saint Petersburg that year). In 1817, the emperor appointed Golitsyn to lead a new Ministry of Religious Affairs and Popular Enlightenment, which oversaw not only the Ministry of Education and the Central Directorate but also the rapidly expanding Bible Society and even the Synod of the Orthodox Church. Under this new regime, religious polemics were prohibited by the state on the grounds that they violated "the union of love that unites all Christians in a single spirit"; in 1817, Lutherans in Russia were authorized to commemorate the

35. Paul W. Werth, "The French Connection and the Holy Alliance: Two Sources of Imperial Russia's Multiconfessional Establishment," in *Die Heilige Allianz: Entstehung, Wirkung, Rezeption*, ed. Anselm Schubert and Wolfram Pyta (Stuttgart: Verlag W. Kohlhammer, 2018), 133–34. Similarly, Susan Crane describes the Holy Alliance as "representative of the awakened Christian movement across Europe and North America." Susan A. Crane, "Holy Alliances: Creating Religious Communities after the Napoleonic Wars," in *Die Gegenwart Gottes in der modernen Gesellschaft: Transzendenz und religiöse Vergemeinschaftung in Deutschland*, ed. Michael Geyer and Lucian Hölscher (Göttingen: Wallstein, 2006), 49–50. For the longer history of the Russian religious establishment, see Paul W. Werth, *The Tsar's Foreign Faiths: Toleration and the Fate of Religious Freedom in Imperial Russia* (Oxford: Oxford University Press, 2016). On "mysticism" reconsidered in a broader context and correcting widespread assumptions about its inherently conservative or invariably nationalistic political implications, see also Stewart J. Brown, "Movements of Christian Awakening in Revolutionary Europe, 1790–1815," in *Enlightenment, Reawakening and Revolution, 1660–1815*, ed. Stewart J. Brown and Timothy Tackett, vol. 7, Cambridge History of Christianity (Cambridge: Cambridge University Press, 2006), 575–95; Hartmut Lehmann, "Pietistic Millenarianism in Late Eighteenth-Century Germany," in *The Transformation of Political Culture: England and Germany in the Late Eighteenth Century*, ed. Eckhart Hellmuth (London: German Historical Institute, 1990), 327–38; Max Geiger, "Politik und Religion nach dem Programm der Heiligen Allianz," *Theologische Zeitschrift* 15 (1959): 107–25. More generally, see also Dan Edelstein, ed., *The Super-Enlightenment: Daring to Know Too Much* (Oxford: Voltaire Foundation, 2010); David Bates, "The Mystery of Truth: Louis-Claude de Saint-Martin's Enlightened Mysticism," *Journal of the History of Ideas* 61, no. 4 (2000): 635–55; Clarke Garrett, "Swedenborg and the Mystical Enlightenment in Late Eighteenth-Century England," *Journal of the History of Ideas* 45, no. 1 (1984): 67–81; W. H. Oliver, "Owen in 1817: The Millennialist Moment," in *Robert Owen: Prophet of the Poor*, ed. Sydney Pollard and John Salt (London: Macmillan, 1971), 166–87.

tricentenary of the Reformation, provided they did so "without addressing disputes about the superiority of one Christian church over another," since the Russian government "protects all confessions equally."[36]

This was the new Russian religious establishment that, in Werth's estimation, "represented the principal domestic manifestation of the Holy Alliance."[37] Though it was indeed perceived that way by many foreign liberals (and also, as chapter 5 will discuss, by Catholic critics of the Holy Alliance like Joseph de Maistre), it proved short-lived within Russia itself. Golitsyn's Ministry was dismantled in 1824; the Bible Society was closed in 1826; and by 1832, the Orthodox Church had reasserted its status as the "predominant and ruling faith" and begun to forge an identity as a more explicitly national faith.[38] In Russia, the liberal view of the Holy Alliance associated with Golitsyn's Ministry and the Russian Bible Society was contested by Alexander Stourdza. Stourdza came from a prominent Moldavian Greek family and had served as the secretary of Ioannis Kapodistrias (the Russian foreign minister who later became the first head of state of an independent Greece). Stourdza had been entrusted with the emperor's penciled first draft of the treaty of the Holy Alliance; his sister Roxandra had become a key member of the emperor's religious circle and his conduit to religious figures, including Krüdener, who played an important part in the promulgation and reception of the Holy Alliance. For Stourdza, as Stella Ghervas has explained, the efficacy of the Holy Alliance ultimately derived from the renewal of the Orthodox Church as the guardian and true inheritor of the original unity of Christianity.[39] In 1818, Stourdza caused an uproar in Germany with a report condemning its universities as incubators of antisocial revolutionary passions that he described as deeply embedded in German culture; Krug condemned him, in return, for violating the true liberal and ecumenical spirit of the Holy Alliance.[40] The next year, however—following his flight from Germany after the assassination of the playwright and Russian asset August von Kotzebue—Stourdza was tasked with drafting an anonymous defense of the Holy Alliance as the

36. Werth, "The French Connection and the Holy Alliance," 136.

37. Ibid.

38. Ibid., 138–39.

39. Ghervas, Réinventer la tradition, 194–98, 332. See also Alexander M. Martin, Romantics, Reformers, Reactionaries: Russian Conservative Thought and Politics in the Reign of Alexander I (DeKalb: Northern Illinois University Press, 1997), 169–98.

40. Alexander Stourdza, Mémoire sur l'état actuel de l'Allemagne (Paris: La librairie grecque-latine-allemande, 1818); Wilhelm Traugott Krug, État actuel de l'Allemagne: Ou examen et réponse au Memoire de M. de Stourdza (Leipzig: Brockhaus, 1819); Ghervas, Réinventer la tradition, 204–17.

true alternative to both revolution and reaction: commissioned by the emperor, to be published abroad for a foreign audience. In the end, the project was overtaken by events (the uprising in Naples) and remained unpublished, even though Stourdza had fulfilled his instructions, which were to distance the emperor from all those who had mistakenly identified him as a partisan of either "liberal ideas" or "absolute power."[41]

If the future of the Holy Alliance could be redemptive as well as apocalyptic, the scope of that redemption could also be national or international. A more narrowly nationalistic Holy Alliance appears in an engraving from Nuremberg titled *The Holy Alliance or Victory Celebration of October 18, 1814*, which was the first annual commemoration of the Battle of Leipzig (figure 3). Here an eye of providence surveils a heavenly trinity featuring a Germanic Hercules—a guise in which Luther had famously been portrayed by Hans Holbein the Younger in 1519, using his club to slay the hydra of the Roman Church. Below, instead of the victims, are the victors: but the three allied kings are not alone. They are surrounded by their generals, and their armies, all arrayed around a stone altar presided over by a cleric—possibly Luther himself, according to one commentator.[42] This is a Holy Alliance closely associated with military victory and the popular mobilization that had achieved it; the individuality of the monarchs and of many of their generals is very much apparent, even if the nation they had summoned to defeat Napoleon's new Rome recedes into the landscape and ultimately into the figure of the Germanic Hercules. Interestingly, this engraving has been dated to 1814, which might be incorrect (since news of the Holy Alliance did not begin to appear in the German press until early 1816).[43] But it is also possible that the engraving took its title directly from the Book of Daniel or Fénelon's *Adventures of Telemachus*, and really does predate the Russian emperor's treaty altogether: the scene recalls the spectacular commemoration of the Battle of Leipzig staged during the Congress of Vienna in 1814, as well as the extensive merchandizing that accompanied it.[44]

By contrast, a more emphatically international and less emphatically Protestant Holy Alliance appears in a French engraving published in 1817, titled *The Holy Alliance placed under the protection of Religion by the tute-*

---

41. Martin, *Romantics, Reformers, Reactionaries*, 176.

42. Bettina Brandt, *Germania und ihre Söhne: Repräsentationen von Nation, Geschlecht und Politik in der Moderne* (Göttingen: Vandenhoeck & Ruprecht, 2010), 184.

43. For the dating of the engraving to 1814, see http://resolver.staatsbibliothek-berlin.de/SBB0002050700000000 and https://gallica.bnf.fr/ark:/12148/btv1b8413755n.

44. Vick, *The Congress of Vienna*, 30–37.

FIGURE 3. Leonhard Schlemmer, *Die heilige Allianz, oder Sieges-Feyer den 18ten Oct 1814*, engraving after a drawing by Johann Georg Rögner. Nürnberg: Leonhard Schlemmer, 1814. Bibliothèque nationale de France, Paris.

lary angels of the allied Powers (figure 4). This engraving was done by the royal engraver (François Anne David) after a drawing by the royal illustrator (Charles Monnet)—a duo that had previously collaborated on a *History of Russia* as well as a *History of France under the Empire of Napoleon the Great* (a project left unfinished in 1813).[45] This is not a militaristic Holy

45. Alexandre Joseph Guyot, *Histoire de France sous l'empire de Napoléon le Grand représentée en figures accompagnées d'un précis historique*, 6 vols. (Paris: Chez l'auteur, David, graveur, 1809); Adrien Michel Hyacinthe Blin de Sainmore, *Histoire de Russie,*

FIGURE 4. François Anne David, *La Sainte Alliance mise sous la protection de la Religion par les anges tutélaires des Puissances alliées*, engraving after a drawing by Charles Monnet. Paris: chez Crousel, 1817. Bibliothèque nationale de France, Paris.

Alliance: unlike the previous engraving, the only weaponry remaining in this one is the sword in the hand of Justice. In 1817, the armies of Russia, Prussia, and Austria still occupied France, but here they are represented by angels, offering up the text of the Holy Alliance to Jesus Christ (who is already holding the gospel along with the cross); and they are now assisted by the angelic representatives of the restored Bourbon monarchies of France and Spain. The inscription on the engraving makes a point of specifying that the treaty of the Holy Alliance had been concluded in Paris. At the very top is a series of rondels listing some of the other states (notably including even neutral and republican Switzerland) that had formally acceded to the Holy Alliance over the course of 1816 and 1817. There is a conspicuously blank rondel at the top—just as there is an allied power conspicuously missing at the bottom of the engraving: Great Britain was the only European state, apart from the pope and the Ottoman Empire, that never acceded to the Holy Alliance. For many liberals, the Holy Alliance was an opportunity to realize ideals that Napoleon had betrayed but that Britain had monopolized for itself. From an ex-Bonapartist perspective, especially, the Holy Alliance was easily linked to earlier aspirations to closer European integration in spite of British objections. According to Krug, the Holy Alliance would help dismantle Britain's commercial monopoly through a corrected version of Napoleon's continental system (the closure of European markets to British trade), now reorganized according to "the principle of national equality of rights."[46] According to Emmanuel, comte de Las Cases, a chief expositor of the potent nineteenth-century legend of a liberal Napoleon (whom he had accompanied on his final exile to Saint Helena in the South Atlantic), even the "prince of liberal ideas" himself had claimed the Holy Alliance as his own: "I too should have had my congress and my holy alliance. These are plans which were stolen from me."[47]

Finally, the Holy Alliance as Krug's "most liberal of all ideas" is best represented on the front cover of a remarkable collection called the *Archive of the Holy Alliance* (figure 5). The *Archive* was published in Munich, in two volumes that appeared in 1818 and 1819; though the preface mentions an editorial collaboration, the only extant attribution is to

représentée par figures, accompagnées d'un précis historique, 2 vols. (Paris: Imprimerie de Boiste, 1797).

46. Krug, _La sainte alliance_, 46.

47. Emmanuel-Auguste-Dieudonné comte de Las Cases, _Mémorial de Sainte Hélène: Journal of the Private Life and Conversations of the Emperor Napoleon at Saint Helena_, vol. 3 (London: H. Colburn and Company, 1823), 265. On the liberal legend of Napoleon, see Sudhir Hazareesingh, _The Legend of Napoleon_ (London: Granta, 2004).

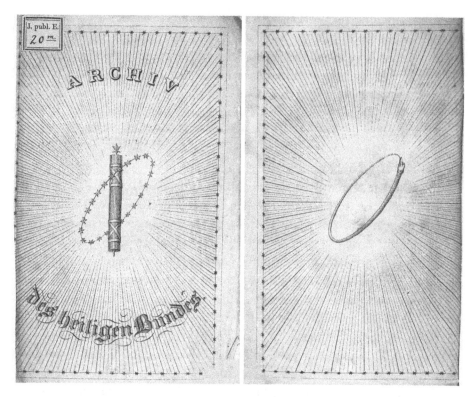

FIGURE 5. *Archiv des Heiligen Bundes: Enthaltend die denselben betreffenden Aktenstücke, Literatur, Nachrichten u. Urtheile,* front cover (*left*) and back cover (*right*). München: Thienemann, 1818. Bayerische Staatsbibliothek, München, J.publ.e 20 m-1/2, urn:nbn:de:bvb:12-bsb10555183-6.

Adolph Heinrich Friedrich Schlichtegroll, the secretary of the academy of sciences in Munich, best known as the first biographer of Wolfgang Amadeus Mozart.[48] Apart from appearing in the bibliographies of a few nineteenth-century treatises on political science and international law, the *Archive* appears to have been entirely neglected by posterity—even though it was expressly designed to supply present and future historians with a comprehensive repository of all the relevant public documents and contemporary responses to "one of the most notable events in history."[49] In

48. *Archiv des Heiligen Bundes: Enthaltend die denselben betreffenden Aktenstücke, Literatur, Nachrichten und Urtheile,* vol. 1 (München: Thienemann, 1818), vi, http://mdz-nbn-resolving.de/urn:nbn:de:bvb:12-bsb10555183-6. For the attribution, see Oskar Ludwig Bernhard Wolff, *Encyclopädie der deutschen Nationalliteratur: Oder, Biographisch-kritisches Lexikon der deutschen Dichter und Prosaisten seit den frühesten Zeiten, nebst Proben aus ihren Werken,* vol. 6 (Leipzig: O. Wigand, 1835), 458.

49. *Archiv des Heiligen Bundes,* 1:iii–iv.

terms of its format and presumably its target audience, the *Archive* closely resembles the *Reformation Almanac* published in 1817 by the Erfurt bookseller Friedrich Keyser, in connection with tricentenary commemorations of the Reformation: Keyser's aspirations likewise extended to supplying "an archive for Reformation history" for the benefit of historians and others seeking to learn about a great moment in world history.[50]

The Holy Alliance that appears on the front cover of the *Archive* is strikingly impersonal. There is no trace of the three original signatories— the emperor of Russia, the emperor of Austria, or the king of Prussia. Instead, the abstraction of this emblem points toward the kind of liberal theology embraced by many liberals at the time, like Benjamin Constant: it suggests an abstract vision of redemption as the realization of humanity's moral potential.[51] This was the theory of progress developed along Kantian lines by Krug, who featured prominently in the *Archive*. The front cover shows the Roman fasces within a ring of stars, at the center of a glory of divine light: the technology of the state, the instruments of force bound up in legal authority, now infused with providential purpose and transformed into an ethical community. The stability achieved by this reinforcement and modulation of temporal authority through religion is suggested on the back cover by the ouroboros, the serpent devouring its own tail and renewing itself. Though the *Archive* aspired to impartiality and comprehensiveness, the perspective on the Holy Alliance it favored most was in fact Krug's liberal faith in the capacity of enlightened public opinion, channeled through representative institutions, to transform the state into a durable engine of progress.

For Krug, the Holy Alliance marked the emergence of the kind of ethical community theorized by Kant: a community whose universal principles could

50. Friedrich Keyser, *Reformations Almanach für Luthers Verehrer: Auf das evangelische Jubeljahr, 1817* (Erfurt: G. A. Keysers Buchhandlung, 1817), x, https://catalog .hathitrust.org/Record/009707246. The volume on Martin Luther was followed in 1819 by a second devoted to Zwingli; the third, on Calvin, appeared in 1821 after Keyser's death. I am grateful to Michael Printy for this reference, and for his insight into Keyser's project and its place in the history of Protestantism that he develops in his forthcoming book, *Enlightenment's Reformation: Religion and Philosophy in Germany, 1750–1830*.

51. Rosenblatt, *Liberal Values*, 3. See also Laurence Dickey, "Constant and Religion: 'Theism Descends from Heaven to Earth,'" in *The Cambridge Companion to Constant*, ed. Helena Rosenblatt, Cambridge Companions to Philosophy (Cambridge: Cambridge University Press, 2009), 313–48; Bryan Garsten, "Constant on the Religious Spirit of Liberalism," in *The Cambridge Companion to Constant*, ed. Helena Rosenblatt, Cambridge Companions to Philosophy (Cambridge: Cambridge University Press, 2009), 286–312; Bryan Garsten, "Religion and the Case against Ancient Liberty: Benjamin Constant's Other Lectures," *Political Theory* 38, no. 1 (2010): 4–33.

unify an ineluctably pluralistic political world divided up into independent states. For others in the 1820s, however, the Holy Alliance represented the first stage in the unification of Europe, through the formation of a pan-European civic identity and the institutional development of a federal European state. The variety of possible forms of community associated with the Holy Alliance reflects the variety of new forms of religious community that accompanied the spread of "awakened Christianity" around the turn of the nineteenth century. As Susan Crane has emphasized, the turn to more "personalized" forms of spirituality also led to more "universalizing" notions of community: notions that were not as necessarily or inevitably linked to the consolidation of the nation-state as has often been supposed. On the contrary, in releasing many Germans from established forms of local community and authority, they also opened up a path to migration—across the Atlantic but also to the Russian Empire.[52] In North America, the "frontier revivalism" of such migrant communities clashed with the "national evangelism" emanating from New England; in Europe, it clashed with aspirations that, in their grandest form, linked the Holy Alliance to the formation of a pan-European "Christian nation" expanding across the territories of the Russian Empire.[53] The circumstances and outcomes of these clashes were different, but putting them into comparative perspective connects the Holy Alliance to the imagining of new "civic spaces" beyond the scale of a European nation-state—and connects such imaginings to the Holy Alliance.[54]

Though Britain was missing from the Holy Alliance, it was not missing from the *Archive of the Holy Alliance*. The first volume featured a complete German translation of *Remarks on the Holy League*, an 1816 pamphlet by Robert Hindmarsh, leader of the Swedenborgian Church in Manchester. Hindmarsh's pamphlet was an instance of a whole genre of early responses to the Holy Alliance: a close exegesis of the published text of the treaty (often together with the czar's accompanying manifesto) to discern the

52. Crane, "Holy Alliances," 37. Eighteenth-century cosmopolitanism has likewise been redescribed as projecting a wide range of potential civic identities: see Sophia Rosenfeld, "Citizens of Nowhere in Particular: Cosmopolitanism, Writing, and Political Engagement in Eighteenth-Century Europe," *National Identities* 4, no. 1 (2002): 25–43.

53. On the former, see Sam Haselby, *The Origins of American Religious Nationalism* (Oxford: Oxford University Press, 2015).

54. On the imagining of "civic spaces" on an imperial scale in this period, see Lauren Benton and Aaron Slater, "Constituting the Imperial Community: Rights, Common Good and Authority in Britain's Atlantic Empire, 1607–1815," in *Revisiting the Origins of Human Rights*, ed. Pamela Slotte and Miia Halme (Cambridge: Cambridge University Press, 2015), 140–62.

content of its fundamental principles. According to Hindmarsh's distinctive reading, the Holy Alliance was a profession of the antitrinitarian doctrine of the Church of New Jerusalem, which was the only truly universalistic expression of Christianity. Hindmarsh was also hopeful that the recently announced Prussian commission for liturgical reforms would at least start to move in the same direction. His broader point was that the Holy Alliance expressed a rising tide of "genuine radical reform in the *first principles* of religion." Those who mistook the Holy Alliance for "a revival of the hateful spirit of persecution and fanaticism" of a bygone age were simply blind to the social power of this new religious current: "They are the men, who can perceive no corruptions or abuses, except in the Civil State; no necessity for a reform, except in Elections and Parliamentary Representation." It was the Holy Alliance that promised to transform the end of the Napoleonic wars into "a general reformation both in religious principle and in moral life" of nations as well as individuals: an achievement "of far greater importance to the real welfare and happiness of mankind" than either Luther's Reformation or the Emperor Constantine's conversion to Christianity had been.[55] For Hindmarsh, Britain's failure to accede to the Holy Alliance, despite the professed endorsement of its principles by its monarch and his ministers, was a sign that political progress in Britain was likely to be slower than elsewhere. The greater progress of liberty in Britain, as reflected in its constitutional achievements, would actually make it much more difficult to dismantle the entrenched and divisive hierarchy of the established Church of England (the Test and Corporation Acts still barred dissenters such as Hindmarsh from full participation in civic life). Whereas the continental monarchs could immediately deploy their relatively unchecked power to introduce rapid reforms from the top down—converting the "relative imperfection" of their societies "into a national benefit"—Britain would have to wait for the new religious spirit to diffuse upward into its political class, who could then legislate accordingly. If they failed to follow the example set by the Holy Alliance, Hindmarsh warned, then "the new and true Christian religion must remain in a state of relative depression in this the proper land of it's nativity," and England's religious future would be exiled across the Atlantic.[56]

55. Robert Hindmarsh, *Remarks on the Holy League Lately Entered into by Their Majesties the Emperor of Austria, the King of Prussia, and the Emperor of Russia: Wherein They Openly Proclaim and Recommend to Their Own Subjects, and to the Christian World at Large, the Two Essential and Distinguishing Articles of the New Church, Called the New Jerusalem* (Manchester: F. Davis, 1816), 14–16.

56. Ibid., 22–24.

Hindmarsh's pamphlet represents one of many contemporary assessments of the Holy Alliance that disappear from view when its religious context is too narrowly drawn or when its political context is restricted to the diplomatic negotiations that produced the postwar settlement of 1815. "An uncommon event must, in writing and in life, give rise to the most varied, contradictory judgments," observed the preface to the *Archive of the Holy Alliance*: some immediately discerned "the salvation of the age" in the Holy Alliance, while others immediately dismissed it as altogether empty of content or consequences. The aim of the *Archive* was to enable contemporaries and posterity alike to form a balanced judgment of the Holy Alliance by compiling published diplomatic documents together with a selection of literature and topical commentary "for, against, and about" the Holy Alliance.[57] To one correspondent, the great intensity of the initial response to the appearance of the Holy Alliance recalled reactions across Germany to news of the storming of the Bastille at the outset of the French Revolution in 1789: a compilation like the *Archive* ought to have been organized then.[58] To posterity, contemporary assessments of the transformative potential of events in 1789 have remained intelligible in a way that the liberal idea of the Holy Alliance has not. Showing how the Holy Alliance could be understood in this way—and even be recognized as the realization of the ideals of 1789—also requires a broader perspective on the invention of the Holy Alliance, not just as a religious or moral idea but as a political one too.[59]

Bruin Become Mediator

The Holy Alliance was supposed to inaugurate a new era of European politics. It enlisted international public opinion to authorize and guide the interventions necessary for ensuring that the European balance of power would operate peacefully, within legally defined channels. As the German Danish banker Conrad Friedrich von Schmidt-Phiseldek put it in the early 1820s, the Holy Alliance was a "declaration of intent," or *Willenserklärung*, expressing the commitment of the signatories to a shared set of constitutional principles: a commitment that amounted to a "standing norm and instruction" to guide future political action. At the same time, the

57. *Archiv des Heiligen Bundes*, 1:vii, x.

58. Ibid., 1:162.

59. Cf. Keith Michael Baker, *Inventing the French Revolution: Essays on French Political Culture in the Eighteenth Century* (Cambridge: Cambridge University Press, 1990).

Holy Alliance was also the "federal act," or *Bundesakt*, "constituting the Christian nation." In Schmidt-Phiseldek's view, "there lies undeniably in the Holy Alliance the idea of a European federation [*eines Europäischen Staatenbundes*] which now has to be realized."[60] The kind of textual interpretation applied to the Holy Alliance by Schmidt-Phiseldek, Hindmarsh, Krug, and others was not unprecedented. The United States Declaration of Independence of July 4, 1776 (which Schmidt-Phiseldek considered a world-historical turning point), is another document whose diplomatic function did not prevent it from acquiring constitutional meanings through such readings.[61] In the case of the Holy Alliance, however, such interpretations appeared in spite of determined efforts to preclude them, undertaken by two leading figures: Castlereagh and Metternich, the British foreign secretary and his Austrian counterpart. Exposing these efforts and their outcomes helps clarify the contested relationship of the Holy Alliance to the postwar settlement of 1815, by identifying the Holy Alliance as a revival of a form of politics whose emancipatory potential had been extensively discussed in the 1780s. Its application to Russia had been attempted by La Harpe and Czartoryski at the outset of Alexander's reign after 1801, and had been revived once again as Napoleon retreated from Russia after 1812. Considered in this context, the history of the Holy Alliance as a liberal idea becomes a window into the promise and problems of federative politics more generally.

Castlereagh's oft-quoted description of the Holy Alliance as "a piece of sublime mysticism and nonsense" appeared in a report to London dated only two days after the treaty had been privately signed in Paris on September 14/26, 1815, by the czar, the Prussian king, and the Austrian emperor. Castlereagh's remark predated Alexander's publication of the treaty with his manifesto: it did not represent a retrospective evaluation of a completed political act but an intervention in an ongoing one, aiming to redefine it as a purely personal expression of religious sentiment. In his letter to Lord Liverpool, Castlereagh reported that "this rather novel proceeding" had "entirely originated with the Emperor of Russia, whose mind has latterly taken a deeply religious tinge": Alexander had sprung his treaty upon his unsuspecting wartime allies after falling under the influence of "a Madame de Krudener, an old fanatic, who has a considerable

60. Conrad Friedrich von Schmidt-Phiseldek, *Die Politik nach den Grundsätzen der heiligen Allianz* (Kopenhagen: Friedrich Brummer, 1822), 27, 31, https://mdz-nbn -resolving.de/urn:nbn:de:bvb:12-bsb10725782-6.

61. David Armitage, *The Declaration of Independence: A Global History* (Cambridge, MA: Harvard University Press, 2007).

reputation amongst the few highflyers in religion that are to be found in Paris." In order to extract the prince regent of Great Britain from this "scrape," while preserving "the harmony which subsists between him and his Allies," Castlereagh recommended that he join the Prussian king and Austrian emperor in signing Alexander's treaty, while construing it as a "communication of sentiment between Sovereign and Sovereign, binding upon their own consciences in the general management of their affairs": in fact, Castlereagh reported, he had intervened together with Metternich to "keep it, if it must go forward, in this channel," rather than allowing it to acquire "an official character" that "might have rendered its production as a State document necessary," which would have "exposed" this private agreement among sovereigns "to public discussion as an act advised by their Ministers."[62] Despite this intervention, the Holy Alliance did not quite proceed according to Castlereagh's plan. Instead of formally signing the treaty, the prince regent circulated his own letter "conveying to the august sovereigns who have signed it, my entire concurrence in the principles which they have set forth."[63] After the Russian emperor publicized the Holy Alliance on Christmas 1815, Castlereagh did find himself having to defend the treaty in Parliament: against allegations by the Whig opposition that what Castlereagh had described as an anodyne declaration of religious and moral principles was cover for a secret pact with sinister political implications.[64]

Unlike Castlereagh's remark, Metternich's equally famous description of the Holy Alliance as "a loud-sounding nothing" was not a contemporary response but a retrospective assessment composed in 1852 and delivered in his memoirs. Following Castlereagh, Metternich also cast the Holy Alliance as a "moral manifestation" that was not political but merely an "effusion" of Alexander's "pietistic disposition." It was an expression of Alexander's personal religious proclivities, influenced by the company

62. Charles K. Webster, *British Diplomacy, 1813–1815: Select Documents Dealing with the Reconstruction of Europe* (London: G. Bell and Sons, 1921), 382–84.

63. "Letter of the Prince Regent to the Emperor of Russia, the Emperor of Austria and the King of Prussia," October 6, 1815, in Werner Näf, *Zur Geschichte der Heiligen Allianz* (Bern: Paul Haupt, 1928), 41.

64. To some on the outside, the initial parliamentary debate about the Holy Alliance in Britain revealed more about the British system of government than it did about the Holy Alliance. As Germaine de Staël had observed, a "peculiarity of the English constitution" was "the necessity in which the opposition believe themselves placed of opposing the government on all possible grounds." Anne-Louise-Germaine de Staël, *Considerations on the Principal Events of the French Revolution*, ed. Aurelian Craiutu (Indianapolis: Liberty Fund, 2008), 709.

of religious mystics like Krüdener in Paris, which did not belong in a diplomatic instrument; it could do no good in that form and was likely to be misinterpreted. Metternich's recollections were misleading in another respect: he was wrong that the treaty of the Holy Alliance was never again mentioned in diplomatic correspondence after its initial appearance (and that its notoriety was therefore entirely manufactured by liberals who appropriated the label as a rhetorical weapon against monarchy).[65] In other respects, however, Metternich's recollections are quite revealing. His description of the treaty as "a philanthropic aspiration clothed in religious garb" captures the reason why a patriot like La Harpe could still recognize the Holy Alliance as a form of emancipatory politics while recoiling at its religious idiom; his further description of the treaty as the product of "a combination of religious and political-liberal elements" mirrors Krug's claim that what made the Holy Alliance "the most liberal of all ideas" was the way in which it combined the political and religious dimensions of liberalism.

Metternich's memoirs also reveal that he had intervened not only to alter the process of the treaty's promulgation (as Castlereagh had described) but also to change its content. Metternich reported that he had been deputized by the Austrian emperor and Prussian king to negotiate with the "author of the project": a difficult conversation with the Russian emperor in which he had insisted on making certain "absolutely necessary changes to the text."[66] Metternich's changes are recorded in a document that was discovered in the Austrian state archives in the 1920s and published by a Swiss historian, Werner Näf: a two-column comparison, annotated in Metternich's hand, of the "Text originally written and proposed by the Emperor Alexander" with the "Text corrected by the Emperor Franz and adopted by the 3 sovereigns."[67] Alexander's treaty began with a preamble declaring that the exclusive purpose of the document was to make a public

65. Clemens Wenzel Lothar Metternich, *Aus Metternich's nachgelassenen papieren*, vol. 1 (Wien: W. Braumüller, 1880), 214–16. On references to the "acte de 14 (26) septembre" in official Russian diplomatic documents, particularly during the Congress at Aix-la-Chapelle in 1818, see Wolfram Pyta, "Idee und Wirklichkeit der 'Heiligen Allianz,'" in *Neue Wege der Ideengeschichte: Festschrift für Kurt Kluxen zum 85. Geburtstag*, ed. Frank-Lothar Kroll (Paderborn: Ferdinand Schöningh, 1996), 315–45; Menger, "Die Heilige Allianz: 'La garantie du nouveau système Européen'?" 218.

66. Metternich, *Aus Metternich's nachgelassenen papieren*, 1:215.

67. Näf, *Zur Geschichte der Heiligen Allianz*. See also Ley, *Alexandre Ier et sa Sainte-Alliance*, 149–53. There is also a copy of the two-column comparison in Castlereagh's papers: "Projet of a Holy Alliance between the Tsar, the Austrian Emperor and the King of Prussia," Public Record Office for Northern Ireland, D3030/4715.

commitment ("manifester à la face de l'univers") to govern according to the Christian standard of "justice, charity, and peace": principles that were not merely applicable to private life but ought to govern the conduct of all internal and external political relations as well. Alexander's original version had framed this commitment as an "urgent" break with the past: the commitment to "the future" was grounded in a general condemnation of the "previous" form of politics—not just in France but universally—that lacked this religious foundation. Metternich's revision eliminated these references to past and future. Instead, it reframed the treaty as a statement dedicated to securing the present.

Metternich made another major intervention in the first article of the treaty, which turned a union of peoples into an alliance of their monarchs only. In Alexander's text, applying Christian principles to politics had meant considering the subjects of the different states to be "compatriots," united by "true *fraternité*," and their respective armies as "part of the same army called to protect religion, peace and justice." Metternich's version restricted this invocation of revolutionary unity to the monarchs alone while reasserting a patrimonial relation between princes and peoples: it was the monarchs who were to be united as brothers, while acting like fathers to their subjects and their armies. The treaty's second article—which Krug, Schmidt-Phiseldek, and other liberal readers would interpret as a commitment to introduce constitutional government and representative institutions—called for all governments and subjects alike to "consider themselves only as members of the same nation, called the Christian nation." Monarchs were to see themselves as "delegated by Providence to govern three provinces of that same nation" and "thus confess that the essentially one Christian nation has no other sovereign" but God (an understanding of sovereignty later embraced by François Guizot). Here Metternich's changes were limited to reasserting a more traditional religious discourse (he added the word "God" to Alexander's invocations of "the Word of the Most High, the Word of Life") and to reaffirming a patrimonial view of politics ("provinces of the same nation" became "branches of the same family"). Finally, the third article of the treaty—which liberal readers would welcome as an important sign of the universality that would foster postwar reconciliation—remained unchanged: it invited all states that accepted the principles set out in the treaty to accede to the alliance.[68]

68. Näf, *Zur Geschichte der Heiligen Allianz*, 34–37.

Although the published version of the treaty reflected Metternich's revisions, the manifesto which Alexander published alongside it did not. As Näf showed, Alexander's manifesto reproduced the sense of the original treaty in compressed form: it restored the contrast between past and future forms of politics and applied the principles of Christianity to subjects and monarchs alike. (It also added a warning to the other signatories not to "have the temerity to detach themselves" from the alliance.)[69] Alexander's publication of the treaty and the additional appearance of his manifesto seem incongruous only from the perspective of Castlereagh's and Metternich's hidden diplomatic efforts to reframe the treaty as a purely private and apolitical act among monarchs.[70] The two texts were encountered together and interpreted as moments in a single process by everyone else, including by Noah Worcester, a close associate of William Ellery Channing who had founded the Massachusetts Peace Society and conducted a well-publicized exchange of letters with Alexander and Golitsyn in 1817. "The Manifesto is an admirable document," Worcester enthused, "and may be regarded as expressing the ground, the spirit, and the object of the Alliance."[71] One German writer excerpted in the *Archive of the Holy*

69. Ibid., 33.

70. The diplomat Friedrich Gentz, who had been tasked by Metternich with keeping the princes of Wallachia informed about political developments, described the Holy Alliance to them in a pair of dispatches in January and February 1816. In this rendition, the Holy Alliance was a "most secret" treaty which Alexander had wanted to publish in October 1815, but his reluctant allies had done "everything possible to prevent it"; Gentz implied that Alexander had broken a promise not to publish it without the consent of all the signatories. Gentz assured his correspondents that the treaty was not directed against the Ottoman Empire but was in fact "a political nullity" with no "real aim": it was merely "a theater decoration imagined in a spirit of devotion that is perhaps misunderstood but above all very badly expressed." Friedrich von Gentz, *Dépêches inédites du chevalier de Gentz aux hospodars de Valachie: Pour servir à l'histoire de la politique européenne (1813 à 1828)*, vol. 1 (Paris: Plon, 1877), 214–24. In his dispatch of January 15, 1815, Gentz, like Castlereagh and Metternich, attributed the treaty to Krüdener's "bizarre" spirituality. However, on September 27, 1815 (the day after the initial signing), Gentz had complained to another correspondent that Krüdener had "played a part on the world stage [*Weltrolle*]" and "accomplished more than all ministers put together." Friedrich von Gentz, *Briefe von Friedrich von Gentz an Pilat: Ein Beitrag zur Geschichte Deutschlands im XIX. Jahrhundert*, ed. Karl Mendelssohn-Bartholdy, vol. 1 (Leipzig: F.C.W. Vogel, 1868), 194. On Gentz's correspondence with the princes of Wallachia, see Constantin Ardeleanu, "Friedrich von Gentz and His Wallachian Correspondents: Security Concerns in a Southeastern European Borderland (1812–28)," in *Securing Europe after Napoleon: 1815 and the New European Security Culture*, ed. Beatrice de Graaf, Ido de Haan, and Brian Vick (Cambridge: Cambridge University Press, 2019), 251–70.

71. Philo Pacificus, "The Friend of Peace, No. X," in *The Friend of Peace*, vol. 1 (Boston: J. T. Buckingham, n.d.), 24, https://hdl.handle.net/2027/hvd.hxj9mf.

Alliance asserted what other commentators also set out to establish: even "a cursory glance" at the treaty and manifesto made it clear that the principles they had articulated "cannot be reconciled with a great many existing (and still persisting) institutions and forms."[72]

Underlying such perceptions of the Holy Alliance was a set of claims about sovereignty and the balance of power that had developed over the course of the eighteenth century. The key idea was for one or more states to legislate a new treaty system that would better align their respective interests with the needs of collective security and prosperity. As other states joined this new system, it would increasingly exclude the destructive forms of international competition over markets and territory that were still permitted under existing European treaty law. This strategy avoided asserting a higher legal authority over sovereign states, even though it relied on a particular state or states to legislate the new treaty system. It amounted to an expansive reinterpretation of two roles frequently performed in European politics: the mediator intervening to end a conflict and the guarantor tasked with upholding the settlement that resolved it. The idea of a guarantor figured in the postwar settlement negotiated at the Congress of Vienna, including in constitutional provisions for Switzerland and the German Confederation. It also came to figure in a wide variety of constitutional theories, from the constitutional balancing function theorized by Benjamin Constant to the nested system of mutual guarantees theorized by Pierre-Joseph Proudhon.[73] The role of the Holy Alliance was to authorize and guide the interventions of the guarantors of the entire European treaty system: the system of collective security whose emergence in 1815 was influentially described as the "transformation of Europe" by the diplomatic historian Paul Schroeder.[74]

In the 1820s, the underlying questions raised by this form of politics came to be posed—for neither the first nor the last time—in highly polarized terms. The possibility of legal relations between states came to be

72. Friedrich Gottfried Cramer, *Betrachtungen über das heilige Bündniss besonders in Vergleich mit ähnlichen Ereignissen des sechszehnten Jahrhunderts* (Hamburg: Hoffmann und Campe, 1817), 15.

73. Benjamin Constant, *Réflexions sur les constitutions, la distribution des pouvoirs et les garanties, dans une monarchie constitutionnelle* (Paris: H. Nicolle, 1814); Pierre-Joseph Proudhon, *Du principe fédératif et de la nécessité de reconstituer le parti de la révolution* (Paris: E. Dentu, 1863). On the development of Constant's theory of the "neutral power," see especially William Selinger, *Parliamentarism from Burke to Weber* (New York: Cambridge University Press, 2019), chap. 4.

74. Paul W. Schroeder, *The Transformation of European Politics, 1763–1848* (Oxford: Clarendon Press, 1994).

understood in terms of a sharply drawn distinction based on the location of sovereignty: the distinction between a *Staatenbund*—a federation of states, each of which retained its sovereignty—and a *Bundesstaat*, where many government functions might be devolved to member states but where sovereignty was ultimately located in the federal state.[75] The most incisive critic of this enduringly influential formal distinction was the twentieth-century German jurist Carl Schmitt. In the 1920s, Schmitt's reflections on the League of Nations as well as the Weimar Constitution of 1919 prompted him to rethink the nature of federative politics. This rethinking shaped Schmitt's assessment of the Holy Alliance—and (as we shall see later on) also went on to shape how some prominent liberals thought about Cold War politics in terms of the Holy Alliance. According to Schmitt, the formal distinction between a *Staatenbund* and a *Bundesstaat* merely described the possible outcomes of a breakdown of federative politics. In his *Constitutional Theory* of 1928, Schmitt claimed that federative politics as such was actually defined by the indeterminate location of sovereignty: "the question of sovereignty between federation and member states always remains open as long as the federation as such exists alongside the member states as such." The "constitutional contract" that gave rise to this form of politics was "an act of the constitution-making power" of each member state. This act produced the "content of the federation constitution" while simultaneously transforming the "comprehensive status" of state constitutions by altering their "fundamental presuppositions" with regard to sovereignty. Federative politics always harbored the possibility of an "existential" clash between state sovereignty and the interventions required by the federal "guarantee" of collective security. This outcome could only be forestalled by maintaining the "homogeneity" of the federation's members: such "homogeneity" was therefore explicitly guaranteed by most federative constitutions.[76]

Federative politics has sometimes been described as a transitional stage (particularly pronounced in Germany) between the absolutism of the old regime and the popular sovereignty characteristic of modern constitutionalism. But it is better understood as a form of constitutional politics in its own right—and as an ideal of liberal modernity alongside

75. On the origins and career of this distinction, see Murray Greensmith Forsyth, *Unions of States: The Theory and Practice of Confederation* (Leicester: Leicester University Press, 1981); Michael Sonenscher, *Jean-Jacques Rousseau: The Division of Labour, the Politics of the Imagination and the Concept of Federal Government* (Leiden: Brill, 2020).

76. Carl Schmitt, *Constitutional Theory*, ed. Jeffrey Seitzer (Durham: Duke University Press, 2008), 385–95. Cf. U.S. Constitution, art. 4, sec. 4.

the ideal of a liberal nation-state.[77] A striking feature of La Harpe's and Czartoryski's careers is that they embraced the emancipatory potential of federative politics during the revolutionary ferment of the 1780s and were still able to describe the Holy Alliance as an ill-fated instance of this kind of politics four decades later. From this perspective, the repressive interventions imposed by members of the Holy Alliance in Germany, Italy, and Spain—alongside the emancipatory intervention they did not undertake in Greece—ultimately demonstrated the incapacity of the Holy Alliance to deliver collective security and prosperity to Europe without instigating existential clashes over sovereignty. A final set of early nineteenth-century images illustrates how the fundamental ambiguities of federative politics played out in the history of the Holy Alliance.

The promise of federative politics—what La Harpe called the "initial conception" of the Holy Alliance, as opposed to its "subsequent development"—is best illustrated in *Bruin become Mediator*, an 1803 print by Isaac Cruikshank, the father of George Cruikshank (figure 6).[78] Here, the Russian emperor appears as a bear serving as a mediator between Britain and France, saying, "I wonder you civilized folks could not agree upon matters without reference to me whom you have ridiculed as a Barbarian.—But I suppose you think I must have more sense than yourselves because I come farther North." The civilized folks are not so civilized themselves: the bear is making peace between John Bull (an actual bull) and Napoleon (a monkey), who are enumerating their respective negotiating positions. The act of mediation caricatured in this print represents an ephemeral diplomatic conjuncture in the early years of Alexander's reign: after Napoleon had invited Alexander to help negotiate a potential settlement between Britain and France but before Russia had joined Britain and Austria in a third coalition against Napoleon—a coalition that soon ended in defeat at the Battle of Austerlitz in 1805. But the mediation caricatured here also represents a whole series of efforts to realize the promise

77. Cf. Horst Dreitzel, *Absolutismus und ständische Verfassung in Deutschland: Ein Beitrag zu Kontinuität und Diskontinuität der politischen Theorie in der frühen Neuzeit* (Mainz: Verlag Philipp von Zabern, 1992), 128–29. Similarly, enlightened religion and liberal theology have been described as transitional stages in a secularizing process leading from orthodoxy to unbelief but are better understood as modern forms of religious life in their own right. See David Sorkin, *The Religious Enlightenment: Protestants, Jews, and Catholics from London to Vienna* (Princeton: Princeton University Press, 2008), 17; Dickey, "Constant and Religion."

78. E. B. Krumbhaar, *Isaac Cruikshank: A Catalogue Raisonné, with a Sketch of His Life and Work* (Philadelphia: University of Pennsylvania Press, 2017), 41. A different version of the same scene, also printed by Thomas Williamson but without Cruikshank's autograph, can be found in the collection of the British Museum.

FIGURE 6. Isaac Cruikshank, *Bruin become Mediator*, hand-colored etching. London: T. Williamson, 1803. The Bodleian Libraries, University of Oxford, Curzon b.4(19).

of federative politics via Russia, after the failures of Britain and France to fulfill the role of guarantors of European collective security. The geographical scope and imaginative potential of this type of politics, and its renewed association with Russia after 1812, is illustrated by *Bruin become Mediator or Negociation for Peace*, an American reworking of Cruikshank's original by the Scottish-born Philadelphia illustrator William Charles (figure 7). John Bull is the real beast in this one; Napoleon has been replaced by Columbia, who is saying, "I thank you Mr Bruin but I cannot trust the Bull" until he has retracted his horns, or in other words agreed to free trade for American shipping (Charles falsely implied that Alexander's offer of mediation in the War of 1812 was sought by the British, when in fact it was welcomed only by the United States).[79]

79. It was the American government that responded to Alexander's offer by immediately sending representatives to Saint Petersburg without waiting for the British to agree to Russian mediation (which they never did). Alexander later did mediate between Britain and the United States in a famous case about compensation over slaves who had fled to British lines during the War of 1812: see Bennett Ostdiek and John Fabian Witt, "The Czar and the Slaves: Two Puzzles in the History of International Arbitration," *American Journal of International Law* 113, no. 3 (July 2019): 535–67.

FIGURE 7. William Charles, *Bruin become Mediator or Negociation for Peace*, etching, ca. 1813. Yale University Art Gallery, New Haven, Conn.

Where La Harpe sought to distinguish the "initial conception" of the Holy Alliance from its "subsequent development," another observer contrasted the "reality of the Holy Alliance" with the "imaginary world" invoked most enthusiastically by the contributors to the *Archive of the Holy Alliance*. The Baron Bignon was a former French diplomat under Napoleon whose experience in the Rhineland and Prussia had left him well equipped to engage with the German literary world. In 1823, Bignon ridiculed the contributors to the *Archive* for exalting the Holy Alliance into a *Bund*, or federation, rather than a mere *Allianz*. While German philosophers (true to form) lost themselves in their ideals, Bignon charged, the deliberations at the Congress of Verona had exposed the "reality of the Holy Alliance."[80] This reality is illustrated by a well-known satirical print of 1823 called *A Hasty Sketch at Verona, or the Prophecies of Napoleon Unfolding*, by the English caricaturist John Lewis Marks (figure 8). A year after the Congress of Laibach and the Austrian intervention in Naples, the allies had

80. Louis-Pierre-Édouard Bignon, *Les cabinets et les peuples, depuis 1815 jusqu'à la fin de 1822*, 2nd ed. (Paris: Béchet ainé, 1823), 15.

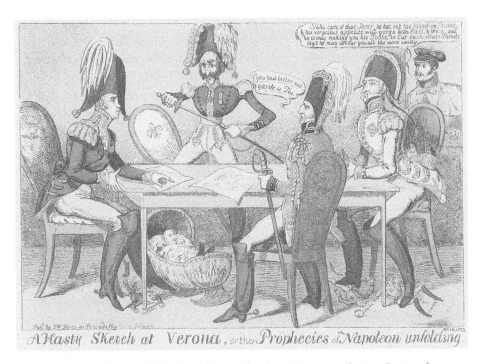

FIGURE 8. John Lewis Marks, *A Hasty Sketch at Verona, or the Prophecies of Napoleon Unfolding*, hand-colored etching. London: S. W. Fores, 1823. British Museum, London. © Trustees of the British Museum.

met again to discuss intervening to suppress the liberal constitution in Spain: whether it would be conducted with the participation of a large Russian army or (as transpired) by the French alone. The possibility of further such actions loomed, perhaps even to restore Spanish rule in the Americas. The reality revealed by *A Hasty Sketch at Verona* was the postwar continuation of the rivalries that had shaped the power politics of the old regime. The conference table is split one way by the British perception of French aggression and the other way by the Austrian perception of Russian expansionism. The Duke of Angoulême (who later commanded the French army that invaded Spain) has sprung to his feet, overturned his chair, and begun to draw his sword; the Duke of Wellington (who did not actually participate in the discussions but opposed the invasion) grips his sword and says, "You had better not—Garde a Toi." Meanwhile, the two emperors and their dependents face off: Alexander is rocking a cradle under the table containing a baby king of Prussia, there are several other small kings underfoot, and Franz has a couple more in his pocket, too. Alexander is gesturing toward a map of Spain while Franz eyes him warily;

behind him is Metternich, with a warning. "Take care of that Bear, he has set his Mind on Blood, & his voracious appetite will gorge both East, & West, and he is only making you his Tools, to Cut each others Throats that he may devour you all the more easily."

From one perspective, the imaginary world of liberal ideas served to mask the political reality of the Holy Alliance. But from another perspective, the emancipatory politics of the Holy Alliance degenerated into the very kind of politics that the Holy Alliance had been designed to supersede. Writing in anticipation of the Congress of Verona, another French liberal charged that nothing was left of Alexander's Holy Alliance but "its form and its name." The original goal of Alexander's alliance had been to lock into place a "perpetual peace," wrote Alphonse Mahul, but it was the Holy Alliance itself that had changed: now it belonged to Metternich, for whom "peace is just a means for waging the war of power against peoples."[81] Even for La Harpe—whom Metternich had suspected (perhaps not without reason) of being a liberal agent serving a Russian plot to wrest Italy from Austrian rule—the Congress of Verona was "the crossing of the Rubicon": the point of no return, he later recalled, that put an end to decades of effort dedicated to helping Alexander turn Russia into an agent of universal emancipation.[82] La Harpe warned Alexander in 1820 that the Holy Alliance had mainly served his enemies as an instrument for turning liberal public opinion against him: "a means of rendering suspect the philanthropic intentions of its author." In his efforts to hold the alliance together, Alexander had accommodated Russian power to Metternich's agenda—and set himself up to be blamed for all the problems it had produced. Metternich's appropriation of the Holy Alliance aside, La Harpe bitterly complained to Alexander, "the friends of justice, enlightenment, and liberal institutions" genuinely had "lost their protector."[83]

Viewed from the vantage point of contemporary liberals like La Harpe or Mahul, the fate of the Holy Alliance illustrates the transformation of federative politics into a font of reaction rather than progress. A final image of the Holy Alliance illustrates the transformation of religious association

81. Alphonse Jacques Mahul, *De la Sainte-alliance et du prochain congrès* (Paris: Chez l'Editeur, 1822), 8, 6, 31.

82. *Lettres inédites de Frédéric-César de La Harpe à Etienne Dumont et à la famille Duval (1822 à 1831)*, ed. Jean Martin (Lausanne: s.n., 1929), 35–38; *Correspondance de Frédéric-César de La Harpe et Alexandre Ier: Suivie de la correspondance de F.-C. de La Harpe avec les membres de la famille impériale de Russie*, ed. Jean Charles Biaudet and Françoise Nicod (Neuchâtel: Éditions de la Baconnière, 1978), 1:230.

83. La Harpe to Alexander I, August 28, 1820, *Correspondance de La Harpe et Alexandre Ier*, 3:440.

into a force undermining rather than unlocking the emancipatory potential of federative politics. In *The Holy Alliance, or, Satan's Legion at Sabbath Pranks*, the Philadelphia printer James Akin invoked the Holy Alliance to oppose a powerful social movement that had mobilized to condemn postal service on Sundays in the United States of America (figure 9). At first, as Richard John has explained, the 1810 federal law that required postal service throughout the week was perceived by a broad spectrum of Protestants as a threat to the moral basis of communal life as well as an unprecedented violation of local self-government. Though William Ellery Channing had voiced his opposition to this law in 1811, he later came to fear the growing power of the "Sabbatarian" movement. For Channing, this movement served as an example of the danger that public opinion, "when shackled and stimulated by vast associations," might become "a steady, unrelenting tyrant, brow-beating the timid, proscribing the resolute, silencing free speech, and virtually denying the dearest religious and civil rights." Such associations "create tyrants as effectually as standing armies," he warned: "it will be as perilous to think and speak with manly freedom, as if an inquisition were open before us."[84] Such fears were raised to a fever pitch in Akin's "Anti-Sabbatarian" lithograph of 1830, in which a mob of pitchfork-wielding fanatics tries to block the path of a mail coach. The mob, whose "pretended Pietism" threatens "ecclesiastical domination," is incited by Calvinist clergy as well as Catholic priests and other diabolical clerics, some of whom are drawn in the style of George Cruikshank.[85] The mail coach, upholding "the free exercise of all the noble rights that freemen love," is enveloped by the spirit of the U.S. Constitution and its authors; looming in the background is the Capitol, its facade emblazoned with the text of the First Amendment's prohibition of established religion and protection of free speech. "Look out for your Liberties my Boys!" exclaim a pair of immigrants surveying the scene, "thats just the way they wanted to shackle us in Ireland!!!" Though Akin drew on Cruikshank for inspiration, his depiction of the Holy Alliance also reflects a significant modification of liberal argument. In his review of Cruikshank and Hone's attack on the Holy Alliance, the radical critic

84. William Ellery Channing, "Remarks on Associations," in *The Works of William E. Channing, D.D.*, 11th ed., vol. 1 (Boston: G. G. Channing, 1849), 306–7, 326, cited in Richard R. John, "Taking Sabbatarianism Seriously: The Postal System, the Sabbath, and the Transformation of American Political Culture," *Journal of the Early Republic* 10, no. 4 (1990): 517–67. I am grateful to Richard John for bringing Akin to my attention.

85. On Akin and Cruikshank, see Maureen O'Brien Quimby, "The Political Art of James Akin," *Winterthur Portfolio* 7 (1972): 59–112.

FIGURE 9. James Akin, *The Holy Alliance, or, Satan's Legion at Sabbath Pranks*, colored lithograph. Philadelphia: James Akin, 1830. American Antiquarian Society, Worcester, Mass.

Leigh Hunt had appealed to the power of public opinion, communicated ever more efficiently and effectively, to defend liberty from the tyrannical state power represented by the Holy Alliance. For Akin, by contrast, the Holy Alliance represented the tyranny of public opinion, poisoned by religious fanaticism and bigotry, and the danger it posed to the free communication guaranteed by state institutions.

Reductive historical analogies, like those which merely invoke the Holy Alliance as an atavistic obstacle to progress, are poorly equipped to grapple with the political complexities that they purport to clarify. Closer attention to how the image of the Holy Alliance was deployed in a variety of contemporary political arguments suggests how the problems it confronted have continued to appear in new forms, rather than vanishing with the triumph of the liberal nation-state. Initially, as the following chapters will show, the Holy Alliance was widely perceived across the northern (and mainly but not exclusively Protestant) European world as a combination of Christianity with federative politics that would advance liberal goals. The conflict over the Holy Alliance that became a clash between Western liberalism and Eastern reaction was initially also an instance of a recurring clash between liberalisms: a liberalism of the North (the liberal idea of the Holy Alliance) against an emergent "liberal international" of the South (which came to include Mazzini), with France as a key battleground state.[86] Considered in this way, the liberal idea of the Holy Alliance, systematically theorized in Kantian form by Wilhelm Traugott Krug, raises the kinds of questions that would be reformulated with the invention of "global justice"—again in Kantian form, now in the context of a mainline Protestant response to the challenge posed by the postcolonial New International Economic Order of the 1970s.[87] At the same time, looking forward from the eighteenth century, rather than backward from the twentieth, turns the liberal idea of the Holy Alliance into "the first attempt to transform plans for a perpetual peace into reality."[88] The Holy Alliance was still widely recognizable, from Denmark to Haiti, as an enactment (though possibly an eccentric one) of Enlightenment politics, as well as a performance of Enlightenment authorship. The fact that this performance was being staged by a Russian bear was a vindication

86. For the idea of a "Protestant International," see Christopher Clark and Michael Ledger-Lomas, "The Protestant International," in *Religious Internationals in the Modern World: Globalization and Faith Communities since 1750*, ed. Abigail Green and Vincent Viaene (Houndmills: Palgrave Macmillan, 2012), 23–52. On the "liberal international" of southern European liberalism, see Maurizio Isabella, "Mazzini's Internationalism in Context: From the Cosmopolitan Patriotism of the Italian Carbonari to Mazzini's Europe of the Nations," in *Giuseppe Mazzini and the Globalisation of Democratic Nationalism, 1830-1920*, ed. C. A. Bayly and Eugenio F. Biagini (Oxford: Oxford University Press, 2008), 37–58; Maurizio Isabella, *Risorgimento in Exile: Italian Émigrés and the Liberal International in the Post-Napoleonic Era* (Oxford: Oxford University Press, 2009); Elisabetta Fiocchi Malaspina, "Vattel's Law of Nations in Late Eighteenth- and Early Nineteenth-Century Greece and Italy," in *Concepts and Contexts of Vattel's Political and Legal Thought*, ed. Peter Schröder (Cambridge: Cambridge University Press, 2021), 239–57.

87. Samuel Moyn, "The Political Origins of Global Justice," in *The Worlds of American Intellectual History*, ed. Joel Isaac et al. (Oxford: Oxford University Press, 2016), 133–52.

88. Reinhart Koselleck, "Die Restauration und ihre Ereigniszusammenhänge 1815-1830," in *Das Zeitalter der europäischen Revolution 1780-1848*, by Louis Bergeron, Reinhart Koselleck, and François Furet (Frankfurt am Main: Fischer Bücherei, 1973), 220.

of a whole complex of arguments about why Russia could avoid reproducing the pathologies of more "civilized" European states and empires: about why it could acquire the capacity, motivation, and authority to play the roles of mediator and guarantor in a globally emancipatory fashion. These arguments, which are reflected in the images of bruins becoming mediators, were still being reprised in the early 1820s—but they had been forged in the eighteenth century.

CHAPTER TWO

Friend of Mankind

Today, enlightenment comes to us from the north.

—VOLTAIRE, "LETTER TO THE EMPRESS OF RUSSIA"[1]

TWO YEARS AFTER the burning of Moscow, Paris was won over by a spectacle of magnanimity. On the last day of March in 1814, the emperor of Russia issued a proclamation announcing his army's peaceful entry into the French capital. Alexander—who had, over the course of 1813, pressured his allies not to negotiate or pursue a separate peace—now assured the public that the aim of the victorious allies was not limited to eliminating the threat posed by Napoleon. They also intended to "recognize and guarantee the constitution that the French nation will adopt," since "for the happiness of Europe, France must be great and strong."[2] Two days later, in an address to the French Senate, Alexander declared himself the "friend of the French people"—a claim reinforced by the strict discipline maintained by the Cossacks camping on the Champs-Elysées and the ecumenical thanksgiving service celebrated in the Place de la Concorde (where Louis XVI had been guillotined in 1793).[3] Alexander's subsequent efforts to foster reconciliation within France under a newly restored Bourbon monarch produced a wave of popular enthusiasm and liberal infatuation

1. Voltaire, "Épître à l'impératrice de Russie," ed. John Pappas, in *Writings of 1771,* ed. Nicholas Cronk, Les Oeuvres complètes de Voltaire, vol. 73 (Oxford: Voltaire Foundation, 2004), 444.

2. Cited in Marie-Pierre Rey, *Alexander I: The Tsar Who Defeated Napoleon,* trans. Susan Emanuel (DeKalb: Northern Illinois University Press, 2012), 268–69. See also Raymond McNally, *Das Russlandbild in der Publizistik Frankreichs zwischen 1814 und 1843,* Forschungen zur osteuropäischen Geschichte 6 (Berlin: Osteuropa Institut an der Freien Universität Berlin, 1958).

3. Cited in Rey, *Alexander I,* 274.

as well as resentment among many reinstated royalists. Though Alexander failed to persuade Louis XVIII to embrace the revolutionary tricolor, he did succeed in pressuring him to grant a constitutional charter underwritten by "liberal ideas": as the idiosyncratic royalist François-René de Chateaubriand later observed, "he alone of all the sovereigns of Europe had understood that France at the age of civilization it had reached could only be governed thanks to a free constitution."[4] A similar response greeted Alexander in London later that spring, where his public appearances attracted enormous crowds together with the suspicion of many political elites; but his support for international action against the slave trade prompted the abolitionist William Wilberforce to praise him in the House of Commons as "the benefactor, not of Europe only, but of the human race."[5]

In his triumphant tour of Paris and London, Alexander had assumed the role of "friend of mankind"—an epithet that had been marked out for him years earlier by his former Swiss tutor, Frédéric-César de la Harpe.[6] This eighteenth-century idiom was still meaningful a century later to the foreign head of state who followed in Alexander's footsteps and entered Paris to a hero's welcome at the conclusion of World War I. In order to extract themselves from the logic of "competitive interest," President Woodrow Wilson explained in February 1919, Europeans "resort to that nation which has won the enviable distinction of being regarded as the friend of mankind." This distinction reflected both the spectacle of American power and the moral authority conferred by its deployment in the spirit of impartial empathy for Europe's predicament. Wilson faithfully reproduced the moral character that defined the eighteenth-century friend of mankind: "I do not see how any man can fail to have been subdued by these pleas, subdued to this feeling that he was not there to assert an individual judgment of his own but to try to assist the cause of humanity."[7]

4. Ibid., 275.

5. *Hansard Parliamentary Debates*, House of Commons, June 6, 1814, 1st ser., vol. 27, c. 1081, https://api.parliament.uk/historic-hansard/commons/1814/jun/06/treaty-of-peace.

6. La Harpe to Alexander I, February 13, 1803, *Correspondance de Frédéric-César de La Harpe et Alexandre Ier: Suivie de la correspondance de F.-C. de La Harpe avec les membres de la famille impériale de Russie*, ed. Jean Charles Biaudet and Françoise Nicod (Neuchâtel: Éditions de la Baconnière, 1978), 2:27.

7. Woodrow Wilson, "An Address in Boston, February 24, 1919," in *The Papers of Woodrow Wilson, Volume 55: February 8–March 16, 1919*, ed. Arthur S. Link (Princeton: Princeton University Press, 1986), 239–40. On Wilson's brief global appeal, see Erez Manela, *The Wilsonian Moment: Self-Determination and the International Origins of Anticolonial Nationalism* (Oxford: Oxford University Press, 2009). Interestingly, the eighteenth-century idiom of the "friend of mankind" lingered long enough to be used by another Southern Democrat, the Arkansas senator J. William Fulbright. In 1966, Fulbright declared that "I prefer to see

The character that Wilson summoned in 1919, following in the footsteps of Alexander in 1814, was originally constructed during the eighteenth century, in the context of efforts to resolve the rivalry between Britain and France. Though the projection of this originally Anglo-French idea onto America may be more familiar than its projection onto Russia, in fact the Enlightenment's "mirage in the West" and its *mirage russe* share a common origin.[8] Alexander's 1814 performance of a peacemaking "friend of mankind" was urgently fashioned over the course of the military campaign of 1813 by drawing explicitly on the extensive eighteenth-century literature on "perpetual peace," which addressed the problem of destructive competition among European states.[9] But Alexander's performance was also the product of much longer efforts undertaken by his tutor, La Harpe, as well as his former foreign minister, Adam Jerzy Czartoryski. Their efforts, which are the subject of the following two chapters, rested in turn on a series of eighteenth-century debates: not only about perpetual peace and relations between states but also about the implications of Russia's development for the progress of what had come to be called "civilization." This constellation of eighteenth-century debates about Russia and "civilization" generated complex claims about the relationship between Russian and European history that continued to frame assessments of the Holy Alliance through the 1820s. The idea of a Russian "friend of mankind" emerged at the intersection of all these debates, and it raised further questions about Alexander's intentions, Russia's capacities, and the kinds

---

my country in the role of sympathetic friend to humanity rather than its stern and prideful schoolmaster." Fulbright lamented that the "democratic humanism" of the former had given way to the "spirit of a righteous crusade" that had been "dredged up from the depths of a puritan soul" to fight two world wars and that remained the dominant style of "professional patriots." J. William Fulbright, *The Arrogance of Power* (New York: Random House, 1967), 250–57.

8. Durand Echeverria, *Mirage in the West: A History of the French Image of American Society to 1815* (Princeton: Princeton University Press, 1957); Albert Lortholary, *Les "philosophes" du XVIIIe siècle et la Russie: Le mirage russe en France au XVIIIe siècle* (Paris: Éditions contemporains, Boivic, 1951). Both of these 1950s studies were concerned to address the affinity of many twentieth-century Western intellectuals for the Soviet Union. For a contrasting post-1989 perspective, concerned to address Western condescension toward Eastern Europe, see Larry Wolff, *Inventing Eastern Europe: The Map of Civilization on the Mind of the Enlightenment* (Stanford: Stanford University Press, 1994). For criticism of both approaches, see Reto Speck, "The History and Politics of Civilisation: The Debate about Russia in French and German Historical Scholarship from Voltaire to Herder" (PhD diss., Queen Mary University of London, 2010).

9. Maria Mayofis, "After the Napoleonic Wars: Reading Perpetual Peace in the Russian Empire," in *Cosmopolitanism in Conflict: Imperial Encounters from the Seven Years' War to the Cold War*, ed. Dina Gusejnova (London: Palgrave Macmillan, 2018), 85–110.

of Russian interventions in European politics that might bring about "perpetual peace." The purpose of this chapter is to explain the framework within which such questions came to be posed following Napoleon's retreat from Russia in 1812, Alexander's entry into Paris in 1814, and his proclamation of the Holy Alliance in 1815.

Perpetual Peace and the Peacemaking State

The moral character who figured as the "friend of mankind" has been assigned a prominent place in the attempt to write the history of human rights as an eighteenth-century invention that was temporarily eclipsed by the rise of nationalism before reemerging in the second half of the twentieth century.[10] The endurance and proliferation of the "friend of mankind" idiom points instead toward the history of a political strategy for imposing moral limits on the competitive behavior of European states: an approach that connects, rather than isolating as ideological opposites, the histories of eighteenth-century cosmopolitanism and republicanism with the histories of nineteenth-century nationalism, internationalism, pan-nationalism, and imperial liberalism.[11] As many contributors to the eighteenth-century literature on "perpetual peace" pointed out, the seventeenth-century language of natural rights had produced a powerful way to theorize the state as a collective personality. But when multiple states found themselves locked into highly competitive relations with one another, the resulting instability of these personalities became a central problem of political theory. As the Scottish republican Andrew Fletcher asserted in 1704 (possibly channeling a remark cited by the jurist Hugo Grotius), those who defended the suppression of Ireland's and Scotland's economic potential as necessary for England's security were admitting that "no man can be a good citizen

10. See Lynn Hunt, *Inventing Human Rights: A History* (New York: W. W. Norton, 2007).

11. For some recent approaches to the eighteenth-century literature on perpetual peace and its nineteenth-century legacies, see Antoine Lilti and Céline Spector, eds., *Penser l'Europe au XVIIIe siècle: Commerce, civilisation, empire* (Oxford: Voltaire Foundation, 2014); Sylvie Aprile et al., eds., *Europe de papier: Projets européens au XIXe siècle* (Villeneuve-d'Ascq: Presses universitaires du Septentrion, 2015); Thomas Hippler and Miloš Vec, eds., *Paradoxes of Peace in Nineteenth Century Europe* (Oxford: Oxford University Press, 2015); Béla Kapossy, Isaac Nakhimovsky, and Richard Whatmore, eds., *Commerce and Peace in the Enlightenment* (Cambridge: Cambridge University Press, 2017); David Armitage and Stella Ghervas, eds., *A Cultural History of Peace in the Age of Enlightenment* (London: Bloomsbury Academic, 2020); John Shovlin, *Trading with the Enemy: Britain, France, and the 18th-Century Quest for a Peaceful World Order* (New Haven: Yale University Press, 2021).

of a particular commonwealth, and a citizen of the world; no man can be a true friend to his country and to mankind at the same time."[12] "In uniting ourselves to particular men," warned the Genevan philosopher Jean-Jacques Rousseau in a similar vein in 1760, "we really become the enemies of humankind."[13] In the eighteenth century this kind of competitive politics was often diagnosed as "Machiavellism," and many worried that it was seeping into broader cultures, producing a deformation of patriotism that became known, initially in German, as "nationalism."[14]

The character of the "friend of mankind" was supposed to supply the antidote to such deformation. The *hostis humani generis*, or "enemy of mankind," was an old Roman term that came to designate violators of natural law like pirates. Its use proliferated in the eighteenth century, and it was invoked at the trial of Louis XVI of France before being applied to Napoleon.[15] The "friend of mankind," by contrast, came to serve as a label for a moral character who emerged around the turn of the eighteenth century: someone whose capacity for emotional identification with others was not limited by arbitrary or conventional boundaries. Such an agent practiced a

12. Andrew Fletcher, "Account of a Conversation Concerning a Right Regulation of Governments for the Common Good of Mankind. In a Letter to the Marquiss of Montrose, the Earls of Rothes, Roxburg and Haddington, from London the First of December, 1703," in *Political Works*, ed. John Robertson (Cambridge: Cambridge University Press, 1997), 206. Cf. the remark cited by Grotius in section 25 of the Prolegomena to his famous 1625 treatise *The Rights of War and Peace*: "Themistius, in his Oration to Valens, says very elegantly, that Kings, who conduct themselves by the Rules of Wisdom, take Care, not only of the Nation whose Government they are entrusted with, but of all Mankind; and are, as he expresses himself, not φιλομακέδονες Friends to the Macedonians only, or φιλορωμαίοι to the Romans, but φιλάνθρωποι to all Men without Exception." Hugo Grotius, *The Rights of War and Peace*, ed. Richard Tuck (Indianapolis: Liberty Fund, 2005), 1:100–101.

13. Jean-Jacques Rousseau, *A Project for Perpetual Peace* (London, 1761), 3.

14. On "Machiavellism," the deformation of patriotism, and nationalism, see Istvan Hont, "The Permanent Crisis of a Divided Mankind: 'Contemporary Crisis of the Nation State' in Historical Perspective," in *Jealousy of Trade: International Competition and the Nation-State in Historical Perspective* (Cambridge, MA: Harvard University Press, 2005), 447–528. See also Isaac Nakhimovsky, introduction to *Addresses to the German Nation*, by Johann Gottlieb Fichte, ed. Isaac Nakhimovsky, Béla Kapossy, and Keith Tribe (Indianapolis: Hackett, 2013), ix–xxx.

15. On the Roman term and its subsequent career, see Harry D. Gould, "Cicero's Ghost: Rethinking the Social Construction of Piracy," in *Maritime Piracy and the Construction of Global Governance*, ed. Michael J. Struett, Jon D. Carlson, and Mark T. Nance (New York: Routledge, 2012), 23–46. On the significance of the term during the French Revolution, see Dan Edelstein, "Hostis Humani Generis: Devils, Natural Right, Terror, and the French Revolution," *Telos: A Quarterly Journal of Critical Thought* 141 (2007): 57–81; Dan Edelstein, *The Terror of Natural Right: Republicanism, the Cult of Nature, and the French Revolution* (Chicago: University of Chicago Press, 2009). See also Walter Rech, *Enemies of Mankind: Vattel's Theory of Collective Security* (Leiden: Martinus Nijhoff, 2013).

worldly kind of virtue, a benevolence that was not entirely selfless but was linked to a healthy desire for approbation: "his whole delight is in doing good," explained the printer and novelist Samuel Richardson, "And to mend the hearts, as well as fortunes, of men, is his glory."[16] To affirm this principle of sociability was also to assume the title of "friend of mankind," whereas to challenge it was to be labeled, along with Thomas Hobbes, an "enemy of the human race."[17] The term "friend of mankind" was particularly associated with educational reform and the emergence of an enlightened and polite civic culture, and it also became a way of signaling opposition to slavery.[18] It was generally used to express an individual commitment to collective security and prosperity, projecting a morally attractive alternative to established power structures. It had this meaning in the realm of international relations as well. As the heroine of Richardson's 1753 novel *The History of Sir Charles Grandison* put it, "How much more glorious a character is that of *the friend of mankind*, than that of *the conqueror of nations!*"[19] Read as a political allegory, the "friend of mankind" who was the eponymous hero of Richardson's novel was "all that Charles Stuart should have been": "a corrective and hopeful image" of "the Tory Prince who never came" to tame the excesses of the post-1688 Whig regime.[20]

The most important and enduringly influential image of such a peacemaking prince appeared in *Adventures of Telemachus*, by François de Salignac de la Mothe-Fénelon, archbishop of Cambrai. Fénelon was Louis XIV's greatest

16. Samuel Richardson, *The History of Sir Charles Grandison. In a Series of Letters Published from the Originals, by the Editor of Pamela and Clarissa. In Seven Volumes* (London, 1754), 3:88.

17. Jean-Jacques Rousseau's greatest critic in the 1750s was the Swiss republican reformer Isaak Iselin, whose refutation of Rousseau's "Discourse on the Arts and Sciences" was titled *Patriotic Dreams of a Friend of Mankind* (1755): see Béla Kapossy, *Iselin Contra Rousseau: Sociable Patriotism and the History of Mankind* (Basel: Schwabe, 2006). On Denis Diderot's identification of the Hobbesian principle of natural unsociability with the "enemy of humankind," see his article "Droit naturel," in *Encyclopédie, ou Dictionnaire raisonné des sciences, des arts et des métiers, par une société de gens de lettres*, ed. Denis Diderot and Jean Le Rond d'Alembert, vol. 5 (Paris, 1755), 116. On the identification of Rousseau (at least in Rousseau's own eyes) with this "violent reasoner," see *The Political Writings of Jean Jacques Rousseau*, ed. Charles Edwyn Vaughan (Cambridge: Cambridge University Press, 1915), 1:427–28.

18. G. Felicitas Munzel, "Menschenfreundschaft: Friendship and Pedagogy in Kant," *Eighteenth-Century Studies* 32, no. 2 (1998): 247–59; Miles Mark Fisher, "Friends of Humanity: A Quaker Anti-Slavery Influence," *Church History: Studies in Christianity and Culture* 4, no. 3 (1935): 187–202.

19. Richardson, *The History of Sir Charles Grandison*, 3:101.

20. Margaret Anne Doody, "Richardson's Politics," *Eighteenth-Century Fiction* 2, no. 2 (1990): 125.

critic, and his many admirers included a wide variety of British critics of the Whig establishment.[21] Fénelon had served as the tutor of Louis XIV's grandson (the successor to French throne); he had composed *Telemachus* (first published anonymously in 1699) in the hope that his pupil's reign would be nothing like his grandfather's. In *Telemachus* as well as his other writings, Fénelon asserted the possibility of a moral alternative to Louis XIV's Machiavellian pursuit of glory through conquest.[22] Fénelon claimed that princes who subordinated their own interests to the "true needs of the state" and ensured the people's security and prosperity would earn their love as well as true glory—and would thereby acquire far greater power than Louis XIV.[23] In Fénelon's thinly veiled allegory, Telemachus and his tutor Mentor helped persuade a powerful king to abandon his misguided quest for false glory and devote himself to reforming his country; he then reconciled with the alliance that had originally formed to resist his unjust ambitions for conquest, and joined them in combating the real menace to them all, another king "who despised the gods, and sought only to deceive mankind."[24] This was the "holy alliance, of which the gods will be witnesses and guarantees," which Mentor promised would become the foundation of a more peaceful world:

> Your several nations for the future will be but one, under different names and governors. Thus it is, that the just gods, who formed and love the human race, would have them united in an everlasting bond of

21. On Fénelon and his eighteenth-century reception, including in Britain, see Albert Chérel, *Fénelon au XVIIIe siècle en France (1715-1820): Son prestige, son influence* (Fribourg: Imp. Fragnière frères, 1917); Istvan Hont, "The Luxury Debate in the Early Enlightenment," in *The Cambridge History of Eighteenth-Century Political Thought*, ed. M. Goldie and R. Wokler (Cambridge: Cambridge University Press, 2006), 379–418; Christoph Schmitt-Maaß, Stefanie Stockhorst, and Doohwan Ahn, eds., *Fénelon in the Enlightenment: Traditions, Adaptations, and Variations* (Amsterdam: Rodopi, 2014); Andrew Mansfield, *Ideas of Monarchical Reform: Fénelon, Jacobitism, and the Political Works of the Chevalier Ramsay* (Manchester: Manchester University Press, 2015); Ryan Patrick Hanley, *The Political Philosophy of Fénelon* (New York: Oxford University Press, 2020).

22. On Fénelon and late seventeenth-century reason of state theory, see Isaac Nakhimovsky, "The Enlightened Prince and the Future of Europe: Voltaire and Frederick the Great's *Anti-Machiavel* of 1740," in *Commerce and Peace in the Enlightenment*, ed. Béla Kapossy, Isaac Nakhimovsky, and Richard Whatmore (Cambridge: Cambridge University Press, 2017), 44–77.

23. Fénelon preferred the language of "true needs" to that of interest: see Lucien Jaume, "Fénelon critique de la déraison d'Etat," in *Raison et déraison d'Etat*, ed. Yves Charles Zarka (Paris: Presses Universitaires de France, 1994), 403.

24. François de Salignac de la Mothe-Fénelon, *Telemachus, Son of Ulysses*, ed. Patrick Riley (Cambridge: Cambridge University Press, 1994), 214.

perfect amity and concord. All mankind are but one family dispersed over the face of the whole earth. All nations are brethren, and ought to love one another as such.[25]

It was a sentiment that Alexander would translate into his own holy alliance—and was already expressing in the wake of the French army's retreat from Russia in December 1812:

> Why, the emperor said, do not all the sovereigns and nations of Europe agree among themselves to love and live as brothers, by helping each other in their reciprocal needs? Trade would become the general good of this great society whose members, no doubt, would have different religions, but the spirit of tolerance would unite all faiths.[26]

As Alexander's reference to trade indicates, the peacemaking agent who became the eighteenth-century ideal of a "friend of mankind" was not just a moral character. It was an agent whose constitution and conduct were the subject of a much broader set of discussions concerning political economy and forms of government. The underlying problem these discussions addressed was the one identified by the Scottish republican Andrew Fletcher in 1704: England's pursuit of maritime and commercial empire, no less than France's pursuit of continental empire, had made it impossible to be "a true friend to his country and to mankind at the same time."[27] Underlying the moral vision advanced in *Telemachus* was Fénelon's criticism of Louis XIV's minister Jean-Baptiste Colbert, who had sought to pay for Louis XIV's wars by accelerating the development of French manufacturing and trade in competition with the Dutch and English. Fénelon charged that the result was a destabilizing pattern of development that had produced excessive urbanization and rising inequality. A more stable form of international competition required sweeping state interventions to reverse Colbert's policies by restoring the primacy of agricultural production over the growth of manufacturing. In an essay published posthumously in 1719 and immediately translated into English, Fénelon described how Louis XIV had left France facing two unappealing alternatives: either it would be weakened by the alliance that had formed to resist it, or it would mount another disastrous

25. Ibid., 146–47.

26. Sophie de Tisenhaus de Choiseul-Gouffier, *Mémoires historiques sur l'empereur Alexandre et la cour de Russie* (Bruxelles: A. Wahlen and H. Tarlier, 1829), 134–35, cited in Rey, *Alexander I*, 266–67.

27. Fletcher, "Account of a Conversation," 206.

bid for supremacy.[28] Fénelon's alternative was a new kind of balance of power: a state was "the wisest and happiest of all," he explained, when it had "a Force nearly equal to that of another neighbouring State, together with which it maintains all in Peace, by a kind of Balance, which it preserves without Ambition, and with exact Faith."[29] Rather than vying for military advantage, an agriculturally self-sufficient France could maintain an equilibrium with Britain while pursuing the "other kind of Superiority" that was "Inward and Substantial": a larger and more productive population that, Fénelon claimed, would follow from erasing Colbert's legacy.[30]

Several variations on Fénelon's moral vision became associated with the role of a peacemaking "friend of mankind" over the course of the eighteenth century, before becoming connected to Alexander. One such variation appeared in *The Friend of Mankind*, a famous treatise on political economy by Victor Riqueti, Marquis de Mirabeau, which appeared at the outset of the Seven Years War in 1756. Mirabeau's treatise was, among other things, a monumental effort to show how France could assume the titular role by imposing Fénelon's moral vision on Britain as well as itself. Having increased its agricultural productivity by liberalizing its markets, Mirabeau explained, it would be in France's interest to establish a new international system based on the principle of free trade. The members of this new federation would collectively impose an embargo on English goods until England surrendered its monopolistic position and joined the "universal confraternity in commerce." If this strategy led to war with Britain, as Mirabeau assumed, it would be apparent that the French "friend of mankind" was fighting on behalf of "the cause of humanity."[31] Several versions of this embargo strategy were revived at the turn of the

28. [François de Salignac de la Mothe-Fénelon], "Sentiments on the Ballance of Europe. Written by the Late Archbishop of Cambray," in *Two Essays on the Ballance of Europe* (London: John Darby, 1720), 22. On the English translation, see Clare Jackson, "Revolution Principles, Ius Naturae and Ius Gentium in Early-Enlightenment Scotland: The Contribution of Sir Francis Grant, Lord Cullen (c. 1660–1726)," in *Early Modern Natural Law Theories: Context and Strategies in the Early Enlightenment*, ed. T. Hochstrasser and P. Schröder (Dordrecht: Springer, 2003), 124; Doohwan Ahn, "From Idomeneus to Protesilaus: Fénelon in Early Hanoverian Britain," in *Fénelon in the Enlightenment: Traditions, Adaptations, and Variations*, ed. Christoph Schmitt-Maaß, Stefanie Stockhorst, and Doohwan Ahn (Amsterdam: Rodopi, 2014), 99–128.

29. Fénelon, "Sentiments on the Ballance of Europe," 24.

30. Ibid., 26–27.

31. Victor de Riqueti, marquis de Mirabeau, *L'ami des hommes, ou Traité de la population* (Avignon, 1756), 3:271. On Mirabeau's strategy, see Michael Sonenscher, *Before the Deluge: Public Debt, Inequality, and the Intellectual Origins of the French Revolution* (Princeton: Princeton University Press, 2007), chap. 3.

nineteenth century—including by Thomas Jefferson, who (as chapter 3 will discuss) had also entered into correspondence with Alexander before trying to impose free trade on both Britain and France after 1807. Writing to Germaine de Staël in 1813, Jefferson observed that if Alexander, having defeated Napoleon, also succeeded in defeating Britain's monopolistic approach to trade, "it will prove that the immortal character, which has first stopped by war the career of the destroyer of mankind, is the friend of peace, of justice & of human happiness, and the patron of unoffending and injured nations." The "virtuous Alexander," Jefferson hoped, was "too honest and impartial to countenance propositions of peace derogatory to the freedom of the seas."[32]

In his posthumous *Sketch for a Historical Picture of the Progress of the Human Mind* of 1795, the French philosopher the Marquis de Condorcet outlined another version of the role of "friend of mankind" that also came to be connected to Alexander. Condorcet described how constitutional reforms could lead to Britain and France becoming the joint creators of a new Atlantic economy by abolishing the slave trade and investing in the economic development of Africa:

> Already, in Great Britain, some friends of humanity have set the example; and if its Machavelian government, forced to respect public reason, has not dared to oppose this measure, what may we not expect from the same spirit, when, after the reform of an abject and venal constitution, it shall become worthy of a humane and generous people? Will not France be eager to imitate enterprises which the philanthropy and the true interest of Europe will equally have dictated?[33]

Led by governments worthy of "friends of mankind," Britain and France would acquire the moral authority as well as the economic power that came from abolishing the practices that had been "destroying that sentiment of respect and benevolence which the superiority of our commerce had at first obtained" among Africans: "no longer exhibiting to the view of these people corruptors only or tyrants, we shall become to them instruments of benefit, and the generous champions of their redemption from

32. Thomas Jefferson to Germaine de Stäel, May 28, 1813, *The Papers of Thomas Jefferson, Retirement Series, Volume 6: 11 March to 27 November 1813*, ed. J. Jefferson Looney (Princeton: Princeton University Press, 2009), 144.

33. Jean-Antoine-Nicolas de Caritat marquis de Condorcet, *Outlines of an Historical View of the Progress of the Human Mind: Being a Posthumous Work of the Late M. de Condorcet* (London: J. Johnson, 1795), 321–22.

bondage."[34] The role of "friend of mankind" that Alexander assumed in Paris and London in 1814 was also tied to his commitment to constitutional principles and the abolition of the slave trade. "It is tempting to believe oneself transported somewhere supernatural when one sees these principles professed by the sovereign of an empire where absolute power has existed for so long," wrote the Swiss liberal Benjamin Constant to La Harpe. "I have rarely experienced such strong emotion as when I saw his superb face animated by a noble indignation in speaking about the slave trade."[35] Likewise, to the abolitionist Thomas Clarkson, Alexander declared himself "the friend of the poor Africans" and "an Enemy to the Slave Trade."[36]

Fénelon was identified as the ultimate source of the character that Alexander had adopted by Robert Wilson, the British military attaché who had accompanied the Russian army under General Kutuzov in 1812 and went on to become a Liberal Member of Parliament. As Wilson recalled in 1817, Alexander had been fashioned in the mold of Fénelon's ideal prince by his Swiss tutor, La Harpe:

> As the pupil of La Harpe, expectation was raised high as to his capacity for government. The "Telemachus of the North" was not then inebriated with power, but, instructed in his duties by a Mentor endowed with intelligence and virtue, exercised the authority of a despotic sovereign to establish philanthropy as the basis of his throne.[37]

From Wilson's perspective, this was an expectation that Alexander had ultimately failed to meet, as his inability to make good on the promise of constitutional reform showed:

> If, indeed, Alexander had resisted the enemies of liberty and human happiness—if he had persevered in the wish he once professed, to see governments and nations so constituted, that sovereigns should be only the *executive* representatives of *represented* states, whose action depended not on the *character* of the individual chief, but on *general,*

34. Ibid.

35. Constant to La Harpe, May 26, 1814, cited in Francis Ley, *Alexandre Ier et sa Sainte-Alliance: 1811–1825, avec des documents inédits* (Paris: Fischbacher, 1975), 83.

36. *Thomas Clarkson's Interviews with the Emperor Alexander I of Russia at Paris and Aix-La-Chapelle in 1815 and 1818 as Told by Himself*, ed. Priscilla Peckover (London: Slavery and Native Races Committee of the Society of Friends, 1930), 9.

37. Robert Thomas Wilson, *A Sketch of the Military and Political Power of Russia, in the Year 1817* (New York: Kirk and Mercein, 1817), 12.

fixed, and self-operating principles; he would have added to his glory, the more illustrious and imperishable title of the "Benefactor to Mankind."[38]

Instead, in Wilson's view, the would-be "Telemachus of the North" had devolved into yet another conqueror—the only remaining question was where and how far his pursuit of power would take him (and, Wilson wondered, whether it would threaten British rule over India). But many liberals took a different view of Alexander's trajectory—including Germaine de Staël.

In her *Considerations on the Principal Events of the French Revolution*, published posthumously in 1817, Staël defended Alexander's cautious approach to constitutional reform as an expression of his quintessentially liberal acknowledgment of the limits of power. She related a conversation with him in Saint Petersburg in 1812, where she had fled after her exile from France by Napoleon, whose army was then closing in on Moscow. Alexander pointed out to her that "Russian peasants are slaves" and that his efforts to improve their condition met with "obstacles which the tranquility of the empire enjoins me to treat with caution." When Staël responded with a reference to his good character—"I know that Russia is at present happy, although she has no other constitution than the personal character of your Majesty"—Alexander delivered a reply that, in her estimation, was "worthy of being consecrated": "'Even if the compliment you pay me were true,' replied the Emperor, 'I should be nothing more than a fortunate accident.'" This acknowledgment of the limits of political power to effect moral change was all the more remarkable, Staël concluded, given the situation of the individual who had made it, which "could blind him in regard to the condition of men." Alexander was correct, Staël concluded, that "the most enlightened kings, if they are absolute, could not, if they would, encourage in their nation strength and dignity of character. God and the law alone can command man in the tone of a master without degrading him."[39] Staël's positive judgment of Alexander extended to the Holy Alliance itself. In her *Considerations*, she singled out its commitment to the "fraternity of all Christian communities." According to Staël, those who condemned it were "these partisans of despotism and of intolerance, these enemies of knowledge, these adversaries of humanity, when

38. Ibid., 152.
39. Anne-Louise-Germaine de Staël, *Considerations on the Principal Events of the French Revolution*, ed. Aurelian Craiutu (Indianapolis: Liberty Fund, 2008), 731–32.

it bears the name of people and nation! Whither could one fly were they to have command?"[40] The object of their condemnation, by imputation, was the act of a friend of mankind.

Civilization and Barbarism

As Staël's exchange with Alexander indicates, the identification of the emperor of Russia with the moral character of a "friend of mankind" raised a further set of questions about Russian history, its relationship to European history, and the nature of progress. The emergence of a Russian "friend of mankind" could be attributed to the exceptional character of its ruler, but it was also linked to a range of widely debated eighteenth-century accounts of Russian history. From one perspective, the unprecedented pace of Russia's development pointed to its emergence as the future center of European "civilization"; from another, it meant that the same pathologies which had turned Britain and France into "enemies of humanity" were turning Russia into the unstoppable agent of Europe's impending relapse into "barbarism." From yet another perspective, however, it was precisely Russia's lingering "barbarism" that created the opening for its ruler to avoid retracing the self-destructive trajectory associated with Britain and France—and created the possibility of rescuing all of Europe and even the rest of the world from its consequences.

The connection between such questions about Russian history and the problem of destructive competition between Britain and France was forged by the prolific French writer François Marie Arouet de Voltaire. In the 1720s and 1730s, Voltaire had embarked on a major revision of Fénelon's account of the reforms that would equip France to participate in a stable balance of power with Britain. According to Voltaire, reversing Colbert's policies, as Fénelon had suggested, would not produce an escape from a Machiavellian world: it would destroy the possibility of constructing an alternative to it.[41] Louis XIV was not a failed conqueror but the true founder of the kind of alternative balance of power that Fénelon had described: in stabilizing the French monarchy and greatly enhancing its internal capacities, Louis XIV had spurred his rivals to do the same, establishing the basis for a balance of power that operated primarily according

40. Ibid., 745.
41. On Voltaire's revision of Fénelon, see especially Hont, "The Luxury Debate in the Early Enlightenment"; Sonenscher, *Before the Deluge*, chap. 2; Nakhimovsky, "The Enlightened Prince and the Future of Europe."

to the "spirit of commerce" rather than the "spirit of conquest."[42] Locked into a system of deepening diplomatic and commercial relations, France and Britain both had an interest in moving beyond their respective quests for imperial dominance on land and sea. Internally, the tremendous wealth they were generating supported the development of the arts and sciences and the emergence of a polite society with a taste for civility and tolerance. Externally, their competition might still produce wars, but they were each so well defended that these wars would remain bounded conflicts rather than becoming existential struggles. Though Britain enjoyed some institutional advantages over France, Voltaire claimed that the French monarchy was also well equipped to practice this new kind of anti-Machiavellian politics, in tandem with Britain.

Voltaire was a pioneer of what J.G.A. Pocock called "Enlightened narrative," which traced how the stifling rule of priests and feudal lords across Europe had given way to sovereign states that served as powerful engines of prosperity and culture.[43] The Anglo-French détente that followed the Treaty of Utrecht in 1713 pointed toward the sequel to that historical narrative: the transformation of Europe since the "Age of Louis XIV" into "a kind of great republic divided into many states."[44] The claims about monarchy, the arts and sciences, and the balance of power that underpinned this narrative were packaged together in the *Anti-Machiavel*, Voltaire's collaboration with Frederick II of Prussia, published in 1740. Voltaire himself claimed that the *Anti-Machiavel* had superseded Fénelon's *Adventures of Telemachus* by translating its moral vision into the idiom of real history and the historical context of real politics.[45] The *Anti-Machiavel* further claimed that extending this Anglo-French model of a new balance of power to the rest of Europe involved redrawing the map of the Holy Roman Empire: the aim was to consolidate its complex and archaic patchwork into modern states more like Britain and France, which would be capable of participating in a balance of power that operated according to the "spirit of commerce," instead

42. These terms were introduced by Jean-François Melon in 1735. On Melon and Voltaire, see Hont, "The Luxury Debate in the Early Enlightenment."

43. J.G.A. Pocock, *Barbarism and Religion, Vol. 2: Narratives of Civil Government* (Cambridge: Cambridge University Press, 1999). See also Karen O'Brien, *Narratives of Enlightenment: Cosmopolitan History from Voltaire to Gibbon* (Cambridge: Cambridge University Press, 1997); Dan Edelstein, *The Enlightenment: A Genealogy* (Chicago: University of Chicago Press, 2010).

44. François Marie Arouet de Voltaire, *Le Siècle de Louis XIV*, in *Oeuvres historiques*, ed. René Pomeau (Paris: Gallimard, 1968), 620.

45. Nakhimovsky, "The Enlightened Prince and the Future of Europe," 48–49.

of generating dynastic struggles that invited manipulation by outside interests. In this respect, the *Anti-Machiavel* posed a challenge to the alternative approach to stabilizing international competition in Europe advanced
most famously by the Abbé de Saint-Pierre (who shared Voltaire's views on
political economy but not his admiration for Louis XIV) as well as Gottfried
Wilhelm Leibniz: an approach premised on reinforcing or abstracting and
generalizing the legal framework of the Holy Roman Empire. From this
perspective, the legal structure of the Holy Roman Empire was not an obsolete artifact hindering the emergence of a more stable form of modern state
politics, as Voltaire and Frederick maintained, but a crucial instrument for
containing the relations between states within legal limits. This was the
approach the Holy Alliance was later understood to be implementing;
its premises were captured most concisely by the Genevan philosopher
Jean-Jacques Rousseau in his summary of Saint-Pierre's ideas. As Rousseau put it, the real stabilizing factor in European politics was not the
calculating diplomacy that produced the balance of power between rival
states. Rather, it was the limits that the Holy Roman Empire served to
impose on such calculations:

> the Germanic Body, placed almost at the center of Europe, which keeps
> all the other parts in check, and perhaps serves to maintain its Neigh-
> bors even more than its own members: a Body formidable to Foreign-
> ers by its extent, by the number and valor of its Peoples; but useful to
> all by its constitution, which, depriving it of the means and the will of
> conquering anything, makes it into a stumbling block for Conquerors.
> In spite of the defects of this constitution of the Empire, it is certain
> that, as long as it exists, the equilibrium of Europe will never be broken,
> no Potentate will have to fear being dethroned by another, and that,
> among us, the Treaty of Westphalia will perhaps always be the basis of
> the political system. Thus, public Right, which the Germans study with
> such care, is even more important than they think, and is not only Ger-
> man public Right, but in certain regards, that of the whole of Europe.[46]

The Anglo-French model at the core of Voltaire's vision of Europe
was torn apart by the escalating imperial rivalries that culminated in the
Seven Years War, which was fought in South Asia and North America
as well as Central Europe. In response, Voltaire reasserted his model on

---

46. Jean-Jacques Rousseau, *The Plan for Perpetual Peace, On the Government of
Poland, and Other Writings on History and Politics*, ed. Christopher Kelly (Hanover, NH:
Dartmouth College Press, 2005), 35.

an even grander scale in 1760 with his *History of the Russian Empire under Peter the Great*. Relying on sources made available to him by the Academy of Sciences that Peter I had founded in Saint Petersburg, Voltaire developed a highly Europeanized account of Russian history.[47] By mapping Russian history (with considerable strain) onto the structure of his "Enlightened narrative," Voltaire was able describe Peter as a heroic reformer who had overcome, in record time, the feudal and priestly shackles that had mired Russia in barbarism. In other words, Peter had compressed into mere decades what had taken over four centuries to transpire in Voltaire's account of European history. In addition to constructing a modern state and integrating it into the European balance of power, Peter had also entered into relations with China: an erosion of the boundary between Europe and Asia that Voltaire regarded as a momentous turning point in the emergence of a global (but still very much Eurocentric) civilization.[48] Among those who echoed Voltaire's account of Russian history was Adam Smith, who cited Peter's reforms in *The Wealth of Nations* of 1776 to demonstrate the military origins of all civil order:

47. Pocock, *Narratives of Civil Government*, chap. 5; Speck, "The History and Politics of Civilisation," 45–63. On the origins of Voltaire's interest in Russia and the legacy of Peter I, and his efforts to acquire the support of the Empress Elizabeth for the project, see Carolyn H. Wilberger, *Voltaire's Russia: Window on the East* (Oxford: Voltaire Foundation, 1976), chap. 2. On the evolution of the Saint Petersburg Academy of Sciences (founded in 1724) and its role in the development of state power in the eighteenth century, see Simon Werrett, "The Schumacher Affair: Reconfiguring Academic Expertise across Dynasties in Eighteenth-Century Russia," *Osiris* 25 (2010): 104–25; Willard Sunderland, "Imperial Space: Territorial Thought and Practice in the Eighteenth Century," in *Russian Empire: Space, People, Power, 1700–1930*, ed. Jane Burbank, Mark von Hagen, and Anatolyi Remnev (Bloomington: Indiana University Press, 2007), 33–66. Voltaire's turn to Russia was anticipated by Leibniz, who aspired to transcend the division of Christian societies and solve the problems of European politics by founding a new kind of academy whose universal expertise would reunify humanity. See Hartmut Rudolph, "Scientific Organizations and Learned Societies," in *The Oxford Handbook of Leibniz*, ed. Maria Rosa Antognazza (Oxford: Oxford University Press, 2013), 543–62. In 1711, Leibniz met Peter I and tried to found his ideal academy in Saint Petersburg. As Leibniz remarked in 1712, "I would rather see the sciences made very fruitful in Russia than see them poorly cultivated in Germany. The country where it will go best, will be the one dearest to me, since all humankind will always benefit from it, and its true treasures will be increased by it." Gottfried Wilhelm Leibniz to Alexander von Golowkin, January 16, 1712, Gottfried Wilhelm Leibniz Bibliothek-Niedersächsische Landesbibliothek, Hanover. The citation is from Malte-Ludolf Babin and Renate Essi, eds., "Transkriptionen des Leibniz-Briefwechsels 1712 für die Leibniz-Akademie-Ausgabe (nicht überprüft)" (Online-Veröffentlichung, October 28, 2020), 23, https://doi.org/10.26015/adwdocs-1948.

48. Pocock, *Narratives of Civil Government*, 79–80.

Peter's path was in fact the only way "that a barbarous country can be suddenly and tolerably civilized."[49]

When Catherine II seized power in 1762, she immediately struck up an extensive correspondence with Voltaire—the first of many such relationships she conducted with European philosophes, including, as we shall see in chapter 3, La Harpe.[50] If entering into correspondence with Frederick had presented Voltaire with an opportunity to export his model of the French monarchy, Catherine now supplied him, and his fellow philosophes, with a potent model for criticizing the French government. Catherine donated to the family of Jean Calas, the executed French Protestant whom Voltaire had fought to exonerate as an innocent victim of religious intolerance. When French censorship appeared to threaten the completion of the *Encyclopédie*, Catherine offered to publish it— without censorship—in Saint Petersburg. "What times we live in!" Voltaire wrote in 1762 to Denis Diderot (the editor, together with Jean Le Rond d'Alembert, of the *Encyclopédie*). "It is France that persecutes philosophy! And it is the Scythians that show it favor!"[51] Voltaire helped polish Catherine's image, publishing selections from their correspondence in a Swiss newspaper with a wide French readership, the *Gazette de Berne*.[52] Voltaire also justified Catherine's intervention in Poland and invasion of the Ottoman Empire as noble civilizing missions.[53] Finally, Voltaire presented Catherine as Peter's true heir. By building on Peter's reforms, and continuing his patronage of the arts and sciences, Catherine was supplying a compelling new model for France and other European states to emulate

---

49. Adam Smith, *An Inquiry into the Nature and Causes of the Wealth of Nations*, ed. A. S. Skinner and R. H. Campbell (Indianapolis: Liberty Classics, 1981), 2:706 (V.i.a). On this aspect of Smith's thought, see Istvan Hont, *Politics in Commercial Society*, ed. Béla Kapossy and Michael Sonenscher (Cambridge, MA: Harvard University Press, 2015); Dimitrios Ioannis Halikias, "Adam Smith on the Scottish Highlands and the Origins of Commercial Society," *History of Political Thought* 41, no. 4 (2020): 622–47; Paul Sagar, *Adam Smith Reconsidered: History, Liberty, and the Foundations of Modern Politics* (Princeton: Princeton University Press, 2022).

50. On Catherine's prolific correspondence, see Kelsey Rubin-Detlev, *The Epistolary Art of Catherine the Great* (Oxford: Voltaire Foundation, 2019).

51. Voltaire to Denis Diderot, September 25, 1762, in François Marie Arouet de Voltaire, *Correspondence and Related Documents, Vol. 25: June 1762–January 1763*, ed. Theodore Besterman, Les Oeuvres complètes de Voltaire, vol. 109 (Oxford: Voltaire Foundation, 1973), D10728.

52. A. Lentin, ed., *Voltaire and Catherine the Great: Selected Correspondence* (Cambridge: Oriental Research Partners, 1974), 15.

53. Voltaire, "Épître à l'impératrice de Russie," 437–39.

in turn. "Today," Voltaire wrote in praise of Catherine in 1771, "enlightenment comes to us from the north."[54]

Far from representing an Enlightenment consensus, however, Voltaire's account was widely contested. It gave rise to a highly varied literature debating Peter's reforms, the relationship between Russian and European history, and the nature of what had just begun to be called "civilization." This term was first coined in the 1750s by Mirabeau, who used it in *The Friend of Mankind*, Michael Sonenscher has explained, to show "the way by which genuine morality might come to inform the otherwise shallow veneer of civility and politeness to be found in modern life."[55] In this initial guise, civilization meant the opposite of civility: it resembled the German term *Kultur*, and implied a criticism of the kind of modern society celebrated by Voltaire.[56] Among Voltaire's many critics was Rousseau—who was also, however, deeply skeptical of the plans for moral regeneration developed by Mirabeau and the group of reformers who became known as *économistes* or Physiocrats. According to Rousseau, the states that Voltaire regarded as engines of prosperity and culture were racing toward disaster without any usable brakes. "We are approaching the state of crisis and the age of revolutions," Rousseau warned in his novel *Emile* (published in 1762, under the shadow of the Seven Years War). "I consider it impossible that the great monarchies of Europe will last much longer."[57]

Underlying Rousseau's diagnosis was the analysis of rising inequality, moral hypocrisy, and imploding legitimacy that had made him famous in the 1750s—including his notorious argument that, because the flourishing of the arts and sciences since the Renaissance was intimately bound up with these processes, it was a mistake to count on them to stabilize the self-destructive behavior of European states. If these states did not collapse internally, they would succumb to external predation. Either way, civilized Europe was doomed to repeat the decline and fall that had destroyed

54. Ibid., 444. Cf. Voltaire's earlier remark to Catherine in a letter from 1767: "Un temps viendra, Madame, je le dis toujours, où toute la lumière nous viendra du nord." Voltaire to Catherine II, February 27, 1767, in François Marie Arouet de Voltaire, *Correspondence and Related Documents, Vol. 31: October 1766–March 1767*, ed. Theodore Besterman, Les Oeuvres complètes de Voltaire, vol. 115 (Oxford: Voltaire Foundation, 1974), D13996.

55. Sonenscher, *Before the Deluge*, 219. On the eighteenth-century context and trajectory of the term, see also Bertrand Binoche, ed., *Les équivoques de la civilisation* (Seyssel: Champ Vallon, 2005).

56. For an account of how *Kultur* and civilization later became opposites, see Raymond Geuss, "Kultur, Bildung, Geist," *History and Theory* 35, no. 2 (1996): 151–64.

57. Jean-Jacques Rousseau, *Oeuvres complètes*, ed. Bernard Gagnebin and Marcel Raymond (Paris: Gallimard, 1964), 4:468.

ancient Rome. In *On the Social Contract*, also published in 1762, Rousseau turned Voltaire's praise of Peter on its head, claiming that Peter's premature and misconceived projects had implicated Russia in this broader fate. By exposing Russia to the dynamics of competitive industrialization that were already gripping European monarchies, Peter had foreclosed the possibility of pursuing sounder, more inward-focused development strategies that aimed to cultivate greater economic self-sufficiency. Both Russia and Europe would pay the price. "Russia will never be civilized," Rousseau declared, "because it was civilized too soon."

> Peter had a genius for imitation, but he lacked true genius, which is creative and makes all from nothing. He did some good things, but most of what he did was out of place. He saw that his people was barbarous, but did not see that it was not ripe for civilization: he wanted to civilize it when it needed only hardening. His first wish was to make Germans or Englishmen, when he ought to have been making Russians; and he prevented his subjects from ever becoming what they might have been by persuading them that they were what they are not. In this fashion too a French teacher turns out his pupil to be an infant prodigy, and for the rest of his life to be nothing whatsoever. The empire of Russia will aspire to conquer Europe, and will itself be conquered. The Tartars, its subjects or neighbors, will become its masters and ours, by a revolution which I regard as inevitable. Indeed, all the kings of Europe are working in concert to hasten its coming.[58]

The Anglican cleric John Brown shared Rousseau's bleak assessment of Europe's trajectory. Brown had become famous for his *Estimate of the Manners and Principles of the Times*, a scathing 1757 condemnation of the moral decline of England's elites. He blamed their corruption for the early military failures of the Seven Years War and warned of a general collapse of social order. However, Brown also saw a clear path toward reversing this trajectory and establishing a solid moral basis for civilization (he was one of the first to use the new term in English).[59] Like Mirabeau's, Brown's path

---

58. Jean-Jacques Rousseau, *The Social Contract and Other Later Political Writings*, ed. Victor Gourevitch (Cambridge: Cambridge University Press, 1997), 73; Rousseau, *Oeuvres complètes*, 4:386.

59. Michael Sonenscher, *Sans-Culottes: An Eighteenth-Century Emblem in the French Revolution* (Princeton: Princeton University Press, 2008), 191. On Brown's political theory and the strongly critical reaction it provoked from Joseph Priestley, see Peter N. Miller, *Defining the Common Good: Empire, Religion and Philosophy in Eighteenth-Century Britain* (Cambridge: Cambridge University Press, 1994), 333–48.

to civilization relied on religion as the basis for moral regeneration. Unlike Mirabeau, whose *The Friend of Mankind* had identified France as the agent of this regeneration, Brown came to assign that role to Russia. According to Brown, communal worship expressed feelings of the sublime that originated in an aesthetic response to nature. These feelings provided an emotionally pure basis for communal identity and social order, uncontaminated by the utilitarian distortions that accompanied the other arts and sciences. In time, Brown held, these feelings would providentially develop into their fullest expression as the precepts of Christianity.[60] In Russia, Brown saw a nation advanced enough to have acquired "the two great engines of power, by which all reformations are to be accomplished"—namely, a sovereign state that had fully consolidated political authority and an established Church committed to the Gospel—but not so advanced as to have acquired the cultural and institutional obstacles to reform that plagued European monarchies.[61] In 1765, Brown's writings on education earned him an invitation to correspond with Daniel Dumaresq, the chaplain of the English factory in Saint Petersburg and a member of Catherine's commission on educational reform.[62] Brown seized the opportunity to expound his views not only on schools but on "the effectual improvement and general civilization of the whole empire."[63] A disconcerted Dumaresq passed these along to Nikita Panin, Catherine's powerful advisor, and Brown soon found himself with an invitation to Saint Petersburg together with a thousand pounds to cover his travel expenses. Both an echo of Voltaire's globalized "Enlightened narrative" and an anticipation of the liberal idea of the Holy Alliance appear in a letter Brown wrote at the time to a friend. "If you will indulge me in carrying my imagination into futurity," he enthused,

60. On Brown's aesthetic and moral theories, and their bearing on politics, as well as an illuminating discussion of how Brown compared to Rousseau in contemporary eyes, see Sonenscher, *Sans-Culottes*, 178–95.

61. Andrew Kippis, ed., "Brown, John," in *Biographia Britannica, or, The Lives of the Most Eminent Persons Who Have Flourished in Great Britain and Ireland, from the Earliest Ages, to the Present Times: Collected from the Best Authorities, Printed and Manuscript, and Digested in the Manner of Mr. Bayle's Historical and Critical Dictionary* (London: W. and A. Strahan, 1778), 664.

62. In addition to Kippis's biographical account, see N. Hans, "Dumaresq, Brown, and Some Early Educational Projects of Catherine II," *Slavonic and East European Review; London, Etc.* 40, no. 94 (1961): 229–35; John H. Appleby, "Daniel Dumaresq, D.D., F.R.S. (1712–1805) as a Promoter of Anglo-Russian Science and Culture," *Notes and Records of the Royal Society of London* 44, no. 1 (1990): 25–50; Marcus C. Levitt, "An Antidote to Nervous Juice: Catherine the Great's Debate with Chappe d'Auteroche over Russian Culture," *Eighteenth-Century Studies* 32, no. 1 (1998): 49–63.

63. Kippis, "Brown, John," 664.

I can fancy that I see civilization and a rational system of Christianity extending themselves quite across the immense continent, from Petersburg to Kamchatka. I can fancy that I see them striking farther into the more southern regions of Tartary and China, and spreading their influence even over the nations of Europe, which, though now polished, are far from being truly Christian or truly happy. Nay, I am sometimes fantastic enough to say with Pitt, that as America was conquered in Germany, so Great Britain may be reformed in Russia.[64]

In the end, poor health prevented Brown from undertaking the voyage to Saint Petersburg. He returned the travel remittance, and on September 23, 1766, he killed himself. A few weeks before he cut his own throat, however, Brown addressed a long letter to Catherine, spelling out a strategy that diverged fundamentally from the course taken by Peter and celebrated by Voltaire.

In his haste to civilize Russia, Brown observed to Catherine, Peter had started by building a navy, promoting foreign trade, and indiscriminately opening the country to new cultural influences. This misguided strategy, Brown claimed, had caused the Russian nobility to pass directly from "ignorance and barbarism" to "the opposite extremes of luxury and irreligion" without "the natural intervention of that salutary medium of useful knowledge, sound religion, virtue, public spirit, and rational civilization, which your Imperial Majesty is now labouring to introduce."[65] To attain this "natural intervention," Brown maintained, the development of Russian civilization had to follow a natural progression, building up from improvements to agricultural production for domestic consumption rather than leaping directly into technologically demanding manufacturing in pursuit of "foreign emoluments":

> I call this a natural intervention, because it appears from the history of mankind, that when the improvement and civilization of a kingdom proceeds by a more gradual and unforced progress of things; that is, when the sovereign engages his nobles and people, first in the practice and improvement of agriculture, by which the honest comforts of life are first obtained and a general spirit of industry is excited throughout the internal parts of the country; when to this is added an application to home-manufactures, in order to make the best of what agriculture hath produced; when population is thus naturally increased, and when

64. Ibid., 667.
65. Ibid., 670.

these improved goods of nature are dispersed through such a country by the arts and conveniencies of a domestic commerce; when such is the natural and unforced progress of things, I believe your Imperial Majesty will find it a truth founded in the history of mankind, that among such a people, an honest simplicity of manners, with a concomitant regard to religious principles, and useful, though bounded, knowledge, do generally, and if attended with a tolerable system of policy, almost spontaneously arise: and from thence the ascent is also easy and natural, nor yet dangerous, up to a higher state of elegance, arts, science, and foreign emoluments, which may then be safely brought in by a guarded communication and commerce with foreign countries.[66]

By starting at the wrong end, Peter had disrupted the natural harmony between the material and moral dimensions of civilization. By corrupting the nobility, he had abandoned the masses to their "native barbarity" and had diminished rather than developed the clergy's potential to exert a moral influence over them. Brown urged Catherine to correct these dangerous problems in order to restore the "natural intervention" of civilization.[67] In addition to controlling Russia's exposure to immoral and irreligious foreign cultural influences, Brown suggested that Catherine lay the groundwork for a comprehensive system of public education: not by inviting foreigners to teach in Russia, as Peter had done, but by sending young Russians to study in England. England was a good choice, he claimed, because the "middling ranks of this kingdom" would furnish these Russian students with a model of useful virtue; and because the moderation of the English church ensured that their religious education could focus on "the great and leading principles of Christianity, which are equally maintained by all Christian churches" without any prejudice to the "doctrines of the Greek church, as it is established in Russia."[68] Upon their return to Russia, these students would be well equipped to build and operate the new educational institutions that Catherine envisaged.

Though Brown's career as Catherine's advisor ended before it began, and d'Alembert declined Catherine's invitation to serve as tutor to her

66. Ibid.

67. Ibid.

68. Ibid., 671. On the longer history of Anglican hopes for union with Orthodoxy, see Hugh Trevor-Roper, "The Church of England and the Greek Church in the Time of Charles I," in *From Counter-Reformation to Glorious Revolution* (London: Secker & Warburg, 1992), 83–112. The reduction of the Church's independence after Peter I made it look like the Church of England to some Anglicans: see also Alexander M. Martin, *Romantics, Reformers, Reactionaries: Russian Conservative Thought and Politics in the Reign of Alexander I* (DeKalb: Northern Illinois University Press, 1997), 144.

son, Diderot did make the voyage to Saint Petersburg in 1773. Catherine had become his benefactor by purchasing his library in 1765, and Diderot became a well-connected and well-informed contributor to ongoing debates about Russia.[69] Against those who investigated the material causes of Russia's barbarous expansionism (in line with the French government's foreign policy at the time), Diderot defended Russia's prospects for "civilization"—adding his voice to a critique of Machiavellism that one of his interlocutors had begun to call "humanism."[70] In his comments on Catherine's *Grand Instructions to the Commissioners Appointed to Frame a New Code of Laws for the Russian Empire* of 1767, which he began writing on his voyage back from Russia in 1774, Diderot warned against empowering the clerical establishment to serve as the moral foundation of civilization, as Brown had advised: "Religion is a buttress which always ends up bringing the house down."[71] Instead, Diderot encouraged Catherine to focus on legislation that would eliminate obstacles to the natural progression of civilization, by aligning the natural liberty of the individual with the general utility of society. Diderot was particularly enthusiastic about Catherine's ambitious plans for encouraging foreign colonists to settle along the Volga River. Investing in communities of Swiss farmers would provide the rest of the population with a much more realistic model of civilization to emulate, he stressed, than the highly skilled foreign workers who were needed to compete with European manufacturers.[72]

69. On these debates and connections, many of which revolved around Catherine's minister in Paris, Dmitrii Golitsyn, see especially Georges Dulac and Ludmilla Evdokimova, "Politique et littérature: La correspondance de Dmitri A. Golitsyn (1760–1784)," *Dix-huitième siècle* 22, no. 1 (1990): 367–400.

70. Cited in Gustave Schelle, *Du Pont de Nemours et l'école physiocratique* (Paris: Alcan, 1888), 100. On Diderot, the civilization of Russia, and the Abbé Baudeau, who introduced the term *humanisme*, see Gianluigi Goggi, "Diderot et l'abbé Baudeau: Les colonies de Saratov et la civilisation de la Russie," *Recherches sur Diderot et sur l'Encyclopédie* 14 (1993): 23–83. On investigations of Russian barbarism, see Levitt, "An Antidote to Nervous Juice"; Gianluigi Goggi, "Alexandre Deleyre et le Voyage en Sibérie de Chappe d'Auteroche: La Russie, les pays du Nord et la question de la civilisation," in *Le mirage russe au XVIIIe siècle: Textes*, ed. Serguei Karp and Larry Wolff (Ferney-Voltaire: Centre international d'étude du XVIIIe siècle, 2001), 75–134.

71. Denis Diderot, "Observations on the Instruction of the Empress of Russia to the Deputies for the Making of Laws," in *Political Writings*, ed. John Hope Mason and Robert Wokler (Cambridge: Cambridge University Press, 1992), 83.

72. On Catherine's colonization projects and Diderot's engagement with them, see Roger Bartlett, "Foreign Settlement in Russia under Catherine II," *New Zealand Slavonic Journal*, no. 1 (1974): 1–22; Roger Bartlett, "Diderot and the Foreign Colonies of Catherine II," *Cahiers du monde russe et soviétique* 23, no. 2 (1982): 221–41; Gianluigi Goggi, "Diderot et la Russie: Colonisation et civilisation. Projets et expérience directe," in *Diderot and European Culture*, ed. Frédéric Ogée and Anthony Strugnell (Oxford: Voltaire Foundation, 2006), 57–76.

Diderot's most pressing concern, however, was to challenge the advice Catherine had received from the French *économistes*. As Graham Clure has shown, Diderot attacked the Physiocrats for taking their polemic against Colbertism too far.[73] Their strategy for restoring the natural priority of agriculture would remove the vital impetus that the manufacturing sector gave to agricultural productivity. It would produce a dreary system in which "the citizen is continually forced to sacrifice his taste and happiness for the good of society."[74] And finally—here Diderot echoed Rousseau's 1767 rejection of Mirabeau's invitation to endorse Physiocracy—deploying the full fiscal power of the state to rebalance the economy would unleash a despotic force that, for all the authority they derived from their scientific knowledge of natural laws, the *économistes* could never be sure of controlling.[75] Instead Diderot urged Catherine to turn her legislative commission into a constituent assembly. "There is no true sovereign except the nation," Diderot declared, "there can be no true legislator except the people."[76] Only by ensuring that she was the last "despot" of Russia could Catherine ensure that Russia avoided replicating the dismal trajectory of European empires. As Diderot detailed in his contributions to *A Philosophical and Political History of the Settlements and Trade of the Europeans in the East and West Indies*, the monumental global history published between 1770 and 1783, this was a trajectory in which rival imperial attempts to monopolize global trade produced intensifying war and class conflict. It was a trajectory that pointed not toward the progress of civilization but toward its decline and fall.[77] In his comments on Catherine's *Grand Instructions*, Diderot warned

73. Graham Clure, "Rousseau, Diderot and the Spirit of Catherine the Great's Reforms," *History of European Ideas* 41, no. 7 (2015): 883–908. For further discussion of the precise target of Diderot's criticisms, see Sergey Zanin, *Utopisme et idées politiques: Visite de Pierre-Paul Joachim Henri Lemercier de La Rivière à Saint-Pétersbourg* (Paris: Classiques Garnier, 2018); Georges Dulac, "À propos du manuscrit physiocratique commenté par Diderot dans les Observations sur le Nakaz," *Recherches sur Diderot et sur l'Encyclopédie*, no. 55 (2020): 53–78.

74. Diderot, "Observations on the Instruction of the Empress of Russia to the Deputies for the Making of Laws," 125.

75. Clure, "Rousseau, Diderot and the Spirit of Catherine the Great's Reforms," 898.

76. Diderot, "Observations on the Instruction of the Empress of Russia to the Deputies for the Making of Laws," 81.

77. On Diderot's contributions to the *Histoire*, see Michèle Duchet, *Diderot et l'Histoire des deux Indes, ou, L'écriture fragmentaire* (Paris: A.-G. Nizet, 1978). On their relationship to Diderot's other writings on Russia, see Speck, "The History and Politics of Civilisation," 64–110. On their criticisms of European empires, see also Sankar Muthu, *Enlightenment against Empire* (Princeton: Princeton University Press, 2003), 72–121; Sunil M. Agnani, *Hating Empire Properly: The Two Indies and the Limits of Enlightenment Anticolonialism* (New York: Fordham University Press, 2013).

that if she was angered by his advice that she "abdicate" her despotic power, then "she has taken herself for a better person than she really is."[78]

Though he differed from Diderot in many respects, the German writer Johann Gottfried Herder shared his interest in Russia as well as his moral outrage at European colonialism. Herder had begun writing about Russia in the 1760s, but he published his last essays on Peter the Great and on development strategies for Russia in 1802. Herder's views on Russia are usually associated with a famous panegyric to the Slavs in his earlier work, *Ideas toward the Philosophy of the History of Mankind*, which predicted their future flourishing and later became influential among nineteenth-century nationalist intellectuals. But as Reto Speck has claimed, this panegyric is best read as a polemical response to a contemporary assertion of German cultural superiority. It does not convey the complexity of Herder's views on the Russian Empire or reflect the extent of his contributions to eighteenth-century debates about Peter's legacy and the development of civilization in Russia.[79] These questions were "the most important" of our age, Herder wrote in 1802, and they were lifelong concerns of his.[80]

Herder had lived in Russian-ruled Riga between 1764 and 1769, and although he never completed his planned history of Russia, for a time he aspired to a career advising Catherine.[81] Though he had become famous for his attack on Voltaire and "Enlightened narrative" in his *Another Philosophy of History for the Education of Mankind* of 1774, Herder did not subscribe to Rousseau's view that Peter's slavishly imitative attempts to import European industry and culture had irredeemably corrupted Russia. On the contrary, Herder presented Peter as a heroic genius who had injected Russia's indigenous cultures with a healthy dose of external dynamism that now needed to be more effectively internalized. Herder's praise for Peter was nearly as fulsome as Voltaire's, and he too supported Catherine's 1768 invasion of the Ottoman Empire as a "civilizing mission."[82] However, for Herder, the moment that Voltaire celebrated as the turning point of Russian history actually represented Peter's sole great mistake: rather than shifting his attention westward, Peter ought to have focused

---

78. Diderot, "Observations on the Instruction of the Empress of Russia to the Deputies for the Making of Laws," 82. A copy of Diderot's manuscript was delivered to Saint Petersburg along with his library after his death in 1784, but it disappeared.

79. Speck, "The History and Politics of Civilisation," 226–27.

80. Johann Gottfried Herder, "Ueber die schnelle Kunstbildung der Völker: Unterredungen auf einem Spatziergange," *Adrastea* 3 (1802): 70.

81. Speck, "The History and Politics of Civilisation," 220.

82. Ibid., 226.

on his conquest of Azov from the Ottoman Empire and built his new capital on the mouth of the Don rather than the Neva river, looking out toward the Black Sea and the Mediterranean rather than the Baltic and the North Atlantic.[83] Herder fervently hoped that Catherine, Alexander, and their remote successors would eventually succeed in orienting Russia toward its true vocation, not only for itself but for the sake of humanity as a whole. With its center on the Black Sea, climate and geography would allow Russia to realize the ideal of cultural plenitude last seen in ancient Greece and make it available to many other nations as well. By forming a new and vital link between Asia and Europe, Russia would be the site for a new cultural synthesis that was beyond the grasp of modern Europe itself: a culture that was rooted and integrated without succumbing to stasis, and dynamic and outward-looking without suffering from alienation.[84] In his final 1802 piece on Russia, Herder enthusiastically imagined what Russia would look like a few centuries into the future:

> Russia had found its midpoint on the Black Sea. Its Asian as well as its European provinces had been made fruitful, useful, arable, and all of its peoples were proportionally cultivated according to their customs. Out of the inaccessible heart of Asia, the aorta of all trade routes was opened; the Ottoman Porte was no more; every coast and harbor of the Mediterranean Sea was, as it should be, a free port of the world, the mediating sea for all nations for world trade with Asia, what a vast, wealthy, powerful, laborious, industrious empire was Russia![85]

Having freed itself from its entanglement in European diplomatic intrigue and economic competition, and having dispatched the Ottoman Empire, the Russia of Herder's imagination had become the heart of a new global order: "In its splendid median between Europe and Asia it made the world peaceful."[86]

These eighteenth-century claims about the progress of civilization and the relationship between Russian and European history were still resonating in the 1820s. A pair of essays about the Holy Alliance, published in 1820 by the rationalist German theologian Heinrich Paulus, illustrates the con-

83. Johann Gottfried Herder, "Peter der Große," *Adrastea* 3 (1802): 61–62; Speck, "The History and Politics of Civilisation," 218–19.

84. Speck, "The History and Politics of Civilisation," 248–63. See also Reto Speck, "Johann Gottfried Herder and Enlightenment Political Thought: From the Reform of Russia to the Anthropology of Bildung," *Modern Intellectual History* 11, no. 1 (2014): 31–58.

85. Herder, "Peter der Große," 79.

86. Ibid., 80.

tinuing attraction of Herder's vision of Russia's future. Paulus cited Staël's account of her conversation with Alexander about constitutional reform in order to make a rather different point: Germans urgently needed to institutionalize the constitutional implications of the Holy Alliance while Russian power remained under the guidance of Alexander's exceptional moral character. Paulus identified the Holy Alliance with the Abbé de Saint-Pierre's approach to international politics. The Holy Alliance would achieve perpetual peace not by imposing it in war but by securing a general guarantee of neutrality for the German Federation established by the Congress of Vienna in 1815. Such a guarantee had been furnished for the Swiss Confederation; extending the same arrangement to the German Federation was the only hope of saving it from becoming a helpless pawn in a destructive rivalry between Austria and Prussia. Paulus undertook an extensive analysis of diplomatic documents connected to Alexander's treaty in order to show that the Holy Alliance was best understood as part of a constitutional process. Alexander had already publicly recognized the German Federation as the "new bulwark" for European security and had been traveling around Europe demonstrating that the best way for sovereigns to address popular demands for representative constitutions with freedom of the press was to satisfy them. Paulus pointed to Alexander's record of promulgating constitutions for France as well as Poland. Poland had been erased from the map by the eighteenth-century partitions, but part of it had now reappeared as a Russian-ruled constitutional monarchy, following contentious negotiations at the Congress of Vienna: "surely the Germans may expect a federal state no less than the Poles, when they helped seize the opportunity for constitutions for France and Poland?" The Holy Alliance had supplied the fundamental norms that could turn the German Federation into the "essence of a union of peoples."[87] A constitutionally secured and institutionalized union of Germany's highly diverse parts would unleash its economic dynamism. Instead of investing in dubious military fortifications on the French border, Europe would acquire a solid guarantee of a European—and perhaps a global—peace: an unconquerable but also unthreatening German core.[88]

87. Heinrich Eberhard Gottlob Paulus, *Sophronizon oder unpartheyisch-freimüthige Beyträge zur neuern Geschichte, Gesetzgebung und Statistik der Staaten und Kirchen* (Frankfurt am Main: bei den Gebrüdern Wilmans, 1820), 62, 47, 139, http://mdz-nbn -resolving.de/urn:nbn:de:bvb:12-bsb10739134-2.

88. On the fortifications and the role of their financing in the post-Napoleonic settlement, see Beatrice de Graaf, *Fighting Terror after Napoleon: How Europe Became Secure after 1815* (Cambridge: Cambridge University Press, 2020), 357–426.

For Paulus, the real implication of Staël's conversation with Alexander was that Russia must never again be "disturbed" from the West, lest its enormous population's expansionist impulses yet again be deflected westward toward the banks of the Seine. Russia's world-historical destiny did not lie to the civilized west but to the south: to Russia, "another half-Europe is entrusted, in an entirely different direction." Left undisturbed, Paulus predicted that Russian history would proceed along the lines that Herder had imagined—even if Russia was no longer guided by Alexander's sentiment of "philanthropy" but only by "the natural law of its global position." The development of the Russian Empire would bridge North and South by uniting the Baltic with the Black Sea. "Just as streams of northern Germanic peoples once sought their south in Italy," Paulus echoed Herder, "so Russia has its own Italy in its southern lands. There is the land where the fruits of the Orient grow for it, and perhaps the ancient spirits of Ionia and Attica might return."[89]

The fate of such expectations was addressed by a former friend of Staël's, the Genevan writer Jacob Frédéric Lullin de Châteauvieux, best known as the anonymous author of an 1817 manuscript purporting to be Napoleon's memoirs.[90] Between 1820 and 1826, Châteauvieux's *Letters from St. James* elaborated an analysis of the unstable combination of European civilization and Russian barbarism under the banner of the Holy Alliance. The pinnacle of "modern civilization," according to Châteauvieux, was England. It had achieved in the Revolution of 1688 what France had sought in 1789 and the rest of Europe was still pursuing in the 1820s: political institutions commensurate with its advancing "social state." The constitutional alliance of crown, aristocracy, and people inaugurated in 1688 had fostered the emergence of a "democratic elite," whose accumulation of capital had given it aristocratic interests even as it exercised the constitutional rights of the people. England had successfully incorporated a stabilizing aristocratic element into democratic society itself: English politics could be divided by opinion while remaining united by interests that aligned the stability of the state with the rights of the people. Thanks to this constitution, England already possessed the political means to address social conflict: like his friend, the eminent liberal political economist J.C.L. Simonde de Sismondi, Châteauvieux traced growing proletarian resentment of England's "plebeian aristocracy" to

89. Paulus, *Sophronizon oder unpartheyisch-freimüthige Beyträge zur neuern Geschichte, Gesetzgebung und Statistik der Staaten und Kirchen*, 131–32.

90. Frédéric Lullin de Châteauvieux, *Manuscrit venu de Sainte-Hélène d'une manière inconnue* (Paris: Gallimard, 1974).

declining wages—and claimed that welfare provision through land reform offered the only genuine escape from the underlying causes of underconsumption and overproduction.[91] By contrast, continental Europe still exhibited various forms of an "anarchic social state": a conflict over the ruling "social and political system" between its "aristocratic" defenders and "the democracy which civilization had developed in society."[92] Since existing political institutions were implicated in this conflict and powerless to rise above it, the stabilizing presence of external "guarantors" was the only way to achieve a new equilibrium and arrive at a new constitutional consensus without replicating the eighty years of revolutionary turmoil it had cost England or the thirty years it had cost France.[93]

For Châteauvieux, the fact that this responsibility had fallen on the Holy Alliance was the contingent result of England's abdication of the leadership befitting its "rank" in "the progress of civilization." The general alliance created to stabilize European politics at the Congress of Vienna had dissolved because its "heterogenous" members had not created a sufficiently robust "federal power" to guarantee their mutual security.[94] With England focused on protecting its colonial empire, responsibility for stabilizing the "anarchic social state" of Europe had devolved onto the states least affected internally by it. The dominant role Russia had suddenly acquired in European politics was not the achievement of an ambitious conqueror like Louis XIV or Napoleon Bonaparte. On the contrary, Russia's defensive response to Napoleon's invasion had revealed the immense power already accumulated by a barbarous population still being formed into "a new people" through the "mechanism of civilization"—and the relative vulnerability of its allies. In Châteauvieux's estimation, Alexander had risen to his "unexpected role" as protector of both what had been accomplished through revolution and what would be destroyed by its recurrence. He had sought to meet the constitutional aspirations of the moment "by stopping the struggle between factions, by fixing their limits, by appeasing the revolutions with their own forces."[95]

Where Herder and Paulus had looked toward Greece in imagining the fulfillment of Russia's world-historical mission, Châteauvieux saw the

---

91. Jacob Frédéric Lullin de Châteauvieux, *Lettres de Saint-James*, 2nd ed. (Genève: J. J. Paschoud, 1822), 1:12, 1:30.

92. Ibid., 3:51, 3:4.

93. Ibid., 2:99.

94. Ibid., 1:11, 2:43–44.

95. Ibid., 3:40, 2:117.

Greek Revolution as a vivid illustration of the contradictions in the role
Alexander had assumed. In February 1821, Alexander Ypsilantis, a Greek
officer in the Russian army, crossed the Russian border into Ottoman-
ruled Moldavia and proclaimed the emancipation of Greece. Russian
backing of the venture was widely assumed; its suppression provoked
widespread unrest and raised fears of war while also intensifying liberal demands that Russia intervene as the guarantor of Christians under
Ottoman rule. ("How will the monarchs be able to talk of a holy alliance,"
complained Czartoryski, "when their hearts are insensitive to the interests of religion?")[96] However, Châteauvieux emphasized, both the example of a successful revolution and the projection of Russian power further
into the Balkans posed a threat to the European states whose internal
stability depended on the external backing of the Holy Alliance. Recognizing this problem, Alexander denounced Ypsilantis at the Congress of
Laibach and insisted Russia would remain at peace with the Ottoman
Empire. Even so, Châteauvieux surmised, the Greek Revolution marked
the beginning of the (possibly very protracted) end of Russian dominance
over European politics. Ultimately, "the mixture made of the material
forces of the Holy Alliance and the moral forces of society" had in fact
exacerbated the conflict it had tried to resolve. It had created an external dependency that inhibited the formation of stabilizing aristocratic
influences within democratic society itself, while simultaneously inflam-
ing revolutionary resistance to existing institutions.[97] From this perspective, the Holy Alliance represented a transitory anomaly. Reflecting on
Alexander's unexpected death while visiting southern Russia in 1825,
Châteauvieux observed that the exceptional emperor had been "for ten
years the only guarantor of the continent; a passing guarantor which a
breeze destroyed." Europe's future once again depended on England, supported by France, reclaiming a role that properly belonged "at the center
of civilization and its moral forces": forming a federal system dedicated
to the progress of civilization through free trade and a mutual guarantee of political stability.[98] An eighteenth-century ideal had reverted to its
Anglo-French roots.

---

96. Cited in W. H. Zawadzki, *A Man of Honour: Adam Czartoryski as a Statesman of
Russia and Poland, 1795–1831* (Oxford: Clarendon Press, 1993), 285.

97. Châteauvieux, *Lettres de Saint-James*, 1822, 3:140.

98. Jacob Frédéric Lullin de Châteauvieux, *Lettres de Saint-James*, vol. 5 (Paris: Paschoud, 1826), 23–24. Cf. Châteauvieux, *Lettres de Saint-James*, 1822, 2:94–108.

Telemachus of the North

Napoleon's retreat from Russia in 1812, and the looming projection of Russian power into Europe, gave new life to the eighteenth-century idea of the Russian "friend of mankind." Three debates reveal the shape assumed by that idea in that moment and how it, in turn, shaped assessments of the Holy Alliance. The first of these debates was about the implications of Russia's military success: whether it represented the emergence of a potential "friend of mankind" or merely a power struggle between two expansionist empires—or, as many French writers had claimed, the impending decline and fall of modern European civilization through a barbarian invasion like the ones that had overwhelmed its classical predecessors.[99] The second debate was about the institution of a new legal order for Europe as theorized by the philosopher Immanuel Kant, and whether it presupposed the intervention of a peacemaking "friend of mankind." The third debate, directly connected to the proclamation of the treaty of the Holy Alliance, was about the role of religion as a source of reconciliation and moral regeneration, and the efficacy of an appeal to it by a peacemaking "friend of mankind." Together, these debates help specify the kind of instrument for liberal progress that the Holy Alliance was initially taken to be—and explain the potential of such instruments to become tools of reaction.

The broader significance of Russia's military victory over France was addressed particularly clearly in an 1813 debate between two members of the Federalist Party in the United States: the South Carolina congressman, general, and later Maryland senator Robert Goodloe Harper and his friend Robert Walsh, a fixture of the Philadelphia literary scene.[100] Harper's June 1813 speech hailing the Russian emperor as "Alexander the Deliverer"

99. A notable statement of the third alternative appeared in the 1812 republication of the "Testament of Peter the Great"—actually written in Poland in 1797—exposing the truth about Russian expansionism. See McNally, *Das Russlandbild in der Publizistik Frankreichs*, 86–87. From that perspective, as Dominique de Pradt was still claiming in 1819, Napoleon's invasion of Russia had not been motivated by self-aggrandizement or French interest but a "European sentiment," namely the necessity of constructing a barrier to defend Europe from barbarism. Dominique Georges Frederic de Pradt, *L'Europe après le Congrès d'Aix-la-Chapelle, faisant suite au Congrès de Vienne* (Paris: F. Béchet ainé, 1819), 106–7.

100. On Walsh, see Drew R. McCoy, *The Last of the Fathers: James Madison and the Republican Legacy* (Cambridge: Cambridge University Press, 1989), 86, 105–13. On Harper, see Eric Robert Papenfuse, *The Evils of Necessity: Robert Goodloe Harper and the Moral Dilemma of Slavery* (Philadelphia: American Philosophical Society, 1997).

provoked a correspondence with Walsh, which the latter published later the same year.[101] According to Harper, France had invaded Russia in pursuit of global dominance, whereas Russia had struggled for "national independence," and its victories were "achieved in the cause of humanity, and of civil society."[102] Had Russia succumbed to the French invasion, Harper maintained, Napoleon would have been able to consolidate his control over all of Europe. With the continent's immense resources at his exclusive command, a successful invasion of the British Isles was only a matter of time. Britain's fall would "seal the fate of the civilized world," dooming both sides of the Atlantic to "the dark and cold night of universal despotism."[103] Instead, Russia's victories would rescue Europe, including France itself, from the "iron yoke" of the French military machine.[104] They would also extract the United States, itself at war with Britain, from its self-defeating role as an accomplice to (and potential future victim of) Napoleon's designs. It was only thanks to Russia's successful resistance, Harper concluded, that "enlightened patriotism does not compel us to grieve over our own victories, which but for those achieved by the arms of Alexander, would be but so many steps towards our own ruin."[105]

Harper's distinction between the two rival empires rested on his military analysis of Russia's victories over France. To an informed observer, he claimed, these victories demonstrated that a government employing "all the lights of modern science" could harness the superior physical force of a still barbarous population to its ends—and these ends were set by an absolute ruler who had given positive evidence of his exemplary moral character.[106] Internally, this combination was allowing Russia to make rapid progress in unlocking its tremendous economic potential. Externally, it was enabling Russia to assume the benign role that France ought to have held, had Napoleon not abdicated it, as "the protectress of other nations; the sword and shield of national independence."[107] Though Walsh joined Harper in celebrating Russia's victories over France, he denied that they indicated anything more than a clash between two empires contending

---

101. Robert Walsh, *Correspondence Respecting Russia, between Robert Goodloe Harper, and Robert Walsh, Jun. Together with the Speech of Mr. Harper, Commemorative of the Russian Victories: Delivered at Georgetown, Columbia, June 5th, 1813: And an Essay on the Future State of Europe* (Philadelphia: William Fry, 1813).

102. Ibid., 26.

103. Ibid., 8–9.

104. Ibid., 27.

105. Ibid.

106. Ibid., 42.

107. Ibid., 46.

for "universal domination," which had resulted in a setback for the latter.[108] While according all due respect to his friend's military expertise, Walsh claimed that Harper's analysis of the victories was controverted by his own extensive reading about the "history, morals, and resources of Russia"—a literature to which he was tempted to make his own contribution.[109] Walsh's preferred authority was Pierre Charles Levesque, whose 1782 *History of Russia* had used medieval chronicles to claim that Voltaire had been wrong about the origins of Russian civilization: according to Levesque, it long predated Peter's reforms, and its historical development had resembled Europe's until the Mongol invasions of the thirteenth century.[110] As Walsh explained, it followed that Peter's reforms had not been nearly as consequential or as transformative as Voltaire and Rousseau alike had made them out to be. Russian civilization had resumed its original, very gradual, and long arrested course of development. But importing modern European methods of administration did not change the fact that Russia remained a despotic state with a primitive economy. Alexander was an improvement on his predecessors because he seemed to understand that real reform entailed the gradual and systematic removal of impediments to civilization, rather than heroic but superficial gestures made as part of a relentless drive to increase the power of the state. But on their own, Alexander's good intentions were powerless to cure Russia of the "old *boulimia* as to power and territory."[111] Any Russian emperor was as much a creature of Russian despotism as Napoleon was of the French military machine.

For Walsh, the French military machine was by far the greater evil. As he had detailed in a book published in 1810, Walsh regarded French domination of Europe as the fulfillment of dire eighteenth-century prophecies

108. Ibid., 32.

109. Ibid., 39, 61. For a lengthy, official Russian rebuttal of Walsh's arguments against Harper, published in Boston and daring Walsh to follow through on his plans to write a history of Russia, see Petr Andreevich Chuikevich, "Strictures on 'The Correspondence Respecting Russia,'" in *Reflections on the War of 1812. With Tables, Shewing the Numerical Force of the Enemy, When He Entered Russia, and the Losses He Sustained in the Subsequent Battles and Actions from the Commencement of the Campaign to the 1st of January 1813; Founded upon Official Documents*, trans. Aleksiei Grigor'evich Evstaf'ev (Boston: Munroe & Francis, 1813), 59–124.

110. Walsh, *Correspondence Respecting Russia*, 71. On Levesque, see Speck, "The History and Politics of Civilisation," 111–65.

111. Walsh, *Correspondence Respecting Russia*, 78. Thomas Hobbes had identified "the insatiable appetite, or *Bulimia*, of enlarging Dominion" as one of the diseases that might afflict a commonwealth. Thomas Hobbes, *Leviathan*, ed. Richard Tuck (Cambridge: Cambridge University Press, 1996), 230.

about the consequences of the financial revolution.[112] Many eighteenth-century observers had been deeply troubled by the increasing reliance of European monarchies on public debt to fund their astronomically expensive wars. David Hume had been among those who feared that this modern system of war finance might give rise to an unprecedented form of despotism. Hume imagined that a government willing to default on a sufficiently large debt would find itself with complete control of its subjects' wealth. In this nightmare scenario, "the whole income of every individual in the state must lie entirely at the mercy of the sovereign." The result of this coup d'état would be "a degree of despotism which no oriental monarchy has ever yet attained."[113] Walsh quoted a prediction made in a similar spirit in 1772 by Jacques Antoine Hippolyte, Comte de Guibert, a writer on military tactics whose many admirers included Frederick II of Prussia and Napoleon Bonaparte himself: "the continent would be speedily enslaved should a nation, with the resources of France, break through the forms and trammels of the civil constitutions of the period; shake off fiscal solicitudes by a general bankruptcy; turn her attention exclusively to military affairs; and organize a regular plan of universal empire."[114]

Walsh concluded that Harper had underestimated French power to the same degree that he had overestimated Russian power. Even after the spectacular destruction of Napoleon's Grande Armée in its retreat from Russia, Walsh warned, it was too early to assume that Napoleon lacked the will or the resources to assemble another. This unprecedented ability to extract the resources of an immensely wealthy society was what made French domination over Europe "transcendently deplorable."[115] By contrast, even if Russia were to achieve an ascendency over Europe,

112. Robert Walsh, *A Letter on the Genius and Dispositions of the French Government: Including a View of the Taxation of the French Empire. By an American Recently Returned from Europe*, 9th ed. (London: Longman, Hurst, Rees, and Orme, 1810). Walsh took his epigraph from Rousseau. On eighteenth-century prophecies, see Sonenscher, *Before the Deluge*; Carl Wennerlind, *Casualties of Credit: The English Financial Revolution, 1620–1720* (Cambridge, MA: Harvard University Press, 2011); John Shovlin, "Jealousy of Credit: John Law's 'System' and the Geopolitics of Financial Revolution," *Journal of Modern History* 88, no. 2 (June 2016): 275–305.

113. David Hume, "Of Public Credit," in *Essays: Moral, Political, and Literary*, ed. Eugene Miller, rev. ed (Indianapolis: Liberty Classics, 1987), 359. See Istvan Hont, "The Rhapsody of Public Debt: David Hume and Voluntary State Bankruptcy," in *Jealousy of Trade: International Competition and the Nation-State in Historical Perspective* (Cambridge, MA: Harvard University Press, 2005), 325–53.

114. Walsh, *A Letter on the Genius and Dispositions of the French Government*, 10–11.

115. Walsh, *Correspondence Respecting Russia*, 34.

the roots of its power would penetrate far less deeply into European society, and the chances of eventually escaping its grasp would therefore be much greater. Walsh, who was a notoriously fervent Anglophile, took comfort in England's survival, which he claimed was far less precarious than Harper had assumed. Thanks to England, the catastrophe of Napoleonic despotism could be confined to continental Europe.[116] The scale of that catastrophe, however, was revealed in the appendix that Walsh added to his published correspondence with Harper. The appendix was written by the Abbé Correa, a Portuguese statesman who had installed himself in Philadelphia and would become ambassador to the United States.[117] Correa developed a rapport with Walsh despite his extensive ties to Walsh's political enemies (Correa was closest to Jefferson and his followers, one of whom professed surprise at finding such a respectable foreign luminary in the company of a "little literary cuckoo" constantly crying "Bonaparte, Bonaparte, Bonaparte").[118]

Walsh published the first half of Correa's "General Considerations upon the Past and Future State of Europe" in 1812, and the sequel together with his correspondence with Harper the following year.[119] Correa's essay was a eulogy for the old European republic of states proclaimed by Voltaire. The achievements of this republic—moderate government, civil liberty, cultural and economic dynamism, and an increasingly humane practice of warfare—had been "but an accidental, evanescent refinement," contingent on a transient balance of power and on the moderating influence of the nobility and clergy.[120] The demise of the old balance of power and the rise of Russia, Correa observed, meant that "the plains of Poland will in all likelihood, be the sanguinary theatre of the mighty wars destined to

116. Ibid., 38.

117. On Correa and his career in the United States, see Richard Beale Davis, "The Abbé Correa in America, 1812–1820: The Contributions of the Diplomat and Natural Philosopher to the Foundations of Our National Life. Correspondence with Jefferson and Other Members of the American Philosophical Society and with Other Prominent Americans," *Transactions of the American Philosophical Society* 45, no. 2 (1955): 87–197.

118. Ibid., 98.

119. José Francisco Correa da Serra, "General Considerations upon the Past and Future State of Europe," *American Review of History & Politics* (October 1, 1812): 354–66; José Francisco Correa da Serra, "An Essay on the Future State of Europe," in *Correspondence Respecting Russia, between Robert Goodloe Harper, and Robert Walsh, Jun. Together with the Speech of Mr. Harper, Commemorative of the Russian Victories: Delivered at Georgetown, Columbia, June 5th, 1813: And an Essay on the Future State of Europe*, by Robert Walsh (Philadelphia: William Fry, 1813), 121–40.

120. Correa da Serra, "An Essay on the Future State of Europe," 128.

signalize the *neighbouring* future."[121] The leveling of social distinctions and the rise of military despotism in France would transform "the physiognomy of Europe" even more fundamentally: "it is to be feared," Correa wrote, echoing Rousseau's pronouncement of the 1750s, "that the future history of Europe will be made up of perpetual oscillations between sedition and despotism."[122] However transient Napoleon's own conquest of Europe turned out to be, the form of government he epitomized would endure and exert a lasting effect on European societies: "after a very few generations have passed away in this state," Correa wrote,

> they will consist, to the eye of the philosopher, of but two classes of beings; the one, an immense multitude devoted to physical wretchedness; the other, a body of favourites of all grades abandoned to moral corruption. . . . As long as there is but one focus for hope and fear, while the whole action and re-action of society is limited to one point, while all that is deemed valuable or noxious emanates from a common centre, we must expect to find no other real division of classes than the oppressor and oppressed.[123]

Correa's prognosis was something of a commonplace in 1813. "Humanity is splitting into two basic groups," lectured the German philosopher Johann Gottlieb Fichte that same year, "the propertied and the propertyless."[124] "In France they say that it is all about war between the plebeians and the patricians," wrote Germaine de Staël to the Scottish Whig politician

121. Ibid., 140. On the "sanguinary theater" this region became in the more distant future, see Timothy Snyder, *Bloodlands: Europe between Hitler and Stalin* (New York: Basic Books, 2010).

122. Correa da Serra, "An Essay on the Future State of Europe," 137. Cf. Jean-Jacques Rousseau, "Discourse on the Origin and Foundations of Inequality among Men," in *The Discourses and Other Early Political Writings*, ed. Victor Gourevitch (Cambridge: Cambridge University Press, 1997), 111–222.

123. Correa da Serra, "An Essay on the Future State of Europe," 135.

124. Johann Gottlieb Fichte, *Die Staatslehre, oder über des Verhältniss des Urstaates zum Vernunftreiche, in Vorlesungen*, in *Sämmtliche Werke*, ed. Immanuel Hermann Fichte (Berlin: de Gruyter, 1965), 4:404. A French translation of Fichte's 1813 lecture "Über den Begriff des wahrhaften Krieges" was published in 1831 by the grandson of the revolutionary Gracchus Babeuf. This edition rendered Fichte's term "Nichteigenthümer" as "prolétaires," so that Fichte's observation "Die Menschheit zerfällt in zwei Grundstämme: die *Eigenthümer*, und die *Nichteigenthümer*" became "L'humanité se devise en deux classes principales: les propriétaires et les prolétaires," anticipating the famous pronouncement of *The Communist Manifesto* seventeen years later. Johann Gottlieb Fichte, *De l'idée d'une guerre légitime*, ed. Louis Babeuf, trans. M. Lortet (Lyon, 1831), 6; Jean-Christophe Goddard, "Fichte est-il réactionnaire ou révolutionnaire," in *Fichte et la politique*, ed. Jean-Christophe Goddard and Jacinto Rivera de Rosales (Milan: Polimetrica, 2008), 484–86.

James Mackintosh the following year. "I think that it is also a war between principles and interests."[125] Though she worried that the postwar politics of Italy, Spain, and France were being shaped by the interests rather than the principles, Staël identified Alexander as the champion of the latter. Less equivocally, the Russian writer Vasilii Malinovskii proclaimed Alexander the liberator of nations and the founder of the federation that would secure the freedom of Europe: "Europe is for the first time divided in only two parts, and the one in the right is now triumphant."[126] However, by the time the French writer Dominique de Pradt described Europe as divided into suzerains and vassals in 1825, this outcome had become "the work of the Holy Alliance": "through it, a new kind of federation, unique and poorly defined, which is convenient for extending its jurisdiction, has raised itself over Europe; it commands in the style of Jupiter, by a nod of the head; it hides its regular action under the forms of liberty."[127] The stage was set for Karl Marx and Friedrich Engels to implicate the Holy Alliance in their famous pronouncement of 1848: "Society as a whole is more and more splitting up into two great hostile camps, into two great classes directly facing each other."[128]

The success of the military campaign that carried Alexander to Paris in 1814 reactivated a further set of questions about the role of a peacemaking agent in legislating a new European political system. To the Prussian writer Konrad Engelbert Oelsner, these questions were best addressed through the idea of "perpetual peace" famously articulated by the Prussian philosopher Immanuel Kant in the 1790s. Oelsner (who was in Paris in 1814 as part of the Prussian diplomatic delegation) translated selections from Kant's *Metaphysics of Morals* and published them in a French journal, annotated with notes referring to the history of the French Revolution and Napoleonic period. "Kant seems to have written out of presentiment; his views are adapted to present circumstances. The allied sovereigns have brought moral civilization into war and politics," Oelsner claimed. "According to what we have witnessed in the space of a few days, it is permitted to hope that the permanent congress which is proposed will not

125. Germaine de Staël to James Mackintosh, May 31, 1814, in Norman King, "Lettres de Madame de Staël à Sir James Mackintosh," *Cahiers Staëliens* 10 (1970): 37.

126. Vasilii Fedorovich Malinovskii, "Obshchii mir," in *Izbrannye obshchestvenno-politicheskie sochineniia*, ed. A. P. Belik (Moskva: Izdatel'stvo Akademii Nauk SSSR, 1958), 94.

127. Dominique Georges Frederic de Pradt, *Vrai système de l'Europe relativement a l'Amérique et à la Grèce* (Paris: Béchet ainé, 1825), 87.

128. Karl Marx and Friedrich Engels, *The Communist Manifesto*, ed. Gareth Stedman Jones (London: Penguin, 2002), 220.

remain a mere wish."[129] In October 1814, these claims received a reply in the form of a letter to the editor from a French official named Charles Mullot. According to Mullot, this German approach to "perpetual peace" needed to be synthesized with its French counterpart. Though it was Kant who had "founded the *theory* of the law of nations in general laws," it was the Abbé de Saint-Pierre who had shown how to "reduce that theory into practice" through political analysis.[130]

Despite Saint-Pierre's reputation as an impractical utopian dreamer, Mullot explained, he was in fact (as more recent scholarship has also emphasized) a theorist of the incentives that diverted those in power away from their interests, or the utility of commercial reciprocity: he was an analyst of the passions or the distorted moral psychology fueling military competition and the pursuit of conquest.[131] Saint-Pierre's plan for a European federation had rested on a theory of "self-interest *well understood* of peoples and kings, the glory and welfare of all," which Mullot described as "the law of nations reduced into action by the *sentimental virtue* of a universal morality." From this perspective, both Britain and France prior to 1789 had behaved as "anti-social" imperial powers; the popular absolutism of the revolutionary republic that had succeeded the French monarchy had not altered this behavior. This neo-Roman militarism had been opposed by neo-Greek anti-imperial federations, but these were narrowly

129. Konrad Engelbert Oelsner, *Traité du droit des gens; dédié aux souverains alliés et à leurs ministres: Extrait d'un ouvrage de Kant* (Paris: Adrien Égron, 1814), avertissement. The extracts appeared in the *Mercure étranger* and were reprinted in two collections by Adrien Égron, who was also the publisher of *On the Reorganization of European Society*, a famous 1814 essay by the philosopher Henri de Saint-Simon and his disciple Augustin Thierry that is discussed in chapter 5. On the friendship between Oelsner and Saint-Simon, see Henri Gaston Gouhier, *La jeunesse d'Auguste Comte et la formation du positivisme* (Paris: J. Vrin, 1933), 329–32.

130. "Lettre de M. Mullot (de la Gironde) à M. le rédacteur du Mercure étranger, 24 octobre 1814," in *Pièces relatives au droit public des nations* (Paris: Adrien Égron, 1815), 52–53, https://gallica.bnf.fr/ark:/12148/bpt6k62922593. For a description of a comparable Dutch discussion of Kant and Saint-Pierre in 1814, see Matthijs Lok, "The Congress of Vienna as a Missed Opportunity: Conservative Visions of a New European Order after Napoleon," in *Securing Europe after Napoleon: 1815 and the New European Security Culture*, ed. Beatrice de Graaf, Ido de Haan, and Brian Vick (Cambridge: Cambridge University Press, 2019), 64.

131. For studies of Saint-Pierre emphasizing his realism, see Olaf Asbach, *Staat und Politik zwischen Absolutismus und Aufklärung: Der Abbé de Saint-Pierre und die Heraus-bildung der französischen Aufklärung bis zur Mitte des 18. Jahrhunderts* (Hildesheim: G. Olms, 2005); Céline Spector, "L'Europe de l'abbé de Saint-Pierre," in *Les projets de l'abbé Castel de Saint-Pierre, 1658–1743: Pour le plus grand bonheur du plus grand nombre*, ed. Carole Dornier and Claudine Poulouin (Caen: Maison de la recherche en sciences humaines, Université de Caen Basse-Normandie, 2011), 39–49.

self-interested and displayed no concern for collective security. By contrast, Mullot concluded, it was the spirit of Saint-Pierre's constitutionalism that had reemerged in 1814. Mullot defined this constitutionalism in terms directly anticipating the language of the treaty of the Holy Alliance a year later. "Thus the publicists of Europe, and the ministers in their proclamations, could, without exposing themselves to ridicule, compare peoples to a great family, in which the monarchs are no more than cherished princes, and the visible delegates of Providence."[132]

The direct antecedent of this hope, Mullot pointed out, was the earlier hope invested in Napoleon. But Napoleon had failed to assume the role of the "protector of a confederation of princes for the reestablishment of the freedom of the seas" (the role, as we have seen, defined by Mirabeau as the "friend of mankind"). Instead of uniting Europe, Napoleon had become the oppressor of kings and peoples, and his confederation had turned against him. Mullot repented for his own prior faith in Napoleon while wondering whether his hope in the allies of 1814 would turn out any differently. The hope of 1814 was that "the political wisdom of Louis, the generous soul of Alexander, and the interest of England" would combine to introduce a new code of the law of nations, founded on the principles of Saint-Pierre and Kant. However, if "social reason" was still drowned out by the distorted pride of kings and peoples—as Saint-Pierre himself had, after all, predicted—then it would be either "the force of things" or "the force of revolutions" (rather than "the force of great men") that would "arise to change the face of the world." In the former case, the weight of injustice would produce suffering that would lead to the desire for peace. In the latter case, peoples would try to liberate themselves by wielding the debris of their chains against their oppressors: but Mullot warned that they would meet either the Polish fate—defeat followed by the imposition of an even stronger yoke—or the English fate: "a constitution which offers only a mockery of liberty founded on a system of division and conquests."[133]

Mullot's response to Oelsner highlights the difficulty of inserting the agency of a peacemaking "friend of mankind" into a Kantian legal framework for international relations: a difficulty that has confronted many twentieth-century interpreters of Kant and that Oelsner himself had already encountered. In the 1790s, Oelsner had become the intimate confidant of Emmanuel Joseph Sieyès, the leading constitutional

132. "Lettre de M. Mullot," 63, 54, 60.
133. Ibid., 68, 72, 66–67.

theorist and architect of the French Revolution. Oelsner was one of several radical German émigrés in Paris who had seen a close philosophical affinity between Sieyès and Kant: according to Oelsner, they were the "Calvin and Luther" of their time, the French revolutionary and German philosopher who would unite to "reform the world."[134] When Kant's famous essay on "perpetual peace" appeared in 1795, it was enthusiastically received by Oelsner and others as an endorsement of Sieyès's efforts to negotiate a peace treaty with Prussia that would mark the emergence of a peaceful new international system: "if by good fortune one powerful and enlightened nation can form a republic," Kant had written, "this will provide a focal point for a federal association among other states."[135] However, Kant was not the same kind of theorist of a peacemaking "friend of mankind" as Oelsner. On the contrary, Kant had gone to considerable lengths to excise that moral character from the legal idea of a "perpetual peace."

Kant did closely identify himself with contemporary educational reformers who had adapted the term *Menschenfreund*, or "friend of mankind"; he described the role of his critical philosophy as educating such educators, providing them with the rational discipline that would prevent them from "going astray" in their efforts to educate good citizens.[136] In his *Doctrine of Virtue* of 1797, Kant provided a precise definition of the "friend of mankind," presenting the concept as "somewhat narrower in its meaning than 'one who merely loves human beings' (a *philanthropist*)." Since friendship implied an equal relationship of mutual obligation rather than the asymmetry of benevolent patronage, Kant explained, the concept served as a guard against "the pride that usually comes over those fortunate enough to have the means for beneficence."[137] However, Kant's

---

134. Emmanuel Joseph Sieyès, *Politische Schriften, 1788-1790: Vollständig gesammelt von dem deutschen Uebersezer nebst zwei Vorreden über Sieyes Lebensgeschichte, seine politische Rolle, seinen Charakter, seine Schriften*, ed. Konrad Engelbert Oelsner (s.l., 1796), 1:cxvi.

135. Immanuel Kant, "Perpetual Peace: A Philosophical Sketch," in *Political Writings*, ed. Hans Reiss, trans. H. B. Nisbet (Cambridge: Cambridge University Press, 1991), 104.

136. Munzel, "Menschenfreundschaft." The quotation is from the concluding lines of the *Critique of Practical Reason* (1788): Immanuel Kant, *Gesammelte Schriften*, Deutsche Akademie der Wissenschaften zu Berlin (Berlin: W. de Gruyter, 1969), 5:163.

137. Immanuel Kant, *Practical Philosophy*, ed. Mary J. Gregor, Cambridge Edition of the Works of Immanuel Kant (New York: Cambridge University Press, 1996), 587–88; Kant, *Gesammelte Schriften*, 6:472–73. See also the discussion in Immanuel Kant, *Lectures on Ethics*, ed. Peter Lauchlan Heath and J. B. Schneewind, Cambridge Edition of the Works of Immanuel Kant (New York: Cambridge University Press, 1997), 189–90; Kant, *Gesammelte Schriften*, 27:430–31.

Groundwork for the Metaphysics of Morals of 1785 had famously denied that the sentiments of a *Menschenfreund* necessarily held moral value.[138] When "affectations of universal philanthropy" were confronted with the empirical behavior of actual human beings, Kant warned in 1793, they were likely to result in hatred of humanity, even if this hatred took the form of peaceful isolation rather than active aggression: "For, however one may try to exact love from oneself, one cannot avoid hating what is and remains evil, especially in deliberate mutual violation of the most sacred human rights: not exactly so as to inflict troubles upon men but still so as to have as little as possible to do with them."[139] When Oelsner and his circle presented him with an opportunity to enter into a direct correspondence with Sieyès, Kant declined—but he did leave an opening for a "purely literary" discussion of how to translate his philosophical works into French.[140] In his essay on "perpetual peace," by contrast, Kant warned that those who attempted to justify the military interventions of a peacemaking agent in legal terms would merely serve as "sorry comforters" adapting their principles to the demands of power.[141]

It was left to others (most importantly Fichte, another German admirer of both Kant and Sieyès) to construct a Kantian theory of a peacemaking "friend of mankind."[142] Kant himself limited his account of "perpetual peace" to specifying the formal legal structure of a federal union among states—and describing how far states would have to limit their behavior in order to become capable of participating in it. Kant also elaborated a model of a historical process, driven by both intensifying wars and intensifying commerce, through which states would learn how to participate in such a federal system. The French Republic's success in repelling its invaders, Kant implied in 1795, was not an opening for a benevolent agent to redraw the map of Europe and impose new legal structures on other states. It marked the emergence of a viable federal system to which other states could independently align themselves. As Kant later explained in 1797, the kind of federal system he had in mind did not amount to a permanent association that was based on a "political constitution" and

---

138. Kant, *Gesammelte Schriften*, 4:398.

139. Immanuel Kant, "On the common saying: That may be correct in theory, but it is of no use in practice," in *Practical Philosophy*, 305; Kant, *Gesammelte Schriften*, 8:307. I have modified Gregor's translation.

140. Alain Ruiz, "Neues über Kant und Sieyès: Ein unbekannter Brief des Philosophen an Anton Ludwig Théremin (März 1796)," *Kant-Studien* 68, no. 4 (1977): 450.

141. Kant, "Perpetual Peace," 103.

142. See Isaac Nakhimovsky, *The Closed Commercial State: Perpetual Peace and Commercial Society from Rousseau to Fichte* (Princeton: Princeton University Press, 2011).

"therefore indissoluble," like the United States of America. Nor would it live up to the ideal of a family of nations. But it would make international relations less arbitrary and more just: "This rational idea of a *peaceful*, even if not friendly, thoroughgoing community of all nations on the earth that can come into relations affecting one another is not a philanthropic (ethical) principle but a principle *having to do with rights*."[143] The idea of a peacemaking "friend of mankind," including the Russian "friend of mankind" which came to be associated with the promulgation of the Holy Alliance, was not confined within the uncompromising boundaries of Kant's distinction between law and morality. On the contrary, it was characterized by what Mullot, referring to Saint-Pierre, had described as "the law of nations reduced into action by the *sentimental virtue* of a universal morality."[144]

After 1815, debates about the Russian "friend of mankind" were further connected to another set of questions about religion. These questions centered on Alexander's association with the Livonian religious figure Juliane von Krüdener, whom Alexander saw regularly in Paris in 1815. The religious idiom promoted by Krüdener, and expressed in the treaty of the Holy Alliance, divided La Harpe from Germaine de Staël and Benjamin Constant: liberals who shared many of the same political goals but subscribed to different understandings of progress. Alexander had met Krüdener in June 1815, shortly before the Battle of Waterloo. The connection had been forged by his wife Elizabeth's lady-in-waiting, Roxandra Stourdza, and they met in Baden, where Elizabeth's grandfather was the Grand Duke. Krüdener had already recognized Alexander as a messianic savior, and their first meeting (according to the account of her Genevan associate Henri Empaytaz) was a three-hour affair in which she exhorted him to atone while he wept.[145] Alexander then arranged for Krüdener and her entourage to join him in Paris; Krüdener may have reviewed a draft of the treaty of the Holy Alliance.[146] Her real triumph, however, was to accompany Alexander to the review of Russian troops he conducted in the presence of the emperor of Austria and king of Prussia in September 1815, in a natural amphitheater in Champagne, eighty miles east of Paris. In her pamphlet commemorating this spectacular celebration of the final victory over Napoleon, Krüdener described how Europe had been punished for its

143. Kant, *Practical Philosophy*, 488–89; Kant, *Gesammelte Schriften*, 6:351–52.

144. "Lettre de M. Mullot," 63.

145. Henri Louis Empaytaz, *Notice sur Alexandre, empereur de Russie* (Genève: Susanne Guers, 1828), 13.

146. Ley, *Alexandre Ier et sa Sainte-Alliance*, 141–43.

sins until redemption had arrived from "the deserts of Asia." "The Eternal called Alexander," Krüdener wrote, and the result was "a hundred and fifty thousand Russians making amends with the religion of love," recalling the reconciliation of French Catholics and Protestants achieved centuries earlier by King Henri IV.[147]

To La Harpe, Alexander's embrace of Krüdener's unconventional religious idiom was a costly error that had burdened Alexander's peacemaking politics with controversy. He warned Alexander in March 1816 that the Holy Alliance was being exploited by the British in order to undermine his well-earned reputation; later that year he castigated his former pupil for failing to give his project "a name that would designate more clearly the purely philanthropic goal that it presents" (while simultaneously celebrating the accession of Switzerland to the alliance).[148] In 1818, La Harpe complained to Alexander that he could only "explain the kind of contradiction which seems to exist between what has happened and your liberal and philanthropic views" by "the supposition that the facts and the truth are imperfectly known to you"—and he did eventually blame Alexander for allowing himself to be misled in this way. After the Congress of Laibach had authorized the Austrian invasion of Naples in 1821, La Harpe later annotated his letter: the Holy Alliance had been "manifested in its horrifying nudity," casting Alexander as "a sovereign enemy of the liberty of peoples, as the defender of the principles of the middle ages."[149] At the end of the 1820s, however, La Harpe tried to reclaim what he called the "initial conception" of the Holy Alliance as the peacemaking project of a "friend of mankind." He was prompted to do so by a review of the account of the origins of the Holy Alliance published by Empaytaz, Krüdener's former associate. The Holy Alliance, as the review had presented it, was the reactionary outcome of Alexander's seduction by religious mystics like Krüdener. It was a mistake, La Harpe warned in reply, for liberals to take Empaytaz's self-serving and undocumented account so seriously. In fact, La Harpe claimed, the same liberal viewpoint that condemned what the Holy Alliance had become would approve of what it had initially been intended to do.

---

147. Juliane von Krüdener, *Le Camp de Vertus, ou la Grande revue de l'armée russe, dans la plaine de ce nom, par l'empereur Alexandre* (Lyon: Guyot Frères, 1815), 7–9, https://gallica.bnf.fr/ark:/12148/bpt6k6100123s.

148. Postscript to La Harpe to Alexander I, March 11, 1816, *Correspondance de La Harpe et Alexandre Ier*, 3:132; La Harpe to Alexander I, August 2, 1816, ibid., 3:155.

149. La Harpe to Alexander I, January 23, 1818, *Correspondance de La Harpe et Alexandre Ier*, 3:292, 3:300.

La Harpe noted only in passing that Alexander's signature intervention in European politics had taken the form of a "solemn appeal to religion." His main concern was to establish that the Holy Alliance had been conceived in the same "generous spirit" as Alexander's emancipatory internal reforms: La Harpe cited Alexander's (more legendary than real) abolition of serfdom in Estonia, Courland, and Livonia, as well as Alexander's description of Poland's new representative institutions as a model for Russia's future. In La Harpe's presentation, Alexander's moral authority as "friend of mankind" had depended on his deployment of Russian power to help bridge the explosive divisions that had opened up within and between European societies. He was supposed to have done so not by appealing to a rather controversial form of Christianity but by establishing the political and economic conditions in which all were free to pursue a shared prosperity. Rather than relying on religion as a source of moral regeneration, La Harpe held that legislation, guided by the accumulated scientific knowledge of the "civilized world," could systematically remove obstacles to the emergence of national cultures characterized by republican virtues. This was how La Harpe envisioned Alexander acting as "friend of mankind": but, in La Harpe's retrospective estimation, Alexander had been undermined by the machinations of European diplomacy thanks to his excessively "generous abnegation" of the "preponderant influence" he had exercised after his victory over Napoleon.[150]

The view of progress informing what La Harpe later recalled as the "initial conception" of the Holy Alliance was most closely connected to claims put forward by the famous French political economist Jean-Baptiste Say. As chapter 3 will elaborate, La Harpe promoted both the 1803 and the 1814 editions of Say's *Treatise on Political Economy* to Alexander; Say dedicated the 1814 edition to Alexander, who presented Say with a medal. Say's *Treatise* claimed to supersede earlier eighteenth-century debates about the priority of agriculture or manufacturing in the development of civilization. It showed how, in a sufficiently integrated economy, increased productivity in one sector would always translate into lower costs for the others. This was why, according to what became known as "Say's Law," production in the aggregate would never be limited by consumption. The result was a path to general prosperity that relied on domestic more than foreign markets, and was therefore more insulated from the demands of power politics, without depending on massive intervention by the fiscal

150. Frédéric-César de la Harpe, "Aux Rédacteurs du Globe," *Le Globe*, August 15, 1829, 517–18.

or monetary power of the state.[151] Say claimed that his *Treatise* supplied "a general plan of administration" that addressed all members of society and was applicable under different forms of government.[152] It approached the science of political economy as a school of citizenship: Say claimed that the broad diffusion of this science in the population would inculcate the practical virtues that formed the moral foundation of a republican political culture.[153] La Harpe spelled out the application of Say's principles to Russia in a memo he wrote for Alexander during the Congress of Vienna in 1815. If Russia devoted itself to becoming a competitive manufacturer of products that the vast bulk of its population could not afford to consume, La Harpe warned Alexander, it would fail to increase its agricultural productivity while also saddling itself with an immiserated urban working class. Like London or Lyon, Russian cities would fill up with "machines known as workers."[154] Instead of following this economically flawed and politically dangerous path, the Russian state should invest its resources in integrating its economy and encouraging production for the domestic market: production that at the outset would mostly, but not exclusively, be undertaken by "the great national manufacture called agriculture."[155] In this way, as Say had shown, Russia would enjoy the "progress of civilization," which La Harpe defined as "the progress of agriculture and industry, public credit and the morality of citizens."[156]

La Harpe was not involved in the drafting or promulgation of the treaty of the Holy Alliance. As he later annotated a letter he had sent to Alexander on September 27, 1815, "Although the author of this letter arrived in Paris the 24th of September 1815, and had the honor of dining twice in a row tête à tête with the Emperor, he was throughout unaware of the convention that was signed in Paris on the 26th of September 1815 between Russia, Prussia and Austria, and published in Saint-Petersburg the day of Christmas." Though they had discussed "the most important and delicate matters," La Harpe further noted, Alexander "did not speak to me about the Holy Alliance, he only told me that they had taken measures that would assure a long peace, which would be taken advantage of in order to

151. On Say's political economy in this context, see Sonenscher, *Before the Deluge*, 334–48.

152. Jean-Baptiste Say, *Traité d'économie politique* (Paris, 1803), 1:xxxii.

153. See Richard Whatmore, *Republicanism and the French Revolution: An Intellectual History of Jean-Baptiste Say's Political Economy* (Oxford: Oxford University Press, 2000).

154. La Harpe to Alexander I, April 24, 1815, *Correspondance de La Harpe et Alexandre Ier*, 3:46.

155. Ibid..

156. Ibid., 3:48; La Harpe to Alexander I, April 7, 1802, *Correspondance de La Harpe et Alexandre Ier*, 1:547.

reform old abuses and prevent new reversals."[157] A letter written by Germaine de Staël on the same day as La Harpe's letter points to a very different liberal response to Krüdener's religious idiom and its expression in the Holy Alliance. Staël was replying to a report about the dramatic effect that Krüdener's pure "power of love" was having on Alexander. "I cannot fathom what Providence will allow to follow from the alliance of these two souls," Madame de Gérando had written to her, "or whether views so holy and so mystical are what best suit this world troubled by storms and passions, but also agitating to achieve a generous goal and recover a noble independence."[158] Staël's reply reflects her admiration for Alexander as well as for the spirituality that he was sharing with Krüdener (whom she had first met in 1802):

> I am very struck by what I have been told and by what you confirm to me of the Emperor Alexander's conversations with Madame de Krüdener. I greatly admire him, and if, unlike ordinary sovereigns, he is less praised than he deserves, it is because the liberal ideas he loves from the bottom of his heart have few partisans in the salons. . . . What a fine thing for the Emperor Alexander to be at the head of the two things nobly perfecting the human race, inward religion and representative government![159]

These divergent responses to Krüdener reflect a wider nineteenth-century debate over liberty and utility that represents another iteration of eighteenth-century debates over the relationship between the material and moral dimensions of "civilization."[160] La Harpe's views were shared by Say and other writers linked to an influential French journal, the *Décade philosophique*; they were challenged by Staël and those in her circle, like Benjamin Constant (or as Say called them in 1829, the "germanico-scolastic sect of duties" who had attacked the principle of utility).[161]

157. *Correspondance de La Harpe et Alexandre Ier*, 3:115, 3:107.

158. Mme de Gérando to Staël, September 1815, in E. Mühlenbeck, *Étude sur les origines de la Sainte alliance* (Paris: F. Vieweg, 1887), 234–36.

159. Staël to Mme de Gérando, September 27, 1815, in Mühlenbeck, *Étude sur les origines de la Sainte alliance*, 234–36.

160. On this continuity, see Michael Sonenscher, "'The Moment of Social Science': The *Decade Philosophique* and Late Eighteenth-Century French Thought," *Modern Intellectual History* 6, no. 1 (2009): 121–46.

161. Emmanuelle de Champs, *Enlightenment and Utility: Bentham in French, Bentham in France* (Cambridge: Cambridge University Press, 2015), 192. See also Cheryl B. Welch, *Liberty and Utility: The French Idéologues and the Transformation of Liberalism* (New York: Columbia University Press, 1984).

As Lucian Robinson has shown, this debate had an important historiographical dimension, dealing with complex arguments about the history of Christianity and its role in the progress of civilization. La Harpe made his position clear in an 1810 exchange with his friend Philipp Albert Stapfer, a Kantian-educated liberal Protestant who was the Swiss ambassador in Paris and an important influence on the early career of the historian and statesman François Guizot (whose connection to the liberal idea of the Holy Alliance, famously alluded to by the *Communist Manifesto*, will be discussed in chapter 5). La Harpe and Stapfer disagreed over whether ancient or modern slavery was worse. La Harpe took the position that ancient slavery had not been as bad as Christian slavery, because "it was never extended to include the whole populace of the nation, whereas under Christian governments, entire nations (en masse) were condemned to the hardest servitude and remain so still"; moreover, "Christianity has never attempted to destroy these monstrous institutions, born and established in these nations after Christianity's introduction in their midst."[162] Stapfer's rejoinder was that La Harpe had misunderstood the nature of Christianity's role in the progress of civilization, which was to gradually and indirectly prepare the moral grounds for the eventual abolition of wrongs like slavery. Staël's views were closer to Stapfer's than La Harpe's. Her 1799 book *The Influence of Literature upon Society* had drawn a parallel between the French Revolution and the barbarism that had descended on Europe after the fall of the Roman Empire: her point was that the fall of the French monarchy, like the fall of Rome, was ultimately conducive to moral progress driven by the natural religious impulse expressed in Protestant Christianity. Staël's views on the religious foundations of liberal politics had also aligned her with the argument of the prize-winning *Essay on the Spirit and Influence of the Reformation of Luther*, written in 1803 by her friend Charles Villers, an important interpreter of Kant in France: Villers had identified the Reformation with "the progress of civilization and Enlightenment," producing a potent new synthesis of "Enlightened narrative" with Protestantism.[163] In her book *On Germany*, first published

162. La Harpe to Philipp Stapfer, July 6, 1810, cited in Lucian Robinson, "Accounts of Early Christian History in the Thought of François Guizot, Benjamin Constant and Madame de Staël 1800–c. 1833," *History of European Ideas* 43, no. 6 (2017): 634.

163. Charles Villers, *An Essay on the Spirit and Influence of the Reformation of Luther*, trans. James Mill (London: C. and R. Baldwin, 1805); Helena Rosenblatt, *Liberal Values: Benjamin Constant and the Politics of Religion* (Cambridge: Cambridge University Press, 2008); Michael Printy, "Protestantism and Progress in the Year XII: Charles Villers's *Essay on the Spirit and Influence of Luther's Reformation* (1804)," *Modern Intellectual History* 9, no. 2 (August 2012): 303–29.

(but suppressed by Napoleon) in 1810, Staël linked the German tendency to mysticism in religion to the tendency to idealism in philosophy: "one puts all the reality of things in the world in thinking; the other puts all the reality of things in the heavens in sentiment."[164] Staël associated this religious current with Fénelon, whom she had begun reading because she was "tired of materialism." Mysticism was "the religion of Fénelon": it was "the reformation of the Reformation," which could generate the morality required by a society of autonomous individuals.[165] It was in this context that Staël wrote to her friend Juliette Récamier in 1814, describing Krüdener as "a forerunner of a great religious epoch which is arising for the human race."[166]

Like Staël, Benjamin Constant also located the moral foundations for liberal politics in German Protestantism and prayed with Krüdener (at least in part because she had promised to help him in his romantic pursuit of Madame Récamier). But as Constant's political writings highlight, these disagreements with La Harpe were compatible with shared political aims grounded in closely related views of Russia's political future. Constant's remarks about Alexander in the 1806 draft of his *Principles of Politics Applicable to All Governments* belong very much in the tradition of eighteenth-century discussions of Russia and civilization (though they were omitted from the version that Constant published during Napoleon's return from exile in 1815). "Of all monarchs who have arrogated to themselves the difficult function of speeding up their peoples' progress toward civilization," Constant wrote, "those of Russia are certainly the most excusable":

> It is only since the beginning of the reign of Alexander that Russia has some chance of enlightenment. This young prince seeks not at all to reform the people but to moderate the government. He does not direct thought; rather he restrains government. Now, thought is strengthened when redundant activity is removed from government. For a people to

164. Anne-Louise-Germaine de Staël, *De l'Allemagne*, ed. Simone Balayé (Paris: Garnier-Flammarion, 1967), 2:270.

165. Rosenblatt, *Liberal Values*, 140, 147; letter to Madame Gérando, September 1815, quoted in John Isbell, *The Birth of European Romanticism: Truth and Propaganda in Staël's "De l'Allemagne," 1810–1813* (Cambridge: Cambridge University Press, 1994), 178.

166. Rosenblatt, *Liberal Values*, 140, 147; Staël to Juliette Récamier, October 27, 1814, in Anne-Louise-Germaine de Staël, *Lettres de Madame de Staël à Madame Récamier*, ed. Emmanuel Beau de Loménie (Paris: Domat, 1952), 262. On the broader history of this current in nineteenth-century French thought, see Michael C. Behrent, "The Mystical Body of Society: Religion and Association in Nineteenth-Century French Political Thought," *Journal of the History of Ideas* 69, no. 2 (2008): 219–44.

progress, it suffices that government does not shackle them. Progress is in human nature. The government which leaves it alone favors it enough. May Alexander persevere in this at once prudent and generous way and protect himself against the mistrust which seeks to interrupt and the impatience which wants to push ahead.[167]

In 1814, as we have seen, Constant amplified his praise of Alexander in a letter to La Harpe seeking the Russian emperor's patronage; however, La Harpe had long been suspicious of Constant and Staël, and had warned Alexander to be cautious when meeting them in 1804; he again warned Alexander against awarding Constant a decoration on the grounds that it would be seen as a contentious intervention in French politics.[168] All the same, Constant's earlier view of Alexander as a model practitioner of Enlightenment politics was still in evidence as late as 1819. That year, Constant revived Voltaire's technique of praising Russia in order to criticize the French government. He published an enticing (but actually false) rumor in the French press: that Alexander had signed a charter establishing "the foundations of representative government by giving a constitution to Russia" that provided for federal government and a bicameral "national representation." "Thus," Constant reported, "while France takes a retrograde step, Russia advances in the career of liberal ideas and civilization."[169]

167. Benjamin Constant, *Principles of Politics Applicable to All Governments*, ed. Etienne Hofmann, trans. Dennis O'Keeffe (Indianapolis: Liberty Fund, 2003), 194, 343. On Constant's 1806 draft, see Etienne Hofmann, *Les "Principes de politique" de Benjamin Constant: La genèse d'une oeuvre et l'évolution de la pensée de leur auteur (1789–1906)* (Genève: Librairie Droz, 1980), vol. 1. Constant added similarly fulsome remarks to the July 1814 edition of *The Spirit of Conquest and Usurpation and Their Relation to European Civilization*, where he praised Alexander for exhibiting the patience that both Emperor Joseph II and the French Constituent Assembly had fatally lacked: "Look instead at Russia since the beginning of the reign of Alexander. The improvements there are slow and gradual; the people are fully and freely enlightened; the laws are perfected in detail, and no-one thinks of subverting the entire system. By preceding theory, practice prepares the spirit to accept it, and the moment arrives when that theory, which is merely the exposition of what must be, will be received even better because it will simply be the explanation of what already is. Honour to that prince who, in his prudent and generous march, favours all natural progress, respects all necessary adjournments, and knows how to protect himself equally from the suspicion that wishes to stop him, and from the impatience which seeks to precede him." Benjamin Constant, *Political Writings*, ed. Biancamaria Fontana (Cambridge: Cambridge University Press, 1988), 152–53.

168. La Harpe to Alexander I, April 3, 1804, *Correspondance de La Harpe et Alexandre Ier*, 2:136; La Harpe to Alexander I, October 14, 1814, ibid., 2:587. See also La Harpe to Alexander I, February 10, 1815, ibid., 2:621.

169. Cited in George Vernadsky, *La charte constitutionnelle de l'Empire russe de l'an 1820*, trans. Sergei Oldenburg (Paris: Librairie du Recueil Sirey, 1933), 77.

Krüdener herself did not share Staël's and Constant's commitment to constitutional reform and representative government. But she did maintain a link with another dimension of eighteenth-century discussions of civilization: the colonization of the Russian Empire. Historians of abolitionism have maintained that "Anglo-American Protestantism during the late eighteenth century tended to square itself with the Enlightenment faith in moral progress, but to reinterpret beneficial change as the workings of divine providence."[170] The progress that was supposed to follow from the colonization of the Russian Empire was reframed in a similar way. For Diderot as for La Harpe, colonization figured as a key element of a strategy for transforming Russia into an agent capable of addressing the problems of European politics. Migration to the Russian Empire acquired a providential meaning not only through the struggle with Napoleon but also in the millenarian atmosphere of the "year without a summer" of 1816 (due to the eruption of Mount Tambora in Indonesia, which caused severe food shortages in southern Germany and Switzerland).[171] As Hartmut Lehmann has explained, some of those inspired by millenarian convictions in that moment merely dissented from their local churches, while others migrated to Pennsylvania; a further contingent identified Odesa as a providentially meaningful destination. While Odesa was not itself the site of the new kingdom of Christ, it was halfway to the Holy Land, and far easier to reach: Alexander's welcoming policy toward settlers "was considered to be a sign from heaven."[172] Krüdener helped inspire thousands of Württemberg pietists to migrate to Odesa; she herself, having become estranged from Alexander, left in 1824 to found a colony in Crimea, where she died shortly after her arrival.[173]

---

170. Christopher Leslie Brown, "Christianity and the Campaign against Slavery and the Slave Trade," in *Enlightenment, Reawakening and Revolution, 1660–1815*, ed. Stewart J. Brown and Timothy Tackett, vol. 7, Cambridge History of Christianity (Cambridge: Cambridge University Press, 2006), 532.

171. See Wolfgang Behringer, *Tambora and the Year without a Summer: How a Volcano Plunged the World into Crisis*, trans. Pamela Selwyn (Cambridge: Polity Press, 2019).

172. Hartmut Lehmann, "Pietistic Millenarianism in Late Eighteenth-Century Germany," in *The Transformation of Political Culture: England and Germany in the Late Eighteenth Century*, ed. Eckhart Hellmuth (London: German Historical Institute, 1990), 334. One member of Krüdener's circle, Marie Kummer, apparently started to lead a group of thirty peasants to the Holy Land on foot; they made it as far as Vienna before they were stopped and Kummer ran off with the group's money. In an earlier prayer session involving Alexander, Kummer had scandalously conveyed a divine message that the emperor would donate funds to her community. Charles Eynard, *Vie de Madame de Krudener* (Paris: Cherbuliez, 1849), 2:41–42.

173. Ernest John Knapton, *The Lady of the Holy Alliance: The Life of Julie de Krüdener* (New York: Columbia University Press, 1939), 142.

As Krüdener's trajectory suggests, the religiously motivated colonization of the Russian Empire was the most enduring element of an originally much more multidimensional picture of Russia's capacity to serve as a peacemaking "friend of mankind" and its relationship to the moral and material progress of civilization. The religious lives of migrants to colonies on Russia's imperial frontier also diverged from the universalistic aspirations of those imagining the progress of civilization and the Russian "friend of mankind" from afar. This divergence is vividly illustrated by the brief Russian career of Franz von Baader, the true successor to the Anglican cleric John Brown's position in the eighteenth-century debate about Russia and civilization. Baader was a Catholic Bavarian mining inspector who later became a professor of religion. His essay about the application of Christian morality to politics, which was sent to Alexander, has often been discussed as an important influence on the religious idiom of the treaty of the Holy Alliance.[174] After 1814, as Susan Crane has recounted, Baader was invited to come to Russia to found a school for training a new ecumenical clergy; he was also offered a post as literary correspondent and asked to help recruit foreign clergy. In 1820, Baader proposed to found an Academy of Religious Science in Saint Petersburg, and he left for Russia in 1822. However, Baader was accompanied by his son-in-law, Boris von Yxkull, who was suspected of liberalism by the Prussian police because of his association with Benjamin Constant; the Austrian minister Clemens von Metternich explicitly warned Alexander not to let them across the border.[175] Though Baader never made it to Russia himself, he did manage to recruit a Bavarian priest, Ignaz Lindl: a charismatic revivalist who was attracting many thousands of peasants (including many Lutherans) to his services. Arrested for his departures from orthodoxy in 1817, he was released from prison by the czar's representative upon Baader's recommendation. Lindl was given permission to emigrate, and in 1822 he founded a community in Sarata, west of Odesa. For Baader, it was the beginning of a movement to reform the Orthodox Church that would result in its reintegration with western Christendom; for its inhabitants, it was an opportunity to live in "brotherly love" and prepare for the millennium. In 1823,

174. Franz von Baader, *Ueber das durch die französische Revolution herbeigeführte Bedürfniß einer neuern und innigern Verbindung der Religion mit der Politik* (Nürnberg: Campe, 1815).

175. Susan A. Crane, "Holy Alliances: Creating Religious Communities after the Napoleonic Wars," in *Die Gegenwart Gottes in der modernen Gesellschaft: Transzendenz und religiöse Vergemeinschaftung in Deutschland*, ed. Michael Geyer and Lucian Hölscher (Göttingen: Wallstein, 2006), 48.

however, a visiting government inspector found Lindl (a Catholic priest) married with a child and concluded that he had organized what amounted to a personal cult; he was expelled from Russia.

As Crane has observed, "Baader's proposal and Lindl's communal experiment marked a zenith in the brief history of postwar ecumenical ambitions."[176] Detached from these ambitions as well as its emancipatory political content, the religious idiom of the Holy Alliance became associated with the repression of dissent and far more exclusionary forms of community. This fate also points toward a much longer history of the "friend of mankind" idea, as well as its connection to an imperial history that has continued to play out on the shore of the Black Sea. In June 2014—shortly after the Maidan Revolution in Ukraine and the Russian annexation of Crimea—a gathering of European and Russian far right extremists took place in Vienna: the occasion was a secret conference, sponsored by a Russian businessman, to commemorate the Congress of Vienna and "revive the spirit of the Holy Alliance."[177]

176. Ibid., 38.

177. Bernhard Odehnal, "Gipfeltreffen mit Putins fünfter Kolonne," *Tages-Anzeiger*, June 3, 2014, https://www.tagesanzeiger.ch/gipfeltreffen-mit-putins-fuenfter-kolonne -335546606907; Gerhard Lechner, "Heilige Allianz gegen die 'Schwulenlobby,'" *Wiener Zeitung*, June 3, 2014, https://www.wienerzeitung.at/nachrichten/politik/europa/635065 -Heilige-Allianz-gegen-die-Schwulenlobby.html. See also Timothy Snyder, "Integration and Disintegration: Europe, Ukraine, and the World," *Slavic Review* 74, no. 4 (2015): 695–707.

CHAPTER THREE

Scripting Revolution

Who knew that that same star of the North which just shone so brilliantly
over the old world would also exert its benevolent influence over the new?

—JUSTE CHANLATTE, *GRATEFUL HAITI*[1]

ON FEBRUARY 27, 1790, the *London Chronicle* published a letter reporting on "the check received lately by the oligarchy of Switzerland."[2] The
Swiss republics, explained "Philanthropus" from Lausanne, were ruled
by a small number of patrician families. The Republic of Bern, the most
powerful in Switzerland, had trampled on the liberties of its subjects in
neighboring Vaud. It had violated their charters, suppressed their industry, and taxed them oppressively while denying them representation.
Inspired by the French Revolution, the people of Vaud had "all put on the
cockade of *Liberty*." They had declared their independence and elected a
new "Sovereign Assembly," which had abolished feudal privileges while
authorizing itself to take any measures necessary for public safety. Two
months after Philanthropus had exhorted readers to "rejoice at seeing a
new altar erected to Liberty," the *London Chronicle* published a reply from
"A Citizen of Bern," pointing out that no such revolution had taken place
and assuring readers that Bern was no more in need of a revolution than
Britain.[3] This rebuttal did not stop the *London Chronicle* from publishing
another six installments of Philanthropus's revolutionary fantasy over the

---

1. Juste Chanlatte, *Hayti reconnaissante, en réponse à un écrit, imprimé à Londres, et
intitulé: L'Europe châtiée et l'Afrique vengée, ou Raisons pour regarder les calamités du siècle comme des punitions infligées par la Providence pour la traite en Afrique* (Sans Souci:
De l'Imprimerie royale, 1819), 10, https://gallica.bnf.fr/ark:/12148/bpt6k315050x.

2. *London Chronicle*, February 25–27, 1790, 199.

3. *London Chronicle*, April 27–29, 1790, 403.

summer of 1790. During July, as the *London Chronicle* covered the action in the real National Assembly in Paris, Philanthropus reported on the new constitution of Vaud. Bern and its subject territories had become a confederation. In the July 20 issue, readers of the *London Chronicle* learned of the landmark reform of the French ecclesiastical establishment—the Civil Constitution of the Clergy—and turned the page to read about the organization of the new militia and courts of Vaud.[4]

The economic arguments and constitutional arrangements set out by Philanthropus echoed several decades of eighteenth-century attempts to transform a transatlantic British empire into a confederation that did justice to the economic interests of the colonies.[5] As a "script" for revolution, however, the "Letters of Philanthropus" hewed most closely to the French example of 1789: they described a sovereign national assembly convening to dismantle the worst abuses of the old regime and write a new constitution.[6] The author of this script was the Vaudois patriot Frédéric-César de la Harpe, writing from Saint Petersburg. A decade earlier, after completing his law degree at the University of Tübingen, La Harpe had been contemplating joining the American struggle for independence, when another

---

4. *London Chronicle*, July 17–20, 1790, 69–70.

5. On the British imperial debates, see Mary Sarah Bilder, *The Transatlantic Constitution: Colonial Legal Culture and the Empire* (Cambridge, MA: Harvard University Press, 2004); Alison L. LaCroix, *The Ideological Origins of American Federalism* (Cambridge, MA: Harvard University Press, 2010); Jack P. Greene, *The Constitutional Origins of the American Revolution* (Cambridge: Cambridge University Press, 2011); Steven Pincus, *The Heart of the Declaration: The Founders' Case for an Activist Government* (New Haven: Yale University Press, 2016). On the arguments employed by Philanthropus, see Andreas Würgler, "Gemeinderevolution—Fiktiv: 'Etats' und 'villes et communautés' in Frédéric-César Laharpes Bericht über die noch nicht geschehene Revolution in der Waadt (1790)," in *Gemeinde, Reformation und Widerstand: Festschrift für Peter Blickle zum 60. Geburtstag*, ed. Heinrich Richard Schmidt, André Holenstein, and Andreas Würgler (Tübingen: Biblioteca Academica, 1998), 138. The letters of Philanthropus were followed by a four-part refutation of the Citizen of Bern by "Helvetius."

6. On the notion of a revolutionary "script," see Keith Michael Baker, "Inventing the French Revolution," in *Inventing the French Revolution: Essays on French Political Culture in the Eighteenth Century* (Cambridge: Cambridge University Press, 1990), 203–23; Keith Michael Baker and Dan Edelstein, eds., *Scripting Revolution: A Historical Approach to the Comparative Study of Revolutions* (Stanford: Stanford University Press, 2015). For a broad overview of the concept of "revolution," see also Reinhart Koselleck, "Revolution: Rebellion, Aufruhr, Bürgerkrieg," in *Geschichtliche Grundbegriffe: Historisches Lexikon zur politisch-sozialen Sprache in Deutschland*, ed. Otto Brunner, Werner Conze, and Reinhart Koselleck, vol. 5 (Stuttgart: Klett-Cotta, 1984), 653–788. On the broad transatlantic circulation of revolutionaries and revolutionary texts in the late eighteenth century, through networks that included La Harpe, see Janet L. Polasky, *Revolutions without Borders* (New Haven: Yale University Press, 2015).

opportunity presented itself.[7] In 1782, he chaperoned a young Russian aristocrat (the younger brother of Empress Catherine II's lover Alexander Lanskoi) on a tour of Italy. An invitation to Saint Petersburg followed. In 1784, Catherine appointed La Harpe to teach French to her grandson Alexander, then accepted his proposal to take charge of Alexander's overall education. When the Bernese government denounced La Harpe to Catherine in 1791, she allowed him to defend himself in a pair of long letters to her.[8] These letters both articulated and enacted a different script for liberating Lausanne that developed well beyond the reenactment of 1789 in the pages of the *London Chronicle*.

La Harpe's new script, which ultimately did liberate Lausanne, also reveals the process through which liberals formulated their expectations of the Holy Alliance. In 1798, La Harpe was one of the founders of the revolutionary Helvetic Republic, which was established following the French invasion of the Republic of Bern; in 1815, he was an important player in the negotiation of a new Swiss Federal Treaty at the Congress of Vienna, which blocked the restoration of Bernese rule over Lausanne and created the independent Canton of Vaud. Between 1798 and 1815, La Harpe fashioned Alexander into a "friend of mankind": the figure discussed in chapter 2, capable of wielding the power (and potential) of the Russian state as a force for universal emancipation. At the same time, La Harpe fashioned himself into the representative of the international public opinion that would empower and authorize his former pupil to play this emancipatory role. La Harpe's scripting of the Russian "friend of mankind" represented a form of Enlightenment politics that involved both the elaboration of detailed plans for joint action and the construction of a moral character through literary craft. When Alexander came to power in 1801, the elaborate plans of action

7. Heinrich Zschokke, "Friedrich Cäsar Laharpe, Director der helvetischen Republick," *Historische Denkwürdigkeiten der helvetischen Staatsumwälzung* 3 (1805): 80. Zschokke was a prominent Swiss journalist and friend of La Harpe's whose source was an autobiographical piece by La Harpe, later published in 1864: Frédéric-César de la Harpe, *Mémoires concernant sa conduite comme Directeur de la République helvétique addressés par lui-même à Zschokke* (Paris: Cherbuliez, 1864). There was also an 1818 French translation of Zschokke's memoir that was aimed at discrediting La Harpe: Charles Monnard, *Biographie de Mr. Frédéric César Laharpe, cidevant directeur de la République helvétique: Suivie d'extraits de ses ouvrages politiques* (s.l., 1818). See also Arthur Boehtlingk, *Frédéric-César Laharpe, 1754–1838* (Neuchâtel: Éditions de la Baconnière, 1969).

8. La Harpe to Catherine II, November 15, 1791, *Correspondance de Frédéric-César de La Harpe et Alexandre Ier: Suivie de la correspondance de F.-C. de La Harpe avec les membres de la famille impériale de Russie*, ed. Jean Charles Biaudet and Françoise Nicod (Neuchâtel: Éditions de la Baconnière, 1978), 3:505–17; La Harpe to Catherine II, November 20, 1791, ibid., 3:520–31.

that La Harpe began sharing with Alexander in Saint Petersburg amounted to a strategic guide for developing the capacities and defining the interests of a "friend of mankind." At the same time, they also served as a method for aligning international public opinion with Russian interests and orienting both around expectations of progress—expectations whose disappointment would register as Alexander's failure to follow the "friend of mankind" script. After 1802, La Harpe focused on extending his collaboration with Alexander to the international network he encountered through the Paris salon of the famous radical English expatriate writer Helen Maria Williams. Her network included the prominent English abolitionist Thomas Clarkson (whose antislavery pamphlet she asked La Harpe to help distribute in Paris in 1814); the literary strategies La Harpe adopted were closely related to the ones he encountered in Williams's circle, including those employed by abolitionists like Clarkson in their campaign to abolish the slave trade.[9] When the treaty of the Holy Alliance appeared in 1815, La Harpe himself criticized its religious idiom—but he also recognized it as a fatally flawed version of the kind of politics he had pursued. Meanwhile others, including Clarkson, were prepared to assume the role that La Harpe had scripted for himself. In Clarkson's hands, the role that La Harpe had scripted for Alexander even came to encompass the cause of postrevolutionary Haitian independence.

The Liberation of Lausanne

La Harpe's new script for revolution first comes into view in his 1791 letters to the empress of Russia. La Harpe had been denounced by the Bernese government because it had intercepted a petition he had written and sent to three officials in Vaud. In his own defense, La Harpe assured Catherine that he had acted only according to his republican principles, which were certainly no secret to her or anyone else: they were the same principles he had promised would guide her grandson's education. La Harpe's summary of the petition in his letters to Catherine is borne out by a document discovered in the Bern State Archives in the 1960s, addressed to the "Illustrious, high, powerful and Sovereign Lords" of Bern.[10] The petition

9. Lionel D. Woodward, *Une adhérente anglaise de la Révolution française: Hélène-Maria Williams et ses amis* (Paris: Honoré Champion, 1930), 180.

10. Ariane Méautis, "Les idées politiques de Frédéric-César de la Harpe: Le projet de requête qu'il destinait à LL.EE. de Berne en 1790," *Schweizerische Zeitschrift für Geschichte* 18, no. 2 (1968): 246–78. La Harpe also describes the petition in his *Supplément à la biographie de Mr Nicolas-Frédéric de Mulinen: Avoyer du Canton de Berne* (Lausanne: Imprimerie des Frères Blanchard, 1837), 11.

invoked the traditional mythology of Swiss liberty, naming national heroes like William Tell, in imploring the Lords of Bern to save the republic by restoring the constitutional rights of their fellow citizens. It also warned that "tumultuous cries of liberty, equality, the rights of man ring out among us," unleashing violence among neighboring peoples "that some timely concessions would have prevented."[11] It closed by citing the example of the Roman Senate, whose magnanimous concessions to the Roman people had only increased their respect for its authority. As La Harpe later explained, "Far from wishing *to revolutionize*, I wanted to prevent a revolution that chronic abuses, become intolerable, announced as imminent, and that, if it broke out all at once, would be accompanied by atrocities; for there would no longer be anything capable of opposing the overflowing torrent of spirited passions and long contained resentments."[12]

In drafting his petition, La Harpe explained to Catherine, he had acted as a patriotic citizen, seeking to advise the government within the proper legal channels on the urgent need for constitutional change. In fact, he explained, when he had sent the draft of the petition to his colleagues, he had appended a detailed set of instructions on "the legal manner of presenting it."[13] The process was to begin with purely "academic" studies based on archival research into the constitutional history of Vaud.[14] These reports would form the basis for lists of grievances and requests for institutional change that would be prepared by private citizens. These would be submitted to the Lords of Bern by each of the communes, who would themselves be acting in the manner of private citizens with respect to the Bernese government, rather than acting collectively like a "seditious league." If the continued intransigence of the patricians subsequently provoked an unauthorized meeting of the estates, this would be a desperate measure of self-defense, reflecting an abdication of authority. Catherine was evidently satisfied by La Harpe's performance. La Harpe later recounted that she found it odd to condemn a Swiss patriot for invoking

---

11. Frédéric-César de la Harpe, "Requête à Leurs Excellences de Berne," *Correspondance de La Harpe et Alexandre Ier*, 3:141. On the role of such references in Swiss political thought, see Marc H. Lerner, *A Laboratory of Liberty: The Transformation of Political Culture in Republican Switzerland, 1750–1848* (Leiden: Brill, 2012).

12. Frédéric-César de la Harpe, *Essai sur la Constitution du pays de Vaud* (Paris: Batittiot frères, 1796), 2:xxvii–xxviii.

13. La Harpe to Catherine II, November 20, 1791, *Correspondance de La Harpe et Alexandre Ier*, 3:524. Cf. Zschokke, "Friedrich Cäsar Laharpe," 84–85; La Harpe, *Mémoires*, 79.

14. La Harpe later mentioned to Alexander that he had written the first part of his *Essai sur la Constitution du pays de Vaud* (published in 1796) in 1792. La Harpe to Alexander I, January 28, 1797, *Correspondance de La Harpe et Alexandre Ier*, 1:206.

the names of his country's founders. She asked only that he abstain from further involvement in Swiss politics while remaining in her service.[15] When La Harpe was finally dismissed from his position in 1794, the decisive factor was not his republicanism but his refusal to implicate himself in Catherine's scheme to alter the succession to the throne in favor of her teenage grandson Alexander.[16]

La Harpe was both invoking and transforming a procedure for political change that had received its sharpest as well as its most familiar formulation in the essay "An Answer to the Question: 'What Is Enlightenment?'" published in 1784 by the German philosopher Immanuel Kant. According to Kant, a revolution might succeed in removing an autocrat or granting relief from oppression, but it would not produce a "true reform in ways of thinking" that permeated public opinion and ultimately produced a change in "principles of government."[17] True reform of this kind presupposed intellectual freedom, so that the public could gradually enlighten itself, or undergo what Kant later referred to as a "revolution . . . in the mode of thought."[18] Paradoxically, Kant claimed, the emergence of civil freedom presupposed intellectual freedom rather than the other way around, and intellectual freedom was most likely to develop where civil authority had been most firmly established. He held out Frederick II of Prussia as a model because Frederick had removed the greatest number of obstacles presently inhibiting the continuation of this process, driven by private individuals exercising their reason publicly. Frederick had shown how it was possible to create a space for the process of enlightenment to continue without being arrested by established despotism on one side or revolutionary despotism on the other. As Kant famously put it, "only a ruler who is himself enlightened and has no fear of phantoms, yet who likewise has at hand a well-disciplined and numerous army to guaran-

15. La Harpe, *Mémoires*, 82.

16. *Le gouverneur d'un prince: Frédéric César de Laharpe et Alexandre Ier de Russie d'après les manuscrits inédits de F. C. de Laharpe, et les sources russes les plus récentes* (Lausanne: Georges Bridel & Cie, 1902), 50. Several other independent sources corroborate La Harpe's claim about Catherine's intentions regarding the succession. See Marie-Pierre Rey, *Alexander I: The Tsar Who Defeated Napoleon*, trans. Susan Emanuel (DeKalb: Northern Illinois University Press, 2012), 61–63.

17. Immanuel Kant, "An Answer to the Question: 'What Is Enlightenment,'" in *Political Writings*, ed. Hans Reiss, trans. H. B. Nisbet (Cambridge: Cambridge University Press, 1991), 55, 59–60.

18. Immanuel Kant, *Religion and Rational Theology*, ed. Allen W. Wood and George Di Giovanni, Cambridge Edition of the Works of Immanuel Kant (Cambridge: Cambridge University Press, 1996), 92.

tee public security, may say what no republic would dare to say: *Argue as much as you like and about whatever you like, but obey!*"[19]

It is far from clear, of course, that La Harpe had limited himself to acting within the legal channels he had described to Catherine. His intercepted draft petition bore the same date as his second letter in the *London Chronicle*, outlining a new federal constitution for Bern. In his letters to Catherine, La Harpe made passing reference to a "series of articles" he had published in order to enlighten public opinion regarding the people's true interests; even setting aside whatever else he may have published anonymously at the time, it is difficult (though perhaps not impossible) to read his "Letters of Philanthropus" as an endeavor in that spirit.[20] However, in presenting this script to Catherine, La Harpe did add an unmistakable revolutionary twist to it. La Harpe stressed to Catherine that he had drafted his petition as a private individual who held no public office and owned no property in Vaud. "Your Imperial Majesty is the only sovereign I recognize," he declared to Catherine, "in every other regard I am a free man, and Messieurs the patricians of Bern are as foreign to me as the mandarins of China."[21] Catherine was the only sovereign judge he would recognize between himself and the seventy-six patrician families who had denounced him. In closing his letters, then, La Harpe turned the tables on the Bernese government by explicitly inviting Catherine to intervene as arbiter of a conflict between the people of Vaud and patricians of Bern: "and the best day of my life would be the one when she accorded me the honor of pleading the cause of my unfortunate homeland before her august throne."[22] In writing his letter to Catherine, La Harpe was already pleading his cause to her, and in doing so, he was demoting the "Illustrious, high, powerful and Sovereign Lords" of his petition.

---

19. Kant, "'What Is Enlightenment,'" 59.

20. Zschokke's 1805 biography mentions that there were fifty other anonymous pamphlets that took "various forms" and were printed in German, Italian, and English; the autobiographical account published in 1864 refers to "more than sixty": Zschokke, "Friedrich Cäsar Laharpe," 84; La Harpe, *Mémoires*, 78. But it remains unclear how many of these were in fact by La Harpe, since he claimed in his *Mémoires* to have recognized only two of those shown to him in Saint Petersburg as his own: La Harpe, *Mémoires*, 82. These may have included a pamphlet, attributed to La Harpe by the Genevan journalist Mallet du Pan and published in Alsace, which was suppressed by Bernese government: "Aux habitans du canton de Berne" was an appeal to the Bernese people to rise up following the French example (they would do better than the French, the pamphlet promised, because they were armed) and promising that the Vaudois would come to their aid. Méautis, "Les idées politiques," 258–62.

21. La Harpe to Catherine II, November 20, 1791, *Correspondance de La Harpe et Alexandre Ier*, 3:521.

22. Ibid., 3:527; Zschokke, "Friedrich Cäsar Laharpe," 86.

In Kant's terms, La Harpe was inviting a change in "principles of government" guided by enlightened opinion. But this change would not be undertaken by the Bernese government itself, nor through an appeal to popular revolutionary action. Instead, it would be undertaken by La Harpe, brokering an alliance with the Empress of All the Russias, acting as a private individual who could also play the part of a representative of the people of Vaud. Considered in this way, La Harpe's letters diverge from accounts of Enlightenment politics that take their cue from the influential rendering of Kant's essay by the twentieth-century philosopher Jürgen Habermas. La Harpe had pled his case against the Bernese government through rhetorical craft rather than pure reason, not only in print and before the court of public opinion but also in a private letter addressed to a foreign sovereign.[23] La Harpe's letters point ahead to an approach to politics he would later encounter in the Paris salon of Helen Maria Williams and apply to Catherine's grandson Alexander after 1802: the sort of approach in which the link between private understandings and public actions is not "a principle of enlightened, critical discussion" but a "dynamic force by which private or intimate topics are subjected to public display."[24] At the same time, La Harpe was still following in the footsteps of Voltaire, who had begun corresponding with Catherine shortly after she took power in 1762; he was elaborating on the kind of "philosophical alliance" that had developed in the second half of the eighteenth century between the Parisian literary establishment and the courts of Europe.[25] La Harpe's letters raised the prospect that Catherine would not merely serve as a critical standard of enlightened leadership but would actively intervene to transform Swiss politics from the outside. Though it is unlikely that Catherine contemplated such action, La Harpe would repeatedly revisit this script in inviting first Napoleon Bonaparte and later Alexander to liberate Lausanne.

La Harpe issued his invitation to Napoleon in 1797. Military considerations—the need to secure the newly created Cisalpine Republic

---

23. Compare the criticisms of Habermas's influential account of publicity summarized in Kirill Abrosimov, *Aufklärung jenseits der Öffentlichkeit: Friedrich Melchior Grimms "Correspondance littéraire" (1753–1773) zwischen der "république des lettres" und europäischen Fürstenhöfen* (Ostfildern: Thorbecke, 2014), 12–13.

24. Antoine Lilti, "Private Lives, Public Space: A New Social History of the Enlightenment," in *The Cambridge Companion to the French Enlightenment*, ed. Daniel Brewer (Cambridge: Cambridge University Press, 2014), 24–25.

25. Abrosimov, *Aufklärung jenseits der Öffentlichkeit*, 16. For a particularly incisive study of such relationships, see Shiru Lim, "Frederick the Great and Jean Le Ronde d'Alembert on Philosophy, Truth, and Politics," *The Historical Journal* 61 (2018): 357–78.

in northern Italy—had concentrated French attention on Switzerland and on Vaud in particular.[26] In December 1797, a petition written by La Harpe was submitted to the Directory of the French Republic, urging it to invoke its historic rights as guarantor of Swiss treaties, as well as "the interest of humanity," in order to secure a representative constitution for Vaud.[27] The role of the French, according to the petition, would be to convene an assembly of elected representatives and "assure the liberty of their choices and deliberations by nominating a commissioner with an accommodating yet firm character who could aid them in reforming abuses and preventing their return by the establishment of a constitution based on liberty, equality, the guarantee of property and independence."[28] Negotiations in Paris ensued, involving La Harpe, members of the French Directory, Napoleon, and Peter Ochs, La Harpe's colleague from Basel. The script played out as intended in Basel, where an assembly met to draft a new constitution. It was approximated in Vaud, where La Harpe warned that lengthy constitutional deliberations might invite more intensive French intervention (the fate of the Dutch) or lead to the partition of Switzerland among the great powers (the fate of the Poles). He urged his colleagues to ratify a provisional constitution already drafted in Paris by Ochs and edited by members of the French Directory.[29] But the other Swiss cantons proved recalcitrant, and La Harpe, now fearing an oligarchic reaction most of all, eagerly supported the French invasion of the Republic of Bern in March 1798. Then, faced with French plans to partition Switzerland with Austria, La Harpe urged the Directory to proclaim a unified and centralized Helvetic Republic under Ochs's Paris constitution. La Harpe went on to serve as a director of the Helvetic Republic, increasingly dismayed that the guarantors of Swiss liberty were becoming its overlords, until he was forced out of office in a French-supported coup in January 1800. In an annotation he added later in life to his final letter to Catherine (part of a vast commentary on his correspondence with the Russian imperial

26. R. R. Palmer, *The Age of the Democratic Revolution: A Political History of Europe and America, 1760–1800* (Princeton: Princeton University Press, 1959), 2:408.

27. La Harpe to the French Directory, December 3, 1797, *Correspondance de Frédéric-César de La Harpe sous la République Helvétique*, ed. Jean Charles Biaudet et al. (Neuchâtel: La Baconnière, 1982), 1:251.

28. Ibid., 1:251.

29. Palmer, *The Age of the Democratic Revolution*, 2:409; *Korrespondenz des Peter Ochs (1752–1821)*, ed. Gustav Steiner (Basel: H. Oppermann, 1927), 2:266n6. For La Harpe's references to the Dutch and Polish experiences, see La Harpe to the representatives of the République Lémanique, February 5, 1798, in *Correspondance de La Harpe sous la République Helvétique*, 1:382.

family, most of which he added in the 1830s), La Harpe observed that since Russia was too distant to endanger Swiss independence, the Lords of Bern would have done well to accept his original proposal to appoint Catherine as arbiter: "Messieurs the patricians would have gained from accepting my proposition, which would perhaps have prevented the explosion of 1798."[30]

The Best Kind of Revolution

In the fall of 1797, as La Harpe was preparing his petition to the French Directory, he received a remarkable letter from Alexander that set the stage for the next production of his script. Catherine's reign had ended with a rising tide of corruption and abuse, Alexander reported to his former teacher, and his father Paul's military inclination and erratic attempts at reform were not going to help. "You know my ideas," Alexander wrote, "which tend to expatriate me."[31] As yet there was no chance of putting these ideas into practice, but Alexander had resolved to lay the groundwork for "the best kind of revolution, carried out by a legal power, ending as soon as the constitution was achieved and the nation had representatives."[32] For the moment, Alexander's plan was to influence public opinion by arranging for the translation of as many "useful books" as possible into Russian, publishing whatever was permitted and saving the rest for later. Alexander also reported that he had gathered around himself an intimate group of enlightened friends: Nikolai Nikolaevich Novosiltsev, Pavel Aleksandrovich Stroganov, and Adam Jerzy Czartoryski. One of them, Novosiltsev, had been dispatched to Switzerland to deliver Alexander's letter, solicit La Harpe's views on his project, and ask him about education systems that would be easiest to establish and do the most to hasten the enlightenment of popular opinion. Once it was his turn to rule, Alexander promised, he would carry out his legal revolution, whereupon he would surrender power and retire to private life.[33] Alexander's turn came in March 1801, following the assassination of his father. Upon receiving the

30. La Harpe to Catherine II, November 20, 1791, *Correspondance de La Harpe et Alexandre Ier*, 3:530.

31. Alexander to La Harpe, September 27/October 8, 1797, 1:215.

32. Ibid., 1:216.

33. Alexander expressed the same fantasy to others, too. See Marc Raeff, *Michael Speransky: Statesman of Imperial Russia, 1772–1839* (The Hague: Martinus Nijhoff, 1957), 33.

news, La Harpe urged Alexander to "hasten slowly" to act on his ideas.[34] Alexander replied that he would devote himself to "making myself worthy of having been your student" and work steadfastly to promote "general utility."[35] The exiled La Harpe set out for Saint Petersburg that summer, lacking a formal invitation and unsure whether the conspirators who had accelerated Alexander's succession to the throne would prevent him from entering the country or ensure that his journey ended in Siberia.[36]

Alexander's script for a "revolution, carried out by a legal power" fits into an established pattern. Several eighteenth-century monarchs—notably Frederick II of Prussia and the Austrian emperor Joseph II—had raised comparable prospects as they prepared for their reigns.[37] A striking contemporary parallel comes from Prussia. In 1799, the Prussian finance minister, Carl August von Struensee, explained to the French diplomat Louis-Guillaume Otto how Prussia would achieve the goals of the French Revolution through the exercise of state power directed by its monarch:

> The very useful revolution which you have made from the bottom upwards will be made gradually in Prussia from the top downwards. The king [Frederick II's successor, Friedrich Wilhelm III] is a democrat in his way; he works without letting up to reduce the privileges of the nobility, and he will follow the plan of Joseph II in this regard, but by gradual means. In a few years there will no longer be a privileged class in Prussia. The nobles will be allowed to keep their ribbons, which

34. La Harpe to Alexander I, April 13, 1801, *Correspondance de La Harpe et Alexandre Ier*, 2:229. This remark, attributed to the Roman emperor Augustus by Suetonius, was also favored by Cosimo I de' Medici in Renaissance Florence and, more recently, by Lee Kuan Yew in Singapore: see Sophus A. Reinert, *The Academy of Fisticuffs: Political Economy and Commercial Society in Enlightenment Italy* (Cambridge, MA: Harvard University Press, 2018), 399–400.

35. Alexander I to La Harpe, May 9/21, 1801, *Correspondance de La Harpe et Alexandre Ier*, 1:240–41.

36. Rey, *Alexander I*, 109. Orders were issued by Count Nikita Panin, without Alexander's knowledge, to deny La Harpe a passport to enter Russia. See also La Harpe to Constantine, February 23, 1828, *Correspondance de La Harpe et Alexandre Ier*, 3:662. On rumors about Siberia, see Peter Ochs to La Harpe, July 23, 1801, *Korrespondenz des Peter Ochs*, 3:24.

37. On Frederick, see Isaac Nakhimovsky, "The Enlightened Prince and the Future of Europe: Voltaire and Frederick the Great's *Anti-Machiavel* of 1740," in *Commerce and Peace in the Enlightenment*, ed. Béla Kapossy, Isaac Nakhimovsky, and Richard Whatmore (Cambridge: Cambridge University Press, 2017), 44–77. On Joseph, see Derek Beales, "Joseph II's Rêveries," in *Enlightenment and Reform in Eighteenth-Century Europe* (London: I. B. Tauris, 2005), 157–81.

often take the place of pensions and relieve our finances; but the need to live in comfort will encourage them to throw themselves into a more lucrative career, that of commerce and industry.[38]

This Prussian script for a top-down revolution led by the monarch was premised on the transformation of international relations through the emergence of a new alliance system centered on France. Initially, so too were the plans that La Harpe offered to Alexander, at the outset of his reign, on how to proceed with his "revolution, carried out by a legal power."

La Harpe arrived in Saint Petersburg in August 1801, and remained there, in close contact with Alexander, until the following May. The voluminous letters and reports he produced for Alexander during this time presented a detailed set of plans for turning Russia into a "friend of mankind" that would extend Alexander's revolution to the rest of Europe as well as the Atlantic world. On the one hand, La Harpe began advising Alexander on what sorts of internal interventions the "legal power" should make, beyond allowing Russians to argue as much as they liked about whatever they liked.[39] At the same time, La Harpe also developed his earlier ideas about how first Catherine and later the French Republic might intervene externally to facilitate constitutional reform, not only in Switzerland but across Europe. Initially, the link between these endeavors was La Harpe himself. In parallel to (but at times in tension with) the "unofficial committee" (*neglasniy komitet*) now constituted by Alexander's friends, which met regularly and in secret with the emperor in the initial years of his reign, La Harpe aimed to supply private guidance for state action that would compensate for the absence of a social basis for organized public opinion in Russia.[40] At the same time, he would also serve as a private "intermediary" brokering an alliance between Alexander and Napoleon on behalf of the general interests of what he called the "civilized world." Following his departure from Russia and his disenchantment with Napoleon, as we shall see, La Harpe devoted himself to developing a much broader set of connections between Alexander and other members of his international networks, which would empower and authorize

38. Louis-Guillaume Otto to Charles-Maurice de Talleyrand, August 13, 1799, Paul Bailleu, ed., *Preussen und Frankreich von 1795 bis 1807: Diplomatische Correspondenzen, Publikationen aus den K. Preussischen Staatsarchiven* (Leipzig: S. Hirzel, 1881), 1:505.

39. A relaxation of press restrictions was one of Alexander's first and most successful measures, producing an explosion of new journals and a vibrant print culture. See Rey, *Alexander I*, 100.

40. On the "unofficial committee" and La Harpe's relationship to it, see ibid., 104–11.

Alexander to act as "friend of mankind" independently of both the French and British governments.

Alexander's great task, as La Harpe defined it in October 1801, was to eliminate the obstacles that prevented the Russian nation from realizing the great potential of its territory and population, and its government from meeting its needs.[41] This is what it meant to advance "civilization," which La Harpe defined as "the progress of agriculture and industry, public credit and the morality of citizens."[42] Such action was a matter of necessity, La Harpe observed, because if the moral aspect of civilization failed to keep pace with material progress, violent revolution was to be expected. Neither social order nor the power of the Russian state could be maintained for long without finding some way to moderate the vast inequalities dividing the masses from the elites who dominated them. Yet such reforms would face resistance from all those invested in the current order, including "all superior authorities," nearly all the nobility and bourgeoisie, and foreign interests. The people, too, in its current condition of ignorance, "would become its own greatest enemy if it were consulted." Alexander would therefore have to rely on his own authority.[43] It was essential, La Harpe lectured, to "faire l'empereur" internally: to play the conventional role of czar in order to establish and maintain the authority he would need to introduce reforms.[44] In this respect, La Harpe diverged sharply from the approach that, as chapter 2 discussed, Denis Diderot had earlier recommended to Catherine. La Harpe deemed it essential that Alexander repel a proposal to cede legislative authority to the Senate, which in his view would merely empower opponents of reform. Russia was fortunate, he repeatedly told Alexander, not to be burdened already with legislative assemblies, and it would be folly to introduce them prematurely. "I have seen these representative assemblies in action," warned the former director of the Helvetic Republic, convened with so much care and effort to bring about reforms. Almost everywhere they have produced only nonsense." Russia was fortunate to have acquired a leader with the power to "procure for his people not the shadow but *the reality of civil liberty,*

41. La Harpe to Alexander I, October 16, 1801, *Correspondance de La Harpe et Alexandre Ier*, 1:320.

42. La Harpe to Alexander I, April 7, 1802, ibid., 1:547.

43. La Harpe to Alexander I, October 16, 1801, ibid., 1:316–18.

44. La Harpe to Alexander I, August 30, 1801, ibid., 1:243. Adam Jerzy Czartoryski later recalled that Alexander's discomfort with ceremony made him "not at all popular during the first years of his reign." *Mémoires du prince Adam Czartoryski et correspondance avec l'empereur Alexandre Ier* (Paris: Plon, 1887), 1:348.

without making it run the risk of disaster with assemblies that unleash the fury of so many heinous passions, strangling the voice of wisdom, moderation and true patriotism." It was "an old friend of liberty, a republican," La Harpe stressed, "who gives this advice to the autocrat of Russia." Representative institutions would be the ultimate result of Alexander's reforms, not the means of achieving them. Reform had to begin with the foundations of society rather than "the decoration of the structure."[45]

Like many earlier commentators on the civilization of Russia, La Harpe advised Alexander to focus his attention on building two fundamental institutions: schools to educate the entire people and independent courts enforcing a systematic code of civil law. He warned against following the example of the French, who built magnificent academies and institutions of higher education but neglected popular education, particularly for the peasantry: an oversight, La Harpe observed, "that made a satire of their revolution, while perhaps preparing them for further ones."[46] It was rather the village schools of Holland, Switzerland, Protestant Germany, England, and the United States of America that provided the best model for Alexander to follow. As for the judiciary, La Harpe recommended beginning with a civil code, to be compiled with the assistance of foreign jurists, before training judges and developing regular judicial procedures. All other legal reforms—Russia desperately needed a penal code as well as legislation to govern taxation, finance, trade, industry, and agriculture—would have to come later.[47] Public law would come last of all, once the sovereign's "legal power" had been reduced to its proper role of exercising oversight of an independent judiciary.[48] A constitution would have to wait until Alexander's reforms had produced a generation of "new Russians" able to serve as "national instruments" to "advance the civilization of Russia."[49] Until then, Alexander would have to rule as an autocrat, and while it was also essential to undertake reforms that would produce a more effective public administration, Alexander would have to ensure that he was empowering ministers responsible to himself rather than forming rival centers of authority.[50]

45. La Harpe to Alexander I, February 25, 1802, *Correspondance de La Harpe et Alexandre Ier*, 1:489. Cf. La Harpe to Alexander I, October 16, 1801, ibid., 1:320.

46. La Harpe to Alexander I, October 16, 1801, ibid., 1:320.

47. Ibid., 1:325.

48. La Harpe to Alexander I, September 3, 1801, ibid., 1:247–48.

49. La Harpe to Alexander I, October 17, 1804, ibid., 2:198. Cf. La Harpe to Alexander I, ibid., February 25, 1802, 1:489–90.

50. La Harpe to Alexander I, August 30, 1801, ibid., 1:244.

Although Alexander's reforms had to rely on royal authority and power, La Harpe also rehearsed the dangers of such an approach. Catherine had followed too closely the example of Joseph II, whose despotic attempts to impose legal and administrative uniformity had outraged local elites, undermining his attempted reforms and nearly toppling his empire.[51] Instead, La Harpe recommended an approach to legal codification like the one pursued in Prussia. He suggested beginning by cataloging local customs among the different nationalities of the empire, and initially making the new civil code supplementary to these. La Harpe conceded that this approach would, like the infamous French *code noir*, have the effect of enshrining slavery in law. But he deemed this a lesser evil than the loss of legitimacy and breakdown of social order that might result from a state-driven attempt to impose an abrupt emancipation from above. Serfdom also posed the greatest obstacle to the introduction of universal education, but here too La Harpe recommended proceeding with great caution, starting with isolated experiments involving state-owned serfs, and following the Danish practice of justifying any emancipatory measures in terms of economic rationalization rather than even mentioning the word "liberty."[52]

The final element of the strategy La Harpe laid out had to do with colonization. Like Diderot and many others before him, La Harpe was fixated on the enormous economic potential of the vast territories that Catherine had conquered from the Ottoman Empire. Fully exploited, La Harpe claimed, the region bordering on the Black Sea would restructure global trade, opening up promising new connections to Asia and the Mediterranean world.[53] The model of colonization that La Harpe urged on Alexander was based not only on Prussian practices in its eastern territories but also on the westward expansion of the United States of America.[54] La Harpe later compared the economic potential of Russia's new southern conquests to that of the Ohio Valley and urged Alexander to undertake its systematic colonization "*à l'américaine*."[55] The first step, La Harpe advised Alexander, was to establish a bureau of agriculture and colonization

51. La Harpe to Alexander I, December 19, 1801, ibid., 1:378.

52. La Harpe to Alexander I, October 16, 1801, ibid., 1:324.

53. La Harpe to Alexander I, January 15, 1802, ibid., 1:423.

54. La Harpe to Alexander I, April 7, 1802, ibid., 1:543.

55. La Harpe to Alexander I, August 30, 1803, ibid., 2:83. Later he also consulted the Duc de Rochefoucauld-Liancourt, an eminent authority on economic reform who had been close to the Marquis de Condorcet and Thomas Jefferson, and whose *Travels through the United States of North America* had appeared in 1799. La Harpe to Alexander I, July 19, 1802, *Correspondance de La Harpe et Alexandre Ier*, 1:641.

following the example of the English and Americans, "who have understood the system of colonization better than others."[56] The ultimate goal, La Harpe explained, was to encourage the formation of local communities, organized like those in Germany and elsewhere in Europe, which would be self-governing within the constraints of state charters ensuring the widely distributed ownership of actively cultivated land.[57] Such an approach, La Harpe promised in February 1802, would put an end to arbitrary government "by the force of things alone." "The nation will gently enlighten and reform itself, without efforts, without disturbances," La Harpe promised. "Better educated, it will learn to esteem the benefits of *civil liberty*, which it does not yet know. It will then dare to develop its faculties, of all kinds," and educated citizens would begin to appear, who would "give the emperor new means to come closer to the great goal that he has set."[58] In other words, as the process of internal colonization helped create the conditions for what Kant had called a "true reform in ways of thinking," changes to the "principles of government" would follow. In an undated annotation to this letter, La Harpe claimed that after 1816, Alexander had eventually begun to apply such policies to serfs in Estonia, Courland, and Livonia: the same examples La Harpe cited in his 1829 letter as evidence of the emancipatory "initial conception" of the Holy Alliance.[59]

For La Harpe, equipping Russia to become a powerful force for emancipation was a matter of significance for the entire "civilized world." In a series of reports he prepared for Alexander after arriving in Saint Petersburg, La Harpe linked his plans for reform to an updated version of the script for liberating Switzerland that he had addressed to the French government in 1797. This script now included parts for both Napoleon and Alexander. In fact, La Harpe later noted, brokering this alliance had been the real purpose of his return to Saint Petersburg in 1801, and he had laid the groundwork for it before his departure by meeting with Joseph Fouché, the French minister of police.[60] The peace treaty that

56. La Harpe to Alexander I, August 13, 1803, *Correspondance de La Harpe et Alexandre Ier*, 2:72.

57. La Harpe to Alexander I, January 15, 1802, ibid., 1:423.

58. La Harpe to Alexander I, February 25, 1802, ibid., 1:491.

59. Frédéric-César de la Harpe, "Aux Rédacteurs du Globe," *Le Globe*, August 15, 1829, 517–18. On "internal colonization" in Russian history, see Alexander Etkind, *Internal Colonization: Russia's Imperial Experience* (Cambridge: Polity, 2011).

60. La Harpe to Alexander I, November 21, 1801, *Correspondance de La Harpe et Alexandre Ier*, 1:354; La Harpe to Alexander I, November 9, 1801, ibid., 1:334–35. See also the lengthy account La Harpe later provided to Alexander's brother Constantine: La Harpe to Constantine, February 23, 1828, ibid., 3:664–66.

Russia and France eventually signed in the fall of 1801 did contain secret articles stipulating a degree of coordination, but La Harpe had initially imagined a transformative alliance. That France remained an expansionist empire was "unfortunately very true," La Harpe advised Alexander.[61] But La Harpe was not alone at the time in believing that Russia was already powerful enough to restrain French ambitions.[62] Russia and France could either clash again or become allies. Though they had no direct conflict of interest, if their other entanglements eventually brought them into opposition, "calamities without number will ensue." If, however, they joined forces, "the peace of Europe is in their hands":

> By helping one another, they can make their respective subjects more prosperous. They can favor the progress of civilization everywhere, and of enlightenment, and force ignorance, superstition and prejudices to return to their cave. They can direct the establishment of a wise liberty, and assure, through institutions protective of this liberty, the existence of all European states. Forty million Russians and thirty million French who have learned to esteem each other, applying concerted measures through their respective governments, will lead other powers to follow their example.[63]

Despite this reference to the French and Russian nations, La Harpe was relying on the personal authority that their respective leaders could derive from the approbation of the "civilized world" (as represented by himself). His plan was not chimerical, he told Alexander, because it required only "the liaison of two men interested to the highest degree in acting in agreement and in sustaining each other, on two men who can get closer to each other and come to an understanding."[64] On November 21, 1801, La Harpe produced a draft of a private letter for Alexander to send to Napoleon, offering the first consul a share of the external authority that Alexander already enjoyed.

---

61. La Harpe to Alexander I, January 20, 1802, ibid., 1:466.

62. Jean-François Reubell, a director of the French Republic who had helped draft the Swiss constitution in 1797, recalled in 1801 that a Russian army had already nearly overrun France once before. Commenting on the Austro-Russian expedition led by Alexander Suvarov, which had chased the French out of Italy in 1799 and nearly out of Switzerland as well, Reubell claimed that had it not been for the Swiss revolution, "Suvarov would have been in Paris." Quoted in Palmer, *The Age of the Democratic Revolution*, 2:413.

63. La Harpe to Alexander I, January 15, 1802, *Correspondance de La Harpe et Alexandre Ier*, 1:443.

64. Ibid.

I do not know, Citizen First Consul, if I am mistaken; but it seems to me that the heads of the two most powerful nations of Europe, animated as they are by the sincere desire to do good, could acquire a solid glory by concerting to protect the weak from the enemies of liberal ideas. This glory, Citizen First Consul, is worthy of one who has done such great things, and I would consider myself happy to see them initiate a liaison between us, from which our two nations and humanity would receive great advantages.[65]

The liaison between Alexander and Napoleon would be effected by a private rather than a public communication from the former to the latter, conveyed by La Harpe, acting as representative of the opinion of the "civilized world" and arbiter of the authority it was able to confer on both leaders. As a "Helvétian," of course, La Harpe held many grievances against Napoleon, but he promised to set this particular interest aside in favor of forging a personal alliance between "two men of liberal ideas" that would make them joint "protectors of enlightenment and of a wise liberty."[66] Reassured about Alexander's intentions through this process, La Harpe hoped, Napoleon would be able to declare victory and turn his attention to stabilizing France's government.[67] Once the alliance had been concluded, the two leaders would find it "easy to settle on the foundations of a political system that will be applicable to their mutual situation."[68]

The first piece of this political system would be to restore constitutional order in Switzerland. Swiss independence was especially critical for Europe's future, La Harpe claimed, because with Switzerland (and Holland) under French control, all of continental Europe was exposed to French power, condemned to relive the plight of ancient Greece under the Macedonian yoke. On the other hand, guaranteeing a new Swiss constitution would present Napoleon with an opportunity to commit himself publicly to his private alliance with Alexander and demonstrate that he too deserved the approbation of the "civilized world." This time around, La Harpe specified that the new constitution should be drafted by Swiss representatives, but that the ultimate power to create it (what the Abbé Sieyès had called the *pouvoir constituent* in 1789) would be shared with

65. La Harpe to Alexander I, "Projet de lettre qui devait accompagner l'envoi au Premier Consul Bonaparte d'un mémoire du 21 novembre relativement à la Suisse, et qui fut adressé avec ce mémoire à l'empereur Alexandre Ier," November 21, 1801, ibid., 1:355.

66. La Harpe to Alexander I, January 20, 1802, ibid., 1:467.

67. Ibid., 1:466; La Harpe to Alexander I, January 15, 1802, *Correspondance de La Harpe et Alexandre Ier*, 1:443.

68. La Harpe to Alexander I, January 15, 1802, ibid., 1:443.

the guarantors, to whom he assigned the right "to fix in a congress the bases of this constitution, in concert with the legitimate representatives of the Helvetic nation."[69] It would be best to elect the Swiss representatives to this congress, but since Swiss politics was dominated by rival factions, La Harpe proposed appointing the last duly elected executive of the Helvetic Republic—namely himself (La Harpe still considered himself a director of the Helvetic Republic and continued to wear the uniform of his office while in Saint Petersburg).[70] "How happy my country would be," La Harpe wrote, echoing his 1791 letter to Alexander's grandmother, "if Your Imperial Majesty could come to an understanding about it with the First Consul."[71]

Beyond Switzerland, the political system La Harpe sketched for Alexander amounted to a fundamental restructuring of European politics. Alexander and Napoleon would collaborate in reining in Prussia and Austria, compelling them to accede to the creation of a new federal state in Germany that was independent of them both.[72] Alexander and Napoleon would also jointly address the most serious source of instability in European politics, which came from England. English power, La Harpe lectured Alexander, was not the natural product of its territory and population but derived instead from its monopoly status as "the great manufacturer of our world."[73] Aside from its dynastic link to Hanover, England had no interest in Europe and showed no concern for the liberty of others.[74] Following its mercantile interest, England had used its ample financial resources to corrupt one continental government after another, and used foreign factories and commercial treaties as "false sacrifices" to head off potential competitors.[75] By contrast, La Harpe claimed, France had recovered from its revolution and had stopped exporting it. In any case, in an age dedicated to "the reform of abuses," it was wrong to stigmatize the French people on the grounds that their government had failed to reform itself in time to preclude a violent revolution.[76] Despite

69. La Harpe to Alexander I, September 30, 1801, ibid., 1:256. Cf. Emmanuel Joseph Sieyès, "What Is the Third Estate?" in *Political Writings*, ed. Michael Sonenscher (Indianapolis: Hackett, 2003), 135–39, 154.

70. Czartoryski, *Mémoires*, 1:271.

71. La Harpe to Alexander I, November 21, 1801, *Correspondance de La Harpe et Alexandre Ier*, 1:349.

72. La Harpe to Alexander I, January 20, 1802, ibid., 1:460, 1:465.

73. La Harpe to Alexander I, January 15, 1802, ibid., 1:435.

74. La Harpe to Alexander I, November 9, 1801, ibid., 1:336.

75. La Harpe to Alexander I, January 15, 1802, ibid., 1:436.

76. La Harpe to Alexander I, January 20, 1802, ibid., 1:465.

the continued instability of its government, postrevolutionary France had succeeded in removing many obstacles to rapid growth. Russia and France shared a fundamental interest in a system of global trade and industry that was not dominated by any one state but allowed for shared prosperity—particularly the prosperity of other states that would help expand markets and help balance the maritime power of England.[77] In short, La Harpe enthused, the alliance he was brokering between Alexander and Napoleon would realize the eighteenth-century ideal of "perpetual peace." As he put it in a later annotation to his correspondence, "This was, if you will, a dream like that of the abbé de Saint-Pierre, with the difference however that I was placed in a way that enabled me to discuss the affair with one of the two principal actors, and that I succeeded in convincing him."[78]

Alexander did entrust La Harpe with a private letter to Napoleon, to be delivered at his own discretion.[79] As La Harpe later noted, "this letter established me momentarily as an intermediary."[80] Even before he left Saint Petersburg for Paris, however, it was already clear to La Harpe that his scheme was doomed. Napoleon, La Harpe complained to Alexander, was failing to play the role of Timoleon: a reference to the Corinthian liberator of Syracuse from Carthaginian-supported tyrants that Alexander might even have been able to recognize, since Timoleon had appeared in the selection of *Plutarch's Lives* that La Harpe told Catherine he would include in the history lessons he offered to Alexander in 1784.[81] La Harpe left Saint Petersburg in May 1802, and as he made his way across Europe toward Paris he sent increasingly despondent dispatches back to Alexander. In the end, La Harpe informed Alexander that he had declined Fouché's offer of an audience with Napoleon. "The Timoleon on whom I had counted has completely disappeared," La Harpe reported. "He is replaced by a man with limitless ambition, full of contempt for the whole of humanity, who sees nothing but

77. La Harpe to Alexander I, January 15, 1802, ibid., 1:442–43; La Harpe to Alexander I, January 20, 1802, ibid., 1:453.

78. La Harpe to Alexander I, "Projet de lettre," November 21, 1801, ibid., 1:356.

79. Alexander I to Bonaparte, May 7/19, 1802, ibid., 1:610–11.

80. La Harpe to Alexander I, January 15, 1802, ibid., 1:448.

81. La Harpe to Alexander I, April 8, 1802, ibid., 1:564; *Le gouverneur d'un prince*, 248. La Harpe's reference to Timoleon as a defender of Greek liberty against Carthaginian-sponsored tyranny gained resonance from the widespread eighteenth-century association of Carthage with British commercial hegemony (and France with neo-Roman imperialism): see Christopher Brooke, "Eighteenth-Century Carthage," in *Commerce and Peace in the Enlightenment*, ed. Béla Kapossy, Isaac Nakhimovsky, and Richard Whatmore (Cambridge: Cambridge University Press, 2017), 110–24.

himself, and thinks that principles, liberty, etc. ought to disappear at his command."[82] Napoleon's abdication of the role of Timoleon left Alexander the sole remaining hope of the "civilized world": "Two men attracted until now the attention of men with liberal ideas, who placed their hopes in them," La Harpe wrote in June 1802. "You alone remain, Sire; do not take away their last recourse."[83] A month later, again claiming to speak for "men with liberal ideas" across England, France, and Germany, La Harpe quoted Voltaire's verse in praise of Catherine, now tinged with despair: "Today enlightenment comes to us from the north."[84] Had he been ten years younger, La Harpe told Alexander, he would have sought to buy land near the Don River in southern Russia, to cultivate himself.[85] Instead he consoled himself by rereading Alexander's undelivered letter to Napoleon, which he promised he would safeguard until the day when it could become part of the history of Alexander's reign, establishing the vast difference between two great men, only one of whom "constantly showed himself to be the friend of mankind, and did not cease to occupy himself with its happiness."[86]

In the end, Napoleon and Alexander did implement the kind of constitutional process that La Harpe had scripted. Apart from the Franco-Russian agreement that led to the territorial restructuring of the Holy Roman Empire in the wake of French conquests, they did so independently rather than jointly. In February 1803, Napoleon's "Act of Mediation" dissolved the Helvetic Republic and replaced it with a Swiss Confederation: La Harpe complained that the result was an illiberal constitution written by illiberal appointees, but he did not raise any procedural objections.[87] Meanwhile, Alexander followed a similar procedure in the Ionian Islands, which had become a French possession after Napoleon conquered the Republic of Venice in 1797, until Turkish and Russian forces seized control in 1798. The 1803 Constitution of the Republic of the Seven Islands was revised in Saint Petersburg by Gustav Rosenkampf, a Baltic German lawyer whom Alexander also appointed to lead his commission

82. La Harpe to Alexander I, July 19, 1802, *Correspondance de La Harpe et Alexandre Ier*, 1:641.

83. La Harpe to Alexander I, June 4, 1802, ibid., 1:621–22.

84. La Harpe to Alexander I, July 19, 1802, ibid., 1:639.

85. La Harpe to Alexander I, February 13, 1803, ibid., 2:24. La Harpe's Basel colleague Peter Ochs also fantasized about retiring to the Crimea: "I do not want to go to America: I want to live under the laws of Alexander." Ochs to La Harpe, January 10, 1802, *Korrespondenz des Peter Ochs*, 3:44.

86. La Harpe to Alexander I, February 13, 1803, *Correspondance de La Harpe et Alexandre Ier*, 2:27.

87. La Harpe to Alexander I, August 7, 1803, ibid., 2:49.

on legal codification in Russia (and whose rivalry with Jeremy Bentham will be discussed in chapter 4).[88]

For his part, after 1802 La Harpe considered the project of reforming European states via Russian intervention to be indefinitely postponed. He no longer drew any moral distinction between the English and French empires—the English were pirates at sea, the French on land—though he grudgingly hoped for England's survival since a successful French invasion would result in "systematic and enduring despotism in this part of the world."[89] La Harpe now urged Alexander to devote himself exclusively to reforming Russia, turning it into an impregnable asylum for European civilization during the coming dark age. "Russia should be the China of Europe," La Harpe advised, avoiding foreign entanglements until a future opportunity for emancipatory intervention presented itself.[90] In 1804, as tensions sharply increased and Russia broke off diplomatic relations with France, La Harpe stressed that Russia must not sacrifice its advantages to serve the narrow interests of Prussia, Austria, or Britain. Instead, it must wait until the inevitable French invasion of Germany allowed Russia to intervene with all its might as the true defender of Europe's liberties against the common enemy. Rather than repeating the "absurdities and irresponsible acts" of the Austro-Prussian coalition that had invaded the French Republic in 1792, it was Russia's mission "to save principles from disaster, and to restrain those who would profit from the circumstances to close forever the gates to the temple of true liberty."[91]

Friends beyond the Seas

The failure of his personal mission to broker an alliance between Alexander and Napoleon prompted La Harpe to shift the focus of his efforts to fashion Alexander into a "friend of mankind." Even before he had reached Paris in the summer of 1802, La Harpe began to imagine private, even emotionally intimate connections forming between Alexander and the wider membership of his "civilized world." Passing through Königsberg

---

88. Rey, *Alexander I*, 148; Norman E. Saul, *Russia and the Mediterranean, 1797–1807* (Chicago: University of Chicago Press, 1970). The islands returned to French control after the 1807 treaty of Tilsit. After 1815 they became a British protectorate called the United States of the Ionian Islands, until 1864 when they were ceded to the Kingdom of Greece.

89. La Harpe to Alexander I, August 13, 1803, *Correspondance de La Harpe et Alexandre Ier*, 2:69.

90. La Harpe to Alexander I, February 13, 1803, ibid., 2:25.

91. La Harpe to Alexander I, July 16, 1804, ibid., 2:149.

that June, La Harpe reported to Alexander that he had reconnected with "an infinitely interesting circle of men distinguished by their merit" who were all hungry to know more about "the Trajan of Russia."

> Ah! Had you heard the wishes that came from their hearts, you would have been touched, for your desire is to belong, through your works, to the society of friends of humankind and of enlightenment, a society invisible but powerful and indestructible, whose members, dispersed on all points of the globe are everywhere reunited to defend the rights of poor humanity against its detractors and its enemies, who will not escape the judgment of posterity, whatever mask they may cover themselves with.[92]

In Paris, La Harpe devoted himself to supplying Alexander with a wide range of new allies. La Harpe's strategy was to use his literary craft to enlist members of this international "society of friends of humankind and of enlightenment" in the project of developing and populating the Russian Empire. As they enhanced the capacities of the Russian state, these allies would also be assuming the function of an international public opinion. They would be authorizing as well as guiding Alexander's interventions as a "friend of mankind." By cultivating this alliance, Alexander's allies would be deploying Russian prestige and power as a tool against entrenched political establishments which no longer met the changing needs of society, and which had remained impervious to internal pressure. Aside from Johann Heinrich Pestalozzi, the celebrated Swiss educational reformer, almost all the allies whom La Harpe attempted to recruit in the years after 1802 were contacts that he made through Helen Maria Williams. Her Paris salon was known especially for its "republicanism" and for being a place where, as one German visitor put it, "you may meet all the important faces of several countries."[93]

---

92. La Harpe to Alexander I, June 23, 1802, ibid., 1:625–26. Unfortunately, La Harpe reported, he was unable to see Immanuel Kant, due to his poor health, but he did meet the philosopher Karl Christian Friedrich Krause: though Krause himself was later quite critical of the Holy Alliance in the 1820s, his views on perpetual peace—first articulated in his *The Ideal of Humanity* of 1811—were closely related to ideas attributed to the Holy Alliance in the 1820s by some of the figures discussed in chapter 5; later the international lawyer James Lorimer (a disciple of Krause) was also identified by his critic Johann Caspar Bluntschli as a theorist of the Holy Alliance. On Krause's importance for nineteenth-century political thought, particularly in the form of *Krausismo* in Spain and Latin America, see Michael Sonenscher, "Krausism and Its Legacy," *Global Intellectual History* 5, no. 1 (2020): 20–40.

93. Deborah Kennedy, *Helen Maria Williams and the Age of Revolution* (Lewisburg, PA: Bucknell University Press, 2002), 171, 174. The visitor was Caroline von Wolzogen, a writer and *salonnière* who was also Friedrich Schiller's sister-in-law. On Pestalozzi, whose many contemporary admirers included Johann Gottlieb Fichte, Robert Owen, and Horace

Williams had established herself as a successful poet in 1780s London, writing sentimental poems that called attention to the suffering caused by war and slavery. Her poetry was admired by Samuel Johnson and Robert Burns, and inspired William Wordsworth to publish his first poem.[94] Williams had inherited her Scottish mother's Presbyterianism, and was well connected in Dissenting circles: visitors to her literary gatherings in the late 1780s included William Godwin, Joseph Priestley, Richard Price, and other prominent radicals.[95] In 1790, Williams left for Paris, where she began publishing *Letters Written in France*: an eyewitness account of the French Revolution for an English audience that made her "perhaps the best-known contemporary author to magazine readers of her generation" and "for more than ten years the principal interpreter and popular spokesman for political changes in the neighboring republic."[96] As Mary Favret has described, Williams staged the French Revolution for an English audience by dramatizing her own emotional responses both to the spectacular events and to the emotions of those witnessing them—and inviting her readers to share in these "common feelings of humanity." A similar interweaving of gendered spheres of public and private, political and domestic, characterized her Paris salon, which was both "the setting for sentimental narratives and the site for dangerous alliances."[97] Williams hosted English radicals like Tom Paine and Mary Wollstonecraft, military leaders like the Irish rebel Edward Fitzgerald and the Spanish American general Francisco de Miranda, as well as important French politicians, including the abolitionist Henri Grégoire as well as Jacques Pierre Brissot and many other members of the Gironde faction.[98] In 1794, having provided both refuge and publicity for persecuted Girondins, and having been imprisoned herself, Williams fled to Switzerland. When La Harpe arrived from Saint Petersburg in 1802, Williams was back hosting one of the most important

---

Mann, see La Harpe to Alexander I, January 25, 1805, *Correspondance de La Harpe et Alexandre Ier*, 2:229–30.

94. Kennedy, *Helen Maria Williams and the Age of Revolution*, 29, 37–38. Wordsworth's first poem, published in 1787, was titled "Sonnet on Seeing Miss Helen Maria Williams Weep at a Tale of Distress."

95. Woodward, *Une adhérente anglaise*, 30.

96. Robert Donald Mayo, *The English Novel in the Magazines, 1740–1815* (Evanston, IL: Northwestern University Press, 1962), 259.

97. Mary A. Favret, "Spectatrice as Spectacle: Helen Maria Williams at Home in the Revolution," *Studies in Romanticism* 32, no. 2 (1993): 280, 275. See also Mary A. Favret, *Romantic Correspondence: Women, Politics and the Fiction of Letters* (Cambridge: Cambridge University Press, 2005).

98. Woodward, *Une adhérente anglaise*, 30.

salons in Paris, frequented by senators, members of the Institut National, and "everyone in the literary line."[99] Among the many international guests were senior Whig politicians (including on one occasion Charles James Fox himself), newly able to travel to Paris thanks to the Peace of Amiens; exiled Irish and Polish revolutionaries; and members of societies devoted to the abolition of slavery and other causes. Since arriving in Paris, La Harpe reported to Alexander in October 1802, he had met many "English ecclesiastics, non-conformists (*dissenters*), members of the philanthropic society founded in England for spreading Christianity among nations that remain savage and for contributing to their civilization, an institution worthy of the praises that do honor to the eighteenth century."[100]

Over the following months, La Harpe attempted to have Alexander appoint Williams as a kind of cultural ambassador for Alexander, tasked with conducting a literary correspondence: one that was to give preference to "objects of general utility" over "those of pure literature," and that was to be "addressed directly to *His Imperial Majesty the Emperor of all the Russias*."[101] Although La Harpe seems to have forwarded at least one issue of Williams's *English Bulletin* to Alexander, nothing more seems to have come of that venture; in his own subsequent correspondence with Alexander, La Harpe took upon himself the task of keeping the emperor appraised of English, French, and German publications.[102] From one perspective, La Harpe was nominating Williams to serve as the successor to Friedrich Melichor Grimm, who had conducted a long literary correspondence with Catherine and famously circulated a private newsletter to her and to many other European monarchs (it was also Grimm who had launched La Harpe's Russian career by recruiting him as a tutor in 1782).[103] At the same time, La Harpe was trying to draw Alexander into the orbit of a literary enterprise closely linked to the *Décade philosophique, littéraire, et politique*: the influential journal long edited by a friend of Williams, the political economist Jean-Baptiste Say, whom La Harpe greatly admired (as chapter 2 already discussed). The *Décade philosophique* was dedicated to the *science sociale* that would provide the grounding for a republican

99. Kennedy, *Helen Maria Williams and the Age of Revolution*, 172, 175.

100. La Harpe to Alexander I, October 4, 1802, *Correspondance de La Harpe et Alexandre Ier*, 1:665.

101. La Harpe to Helen Maria Williams, December 7, 1803, ibid., 2:104.

102. La Harpe to Alexander I, January 11, 1804, ibid., 2:111. See La Harpe's later comment, ibid., 2:48; La Harpe to Alexander I, May 4, 1804, ibid., 2:140; and La Harpe to Alexander I, September 10, 1804, ibid., 2:188.

103. On Grimm, see Abrosimov, *Aufklärung jenseits der Öffentlichkeit*.

theory of civilization.[104] As Bernard Gainot has emphasized, part of what made this theory of civilization cosmopolitan rather than exclusively national in scope was a commitment to finding in language a universal "grammar of civilizations": this in turn empowered literary sensibility to serve as an "instrument of mediation between cultures."[105] Williams was an important contributor to this project, both as a translator and as a translated author, and her work was both translated and reviewed by Say.[106] For both Williams and Say, this literary project was also connected to efforts to shift the axis of global trade away from the North Atlantic and toward Egypt and the Mediterranean. It was also connected to proposals for "new colonization" that would end the system of "modern colonization" based on African slavery and develop colonies of freed former slaves like Sierra Leone.[107] Another important proponent of such "new colonization" was Charles-Philibert de Lasteyrie, a prolific agronomist, inventor, and philanthropist who contributed to the *Décade philosophique*, and whom La Harpe recommended to Alexander as an authority to consult.[108] La Harpe also had an additional role for Say. When Say published his treatise on political economy in 1803, La Harpe immediately hailed it as a "classic work" and urged Alexander to have it translated as soon as possible, with annotations applying it to Russian circumstances.[109] For La Harpe, Say's treatise was the ideal candidate for meeting Alexander's 1797 pledge

104. On Say, the journal, and social science, see especially Michael Sonenscher, "'The Moment of Social Science': The Decade Philosophique and Late Eighteenth-Century French Thought," *Modern Intellectual History* 6, no. 1 (2009): 121–46.

105. Bernard Gainot, "Helen-Maria Williams, médiatrice culturelle dans *La Décade philosophique*," *La Révolution française: Cahiers de l'Institut d'histoire de la Révolution française*, no. 12 (2017): 7.

106. Ibid., 4–5.

107. Bernard Gainot, "La Décade et la 'colonisation nouvelle,'" *Annales historiques de la Révolution française* 339, no. 1 (2005): 99–116. See also Marcel Dorigny, "Mirabeau and the Société des Amis des Noirs: Which Way to Abolish Slavery?" in *The Abolitions of Slavery: From Léger Félicité Sonthonax to Victor Schoelcher, 1793, 1794, 1848*, ed. Marcel Dorigny (New York: Berghahn Books, 2003), 121–32; Anna Plassart, "'Un Impérialiste Libéral'? Jean-Baptiste Say on Colonies and the Extra-European World," *French Historical Studies* 32, no. 2 (Spring 2009): 223–50; Richard Whatmore, "War, Trade and Empire: The Dilemmas of French Liberal Political Economy, 1780–1816," in *French Liberalism from Montesquieu to the Present Day*, ed. Raf Geenens and Helena Rosenblatt (Cambridge: Cambridge University Press, 2012), 169–91.

108. La Harpe to Alexander I, December 19, 1803, *Correspondance de La Harpe et Alexandre Ier*, 2:91; La Harpe to Alexander I, January 11, 1804, ibid., 2:111; and La Harpe to Alexander I, March 16, 1804, ibid., 2:118.

109. La Harpe to Alexander I, August 7, 1803, ibid., 2:59; La Harpe to Alexander I, August 13, 1803, ibid., 2:75.

to translate "useful works" into Russian, and he was unusually persistent (even for him) in promoting it.[110]

La Harpe attempted to establish new connections for Alexander by making contacts through Williams's salon and by emulating her literary methods. Among these attempts were two bids to fill the emancipatory role of Timoleon, vacant after the collapse of La Harpe's earlier scheme of an alliance between Alexander and Napoleon. Each of these new efforts involved a private communication of Alexander's goodwill that was supposed to blossom into an alliance transcending entrenched political divisions. The first involved Thomas Erskine: a lawyer who had become famous defending various radicals in trials for treason in the 1790s, including Tom Paine and the brother of John Hurford Stone, the English printer who had become Williams's lifelong companion and a member of her household in Paris. In 1806, Erskine would briefly serve as Lord Chancellor of England. In 1802, he was among the Whig politicians visiting Williams's Paris salon. That October, La Harpe recounted a conversation with Erskine to Alexander in a set piece of sentimental craft. "You would have enjoyed," La Harpe informed his former pupil, "the impression produced on an independent and generous soul by the account of your deeds."[111] To verify the authenticity of this account, La Harpe recounted, he had shared one of Alexander's private letters with Erskine: the first letter the young monarch had written to him after taking power in 1801, in which Alexander had pledged to "make myself worthy of having been your pupil" and to devote his reign to "general utility."[112] Erskine was overcome with emotion, staining the precious letter with his tears. "It was," La Harpe recounted with satisfaction, "a true *coup de théâtre*."[113] La Harpe closed the scene by reporting that he had deputized Erskine as "an independent and philanthropic statesman" who possessed the confidence of his former employer, the prince regent of Great Britain. "Until now," La Harpe quoted his instructions to Erskine in his letter to Alexander,

> nations have only contracted political alliances, which are too often works of trickery and cunning. It is about time that they contract them

110. See La Harpe to Alexander I, December 19, 1803, ibid., 2:90, 2:99; La Harpe to Alexander I, August 9, 1804, ibid., 2:171; La Harpe to Alexander I, October 17, 1804, ibid., 2:199.

111. La Harpe to Alexander I, October 4, 1802, ibid., 1:665.

112. Alexander I to La Harpe, May 9/21, 1801, ibid., 1:240–41.

113. La Harpe to Alexander I, October 4, 1802, ibid., 1:665. La Harpe later recounted the episode to Alexander's brother: La Harpe to Constantine, February 23, 1828, ibid., 3:664.

for the benefit of civilization, enlightenment, and wise liberty. It is up to the heads [*chefs*] of great nations to begin. You now know the soul of one of them. . . . Please recall this alliance when your friend is in a position that enables him to enter into it, and prepare him for it in advance.[114]

The fact that La Harpe was recounting this whole scene—a script for a future holy alliance—in his letter to Alexander shows how his literary method served both to guide international opinion toward Alexander and to align Russian interests with international opinion: to induce Alexander to perceive Russian interests through liberal eyes and in liberal terms.

The second substitute Timoleon that La Harpe proposed to Alexander was the newly elected president of the United States, Thomas Jefferson. A year earlier, while still in Saint Petersburg, La Harpe had advised Alexander to promote his colonization efforts by sending a team of botanists to North America to study which of its crops could be introduced into cultivation in the southern regions of the Russian Empire: a mission that could rely on the sponsorship of Jefferson, who was known for his botanical interests, botanical friendships, and botanical diplomacy.[115] In the fall of 1802, in the wake of the failed mission to Napoleon, the idea of a botanical mission to America took on additional significance. "It is essential," La Harpe wrote, following his account of the conversation with Erskine, "that you have friends among enlightened and independent men who enjoy, as private as well as public citizens, a proper consideration legitimately achieved." He urged Alexander to use the botanical mission as an occasion to address Jefferson "from man to man, from Alexander to Jefferson": "I would like, Sire, to procure you friends beyond the seas; I would like your name to be spoken by independent and pure mouths, even in the middle of the forests of America."[116] For La Harpe, Jefferson was "one of the most respectable members of the noble society of friends of mankind, who desire enlightenment and liberty for all," whereas the horrific French invasion of Haiti in 1803 prompted him to label Napoleon the "genius enemy of liberty" throughout the Americas—ironically enough, given Jefferson's hostility toward the Haitian Revolution.[117]

La Harpe twice used his contacts in Williams's circle to engineer the connection between Alexander and Jefferson. The first attempt, in the fall

114. La Harpe to Alexander I, October 4, 1802, ibid., 1:666.
115. La Harpe to Alexander I, December 31, 1801, ibid., 1:387–88.
116. La Harpe to Alexander I, October 4, 1802, ibid., 1:666.
117. La Harpe to Alexander I, August 13, 1803, ibid., 2:67. See also La Harpe to Alexander I, May 3, 1805, ibid., 2:241. Jefferson refused to recognize Haitian independence and cut off trade. The United States did not recognize Haiti until 1862.

of 1802, took the form of a letter from John Hurford Stone to Jefferson's friend Joseph Priestley, transmitted to Jefferson by Priestley's son-in-law Thomas Cooper (himself a prominent Anglo-American Dissenter).[118] The second attempt, in the fall of 1803, involved a letter from La Harpe himself to Stone, transmitted to Jefferson by Joel Barlow, the American poet and diplomat who had become a close friend of Williams and Stone in the early 1790s.[119]

In the first case, Stone recounted the same excerpts from Alexander's 1801 letter to La Harpe that had so affected Erskine and proposed the public administration of the United States rather than botany as the subject for a correspondence. In the second, La Harpe was able to directly quote Alexander's July 1803 request for a connection to Jefferson, and Barlow provided Jefferson with a detailed brief that urged him to limit any correspondence to a discussion of political economy. In both cases, however, it was Russia's increasingly evident intention to interpose itself as a mediator between Britain and France (as illustrated by Isaac Cruikshank's 1803 caricature, *Bruin become Mediator*, discussed in chapter 1) that provided the chief motive for Jefferson to entertain the correspondence. With Jefferson's involvement, this mediation might result in a comprehensive peace settlement that saw both belligerents acceding to a new regime of global free trade. As Stone put it in his letter to Priestley,

> We have now two men in the world to whom we look with mingled respect and anxiety. These two men are placed at opposite points of our globe, but their principles, their Sentiments and Conduct appear to be in exact sympathy with each other: The intermediate space is filled up by chiefs of different descriptions of good and evil, tending in general I think rather toward good, but who will not go far astray, when they have two Sentinels such as Jefferson & Alexander to keep them in order.[120]

---

118. Thomas Cooper to Thomas Jefferson, October 25, 1802, *The Papers of Thomas Jefferson, Volume 38: 1 July to 12 November 1802*, ed. Barbara B. Oberg (Princeton: Princeton University Press, 2012), 550–64.

119. Joel Barlow to Thomas Jefferson, February 11, 1804, *The Papers of Thomas Jefferson, Volume 42: 16 November 1803 to 10 March 1804*, ed. James P. McClure (Princeton: Princeton University Press, 2016), 447–50. See also N. Hans, "Tsar Alexander I and Jefferson: Unpublished Correspondence," *Slavonic Review* 32 (1953): 218. Copies of La Harpe's letter to John Hurford Stone of October 20, 1803, are in the Thomas Jefferson Papers at the Library of Congress.

120. John Hurford Stone to Joseph Priestley, August 10, 1802, *The Papers of Thomas Jefferson, Volume 38*, 554.

Barlow's letter to Jefferson contained an even more detailed script for a kind of Russian-American holy alliance—one that resonated strongly with the political thought of Jean-Baptiste Say, who had himself exchanged letters with Jefferson about his recently published *Treatise on Political Economy*.[121] Despite Alexander's sincere republican convictions, Barlow explained to Jefferson, his "exceedingly delicate" position did not allow him to undertake constitutional reforms that would immediately arouse the opposition of a powerful and hostile aristocracy, or even to hint at the complete emancipation of the serfs. Fortunately, Barlow continued, "there are other principles leading directly to civilization, which being slow in their progress and already in some degree admitted in Europe, do not so much alarm the Nobles and priests," like public education and a free press. But it was free trade that Barlow, like Say, considered the most promising republican strategy going forward. "Fortunately for this system it is easy to demonstrate that it is the source of the wealth of nations, and of individuals, as well as the foundation of their peace," Barlow wrote. "And the Arguments are such as to carry more undeniable conviction to ordinary minds than those of most other principles of Republicanism."[122] The role Barlow proposed for Jefferson was not to make the best arguments in the court of public opinion but to present them to Alexander, endowed with the personal authority he held as someone who was both a head of state and a private man of science and letters "nourished in the purest political region in the globe."[123] In corresponding with Alexander, Jefferson would serve as the uniquely authoritative voice of *la science sociale* for a young republican in a rather less pure political region: "You are sensible," Barlow wrote,

> that the best dispositions will produce little effect if the mind has not embraced the simple principles which govern the great work of Civilization, and if it does not perceive them to be demonstrable as those of the exact sciences, And it is hardly to be supposed that so young a man, educated in the midst of Aristocracy can be sufficiently informed to enable him to do all the good that his power might command and that the present State of things requires from his situation.[124]

121. Jean-Baptiste Say to Thomas Jefferson, [before November 3, 1803], *The Papers of Thomas Jefferson, Volume 41: 11 July to 15 November 1803*, ed. Barbara B. Oberg (Princeton: Princeton University Press, 2014), 651–53. Thomas Jefferson to Jean-Baptiste Say, February 1, 1804, *The Papers of Thomas Jefferson, Volume 42*, 380–81.

122. Joel Barlow to Thomas Jefferson, February 11, 1804, *The Papers of Thomas Jefferson, Volume 42*, 448–49.

123. Ibid., 448.

124. Ibid., 447–48.

Turning Alexander into a powerful advocate of free trade would have profound implications worldwide. The tremendous potential represented by the vast territories and rapidly expanding populations of both the Russian Empire and the United States conferred considerable weight on their views of global order. The fact that neither was burdened by the need to defend a global commercial empire, and that the manufacturing powers of Europe were dependent on their agricultural exports for survival, made them both "powerful in their moral as well as their physical means of defence." It was therefore up to Jefferson and Alexander, Barlow concluded, to construct a peaceful new global order based on free trade:

> These circumstances make it peculiarly proper as well as interesting to the world, that their two governments should come forward with a plan for the liberty of the seas which could not be resisted. The effects in favor of humanity to be produced by such a System are incalculable. [T]hey would be no less felt in the interior of every particular nation than in the great scale of public tranquility among the several nations. In which latter View it must certainly be considered as an indispensible [*sic*] step towards a permanent peace.[125]

Though Cooper was skeptical about the propriety of the overtures conveyed by La Harpe and Stone, Jefferson himself was receptive to the communicative strategy they recommended.[126] "An opening has been given me," Jefferson explained to James Monroe at the beginning of 1804, to communicate with Alexander "as from one private individual to another." Though he had not decided "whether to do it or not," Jefferson noted that he valued such "literary correspondence" because it enabled him to "make private friendships instrumental to the public good by inspiring a confidence which is denied to public, and official communications."[127] In his initial reply to Priestley, Jefferson limited himself to observing that "the apparition of such a man on a throne is one of the phaenomena which will distinguish the present epoch so remarkable in the history of man," and questioned how much Alexander would be able to achieve when even the French nation had turned out to be unprepared for self-government.

125. Ibid., 449.

126. "I give credit to Mr Stone's character of Alexander of Russia, sufficiently to wish that you were his correspondent if you be not so," Cooper observed to Jefferson. "But I cannot help regarding Mr Stone, and even M. de la Harpe, as characters too obscure to become in any degree the vehicles of your Correspondence." Cooper to Jefferson, October 25, 1802, *The Papers of Thomas Jefferson, Volume 38*, 552.

127. Thomas Jefferson to James Monroe, January 8, 1804, *The Papers of Thomas Jefferson, Volume 42*, 246.

"Alexander will doubtless begin at the right end," Jefferson told Priestley, echoing La Harpe's own advice to Alexander, not with a new constitution but "by taking means for diffusing instruction & a sense of their natural rights through the mass of his people, and for relieving them in the mean time from actual oppression."[128]

Eventually, Jefferson did initiate a correspondence with Alexander: an exchange of five letters between June 1804 and August 1808 that unfolded "more in a private than public style," along the lines recommended by Barlow.[129] Assistance provided by Russia to an American frigate off the Barbary Coast gave Jefferson an occasion to thank Alexander and to draw a contrast between their shared commitment to free trade and the barbarous conduct of both the pirates of Tripoli and the mercantile empires of Europe.[130] In his next letter, Jefferson recognized Alexander for his commitment to the collective security of "the great European family" and urged him to seize the moment to enshrine free trade in a new regime of international law: "when you shall proceed to the pacification which is to reestablish peace & commerce," Jefferson wrote in April 1806, "the same dispositions of mind will lead you to think of the general intercourse of nations, & to make that provision for it's future maintenance, which in times past it has so much needed."[131] Jefferson hoped that Alexander would come to an agreement with Napoleon about the right of neutral nations to maintain their trade even in wartime—the major source of ongoing conflict between the United States and both Britain and France. Jefferson further hoped that the forthcoming peace settlement would provide for the enforcement of neutral rights through the mechanism of a collective trade embargo imposed on the violator—a mechanism that had been legally codified by the Swiss jurist Emer de Vattel, whom Jefferson once described as the most "enlightened and disinterested" writer on the

128. Thomas Jefferson to Joseph Priestley, November 29, 1802, Thomas Jefferson, *The Papers of Thomas Jefferson, Volume 39: 13 November 1802 to 3 March 1803*, ed. Barbara B. Oberg (Princeton: Princeton University Press, 2012), 85–86.

129. Thomas Jefferson to William Short, March 8, 1809, *The Papers of Thomas Jefferson, Retirement Series, Volume 1: 4 March to 15 November 1809*, ed. J. Jefferson Looney (Princeton: Princeton University Press, 2004), 38–39. For earlier discussions of this correspondence, see Erwin Hölzle, "Zar Alexander I. und Thomas Jefferson: Ein Briefwechsel um die Freiheit der Welt im Zeitalter Napoleons," *Archiv für Kulturgeschichte* 34 (1952): 154–79; Hans, "Tsar Alexander I and Jefferson."

130. Thomas Jefferson to Alexander I, June 15, 1804, *The Papers of Thomas Jefferson, Volume 43: 11 March to 30 June 1804: 11 March to 30 June 1804*, ed. James P. McClure (Princeton: Princeton University Press, 2018), 590–91.

131. Thomas Jefferson to Alexander I, April 19, 1806, in Hans, "Tsar Alexander I and Jefferson," 222–23.

law of nations.[132] Alexander's reply in August 1806 affirmed his commitment to bringing about "an order of things conforming to the common interest of all civilized nations . . . solidly guaranteed against the efforts of ambition and avidity," but the following year presented another instance of two leaders acting independently rather than jointly as La Harpe had hoped.[133] In July 1807, Alexander signed the Treaty of Tilsit, acceding to Napoleon's policy of excluding Britain from European markets (and surrendering the Ionian Islands); in December of that year Jefferson introduced a unilateral Embargo Act prohibiting Americans from trading with either Britain or France.

Although the correspondence between Jefferson and Alexander did not produce the outcome that La Harpe, Stone, and Barlow had foreseen, Jefferson did not lose interest in the relationship. In fact, at the end of his presidency, he attempted to turn the private relationship into a public one. In 1808 he appointed his protégé William Short as ambassador to Saint Petersburg, instructing him to continue the effort "to avail ourselves of the emperor's marked dispositions of friendly regard for us whenever a treaty of peace shall be on the tapis"—but the Senate refused to confirm the appointment.[134] In 1810, Jefferson was still attempting to persuade the republican Philadelphia printer William Duane of Alexander's potential value to the United States. "Alexander is unquestionably a man of an excellent heart, and of very respectable strength of mind," Jefferson assured Duane, and "we possess the most unquestionable proofs" of his republican convictions and admiration for the American form of government. In anticipation of a future comprehensive peace settlement in Europe, Jefferson concluded, it remained "prudent for us to cherish his good dispositions as those alone which will be exerted in our favor when that occasion shall occur. [H]e,

132. Quoted in Vincent Chetail, "Vattel and the American Dream: An Inquiry into the Reception of the Law of Nations in the United States," in *The Roots of International Law: Liber Amicorum Peter Haggenmacher*, ed. Vincent Chetail and Pierre-Marie Depuy (Leiden: Martinus Nijhoff, 2014), 264. On Vattel's codification of commercial embargoes, see Isaac Nakhimovsky, "Vattel's Theory of the International Order: Commerce and the Balance of Power in the Law of Nations," *History of European Ideas* 33 (2007): 157–73; Isaac Nakhimovsky, "Carl Schmitt's Vattel and the 'Law of Nations' between Enlightenment and Revolution," *Grotiana* 31 (2010): 141–64.

133. Alexander I to Thomas Jefferson, August 10, 1806, in Hans, "Tsar Alexander I and Jefferson," 223.

134. "I pray you to place me rectus in curia in this business, with the emperor," Jefferson told Short, "and to assure him that I carry into my retirement the highest veneration for his virtues and fondly cherish the belief that his dispositions & power are destined by heaven to better, in some degree at least, the condition of oppressed man." Jefferson to Short, March 8, 1809, *The Papers of Thomas Jefferson, Retirement Series, Volume 1*, 38–39.

like ourselves, sees, and feels the atrociousness of both the belligerents."[135] However, Jefferson suspected that Britain's maritime hegemony would prove far more difficult to dislodge even than Napoleon's continental hegemony. "Bonaparte will die, and the nations of Europe will recover their independence with, I hope, better governments," Jefferson remarked to Samuel Brown in 1813. "But the English government never dies, because their king is no part of it, he is a mere formality, and the real government is the aristocracy of the country, for their House of Commons is of that class."[136] For Jefferson, it was England, more than France, that was realizing the eighteenth-century nightmare of a globalized military machine hitched to a financial system that was capable of extracting unprecedented levels of resources from the productive economy. "I see no means of terminating their maritime dominion and tyranny," he told Brown, "but in their own bankruptcy, which I hope is approaching."[137]

For his part, La Harpe reacted to Alexander's 1807 realignment with Napoleon with great dismay. He accused Alexander of becoming Napoleon's "vassal" and conjured up dark visions of French attempts to invade first Britain then America, thereby "destroying the final asylum of civilization, of liberty, of letters, and of printing."[138] Meaningful reform of Russia had yet to begin, La Harpe complained, and Alexander had failed to send any visitors to Pestalozzi or show any interest in Say's treatise on political economy.[139] In February 1811, La Harpe declared to his former pupil (from whom he had not heard since 1803) that the alliance with the "civilized world" was finished. La Harpe now compared Russia's condition to Haiti's, and its nobility to the planter class of the former French colony. Russia's sheer size made it "an imposing mass" but "not at all a powerful nation": it had little chance of standing up to the consolidated forces of Europe without a "strongly constituted third estate."[140] La Harpe once again made

135. Jefferson to William Duane, November 13, 1810, *The Papers of Thomas Jefferson, Retirement Series, Volume 3: 12 August 1810 to 17 June 1811*, ed. J. Jefferson Looney (Princeton: Princeton University Press, 2004), 208. Duane later published a commentary on the Holy Alliance: William Duane, *The Two Americas, Great Britain, and the Holy Alliance* (Washington, DC: Edward De Krafft, 1824).

136. Thomas Jefferson to Samuel Brown, July 14, 1813, *The Papers of Thomas Jefferson, Retirement Series, Volume 6: 11 March to 27 November 1813*, ed. J. Jefferson Looney (Princeton: Princeton University Press, 2009), 294.

137. Ibid. On Walsh, see chapter 2.

138. La Harpe to Alexander I, March 31, 1808, *Correspondance de La Harpe et Alexandre Ier*, 2:307.

139. Ibid., 2:304–5, 2:312.

140. La Harpe to Alexander I, February 28, 1811, 2:388.

use of Voltaire's verse to Catherine. "From now on," he informed Alexander, "friends of enlightenment and liberal ideas, whose gaze had long been turned toward the northeast, have turned their gaze to the west."[141]

Star of the North

La Harpe's renunciation of the alliance between Alexander and the "civilized world" lasted only a few months. By the time the Russian army reached the Rhine in January 1814, La Harpe's script for liberating Lausanne had been fully revived. Alexander appointed Ioannis Kapodistrias ("from Corfu, and therefore republican," Alexander assured La Harpe) to serve as the Russian representative in negotiations for a new federal treaty for Switzerland.[142] La Harpe was reunited with Alexander, who introduced him to the Prussian statesman the Baron von Stein as "my second father; it is to him that I owe what I am and what I know."[143] Later that year, La Harpe attended the Congress of Vienna as the elected representative of the Canton of Vaud. Together with Kapodistrias (who later became the first elected leader of an independent Greece), La Harpe succeeded in blocking a full restoration of the old regime in Switzerland: a restoration that would have returned Vaud to its former status as a subject territory of the Republic of Bern.[144] "English diplomacy never intervened in Switzerland except to restore the patricians of the old regime," La Harpe later wrote. "The Swiss people owes it to Russia alone that the federal pact contains the seeds of liberalism."[145] La Harpe also reclaimed his role as the arbiter of the alliance between Alexander and his "civilized world." From the summer of 1814 through the winter of 1815, La Harpe resumed his efforts to connect Alexander to various reformers whom he had first promoted to Alexander over a decade earlier: via La Harpe, Erskine renewed his offer to travel to Russia and advise Alexander on legal reform.[146] La Harpe urged Alexander to bestow a decoration on Say, whom La Harpe introduced to Alexander in Paris in 1814 and who dedicated the second edition of his long suppressed *Treatise on Political Economy* to the Russian

---

141. Ibid., 2:393.

142. La Harpe to Alexander I, January 3, 1814, 2:506.

143. Boehtlingk, *Frédéric-César Laharpe, 1754–1838*, 350.

144. Mark Jarrett, *The Congress of Vienna and Its Legacy: War and Great Power Diplomacy after Napoleon* (London: I. B. Tauris, 2013), 137; Olivier Meuwly, ed., *Le Congrès de Vienne et le Canton de Vaud: 1813–1815* (Lausanne: Bibliothèque historique vaudoise, 2017).

145. *Correspondance de La Harpe et Alexandre Ier*, 3:409.

146. Thomas Erskine to La Harpe, August 1, 1814, 2:585.

emperor. Starting in January 1815, La Harpe sent Alexander voluminous excerpts from Say's *Treatise*, which he described as an indispensable source of guidance for Russia's future development. Though Say himself told Jefferson (whom he was asking at the time for advice about emigrating to the United States) that the dedication to Alexander was merely a strategy to evade further censorship, La Harpe hoped for Say himself to enter the Russian service.[147]

La Harpe also resumed offering Alexander his guidance on how to deploy Russian power and prestige to transform European politics and the Atlantic economy more broadly. At the Congress of Vienna, the fact that France was initially spared war reparations in 1814 was widely attributed to La Harpe's influence.[148] In February 1815, La Harpe wrote a long report for Alexander about Britain, Russia, and world politics. La Harpe warned that "bloody revolutions" were brewing in Spain's American empire, and that in the first instance these revolutions would further entrench British hegemony, opening vast new markets for its manufacturers to monopolize, rather than producing the kind of balanced and complementary free trade envisaged by La Harpe and his allies.[149] La Harpe once again envisaged a role for Russia as the guarantor of American liberty and free trade against British imperialism. La Harpe emphasized the importance of Russian support for both the United States and Portugal, the two powers "whose calling was to contain the dominators of the seas."[150] Centered in Brazil, where the Portuguese court had moved to escape Napoleon's invasion, a revived and reformed Portuguese empire would join the United States ("that future liberator of the seas") in helping to diminish the "burden of monopoly imposed on Europe by England."[151] In the long run, Russia's own economic dependence on Britain would diminish once Alexander's reforms fostered the development of a more integrated national market and opened up new overland trade routes to Persia and India.[152] In the

---

147. Jean-Baptiste Say to Thomas Jefferson, June 15, 1814, *The Papers of Thomas Jefferson, Retirement Series, Volume 7: 28 November 1813 to 30 September 1814*, ed. J. Jefferson Looney (Princeton: Princeton University Press, 2010), 416–21; *Correspondance de La Harpe et Alexandre Ier*, 2:79.

148. Jean de Montenach and Ana Eynard-Lullin, *Vienne 1814–1815: Journaux du Congrès*, ed. Benoît Challand et al. (Fribourg: Société d'histoire du canton de Fribourg, 2015), 135.

149. La Harpe to Alexander I, February 25, 1815, *Correspondance de La Harpe et Alexandre Ier*, 2:632–33.

150. Ibid., 2:636.

151. Ibid., 2:632, 2:635.

152. Ibid., 2:635.

short run, he advised, Russia did not have to risk an open rupture with Britain by openly allying itself with Portugal and the United States, but "it would be wise, at least" to build confidence with them by giving them evidence of Russia's friendship and benevolent intentions.[153]

Alexander's promulgation of the Holy Alliance itself and the campaign of public diplomacy that accompanied it represent further variations on the pattern of politics that La Harpe had scripted. During his visit to London in June 1814, Alexander had conducted a series of meetings with leading reformers like the abolitionist William Wilberforce and a delegation of Quakers—he also made well-publicized visits to a Quaker meeting and a Quaker family's home. These meetings were anticipated by Alexander's efforts to position himself as a force for reconciliation in Paris in 1814, where he had gone so far as to socialize with Napoleon's former wife Josephine, much to the resentment of many royalists; the reaction of many British elites to Alexander's popularity—"there were never less than 10,000 persons stationed around the park and the street where his hotel was located," according to one contemporary account—was similarly wary.[154] The meetings in London anticipated in turn the meetings that Alexander held with Juliane von Krüdener and her religious circle in the months leading up to the promulgation of the Holy Alliance in September through December 1815. All these efforts to ally international public opinion with Russian interventions in European politics took the form of private understandings with Alexander that were expected to issue in concerted public action. The private understandings Alexander extracted from his wartime allies in Paris and subsequently from the newly restored king of France were the prelude to a public proclamation of new "principles of government." The continuities between the ambitions of the Holy Alliance and La Harpe's script are further indicated by the instructions issued to the new Russian ambassador to the United States in May 1817 on how to pursue its accession to the Holy Alliance. A formal invitation could only follow once the government had clarified its intentions and indicated its commitment to the principles of politics articulated by the Holy Alliance. The Swiss precedent suggested that neither republican sensibilities nor constitutional considerations necessarily precluded such a commitment. However, the ambassador was admonished that he must "take no steps without first assuring himself that the adherence of the United States will not be opposed by public opinion in that country."[155]

---

153. Ibid., 2:636.

154. Rey, *Alexander I*, 277.

155. Cited in William Penn Cresson, *The Holy Alliance: The European Background of the Monroe Doctrine* (New York: Oxford University Press, 1922), 52.

As described in chapter 2, La Harpe did not object to the form or objectives of the Holy Alliance: he only criticized his former pupil for adopting a religious idiom that he considered distasteful and ineffective. For others, though, such as the English abolitionist Thomas Clarkson, this idiom was the perfect medium for the kind of politics that La Harpe had practiced. Clarkson was among those inspired by news of Alexander's meetings in London with Wilberforce and others; he himself went on to hold two private meetings with Alexander, one in Paris in 1815 and the other at the Congress of Aix-la-Chapelle in 1818. Clarkson produced manuscript accounts of each of these meetings, and the first circulated widely enough to reach Jefferson in Virginia.[156] Clarkson belonged to La Harpe's world, as attested by their mutual friendship with Williams, as well as La Harpe's enthusiasm for all the "English ecclesiastics, non-conformists (*dissenters*)" and members of the British and Foreign Bible Society whom he had met at her salon.[157] Unlike La Harpe, however, Clarkson was also an admirer of Krüdener: his initial meeting with Alexander in Paris was arranged through her. Clarkson's goal was to enlist Russian power to remake the Atlantic economy by banning the slave trade and guaranteeing the independence of Haiti. The alliance with Alexander that Clarkson pursued employed a new idiom for practicing rhetorical strategies and pursuing political goals that still belonged to the pattern established by La Harpe.

Clarkson's first meeting with Alexander took place in Paris on September 23, 1815: only three days before the initial signing of the Holy Alliance. In his account, Clarkson emphasized the intimacy and sincerity of their conversation, which they held alone, "face to face." It began with an open exchange of religious sentiments: both shared their admiration for Quakers and described themselves as Quakers in spirit if not in the letter.[158] Clarkson's account of Alexander's comportment also made an impression on Jefferson: "it shews great condescension of character on the part of the

---

156. "Thomas Clarkson's account of his conversation with the Emperor of Russia at Paris the 22nd of September 1815" and "Account of an interview with Alexander I, Emperor of Russia by Thomas Clarkson" (1818), Library of the Society of Friends, London, Temp MSS 5/7, Temp MSS 58/5/4. I have cited a published edition: *Thomas Clarkson's Interviews with the Emperor Alexander I of Russia at Paris and Aix-La-Chapelle in 1815 and 1818 as Told by Himself,* ed. Priscilla Peckover (London: Slavery and Native Races Committee of the Society of Friends, 1930). In the 1818 account, Clarkson complained that his previous manuscript had been printed without permission in the United States, but I am not aware of any copies.

157. La Harpe to Alexander I, October 4, 1802, *Correspondance de La Harpe et Alexandre Ier,* 1:665.

158. *Thomas Clarkson's Interviews,* 10.

emperor," Jefferson wrote, "and power of mind also to be able to abdicate the artificial distance between himself and other good and able men, and to converse as on equal ground. [T]his conversation too, taken with his late Christian league seems to bespeak in him something like a sectarian piety."[159] The rest of the conversation was conducted—and narrated for the reader—with sentimental craft. Alexander continued by explaining that he had been inspired to become "the friend of the poor Africans" and "an Enemy to the Slave Trade" by seeing an engraving of the hold of a slave ship.[160] According to Clarkson himself, who had reprinted the famous 1780s engraving of the slave ship *Brookes* in his 1808 history of the abolition of the slave trade, this image had been "designed to give the spectator an idea of the sufferings of the Africans in the Middle Passage, and this so familiarly, that he might instantly pronounce upon the miseries experienced there."[161] In reply, Clarkson reflected Alexander's international reputation back to him: the Russian emperor's feelings were known among "Friends of the Cause in England," and "it had given them pleasure beyond measure to find that this injured People had so powerful a protector and Friend."[162]

---

159. Thomas Jefferson to George Logan, July 23, 1816, Thomas Jefferson, *The Papers of Thomas Jefferson, Retirement Series, Volume 10: May 1816 to 18 January 1817*, ed. J. Jefferson Looney (Princeton: Princeton University Press, 2013), 265–66. Like La Harpe, Jefferson began to suspect that Alexander had been undermined by the powers of old Europe: "I have no doubt that his firmness in favor of France, after the deposition of Bonaparte, has saved that country from evils still more severe than she is suffering, & perhaps even from partition. I sincerely wish that the history of the secret proceedings at Vienna may become known, and may reconcile to our good opinion of him his participation in the demolition of antient and independant states, transferring them & their inhabitants, as farms & stocks of cattle at a market to other owners, and even taking a part of the spoil to himself. it is possible to suppose a case excusing this, & my partiality for his character encorages me to expect it; & to impute to others, known to have no moral scruples, the crimes of that Conclave, who, under pretence of punishing the atrocities of Bonaparte, reacted them themselves, & proved that with equal power they were equally flagitious." After 1820, Jefferson came to suspect Alexander's motives: "I am afraid our quondam favorite Alexander has swerved from the true faith. [H]is becoming an accomplice of the soi-disent holy alliance, the anti-national principles he has separately avowed, and his becoming the very leader of a combination to chain mankind down eternally to the oppressions of the most barbarous ages, are clouds on his character not easily to be cleared away." Jefferson to Levett Harris, December 12, 1821, Early Access Document, Founders Online, National Archives, http:// founders.archives.gov/documents/Jefferson/98-01-02-2499.

160. *Thomas Clarkson's Interviews*, 9.

161. Thomas Clarkson, *The History of the Rise, Progress, and Accomplishment of the Abolition of the African Slave-Trade by the British Parliament* (London: Longman, Hurst, Rees, and Orme, 1808), 2:111.

162. *Thomas Clarkson's Interviews*, 10.

This sentimental negotiation of community was the prelude to proposals for concerted action which once again combined Russian external intervention on behalf of a liberal cause with external investment in Russian development. In 1815, Clarkson was seeking Russian diplomatic pressure to help enforce a universal ban on the slave trade. Though the slave trade had just been declared "repugnant to the principles of humanity and universal morality" at the Congress of Vienna, the end of Britain's wartime enforcement of its own national ban on foreign shipping had enabled France (along with Spain and Portugal) to resume it. The association of the Holy Alliance with an effective universal ban on the slave trade is discussed in chapter 5, in connection with Clarkson's colleague James Stephen and his 1818 work, *Europe Chastened and Africa Avenged, or, Reasons for Regarding the Calamities of the Age as Punishments Inflicted by Providence for the Slave Trade.* In his 1815 conversation with Alexander, Clarkson coupled his request for Russian diplomatic intervention with a discussion of education. Following in the tradition of the eighteenth-century Anglican cleric John Brown (whose proposals to Catherine II are discussed in chapter 2), Clarkson offered to help train Russian practitioners of the latest English innovation in pedagogy (the Lancaster system, whose many enthusiasts also included La Harpe): adopting it, Clarkson promised, would lead not only to moral and religious progress but also to the enhancement of Russian power.[163] For his part, Alexander attributed the limited progress made at the Congress of Vienna in enforcing the ban on the slave trade to the constraint of maintaining the unity and concord of postwar Europe. In encouraging Clarkson to continue their alliance ("I must write to him freely, and without Ceremony, and as to a Friend acting in Union for the same great Object"), Alexander seemed to allude to the Holy Alliance that would be signed three days later:

> He added, "I trust we have so laboured in the Congress that the Result will be very satisfactory to all Christian People."
>
> This last sentence was uttered after a Pause, and as if it had come out unexpectedly, so that I was at a loss to determine whether it related to the Slave-Trade, or whether to some arrangement in the Congress at Paris respecting Religious Toleration, or any other Religious Subject.[164]

Clarkson and Alexander also went on to discuss the Holy Alliance in their second meeting, at the Congress of Aix-la-Chapelle in 1818. Clarkson gave

---

163. Clarkson, *History*, 15.
164. Ibid., 13.

Alexander a copy of William Penn's writings, which he identified with the application of Christian morality to legislation, just as Alexander had proclaimed with the Holy Alliance; and he further encouraged Alexander to proceed to introduce something like Penn's plan for a system of international legal arbitration (he had helpfully left a bookmark in the volume to mark the spot for Alexander). Expressing the sensibility that (as we have seen) had so impressed Germaine de Staël and Benjamin Constant as well as Jefferson, Alexander replied that this had been his original intention "in the Treaty called 'The Holy Alliance'" but that he had omitted it "lest he might be considered as aiming at too much at once. Improvements must be made gradually to become permanent."[165] Alexander adroitly proceeded to pass the initiative back onto his allies and talked about his admiration for the peace movement. Clarkson had brought a letter and literature from the newly founded London Peace Society: Clarkson likened it to the one founded by Noah Worcester in Massachusetts, which Alexander "himself had Patronized" with his correspondence in 1817. Speaking in the register of a "friend of mankind," Alexander declared that "Two such Societies were to him evident Proofs of the moral improvement of the times" and ended the conversation declaring that "he should consider himself as belonging to *each* and *to all of them in whatever Part of the World they were established.*"[166] Alexander's engagements with one of the founders of the London Peace Society, the pharmacist and prominent philanthropist William Allen, followed a similar pattern: a community of shared endeavor forged through intimate Christian fellowship, with investment in Russian education ending up as the most concrete course of action. In June 1814, Alexander had met with a Quaker delegation led by Allen; in 1818, Allen and his colleague Stephen Grellet traveled to Saint Petersburg, where they met twice more with Alexander, discussing penal reform as well as migration and education. According to Grellet's memoirs, Alexander recounted his composition of the Holy Alliance to them, after which they all wept and prayed together, kneeling side by side. After that, Allen and Grellet traveled southward for a long and grueling tour of the Russian Empire, visiting communities of Mennonites, Karaite Jews, and many others in Crimea, before arriving in Odesa in 1819.[167]

---

165. Ibid., 30.

166. Ibid., 28, 31–32.

167. *Memoirs of the Life and Gospel Labours of Stephen Grellet*, ed. Benjamin Seebohm (Philadelphia: H. Longstreth, 1860), 1:321. For Allen's impressions of his meetings with Alexander and Krüdener and his travels in Russia, see *Life of William Allen: With Selections from His Correspondence* (London: C. Gilpin, 1846), vol. 1. On the London

In his 1818 meeting with Alexander at the Congress of Aix-la-Chapelle, Clarkson proposed a further course of joint action by inviting the Russian emperor to inspect "some Articles of African Manufactures." Alexander duly marveled at the quality of the craftsmanship, which he deemed superior to what could be manufactured in Manchester. "'You astonish me, you have given me a new Idea of the state of these Poor People, I was not aware they were so advanced in Society,'" went the reply recorded by Clarkson. "'Africa ought to be allowed to have a fair chance of raising her Character in the Scale of the Civilized World.'"[168] Clarkson's didactic point was to explain that such industry was to be found throughout Africa, suppressed only by the slave trade. If this distortion were removed, the progress of African civilization would naturally follow: this was the argument developed by the Swedish abolitionist Carl-Bernhard Wadström (a friend of Helen Maria Williams), as well as the premise of the colony of Sierra Leone, which Clarkson co-directed. Clarkson's use of these staged objects also highlights a dynamic discerned by Lynn Festa in sentimental literature, particularly when deployed in a colonial context: in drawing a sharp distinction between "who possesses affect and who elicits it," sentimental affirmations of shared purpose operated "not by forging bonds directly between seemingly like individuals, but by creating a shared relationship to a common but excluded object about which the community has feelings."[169] At the same time, however, Clarkson's set piece was the prelude to a rhetorical strategy more similar to the one pursued by La Harpe in his correspondence with Alexander: a strategy serving a scheme to guarantee the independence of Haiti.

Clarkson had embraced the cause of Haiti after 1814, when he was contacted by King Henri Christophe.[170] Christophe was a former revolution-

Peace Society, see Martin Ceadel, *The Origins of War Prevention: The British Peace Movement and International Relations, 1730–1854* (Oxford: Oxford University Press, 1996). On Quaker diplomacy, see Sarah Crabtree, *Holy Nation: The Transatlantic Quaker Ministry in an Age of Revolution*, American Beginnings, 1500–1900 (Chicago: University of Chicago Press, 2016). On Quakers in Russia, see Richenda C. Scott, *Quakers in Russia* (London: M. Joseph, 1964); Arnold B. McMillin, "Quakers in Early Nineteenth-Century Russia," *Slavonic and East European Review* 51, no. 125 (1973): 567–79.

168. *Thomas Clarkson's Interviews*, 23.

169. Lynn M. Festa, *Sentimental Figures of Empire in Eighteenth-Century Britain and France* (Baltimore: Johns Hopkins University Press, 2006), 3–4.

170. On the correspondence between Henri Christophe and Thomas Clarkson, see J. R. Oldfield, *Transatlantic Abolitionism in the Age of Revolution: An International History of Anti-Slavery, c. 1787–1820* (Cambridge: Cambridge University Press, 2013), 242–43; Earl Leslie Griggs and Clifford H. Prator, eds., *Henry Christophe and Thomas Clarkson, a Correspondence* (Berkeley: University of California Press, 1952), 56–61.

ary general who had become the monarch of the northern part of Haiti; he had sought the support of the African Institution in response to French talk of restoring their West Indian empire. Clarkson was no less capable than La Harpe of considering enlightened monarchy to be a necessary condition for progress in certain conditions. Like La Harpe with Alexander, Clarkson responded to Christophe's affirmation of his commitment to a shared cause (advancing civilization through the abolition of the slave trade) by connecting him to a wider network and enlisting its support. Clarkson recruited William Allen to help organize missionary schools in Haiti; and he set to work recruiting Alexander to help protect Haiti from France. Clarkson had prepared for his meeting by sending Alexander a copy of a letter that Christophe had written to him in 1816. Clarkson later recounted the episode in a letter to Christophe:

> I took the liberty . . . of shewing him *confidentially* one of your letters to me, which I had taken with me from England for that purpose. This letter produced upon his Imperial Majesty the effect I had anticipated. He expressed his obligations to me for having shewn it him; for he confessed it had given him new ideas both with respect to Hayti and to your Government. He had been taught by the French and German newspapers (and he had no other source of information) that Hayti was inhabited by a people little better than savages. He now saw them in a very different light. The letter which I had shewn him was a letter of genius and talent. It contained wise, virtuous, and liberal sentiments.[171]

Clarkson reported that the letter had succeeded in authenticating Christophe. "It would have done honour to the most civilized Cabinets of Europe," Clarkson enthused. He later annotated his copy of Christophe's letter: "I lent the original to Alexander at Aix-la-Chapelle, who was so much struck with it that he carried it to the Emperor of Austria and the King of Prussia for their perusal, and they pronounced it as good a letter as any of their own Cabinet-Ministers could have written on the occasion."[172] Where previously it was Alexander himself, now it was Christophe, whose mastery of European forms was paraded as testimony to the civilizing potential of his regime. Like La Harpe, Clarkson reflected this reaction back onto its object by narrating the whole episode to Christophe. "I had to entreat him if an Expedition against Hayti should be seriously intended,

171. Thomas Clarkson to King Henry, October 30, 1818, in Griggs and Prator, *Henry Christophe and Thomas Clarkson, a Correspondence*, 121–22.

172. King Henry to Thomas Clarkson, November 18, 1816, in Griggs and Prator, *Henry Christophe and Thomas Clarkson, a Correspondence*, 97n7.

to use his great Influence, I mean his Mediation, with the King of France to prevent it." Christophe in turn seized the opportunity to assert his own membership in the sentimental community by praising Clarkson for his approach to Alexander: "In that action I saw a new proof of your zeal and devotion to our cause."[173]

To Alexander, Clarkson had emphasized that the threat of another French invasion (perhaps by exploiting the internal division of Haiti) had forced Christophe to maintain a large army rather than devoting all available resources to agriculture. To Christophe, Clarkson speculated about further steps: perhaps in the future Christophe could even offer to contribute Haitian naval power to help enforce a coordinated ban on the Spanish and Portuguese slave trade.[174] More concretely, the next step was a March 20, 1819, letter from Christophe to Alexander, which Clarkson forwarded to Alexander along with a report on Haiti's schools. Christophe's letter appealed to Alexander's "universal benevolence" and cited his stated commitment to be "the most illustrious protector of the African cause."[175] It focused on eliciting pity for the suffering of Haiti as well as wonder and admiration for their valiant struggle for liberty; it also detailed a plan for the progress of civilization to which Christophe's government was committed. This plan followed the general outlines and sequence of the advice La Harpe had given to Alexander: Christophe proposed to start by encouraging agricultural productivity and legislating a code of laws appropriate to Haiti's social state, while seeking English assistance to create a system of public education that would cultivate the virtues of free citizens.

Clarkson's conjuncture of a Russian guarantee for Haitian liberty abruptly evaporated when Christophe's kingdom collapsed in 1820 (following his suicide, likely prompted by a stroke). Before it did, however, it produced one other text: an 1819 pamphlet published by the Haitian writer Juste Chanlatte, responding to *Europe Chastened and Africa Avenged*, by Clarkson's colleague James Stephen. As chapter 5 will discuss, Stephen

173. King Henry to Thomas Clarkson, November 20, 1819, in Griggs and Prator, *Henry Christophe and Thomas Clarkson, a Correspondence*, 164.

174. Thomas Clarkson to King Henry, October 30, 1818, in Griggs and Prator, *Henry Christophe and Thomas Clarkson, a Correspondence*, 122–23. The episode serves to reinforce the point that diplomatic non-recognition of Haiti was not equivalent to complete isolation: here was a potential connection extending beyond the Atlantic world. See Julia Gaffield, *Haitian Connections in the Atlantic World: Recognition after Revolution* (Chapel Hill: University of North Carolina Press, 2015). Clarkson also suggested that Christophe offer to accept Black emigration from the United States in exchange for the United States purchasing the Spanish side of the island and ceding it to Christophe. See Oldfield, *Transatlantic Abolitionism in the Age of Revolution*, 244–46.

175. King Henry to the Emperor Alexander, March 20, 1819, in Griggs and Prator, *Henry Christophe and Thomas Clarkson, a Correspondence*, 132, 135.

had urged the leaders assembled at the Congress of Aix-la-Chapelle to ensure that the salvation of Europe did not spell disaster for Africans, by erecting a new postwar framework for enforcing a universal ban on the slave trade. Chanlatte's response demonstrates that Alexander's performance as a "friend of mankind," originally scripted by La Harpe for an audience of Thomas Erskines and Thomas Jeffersons, was also legible to Haitians—and was also taken as an opportunity by Haitians to assert their equal membership in the audience for this performance. "Who knew," Chanlatte wrote, "that that same star of the North which just shone so brilliantly over the old world would also exert its benevolent influence over the new?" Alexander's role in Europe had furnished a rare example of great power and good intentions coinciding: this, Chanlatte concluded, was the historical record of the emperor who had now publicly declared himself "protector of the oppressed and defender of our cause."[176]

Chanlatte was the chief architect of the 1805 Haitian Constitution, as well as a key contributor to the flourishing print culture of Henri Christophe's court (under the title of the Comte de Rosiers). Like La Harpe, Chanlatte was also adept at incorporating Voltaire's rhetorical flourishes into his own script for revolution. "J'ai vengé l'Amérique" (I have avenged America), the line Chanlatte inserted into a famous 1804 speech by the first leader of an independent Haiti, Jean-Jacques Dessalines, was a refiguring of a scene from a 1736 play by Voltaire: as Chris Bongie has put it, Chanlatte was "appropriating the theatrical words of French Enlightenment in the service of a very real act of vengeance against colonial tyranny."[177] Chanlatte's efforts were amplified by the most important literary figure of Christophe's court, the Baron de Vastey, whose writings were widely reviewed on both sides of the Atlantic. As Marlene Daut has explained, Vastey was engaged in scripting the liberation of Haiti in a historiographical as well as literary and political sense, by positioning it as the realization of the universally emancipatory aspirations of earlier revolutions. "The independence of the United States of America has been a source of good for Europe and for the whole world," Vastey wrote in 1817, "ours will contribute to the happiness of humankind through its moral and political consequences."[178] Vastey also worked to refigure the alliance

176. Chanlatte, *Hayti reconnaissante*, 10.

177. Chris Bongie, "The Cry of History: Juste Chanlatte and the Unsettling (Presence) of Race in Early Haitian Literature," *MLN* 130, no. 4 (2015): 819.

178. Pompée-Valentin de Vastey, *Réflexions politiques sur quelques ouvrages et journaux francais concernant Hayti* (Sans-Souci: L'Imprimerie royale, 1817), 15, cited in Marlene L. Daut, *Baron de Vastey and the Origins of Black Atlantic Humanism* (New York: Palgrave Macmillan, 2017), 4.

with European abolitionists: in an 1816 work, he positioned Haitians not as a passive and excluded object to stimulate the community and agency of others but as actors at the Archimedean point of world politics, building "the fulcrum on which the philanthropists will be able to plant the powerful lever which will lift up the moral world against the enemies of humankind."[179] Concluding on a more skeptical note, however, Daut appeals to the twentieth-century philosopher Frantz Fanon's maxim that "You will never make colonialism blush for shame by spreading little known cultural treasures before its eyes."[180] Read somewhat freely, the same maxim might also serve as a pronouncement on the fate of attempts to shame the colonial powers of Europe by spreading such treasures before the emperor of Russia: a script that had developed through La Harpe's efforts to liberate Lausanne, and upon which Clarkson's appeal to the Holy Alliance still relied. A final appeal to Alexander for help in ending the international slave trade, published by Wilberforce in 1822, prompted Lord Byron to urge that "moral Washington of Africa" to "set the other half of earth to rights": "You have freed the *blacks*—now pray shut up the whites."

> Shut up the bald-coot bully Alexander;
>   Ship off the Holy Three to Senegal;
> Teach them that "sauce for goose is sauce for gander,"
>   And ask them how *they* like to be in thrall?[181]

179. Pompée-Valentin de Vastey, *Réflexions sur une Lettre de Mazères ex-Colon français, adressée à M. J. C. L. Sismonde de Sismondi, Sur les Noirs et les Blancs, la Civilisation de l'Afrique, le Royaume d'Hayti, etc.* (Cap-Henry: Chez P. Roux, imprimeur du Roi, 1816), 4, cited in Daut, *Baron de Vastey and the Origins of Black Atlantic Humanism*, 4.

180. Frantz Fanon, *The Wretched of the Earth* (London: Penguin Books, 2001), 178–79, cited in Daut, *Baron de Vastey and the Origins of Black Atlantic Humanism*, 109.

181. William Wilberforce, *Lettre à l'empereur Alexandre sur la traite des noirs* (London: G. Schulze, 1822); George Gordon Byron, *Don Juan: Cantos XII, XIII, and XIV* (London: John Hunt, 1823), 156. Byron aimed more mockery at Alexander and the Holy Alliance in his "The Age of Bronze," also published in 1823. For a comparison of Byron's mockery with Aleksandr Pushkin's in the fragmentary tenth chapter of his *Eugene Onegin*, see Vladimir Nabokov's commentary in Aleksandr Pushkin, *Eugene Onegin: A Novel in Verse*, ed. Vladimir Nabokov (Princeton: Princeton University Press, 2021), 2:311–75.

CHAPTER FOUR

Federalizing Europe

"You don't know the abbé Morio? He's a very interesting man . . ." she said.

"Yes, I've heard about his plan for eternal peace, and it's very interest-ing, but hardly possible . . ."

"The means are European balance and the droit des gens," *the abbé was saying. "Let a powerful state like Russia, famous for its barbarism, stand disinterestedly at the head of a union having as its purpose the balance of Europe—and it will save the world!"*

—TOLSTOY, *WAR AND PEACE*[1]

IN JANUARY 1788, eighteen-year-old Prince Adam Jerzy Czartoryski spent a sleepless night in Paris, finishing a plan for revolution that he had promised to share with his mother back in Poland. The plan, which he composed together with his well-connected Florentine tutor Scipione Piat-toli, described a "patriotic congress" of Polish magnates, modeled on the American Continental Congress: they would seize an opportune moment to achieve independence from their king and from the power behind the throne, Empress Catherine II of Russia.[2] However, it was the spirit of 1787 more than the spirit of 1776 that was evoked by the new Polish Constitution proclaimed three years later. The Constitution of May 3, 1791, emerged out of an alliance between the patriot party (led by Czartoryski's father) and King Stanisław August Poniatowski: an alliance brokered in part by the

---

1. Leo Tolstoy, *War and Peace*, trans. Richard Pevear and Larissa Volokhonsky (New York: Alfred A. Knopf, 2007), 10, 14.

2. Adam Jerzy Czartoryski, "Pismo do przygotowania wyborów na Sejm Czteroletni, napisane po powrocie z Paryża z rozkazu Xięcia Generała pod dyrekcją Piattolego 6.I.1788," in *Polonia e Russia alla fine del XVIII secolo (Un avventuriero onorato: Scipione Piattoli)*, by Giampiero Bozzolato (Padova: Marsilio, 1964), 135–52.

Abbé Piattoli, who had become the king's secretary in 1790. Drafted by Stanisław August in Piattoli's rooms in the Royal Castle in Warsaw, the Constitution of 1791 followed the example of the United States Constitution of 1787 in strengthening central authority (by making the monarchy hereditary) while enshrining the separation of powers and toleration— and also in deferring any radical change in the status of those denied civil rights.[3] Remarkably, the constitution was praised effusively by both Edmund Burke and Tom Paine—former allies in support of the American Revolution who famously parted ways in attacking and defending the French Revolution of 1789.[4] The new constitution was short-lived. Poland was invaded by Russia and Prussia, the subsequent rebellion led by the American revolutionary hero Tadeusz Kościuszko was suppressed, and Poland was subjected to a third and final partition in 1795, wiping it off the map. John Adams, whose *Defense of the Constitutions of Government of the United States* of 1787 had cited the unfettered power of the Polish aristocracy in making the case for a strengthened executive, later added a note observing that a good constitution may fail because of "circumstances having no necessary connection with its intrinsic excellence": had the United States of America been placed in the "geographical position" of Poland, Adams surmised, it was "at least open to question" whether it would have suffered a comparable fate.[5]

3. For an account emphasizing the influence of the English Constitution on the Polish reform, see Richard Butterwick, *Poland's Last King and English Culture: Stanisław August Poniatowski, 1732–1798* (Oxford: Clarendon Press, 1998). According to a survey of the American, French, and Polish constitutions published in London in 1791, however, "The new Polish constitution appears to have caught its spirit from the American; joined with a little additional power granted to the executive department: it resembles the English constitution only, as that served as for the prototype of the American." "New Constitutions of France, Poland, and America," *The Critical Review, or, Annals of Literature* 3 (1791): 443, cited in R. R. Palmer, *The Age of the Democratic Revolution: A Political History of Europe and America, 1760–1800* (Princeton: Princeton University Press, 1959), 1:429–30.

4. Palmer, *The Age of the Democratic Revolution*, 1:429, 431–32. For Burke, praising the Polish Constitution mainly served as another opportunity to attack the French Revolution and its British admirers. His remark that the Polish Constitution "probably is the most pure and defecated public good which ever has been conferred on mankind" may also serve as an opportunity to learn that this term for eliminating impurities originally had a much wider range of meaning. Edmund Burke, *An Appeal from the New to the Old Whigs, in Consequence of Some Late Discussions in Parliament, Relative to the Reflections on the French Revolution* (London: J. Dodsley, 1791), 102. On Burke's long-standing interest in Poland, see Anna Plassart, "Edmund Burke, Poland, and the Commonwealth of Europe," *The Historical Journal* 63, no. 4 (2020): 885–910.

5. *The Works of John Adams, Second President of the United States: With a Life of the Author, Notes and Illustrations*, ed. Charles Francis Adams (Boston: Little and Brown, 1851), 4:373–74.

Seven years after his Paris debut, Czartoryski arrived in Saint Petersburg, sent into the Russian service to mollify the empress after his family's support for Kościuszko. There, Czartoryski became the intimate friend of Catherine's grandson Alexander (and his wife's lover). Alexander confided his enthusiasm for the French Revolution and sympathy for the Polish cause, and later demanded that Czartoryski draft a proclamation of his republican convictions to be issued at the inauguration of his future reign.[6] When Alexander did take power in 1801, Czartoryski participated in the four-person "unofficial committee" (*neglasnyi komitet*) that met in the new emperor's private apartments for lengthy discussions of policy ideas, and in 1803 the former hostage became foreign minister. Where Kościuszko and other Polish exiles in Paris were drawing the conclusion that a war of national liberation was the only remaining option, Czartoryski committed himself to building the future of Poland in Saint Petersburg.[7] Like Alexander's former tutor, Frédéric-César de la Harpe, Czartoryski set out to fashion Alexander into a "friend of mankind" capable of wielding Russian power to transform European politics (and liberate his country in the process). As he later recalled in his memoirs,

> I had wished that Alexander would become, in one way or another, an arbiter of peace for the civilized world; that he would be the protector of the weak and of the oppressed, the guardian of justice among nations; that his reign would begin a new era in European politics, politics now based on general welfare and individual rights.[8]

La Harpe eventually returned in triumph to his native Canton of Vaud, having secured its independence with Russian help at the Congress of Vienna in 1815; by contrast, Czartoryski landed in permanent exile after the Russian army suppressed the Polish uprising of 1830–31. Despite this difference in outcomes, the strategy for liberating Poland from Saint Petersburg that Czartoryski had pursued through the 1820s also belongs

6. *Mémoires du prince Adam Czartoryski et correspondance avec l'empereur Alexandre 1er* (Paris: Plon, 1887), 1:150–51.

7. Kościuszko and his associates were reacting to the alliance that France was pursuing with Russia after 1799 during the brief reign of Alexander's father, Emperor Paul I. See Józef Pawlikowski, "Can the Poles Attain Their Independence? [1800]," in *The Crucial Decade: East Central European Society and National Defense, 1859–1870*, by Béla K. Király, ed. Emanuel Halicz ([New York]: Brooklyn College Press, 1984), 553–620, cited in W. H. Zawadzki, *A Man of Honour: Adam Czartoryski as a Statesman of Russia and Poland, 1795–1831* (Oxford: Clarendon Press, 1993), 34–35. Kościuszko attended the salon of Helen Maria Williams (discussed in chapter 3).

8. Czartoryski, *Mémoires*, 1:370.

to the same broader pattern: one in which patriot hopes were invested in what John Locke had termed the "federative power," or the capacity of states to construct new external relationships.[9]

Czartoryski's strategy developed into two successive collaborations which are the subject of this chapter: each brings the Holy Alliance into sharp theoretical focus as a form of federative politics. The first was a renewed partnership with Piattoli at the outset of Alexander's reign. In 1803 and 1805, Czartoryski and Piattoli produced a pair of reports for Alexander advocating for Russian intervention in Europe: it was Piattoli who would later serve as inspiration for the Abbé Morio, a character in Leo Tolstoy's novel *War and Peace*.[10] The ideas developed in these proposals were shelved after Napoleon's triumph at the Battle of Austerlitz in 1805, but they resurfaced in 1814–15 and were reasserted once again by Czartoryski in the 1820s: they relied on the legal concepts of mediation and guarantee to explain how Russia could position itself as the liberator of nations—including, of course, Poland—and the founder of a federal Europe. Czartoryski's second collaborator was the radical English philosopher and jurist Jeremy Bentham, whom Czartoryski had also met as a teenager. In 1815, at Czartoryski's instigation, Bentham presented Alexander with a plan for promulgating a new constitution for Poland. This plan for constitutional change did not survive the negotiations over Poland's fate at the Congress of Vienna, but it represents a pivotal moment in Bentham's thinking. In the 1820s, its premises came to be reframed by Bentham—as well as by the American secretary of state, John Quincy Adams, and other leading Anglo-American critics of the Holy Alliance—in terms of a reactionary conspiracy against national sovereignty. However, in *Essay on Diplomacy*, the major treatise he wrote in the 1820s and published in 1830, Czartoryski forcefully reasserted this constitutional theory in terms that still harkened back to the federative politics of the 1780s. Czartoryski's reassertion of these ideas helps explain why the Holy Alliance could be regarded by other liberals (including the ones who will be discussed in chapter 5) as part of an emancipatory legislative process: a method for introducing national representative institutions throughout Europe, for establishing a new legal framework to govern relations between European governments, and for transforming the political economy of the Atlantic world. The enduring importance of these ideas, and

9. John Locke, *Two Treatises of Government*, ed. Peter Laslett (Cambridge: Cambridge University Press, 1988), 365.

10. Kathryn B. Feuer, *Tolstoy and the Genesis of "War and Peace,"* ed. Robin Feuer Miller and Donna Tussing Orwin (Ithaca: Cornell University Press, 1996), 93.

the inadequacy of conventional categories for capturing their place in nineteenth-century political thought, is attested by their much later reappearance in the hands of the French philosopher Pierre-Joseph Proudhon, whom Tolstoy admired and who identified the Holy Alliance as "the first draft of the future constitution of Europe."[11]

Polish Patriots in Saint Petersburg

When Czartoryski became Russia's foreign minister in 1803, he became associated with a strategy of intervening in European politics. This strategy has been examined in the context of Polish history, the history of Russian foreign policy, and the diplomatic history of the third coalition against Napoleon (which ended in defeat at the Battle of Austerlitz in 1805).[12] Considered in connection with Bentham's career in Russia and his collaboration with Czartoryski, it also reveals an important dimension of a series of transatlantic debates, going back to the 1780s, about federal constitutions and the legalization of the external relations of states. Versions of Czartoryski's strategy proliferated across two overlapping international networks which Czartoryski had encountered in the late 1780s and early 1790s in London as well as Paris—and which generated his subsequent collaborations with Bentham and Piattoli. One of these networks centered around the former prime minister of Great Britain, the Earl of Shelburne (later Marquis of Lansdowne), who had been Bentham's patron; the other was connected to the French philosopher the Marquis de Condorcet as well as the American statesman Thomas Jefferson. Both networks were associated with the view that American independence could exert a positive effect on Europe; both were aligned with hopes of turning Britain and France into the core of a peaceful and prosperous new world order, whose legal structure would emerge through the promulgation of treaties

11. Pierre-Joseph Proudhon, *Si les traités de 1815 ont cessé d'exister? Actes du futur congrès* (Paris: E. Dentu, 1863), 44.

12. Jerzy Skowronek, "Le programme européen du prince Adam Jerzy Czartoryski en 1803–1805," *Acta Poloniae Historica* 17 (1968): 137–57; Zawadzki, *A Man of Honour*; Patricia Kennedy Grimsted, *The Foreign Ministers of Alexander I: Political Attitudes and the Conduct of Russian Diplomacy, 1801–1825* (Berkeley: University of California Press, 1969); Patricia Kennedy Grimsted, "Czartoryski's System for Russian Foreign Policy, 1803: A Memorandum, Edited with Introduction and Analysis," *California Slavic Studies* 5 (1970): 19–92; Hildegard Schaeder, *Die dritte Koalition und die Heilige Allianz: Nach neuen Quellen* (Königsberg: Ost-Europa-Verlag, 1934); Uta Krüger-Löwenstein, *Russland, Frankreich und das Reich 1801–1803: zur Vorgeschichte der 3. Koalition*, Frankfurter historische Abhandlungen, Bd. 2 (Wiesbaden: Steiner, 1972).

enshrining the principle of free trade. Situating both of Czartoryski's collaborations within these well-known transatlantic networks makes it possible to cross several historiographical barriers, linking his strategy—and his later assessment of the Holy Alliance—to the patriotic reform politics of the Holy Roman Empire as well as Britain and France.[13]

Czartoryski had greatly impressed members of these networks as a traveling teenager in the late 1780s and early 1790s: though he later described his education as "entirely Polish, and entirely republican," one of his childhood tutors had been the eminent French political economist Pierre Samuel du Pont de Nemours.[14] At the outset of Alexander's reign, Czartoryski held a series of reunions with these contacts in Saint Petersburg. Most importantly, Czartoryski was finally reunited with Piattoli in 1804. Rescued from Austrian imprisonment after the fall of Poland, Piattoli was hired by Dorothea von Medem, Duchess of Courland, and made his way to Saint Petersburg to address the status of her property now within the Russian Empire. Czartoryski was also rejoined in Saint Petersburg by Filippo Mazzei, Jefferson's former neighbor and friend in Virginia. Mazzei had returned to Europe in 1779 on an ill-fated mission as representative of the Commonwealth of Virginia; in 1788 he was recruited by Piattoli (over dinner with Jefferson in Paris, Mazzei later recalled) to serve as Stanisław August's agent, responsible for promoting the Polish cause in the international press.[15] Mazzei had previously been recruited by Jefferson to per-

13. There is one mention of Piattoli in Bentham's correspondence, in a letter from the British chargé d'affaires in Dresden, reporting on what he had heard from Polish exiles (including Czartoryski) of the Russian intervention in Poland and regretting that Britain had failed to block it: "Abbé Piatoli is also here. He had a principal hand in the Polish revolution. He is busy drawing up an account of that affair from the beginning to its fatal termination and perhaps on this subject I may take the liberty at another time to take your opinion with respect to the manner of introducing this detail to English notice." David Gray to Jeremy Bentham, January 15, 1794, *The Correspondence of Jeremy Bentham, Vol. 5: January 1794 to December 1797*, ed. Alexander Taylor Milne, Collected Works of Jeremy Bentham (London: Athlone Press, 1981), 11, http://dx.doi.org/10.1093/actrade/9780485132052.book.1.

14. Czartoryski, *Mémoires*, 1:26–27, 37. In 1811, Czartoryski thanked Du Pont de Nemours, who had emigrated to America, for offering to send him a copy of his 1773 *Table raisonnée des principes de l'économie politique*. In 1814, Du Pont de Nemours wrote to Alexander, thanking him for his service to humanity and his magnanimity to France, and sending him a copy of the same work. Czartoryski to Du Pont de Nemours, April 23, 1811, Du Pont de Nemours to Alexander I, April 28, 1814, and Alexander I to Du Pont de Nemours, May 5/17, 1814, in Du Pont de Nemours Correspondence, Winterthur Manuscripts, Hagley Museum and Library, Wilmington, DE. I am grateful to Graham Clure for sharing these letters with me.

15. *Memoirs of the Life and Peregrinations of the Florentine, Philip Mazzei, 1730–1816*, trans. Howard R. Marraro (New York: Columbia University Press, 1942), 302. See also Jean

form a similar service: the result was his *Historical and Political Researches on the United States of North America* of 1788. This landmark history of the American Revolution was partly translated by the philosopher Sophie de Grouchy, and included important material supplied by Condorcet, who was her husband, including the first European commentary on the proposed Constitution of 1787. In 1802, Mazzei traveled to Saint Petersburg, where he petitioned Alexander to honor the pension he was owed by the former Polish king. Afterward Mazzei updated Jefferson on the improved fortunes of "the good Polish patriots" in Saint Petersburg; described the exciting reforms being discussed in Alexander's "unofficial committee"; and petitioned (unsuccessfully) to be appointed as United States consul responsible for expanding trade through the Black Sea.[16]

Another of Czartoryski's important reunions in Saint Petersburg at the outset of Alexander's reign, which reconnected him with Bentham, was with the Genevan writer Étienne Dumont. Dumont had lived in Saint Petersburg in the 1780s (as minister to the Reformed Church there) before moving to England to work for Lansdowne, who had assembled what Germaine de Staël later called "the most delightful assemblage of enlightened men that England, and consequently the world, can offer."[17] Lansdowne's associates included the exiled leaders of the failed Genevan Revolution of 1782, who had sought to assert popular sovereignty against the executive councils dominated by the wealthiest families of the city: as Richard Whatmore has described, these Genevan *représentants* later

---

Fabre, *Stanislas-Auguste Poniatowski et l'Europe des lumières: Étude de cosmopolitisme*, 2nd ed. (Paris: Ophrys, 1984), 510, 513. Masonic connections linked Piattoli with La Harpe: Piattoli had been recruited by Stanisław August's previous secretary, Pierre Maurice Glayre, an old friend of La Harpe's. Glayre and La Harpe had met at a masonic lodge in Warsaw in 1783 and later became colleagues on the Directory of the Helvetic Republic; however, La Harpe later accused Glayre of betraying him to Napoleon Bonaparte. See *Correspondance de Frédéric-César de La Harpe sous la République Helvétique*, ed. Jean Charles Biaudet et al. (Neuchâtel: La Baconnière, 1982), 1:291, 3:560, 4:71.

16. Filippo Mazzei to Thomas Jefferson, February 15, 1803, Founders Online, National Archives, https://founders.archives.gov/documents/Jefferson/01-39-02-0450; Mazzei to Jefferson, October 25, 1803, Founders Online, National Archives, https://founders.archives .gov/documents/Jefferson/01-41-02-0449; Mazzei to Jefferson, December 15, 1804, Founders Online, National Archives, https://founders.archives.gov/documents/Jefferson /99-01-02-0833; Mazzei to Jefferson, July 24, 1805, in Howard R. Marraro, "Unpublished Mazzei Letters to Jefferson," *William and Mary Quarterly* 2, no. 1 (1945): 77. Elsewhere Mazzei also recorded Czartoryski's enthusiastic reaction to reports of Jefferson's inaugural address: Howard R. Marraro, "Unpublished Correspondence of Jefferson and Adams to Mazzei," *Virginia Magazine of History and Biography* 51, no. 2 (1943): 124.

17. Anne-Louise-Germaine de Staël, *Considerations on the Principal Events of the French Revolution*, ed. Aurelian Craiutu (Indianapolis: Liberty Fund, 2008), 698.

dispersed to Paris and London, where they continued their pursuit of constitutional reform from abroad, by seeking to transform either Britain or France, or both, from predatory great powers into protectors of the economic and political liberty of small states like Geneva.[18] Dumont had dedicated himself to editing and translating the writings of Bentham, who had also entered Lansdowne's orbit in 1781. Both Bentham and Dumont had met Czartoryski during his visit to London in 1790–91; in 1803, Dumont excitedly reported back from Saint Petersburg on the activities of the "unofficial committee" and on the enthusiastic reception of Bentham's writings there ("Could you have believed that as many copies of my Bentham would have been sold in Petersburg as in London?").[19] In fact, as we shall see, Bentham's own interest in both Poland and Russia extended back to the 1770s and was closely connected to his initial explorations of what he began to call "international law."

Czartoryski's federative strategy does not figure in histories of international law that set out to trace its emergence as a distinct discourse and sociological formation, detached from other forms of political thought.[20] In fact, this strategy first appeared at a time when the notion of a "constitution" was often connected to the idea of a federal treaty, and when the separation of powers as a principle of constitutional design could be referred to as "a kind of law of nations."[21] Nor does it fit within histories organized around doctrinal conflicts over the moral foundations of legal order—in Judith Shklar's terms, conflicts between the rival forms

18. Richard Whatmore, *Against War and Empire: Geneva, Britain, and France in the Eighteenth Century* (New Haven: Yale University Press, 2012). See also Richard Whatmore, "'Neither Masters nor Slaves': Small States and Empire in the Long Eighteenth Century," *Proceedings of the British Academy* 155 (2009): 53–81; Richard Whatmore, *Terrorists, Anarchists, and Republicans: The Genevans and the Irish in Time of Revolution* (Princeton: Princeton University Press, 2019).

19. Étienne Dumont to Samuel Romilly, June 10, 1803, in *The Works of Jeremy Bentham*, ed. John Bowring, vol. 10 (Edinburgh: W. Tait, 1843), 406. See also Jeremy Bentham to Samuel Parr, September 16, 1803, *The Correspondence of Jeremy Bentham, Vol. 7: January 1802 to December 1808*, ed. J. R. Dinwiddy, Collected Works of Jeremy Bentham (Oxford: Clarendon Press, 1988), 243–44, http://dx.doi.org/10.1093/actrade/9780198226147.book.1.

20. See Ian Hunter, "About the Dialectical Historiography of International Law," *Global Intellectual History* 1, no. 1 (2016): 1–32.

21. On the link between constitution and federal treaty, see Ernst-Wolfgang Böckenförde, "The Historical Evolution and Changes in the Meaning of the Constitution [1984]," in *Constitutional and Political Theory: Selected Writings*, ed. Mirjam Künkler and Tine Stein (Oxford: Oxford University Press, 2017), 152–68. On the separation of powers as a law of nations, see Jean Louis de Lolme, *The Constitution of England: Or, An Account of the English Government; in Which It Is Compared, with the Republican Form of Government, and Occasionally with the Other Monarchies in Europe* (London: T. Spilsbury, 1775), 438.

of "legalism" articulated by proponents of natural law and their positivist critics—rather than the varied uses to which such doctrines were put.[22] Rather than mapping Czartoryski's respective collaborations with Piattoli (who remained within the natural law tradition) and Bentham (who did not) in relation to such historiographical fault lines, this chapter positions both collaborations in the context of a much wider set of contemporary discussions of federative politics linked to the complex and contested legacy of the Swiss jurist Emer de Vattel. For many late eighteenth-century thinkers—particularly those engaging with Vattel's thought—federative politics held out the possibility of shielding the pursuit of utility (economic activity and private social life more generally) from potentially explosive conflict over elemental questions of sovereignty and justice. Legally codified under the guidance of international public opinion, federative power could potentially supply a pathway for constitutional reform. Czartoryski was among those liberals for whom the Holy Alliance was still recognizable, even in the 1820s, as a version of this kind of strategy—even as others began defining their liberalism in opposition to the Holy Alliance.

The Abbé Morio's Law of Nations

In 1803, the year he became Russia's foreign minister, Czartoryski prepared a report titled "On the political system Russia ought to follow." The only surviving copy of this report is a draft, preserved in Czartoryski's papers, which seems to have been dictated to a secretary with less than perfect French—but the cover of the manuscript notes, in Czartoryski's own hand, that the memorandum was "presented and read to the Emperor the same year."[23] Thanks in part to a garbled account by the nineteenth-century French historian and politician Adolph Theirs, this revealing draft was long confounded with another manuscript, also preserved in Czartoryski's papers: a related report from 1805, in Piattoli's hand, also

---

22. Judith N. Shklar, *Legalism: Law, Morals, and Political Trials*, 2nd ed. (Cambridge, MA: Harvard University Press, 1986). For the varied uses of these discourses in Germany, see Knud Haakonssen, "German Natural Law," in *The Cambridge History of Eighteenth-Century Political Thought*, ed. M. Goldie and R. Wokler (Cambridge: Cambridge University Press, 2006), 251–90.

23. "Sur le Systême politique que devroit suive la Russie presenté et la meme année à l'Empereur Alexandre," ms. 5226/IV, fol. 13, Princes Czartoryski Library, National Museum in Krakow. Though the manuscript is clearly a preliminary draft, Czartoryski's annotation indicates it was read to Alexander; however, no presentation copy has been found. I have cited the version edited and published by Patricia Grimsted as Adam Jerzy Czartoryski, "Sur le Systême politique qui devroit suivre la Russie presenté et lu la meme année à l'Empereur Alexandre," ed. Patricia Kennedy Grimsted, *California Slavic Studies* 5 (1970): 37–91.

advocating for Russian intervention in Europe.[24] Alongside a third report, submitted to Czartoryski in 1804 by a Russian civil servant named Vasilii Federovich Malinovskii, these texts make it possible to specify Czartoryski's approach to the politics of federation with considerable precision and to show its derivation from late eighteenth-century discussions of Vattel and his approach to the law of nations.

Like his predecessors Hugo Grotius and Samuel von Pufendorf, Vattel later came to be designated as an authority on international law.[25] Initially, though, his famous 1758 treatise on the law of nations was read more broadly (including in British North America) as a guide to improving the conduct of the state's political and economic relations, and as an innovative constitutional theory—one of the first to define the legislative power as subordinate to the nation's constitution, or what came to be called its "constituent" power.[26] As a Swiss subject of the king of Prussia in the

24. Scipione Piattoli, "Memoire" (1805), 221–22, ms. 5508, Princes Czartoryski Library, National Museum in Krakow. For Thiers's account, see *Histoire du Consulat et de l'Empire: Faisant suite à l'Histoire de la Révolution française*, vol. 5 (Paris: Paulin, 1845), 319–39. On Czartoryski's authorship of the 1803 memorandum and for a comparison of the two documents, see Skowronek, "Le programme européen du prince Adam Jerzy Czartoryski en 1803–1805"; Grimsted, "Czartoryski's System for Russian Foreign Policy," 22–25.

25. See, e.g., Annabel Brett, "Natural Right and Civil Community: The Civil Philosophy of Hugo Grotius," *The Historical Journal* 45, no. 1 (2002): 31–51; Peter Schröder, "The Constitution of the Holy Roman Empire after 1648: Samuel Pufendorf's Assessment in His *Monzambano*," *The Historical Journal* 42, no. 4 (1999): 961–83. Recent scholarship on Vattel has increasingly expanded beyond the disciplinary perspective as well. See the contributions to Koen Stapelbroek and Antonio Trampus, eds., *The Legacy of Vattel's Droit des Gens: Contexts, Concepts, Reception, Translation and Diffusion* (Cham: Palgrave Macmillan, 2019); Peter Schröder, ed., *Concepts and Contexts of Vattel's Political and Legal Thought* (Cambridge: Cambridge University Press, 2021).

26. Gerald Stourzh, "Constitution: Changing Meanings of the Term from the Early Seventeenth to the Late Eighteenth Century," in *Conceptual Change and the Constitution*, ed. Terence Ball and J.G.A. Pocock (Lawrence: University Press of Kansas, 1988), 45; Antonio Trampus, *Emer de Vattel and the Politics of Good Government: Constitutionalism, Small States and the International System* (Cham: Palgrave MacMillan, 2020), 46–48. On "constituent power," see Lucia Rubinelli, *Constituent Power: A History* (Cambridge: Cambridge University Press, 2020). On Vattel's reception in British North America, see Peter S. Onuf and Nicholas Greenwood Onuf, *Federal Union, Modern World: The Law of Nations in an Age of Revolutions, 1776–1814* (Madison, WI: Madison House, 1993); Vincent Chetail, "Vattel and the American Dream: An Inquiry into the Reception of the Law of Nations in the United States," in *The Roots of International Law: Liber Amicorum Peter Haggenmacher*, ed. Vincent Chetail and Pierre-Marie Depuy (Leiden: Martinus Nijhoff, 2014), 251–300; Mark Somos, "Vattel's Reception in British America, 1761–1775," in *Concepts and Contexts of Vattel's Political and Legal Thought*, ed. Peter Schröder (Cambridge: Cambridge University Press, 2021), 203–19. Vattel was put to particularly intensive use by Peter Leopold, the Duke of Tuscany, whose ambitious constitutional project briefly drew in

service of the elector of Saxony, Vattel was immersed in the constitutional complexities of the Holy Roman Empire and in debates about its political and economic future. The elector of Saxony was also the elected king of Poland, and Vattel also spent several years in Warsaw serving as a tutor to an influential Polish family in the early 1760s: he was an early link in what later became a more extensive network of connections between Swiss patriotic reform societies and the Polish political elite (a network that famously came to include Jean-Jacques Rousseau, whose 1771 *Considerations on the Government of Poland* became a key text for constitutional theory after it was published posthumously in 1782).[27] The intensive engagement with Vattel in the early 1780s by thinkers like the Neapolitan jurist Gaetano Filangieri, whose *The Science of Legislation* became the subject of a major critical commentary by the Swiss liberal Benjamin Constant in the early 1820s, also represents an important legacy of Vattel's political theory beyond the disciplinary boundaries of international law.[28]

Vattel's treatise developed a vision of Europe as "a kind of republic" of independent states whose external relations united them into one "political system."[29] Its distinctive claim was that the collective security and prosperity of this political system could be grounded in judgments of national interest by particular states, without invoking the guidance of what his predecessor Christian Wolff had termed the *civitas maxima*: the legal fiction of a universal republic whose civil law was instituted by

---

Mazzei in the early 1780s: Trampus, *Emer de Vattel and the Politics of Good Government*, 80–86. (Mazzei was in Florence trying unsuccessfully to secure recognition and a loan from the duke for the Commonwealth of Virginia.)

27. On Vattel in Poland, see Tetsuya Toyoda, *Theory and Politics of the Law of Nations: Political Bias in International Law Discourse of Seven German Court Councilors in the Seventeenth and Eighteenth Centuries* (Leiden: Nijhoff, 2011), 161–90; Radoslaw Szymanski, "Vattel as an Intermediary between the Economic Society of Berne and Poland," in *The Legacy of Vattel's Droit Des Gens: Contexts, Concepts, Reception, Translation and Diffusion*, ed. Koen Stapelbroek and Antonio Trampus (Cham: Palgrave MacMillan, 2019), 29–52. On Vattel and Rousseau, see Theodore Christov, "Vattel's Rousseau: Ius Gentium and the Natural Liberty of States," in *Freedom and the Construction of Europe: Volume 2, Free Persons and Free States*, ed. Quentin Skinner and Martin van Gelderen (New York: Cambridge University Press, 2013), 167–87. The most illuminating discussion of Rousseau's engagement with Poland and its broader significance which I have encountered is in the currently unpublished work of Graham Clure.

28. Trampus, *Emer de Vattel and the Politics of Good Government*, 104, 113–14, 156–59.

29. Emer de Vattel, *The Law of Nations, or, Principles of the Law of Nature, Applied to the Conduct and Affairs of Nations and Sovereigns, with Three Early Essays on the Origin and Nature of Natural Law and on Luxury*, ed. Béla Kapossy and Richard Whatmore (Indianapolis: Liberty Fund, 2008), 496 [3.47].

nature.[30] Instead of this ideal of international community, which Vattel regarded as furnishing too ready a pretext for intervention in other states, Vattel presented an alternate ideal, one premised on well-constituted states whose forms of government and economic activity would reliably align their judgments of their interests with the needs of the system. Vattel's treatise came to serve as a fertile source of justifications for international intervention, including for European expropriations of indigenous land; at the same time, as Radoslaw Szymanski has recently shown, Vattel was originally read in Poland as supplying strong arguments against interventions in the domestic affairs of other states.[31] Vattel was a defender of small states against the charge that they were relics of the past which had lost their political, economic, and military viability and would remain a source of political instability until they were consolidated into larger states. Against that view, closely associated in the eighteenth century with Frederick of Prussia and his collaborator Voltaire, Vattel maintained that even small states could update their institutions and practices and learn to participate in a balance of power that operated primarily through economic growth rather than territorial expansion. By exercising their federative powers judiciously, not only to form military alliances but also to enact commercial treaties, Vattel promised, such states could acquire the capacity to pursue their interests in a way that was compatible with the security and prosperity of other members of the European system—and participate in its global expansion.[32]

The tremendous popularity of Vattel's treatise on both sides of the Atlantic was linked to widespread hopes that the outcome of the American

30. Ibid., 76. See Nicholas Greenwood Onuf, "Civitas Maxima: Wolff, Vattel, and the Fate of Republicanism," *American Journal of International Law* 88, no. 2 (1994): 280–303; T. J. Hochstrasser, *Natural Law Theories in the Early Enlightenment* (Cambridge: Cambridge University Press, 2000), 179.

31. Szymanski, "Vattel as an Intermediary," 49–52. While in Warsaw, Vattel himself also wrote a pamphlet developing legal arguments against Russian interventions in the affairs of Courland. On Vattel and European colonialism, see especially Antony Anghie, "Vattel, Internal Colonialism, and the Rights of Indigenous Peoples," in *Freedom and Democracy in an Imperial Context: Dialogues with James Tully* (Abingdon: Routledge, 2014), 81–99; Jennifer Pitts, *Boundaries of the International: Law and Empire* (Cambridge, MA: Harvard University Press, 2018), chap. 3.

32. On Vattel's ideal of a balance of power, see Isaac Nakhimovsky, "Vattel's Theory of the International Order: Commerce and the Balance of Power in the Law of Nations," *History of European Ideas* 33 (2007): 157–73. On the arguments for consolidation advanced by Voltaire and Frederick of Prussia, see Isaac Nakhimovsky, "The Enlightened Prince and the Future of Europe: Voltaire and Frederick the Great's Anti-Machiavel of 1740," in *Commerce and Peace in the Enlightenment*, ed. Béla Kapossy, Isaac Nakhimovsky, and Richard Whatmore (Cambridge: Cambridge University Press, 2017), 44–77.

Revolution would secure the conditions for a political system generally operating in the fashion described by Vattel. However, the challenge to free trade posed by aggressive searches and seizures of "contraband" by belligerent powers (particularly Britain) and the persistent threat of interstate conflict over territory (among the newly independent American states as well as in central Europe) led to a new wave of critical engagement with Vattel's approach to the law of nations. Vattel's appeal to individual judgments of utility seemed too attenuated a basis for securing justice, let alone for addressing exceptional emergencies that threatened the existence of the "political system" itself. Vattel's treatise still expected states to recognize such "manifest violations" of the law of nations and to look beyond their own interests in taking individual responsibility for collective security. But in the absence of a *civitas maxima* or more robust conception of international community, some critics charged, the only remaining source of guidance for such judgments seemed to be existing treaty law serving as a de facto substitute for Wolff's legal fiction: and existing treaty law left ample room for significant restrictions on trade.[33] One response to this problem was to reassert some other version of a *civitas maxima*, as the famed Neapolitan political economist Ferdinando Galiani did in defending the League of Armed Neutrality of 1780: a Russian-initiated convention to protect neutral shipping from British searches and seizures that was imagined by many, such as the Connecticut minister Ezra Stiles, to represent the dawning of "a new chapter in the laws of nations."[34]

Instead of qualifying Vattel's emphasis on sovereignty by reasserting an idea of a *civitas maxima*, or relying on existing treaty law, another possibility was for one or more states to use their federative powers to legislate a new treaty system. Other states would then be inclined to join this system out of self-interest if it was better equipped to maintain collective security, arrive at a shared commercial policy enshrining free trade, and support collaborative expansion. This approach effectively displaced the

33. Isaac Nakhimovsky, "Carl Schmitt's Vattel and the 'Law of Nations' between Enlightenment and Revolution," *Grotiana* 31 (2010): 141–64.

34. Ezra Stiles, *The United States Elevated to Glory and Honor* (New Haven: Thomas & Samuel Green, 1783), 50. On Galiani, see Koen Stapelbroek, "Universal Society, Commerce and the Rights of Neutral Trade: Martin Hübner, Emer de Vattel and Ferdinando Galiani," in *Universalism in International Law and Political Philosophy*, ed. Petter Korkman and Virpi Mäkinen, Studies across Disciplines in the Humanities and Social Sciences 4 (Helsinki: Helsinki Collegium for Advanced Studies, 2008), 63–89. On the League of Armed Neutrality, see Isabel de Madariaga, *Britain, Russia, and the Armed Neutrality of 1780: Sir James Harris's Mission to St. Petersburg during the American Revolution* (London: Hollis & Carter, 1962).

problem of guiding the judgment of each state's federative power in exceptional circumstances to the internal constitution and capacities of the agent legislating the new system. The federal constitution negotiated in Philadelphia in 1787 could be construed in these terms, and part of the immediate and enduring controversy surrounding it had to do with whether the federal government it created represented a vindication or a betrayal of what Peter and Nicholas Onuf once called "Vattelian internationalism."[35] The legislation of a new code governing the external relations between independent states was also the approach embraced by Piattoli, Mazzei, and others linked to Condorcet and Jefferson in Paris in the 1780s.

In his 1788 supplement to Mazzei's *Researches on the United States*, Condorcet criticized the federal constitution negotiated in Philadelphia as an overreaction to the flaws of the 1777 Articles of Confederation: the new constitution's overly complex institutional design obscured accountability, inhibited coherent action, and invited abuse.[36] However, Condorcet was not just a defender of national sovereignty. He continued to assign a significant role to federative power, guided by public opinion in a way that retained a prominent international dimension. In his *Influence of the American Revolution on Europe* of 1786, which was also reprinted in Mazzei's work, Condorcet had envisaged the United States becoming both a model for Europe and an engine for the global diffusion of knowledge and prosperity. According to Condorcet, the United States provided an example of how, rather than limiting their sovereignty by erecting a supranational authority (as the Abbé de Saint-Pierre had proposed in his famous plan for a European Union), independent states could use their federative power to create a new legal code regulating their political and economic relations. At the same time, Condorcet imagined the United States, particularly if it

---

35. Onuf and Onuf, *Federal Union, Modern World*, 95–96, 101. In their assessment, it was ultimately a way of realizing Vattel's ideal via means that were "fundamentally antithetical" to Vattel's conception of the balance of power. For a historiographical overview, see Max M. Edling, "Peace Pact and Nation: An International Interpretation of the Constitution of the United States," *Past & Present* 240, no. 1 (2018): 267–303.

36. Filippo Mazzei, *Recherches historiques et politiques sur les États-Unis de l'Amérique Septentrionale: Où l'on traite des établissemens des treize colonies, de leurs rapports & de leurs dissentions avec la Grande-Bretagne, de leurs gouvernemens avant & après la révolution, &c*, vol. 4 (Paris: Froullé, 1788), 284–364. On Condorcet's authorship of the "Supplement" and for a translation, see Guillaume Ansart, *Condorcet: Writings on the United States* (University Park: Pennsylvania State University Press, 2012), http://muse.jhu.edu /book/14557. Condorcet's "Letters from a Freeman of New Haven to a Citizen of Virginia on the Futility of Dividing the Legislative Power among Several Bodies," which developed related theoretical arguments, also appeared in the first volume of Mazzei's work, though not in the English translation.

met the expectations of international opinion by abolishing slavery, becoming the core of a new treaty system that would expand by emancipating European colonies while also making it increasingly risky for any European power to continue resisting its demands for free trade.[37]

A similar approach to federative power was later elaborated by a close ally of Mazzei and Jefferson, the American poet, land speculator, and diplomat Joel Barlow. Barlow, who had moved to Paris in 1788, did not let his radical republican convictions stop him from expressing his admiration for the Polish Constitution in a 1792 letter to Stanisław August.[38] As chapter 3 described, Barlow later played a key role in realizing La Harpe's hopes of initiating a correspondence between Alexander and Jefferson. His long 1804 letter to Jefferson discussing the propriety of such a correspondence, and the prospect that it might issue in a future alliance to defend global free trade from European colonial powers, ended with a series of striking observations about the underappreciated importance of federalism. If the "Philosophers of Europe" really understood it, Barlow told Jefferson, they would not have lost their faith in progress; if Americans really understood it, they would no longer worry about the dissolution of their union or about the consequences of its expansion.[39] Barlow's remarks alluded to his extensive discussion of federalism in a letter addressed "to his fellow citizens of the United States," published in 1801; these in turn grew out of a 1799 proposal to the French government for a "Declaration of the Rights of Nations," which would enshrine the principle of free trade and position the United States and France (once the latter had recovered from the military exigencies of the revolutionary wars) as the core of a new global trading system.[40] The main target of Barlow's letter about federalism was the Duke of Rochefoucauld-Liancourt, another important associate of Condorcet and Jefferson in the 1780s, who

37. Mazzei, *Recherches historiques et politiques sur les États-Unis de l'Amérique Septentrionale*, 4:237–83.

38. Joel Barlow to Stanisław August Poniatowski, February 20, 1792, in Miecislaus Haiman, *The Fall of Poland in Contemporary American Opinion* (Chicago: Polish Roman Catholic Union of America, 1935), 59–62.

39. Joel Barlow to Thomas Jefferson, February 11, 1804, *The Papers of Thomas Jefferson, Volume 42: 16 November 1803 to 10 March 1804*, ed. James P. McClure (Princeton: Princeton University Press, 2016), 449.

40. *Joel Barlow to His Fellow Citizens of the United States, Letter II: On Certain Political Measures Proposed to Their Consideration* (Philadelphia: W. Duane, 1801), 51–70. Cf. Thomas Paine, *Pacte Maritime, adressée aux Nations neutres, Par un Neutre* (Paris: Imprimerie-Librairie du Cercle-Social, 1800). On the Franco-American trading system, see *Joel Barlow to His Fellow Citizens of the United States of America, Letter I: On the System of Policy Hitherto Pursued by Their Government* (Paris, 1799), 59.

had toured the United States in the 1790s.[41] According to Barlow, the intensity of French fears of disunity and civil war had led Liancourt to mistake "the federalizing of states" for the failure to achieve or maintain a nationally unified constitution. In fact, Barlow claimed, neither liberty nor peace was possible unless "the representative principle" and "the federal principle" were "united in one system, and kept inseparable in their practice." Without federalism, "representative democracy" would succumb to the fiscal and military pressures generated by international competition, ensuring that its history would merely become "the repetition of some indifferent chapter in the great history of despotism and war."[42] Without representation, the history of European federations showed that the interests of governments would diverge from those of their populations, exacerbating class conflict and ultimately leading to the reimposition or retrenchment of aristocracy. The future of civilization in Europe depended on the federalizing of the French Republic and its neighbors until they formed "the United States of Europe"; the future of civilization in America depended on the preservation of a federal union that new states forming through western expansion would still choose to join.[43] As chapter 5 will show, Barlow's claims about "the federal principle" were widely shared— including by liberals who came to see monarchy, rather than democracy, as the best foundation for "the representative principle."

Between 1803 and 1805, Czartoryski and Piattoli sought to theorize a comparable exertion of federative power from Saint Petersburg: one that was compatible with national autonomy and did not amount to an assertion of sovereignty over other sovereigns. In their effort to do so, Czartoryski and Piattoli gave expansive interpretations to two related roles often played by European states in international affairs: the mediator of a conflict and the guarantor of the settlement that resolved it. In addition to their prominence in discussions of the law of nations, both roles had a long history in the public law of the Holy Roman Empire. Mediation had

---

41. *Joel Barlow to His Fellow Citizens of the United States, Letter II*, 8–9; François-Alexandre-Frédéric de la Rochefoucauld-Liancourt, *Voyage dans les États-Unis d'Amérique, fait en 1795, 1796 et 1797*, vol. 7 (Paris: Chez Du Pont, 1799), 221–22, 231. On the French debate about federalism during the early 1790s, see Paul R. Hanson, *The Jacobin Republic under Fire: The Federalist Revolt in the French Revolution* (University Park: Pennsylvania State University Press, 2003).

42. *Joel Barlow to His Fellow Citizens of the United States, Letter II*, 10–11, 20. There was in fact no history of representative democracy without federation, Barlow maintained, because the British Empire had "answered some of the purposes of a federal union" among the North American colonies (19).

43. Ibid., 9.

long been a feature of the empire's legal culture, where arbitration panels or *Schiedsgerichte* served as an important method of conflict resolution.[44] *Médiation* was also the term for successive interventions by France and the Swiss Confederation to resolve constitutional conflicts within eighteenth-century Geneva: interventions echoed by Napoleon Bonaparte's 1803 "Act of Mediation," which resulted in a new constitution for Switzerland. The practice of international mediation to restore the constitutional balance of power in eighteenth-century Geneva had been discussed by prominent authorities on natural law and was even endorsed by Rousseau, who broke on this point with his fellow Genevan defenders of the principle of popular sovereignty.[45] As formalized by Pufendorf, who was followed in this respect by Vattel, mediation represented a more narrowly circumscribed legal basis for external intervention than Grotius's provision of an individual right to punish violations of natural law.[46] Pufendorf had further introduced a distinction between compulsory arbitration, which implied the assertion of a higher legal authority, and "friendly" mediation, which did not. Pufendorf spelled out a procedure by which a coalition of mediators intervening to resolve a conflict could impose their judgment on a belligerent without violating the legal equality of states:

> if it be the Interest of several to have the Quarrel made up, they may enter into Compact jointly to labour for Peace; and, if their Endeavours should prove unsuccessful, they may then mutually prescribe to one another how far each shall make himself a Party in the War. . . . Moreover, two or more, whom it concerns to have an End put to the War, after having weighed the Pretensions of each side, may lawfully agree upon what Terms a Peace ought to be concluded, and then offer them to the Parties with a Manifesto, that they will join forces against him that refuses them. For a Prince does not, by this means, obtrude his Arbitrage upon another against his Will: nor decides another's Quarrel by his own Authority, (both of which are Encroachments upon the Liberty of Nature).[47]

44. See Duncan Hardy, *Associative Political Culture in the Holy Roman Empire: Upper Germany, 1346–1521* (Oxford: Oxford University Press, 2018), chap. 2.

45. Whatmore, *Against War and Empire*, 45–48, 76–79.

46. On Grotius's doctrine and its legacies, see Richard Tuck, *The Rights of War and Peace: Political Thought and the International Order from Grotius to Kant* (Oxford: Oxford University Press, 1999); Gustaaf van Nifterik, "Grotius and the Origin of the Ruler's Right to Punish," *Grotiana* 26, no. 1 (2007): 396–415.

47. Samuel Pufendorf, *Of the Law of Nature and Nations: Eight Books*, ed. Jean Barbeyrac (London, 1729), 556 [5.7].

The role of guarantor had acquired special significance in the case of the Treaty of Westphalia of 1648 because that peace settlement also functioned as constitutional law for the Holy Roman Empire. "Westphalia" has long been associated with the emergence of a norm of non-intervention within a system of sovereign states, but this image has more to do with the eighteenth-century ideal articulated by Vattel than with the settlement negotiated in 1648.[48] In fact, the guarantee process envisioned by the French statesmen Richelieu and Mazarin, and negotiated in 1648, created a collective security mechanism: all parties to the treaties, including France and Sweden, were assigned the right and duty as guarantors to uphold all provisions of the settlement (including all the empire's subsequent treaties referring back to it).[49] The result was a legal process for international intervention to uphold the Imperial Constitution and protect minority rights, as both France and Sweden did in supporting a coalition of Protestant princes against the Habsburg emperor after 1658. As many commentators (including Vattel) worried, the wide scope for intervention created by the guarantee mechanism threatened to expose the internal politics of the empire to the external dynamics of great power rivalry and conflict over territory.[50] But it also carried the potential to confine international power struggles within legal limits (as Saint-Pierre and Rousseau had emphasized in their discussions of the empire's moderating effect on the European balance of power).[51] In the words of the pioneering historian Karl Otmar Freiherr von Aretin, the guarantor role was predicated on "a politics of peace and legality in the sense of the Imperial Constitution," which France had abandoned with Louis XIV's turn to "expansionistic

48. Jennifer Pitts, "Intervention and Sovereign Equality: Legacies of Vattel," in *Just and Unjust Military Intervention: European Thinkers from Vitoria to Mill*, ed. Stefano Recchia and Jennifer M. Walsh (Cambridge: Cambridge University Press, 2013), 143.

49. On the reassessment of the Treaty of Westphalia by historians of international law and of the Holy Roman Empire, see Patrick Milton, "Guarantee and Intervention: The Assessment of the Peace of Westphalia in International Law and Politics by Authors of Natural Law and of Public Law, c. 1650–1806," in *The Law of Nations and Natural Law, 1625–1800*, ed. Simone Zurbuchen (Leiden: Brill, 2019), 186–226; Patrick Milton, "The Mutual Guarantee of the Peace of Westphalia in the Law of Nations and Its Impact on European Diplomacy," *Journal of the History of International Law* 22 (2020): 101–25.

50. Vattel, *Law of Nations*, 396 [2.16].

51. Jean-Jacques Rousseau, *Extrait du projet de paix perpétuelle, de monsieur l'abbé de Saint-Pierre* (Amsterdam: Marc Michel Rey, 1761), 27–28; Peter Schröder, "The Holy Roman Empire as Model for Saint-Pierre's *Projet pour rendre la paix perpétuelle en Europe*," in *The Holy Roman Empire, 1495–1806: A European Perspective*, ed. R.J.W. Evans and Peter H. Wilson (Leiden: Brill, 2012), 35–50.

great power politics."[52] In the eighteenth century, France came to align itself with Prussia and the politics of consolidating the empire into larger states, with the striking exception of the Seven Years War, when France again exercised its constitutional role as guarantor (this time in concert with all the other guarantors, including the emperor) against Prussian aggression.[53]

When Empress Catherine II maneuvered Russia into becoming a guarantor of the Imperial Constitution in 1779, Aretin further claimed, she repeated the mistake of Louis XIV: she failed to understand that France had initially acquired great influence in the empire by supporting the smaller estates against the pretensions of the emperor. Instead of intervening to check both Austrian and Prussian expansionism, Catherine sought Austrian support for her own expansionist designs against the Ottoman Empire and was outmaneuvered by Frederick of Prussia, who repositioned himself as leader of the *Fürstenbund*: a 1785 league of princes that attracted the hopes of many *Reichspatrioten*, or patriotic reformers hoping to revive the Imperial Constitution. Had Aretin ventured a broader comparative perspective, he might have taken note of the clause in the United States Constitution of 1787 identifying "the United States" as guarantor of "every State in this Union."[54] The wording of this clause originated in efforts to resolve disputes between states over western land claims: the most important of these was the "treaty" of 1787 known as the Northwest Ordinance, whose provision for the creation of new states helped turn the territorial expansion of the United States into a collective enterprise.[55] By contrast, the final crisis of the Holy Roman Empire in the

---

52. Karl Otmar Freiherr von Aretin, "Russia as a Guarantor Power of the Imperial Constitution under Catherine II," *Journal of Modern History* 58 (1986): 160. For the full argument, see Karl Otmar Aretin, *Das Reich: Friedensgarantie und europäisches Gleichgewicht, 1648–1806* (Stuttgart: Klett-Cotta, 1986). For an assessment of Aretin's historiographical legacy, see Joachim Whaley, "Federal Habits: The Holy Roman Empire and the Continuity of German Federalism," in *German Federalism: Past, Present, Future*, ed. Maiken Umbach (New York: Palgrave, 2002), 15–41.

53. Milton, "The Mutual Guarantee of the Peace of Westphalia in the Law of Nations and Its Impact on European Diplomacy," 117–18.

54. U.S. Constitution, art. 4, sec. 4.

55. William M. Wiecek, *The Guarantee Clause of the U.S. Constitution* (Ithaca: Cornell University Press, 1972), 15–16. On the Northwest Ordinance as a "treaty," see Peter S. Onuf, *Statehood and Union: A History of the Northwest Ordinance*, Midwestern History and Culture (Bloomington: Indiana University Press, 1987), xviii. Curiously, the constitutional guarantee does not appear to have figured as a comparative subject in a discussion of German and American federalism to which Onuf contributed: Hermann Wellenreuther, Claudia Schnurmann, and Thomas Krueger, eds., *German and American Constitutional*

1790s was precipitated by Prussian and Austrian demands for additional territory as compensation for assuming responsibility for defending the empire from revolutionary France.[56] Had Aretin pursued his study of the guarantee beyond the demise of the empire in 1806, he might also have noted the importance of the concept for liberal constitutional theory, particularly between 1814 and 1830, and recognized the Holy Alliance as part of an attempt to reprise Russia's guarantor role on a grand scale. According to many liberals in the 1820s, this revival once again foundered along the lines identified by Aretin's argument: in their view, Alexander's failure to keep Austrian interests at arm's length had prevented him from positioning Russia as defender of the rights of smaller states, and from turning territorial expansion (supporting the Greek uprising against the Ottoman Empire) into a collective European enterprise.

The closest predecessor of the proposals developed by Czartoryski and Piattoli in Saint Petersburg, which links them to earlier discussions of federalism and the law of nations, was a 1795 work that has been attributed to Piattoli: *Epistle of the Old Cosmopolitan Sirach to the National Convention of France.*[57] Previously, Piattoli had worked closely with Stanisław

---

Thought: Contexts, Interaction, and Historical Realities (New York: St. Martin's Press, 1989).

56. Joachim Whaley, *Germany and the Holy Roman Empire, Volume 2: The Peace of Westphalia to the Dissolution of the Reich, 1648–1806* (Oxford: Oxford University Press, 2012), 570–71.

57. Scipione Piattoli, *Épitre du vieux cosmopolite Syrach à la convention nationale de France* (Sarmatie, 1795), https://mdz-nbn-resolving.de/urn:nbn:de:bvb:12-bsb10421716-6. For the attribution to Piattoli, see Emil Weller, *Lexicon pseudonymorum: Wörterbuch der Pseudonymen aller Zeiter und Völker,* 2nd ed. (Regensburg: Alfred Coppenrath, 1886), 546. German and Polish translations of the text also appeared, as did several other texts that also assumed the identity of Sirach to deliver a related message to a German audience, lamenting Poland's betrayal by Prussia and calling for imperial unity: *Des alten Weltbürgers Syrach christliches Kirchengebet, welches in allen Kirchen des deutschen Reichs feierlich verlesen werden sollte* (Germanien, 1795), https://nbn-resolving.org/urn:nbn:de:bvb:29-bv003567929-7; *Weltbürger Sirach der Sohn an Deutschlands Reichsversammlung: Aus dem Französischen* (Sarmatien, 1795), https://mdz-nbn-resolving.de/urn:nbn:de:bvb:12-bsb10561381-0; *Wahrheit und Licht: Teutschlands Völkern zur Beherzigung ihren Fürsten zur Warnung. Noch ein Wort vom Weltbürger Syrach,* 1795, https://mdz-nbn-resolving.de/urn:nbn:de:bvb:12-bsb10017619-8. The contents of the *Epistle* are compatible with the thought of Piattoli and his connections as well as with his circumstances in 1795, though I am unaware of external evidence of his authorship; however, there does not appear to be any internal or external evidence to support the suggestion that the German version of the text, which was also published in 1795 and announced itself as a translation from the French, was in fact the original, and that the translator identified by Weller (a disgraced Prussian official named Karl Georg Gottfried Glave) was in fact the author. For this suggestion, but also an overview of the various attributions, see Catalog 62 of the Zisska &

August on saving Poland by negotiating a variety of federative schemes involving Prussia.[58] In 1795, Piattoli was in Austrian custody; the *Epistle* was a desperate call for another joint Austro-French intervention that would forestall the final partition of Poland by Prussia and Russia, and introduce a new European treaty system. The best known and most profound analysis of such federative action at this particular juncture was the 1795 essay *On Perpetual Peace* by the Prussian philosopher Immanuel Kant, which also theorized the legislation of a new treaty system. *On Perpetual Peace* was initially read as an endorsement of Prussia's recently concluded separate peace with revolutionary France. At the same time, however, it radically restricted the state's federative power far more than Vattel (whom Kant famously dismissed, together with his predecessors, as a "sorry comforter" whose legal formulas merely served to justify "military aggression"): Kant's target was interventionism of both the revolutionary and counterrevolutionary varieties.[59] In a supplement to his essay (which was formatted as a draft treaty) Kant elaborated that the real "guarantee" of a new treaty system would not be exercised by any particular state or states but by nature itself, acting through a historical process "even against their will and indeed by means of their very discord."[60]

By contrast to Kant's essay, the *Epistle of the Old Cosmopolitan Sirach* called for far-reaching French intervention against Prussia. Appearing in German and Polish as well as French, the *Epistle* was framed as a cosmopolitan corrective to the French government's calculations of its national interest.[61] The *Epistle* endorsed French assessments of the threat that England posed to the economic liberty of the *"Cosmofédération Européen"* but insisted that the looming partition of Germany—foretold by Russia's abuse of its guarantor status and Prussia's betrayal of Poland—represented an even graver threat to collective security. Underlying this argument was an indictment of the approach to "the European law of nations" taken by

---

Schauer Buch- und Kunstauktionshaus (November 6–8, 2013), pt. 2, 196–97, https://issuu .com/schauer/docs/katalog_62_web_t2.

58. Among these schemes was a remarkable bid by Stanisław August to assume the patronage of the Berlin Academy, which (in the spirit of Leibniz) would in turn be transformed into a unifying institution of technocratic governance for a wider federal union. See Fabre, *Stanislas-Auguste Poniatowski et l'Europe des lumières*, 385, 414.

59. Immanuel Kant, "Perpetual Peace: A Philosophical Sketch," in *Political Writings*, ed. Hans Reiss, trans. H. B. Nisbet (Cambridge: Cambridge University Press, 1991), 103.

60. Ibid., 102.

61. On eighteenth-century literary strategies for inventing cosmopolitan identities, see Sophia Rosenfeld, "Citizens of Nowhere in Particular: Cosmopolitanism, Writing, and Political Engagement in Eighteenth-Century Europe," *National Identities* 4, no. 1 (2002): 25–43.

Vattel, which had failed to define clear limits on the federative powers of states.[62] In its place, the *Epistle* called for the legislation of new constitutions for Germany, Poland, and Italy, as well as a new "general constitution of Europe," which would secure territorial integrity and free trade. It would also forbid military alliances with non-European powers (including Russia) and fix the territorial limits of large states (whereas small states would retain the right to federate with one another). All this legislation would proceed under the guidance of a new comprehensive science of politics, to be called "*Kratosophie*," which the Americans had been the first to practice and which the French were now in a position to develop.[63]

The plans developed by Czartoryski and Piattoli in Saint Petersburg in 1803–5 also proposed the legislation of a new law of nations for Europe: not as a response to the threat posed by Russian power, as the *Epistle* had argued in 1795, but rather to enlist Russian power in service of collective security and national autonomy. By interposing itself as mediator between France and Britain, Russia would bring about a general peace settlement and a transition from what Aretin called "expansionistic great power politics" to "a politics of peace and legality."[64] These plans appeared in the context of a Russian foreign policy debate at the outset of Alexander's reign: Czartoryski and his associates argued for "active" engagement in European politics as opposed to a "passive" detachment that would allow the new emperor to devote himself entirely to internal development.[65] They were also part of a wider debate about how a new treaty system could prevent all political and economic relations between states from becoming implicated in the great power rivalry between Britain and France. Kant's radically restrictive approach to federative power was the most philosophically systematic treatment of the "passive" option, but as his follower Johann Gottlieb Fichte soon pointed out, this path presumed the radical expansion of the state's capacity to intervene effectively in economic life in order to secure a high degree of economic independence.[66] The premise of Czartoryski's draft memorandum of 1803, "On the political system Russia ought to follow," was that Russia

62. Piattoli, *Épitre du vieux cosmopolite Syrach à la convention nationale de France*, 116, 142.

63. Ibid., 16.

64. Aretin, "Russia as a Guarantor Power," 160.

65. Grimsted, "Czartoryski's System for Russian Foreign Policy," 27.

66. Isaac Nakhimovsky, *The Closed Commercial State: Perpetual Peace and Commercial Society from Rousseau to Fichte* (Princeton: Princeton University Press, 2011).

was far too big to remain a "passive" participant in either a British- or French-dominated trading system without becoming the object of contestation among foreign interests.[67]

Czartoryski and Piattoli ventured various assessments of the political conjunctures in which either Britain or France might be persuaded or compelled to collaborate in introducing a new federal system—one that restrained both of their respective ambitions for continental or maritime dominance while also restraining Prussian and Austrian expansionism. They envisaged a new legal order based on the principles of free trade and nationality (Czartoryski, who had met the German philosopher Johann Gottfried Herder in the 1780s, understood nations to be natural communities formed by ties of language and culture, as distinct from the regimes whose machinations drew them into political conflict).[68] France would remain the core of a new federal system in western Europe; Russia would organize what Czartoryski called "a union of Slavic peoples" (tactfully remaining ambiguous about whether Russia would incorporate Poland and the Balkans into an expanded empire, or whether this Slavic union would take a more confederal form); and Germany and Italy would become federal states as well, independent of both Prussia and Austria.[69] Meanwhile the restoration of a maritime balance of power and the commitment to free trade would ensure that all of Europe could participate in expanding trade with the Americas, opening new markets across the Black and Caspian seas, and undertaking the collective European colonization of the Mediterranean, Asia, and Africa.

Where the proposals diverged was in their conceptions of mediation and over whether or how Russian intervention had to appeal to a form of *civitas maxima* or an ideal of international community. Czartoryski's 1803 draft memorandum, which made no such appeal, remained closest in spirit to Vattel: it already shows how Czartoryski and others could later regard the Holy Alliance as a development of "Vattelian internationalism" gone awry, rather than a repudiation of its principles. Czartoryski's Europe was not a political community but merely an "agglomeration of states" whose regular and intensive communication over a long period had equipped

67. Czartoryski, "Sur le Système politique," 52.

68. Czartoryski, *Mémoires*, 1:31. On Czartoryski's interest in and familiarity with Slavic cultural studies, see W. H. Zawadzki, "Adam Czartoryski: An Advocate of Slavonic Solidarity at the Congress of Vienna," *Oxford Slavonic Papers* 10 (1977): 73–97.

69. Czartoryski, "Sur le Système politique," 84–85.

them to identify their interests with "the general good of nations": this was the core principle of "the science of true external politics."[70] Russia's intervention in Europe would be guided in this way, by the pursuit of Russia's "true interest." This alignment between utility and justice would become increasingly strong as European states acquired increasingly "liberal" governments capable of maintaining a balance of power through the internal development of their fundamental capacities.[71] They would do so, Czartoryski claimed, partly by developing national institutions of government, education, and industry, but also by participating in international networks: the guidance of international public opinion, shaped by the overarching process of the economic and cultural development of European "civilization," would, over the long run, help correct temporary fluctuations in national opinion and government policy like the one which had recently disfigured the external conduct of the French Republic.[72]

A contrasting approach to mediation was elaborated in the report submitted to Czartoryski in 1804 by Vasilii Federovich Malinovskii, a Russian civil servant best known for later serving as the first director of the school whose initial pupils included the poet Alexander Pushkin. Like Czartoryski's memorandum, Malinovskii's report also originated in the thoughts of a sleepless night fifteen years earlier. Malinovskii had been appointed to the Russian embassy in London in 1789, where he (like Czartoryski) attended the trial of Warren Hastings, the impeached governor-general of Bengal. One night that August he began writing an essay on perpetual peace by candlelight in Richmond (outside London), which he eventually finished in Saint Petersburg in 1803.[73] What began as a sweeping moral condemnation of war expanded into a formal plan for legislating a new law of nations. Like Czartoryski, Malinovskii cast Russia as founder of a new fed-

70. Ibid., 49, 43.

71. Ibid., 41.

72. Ibid., 44–46.

73. Paola Ferretti, *A Russian Advocate of Peace: Vasilii Malinovskii (1765–1814)* (Dordrecht: Kluwer, 1998). The first two parts of Malinovskii's report appear in Vasilii Federovich Malinovskii, "Rassuzhdenie o mire i voine," in *Izbrannye obshchestvenno-politicheskie sochineniia,* ed. A. P. Belik (Moskva: Izdatel'stvo Akademii Nauk SSSR, 1958), 41–93. The third part was discovered by Jerzy Skowronek and published separately by him in "Rozważania o pokoju i wojnie Wasyla F. Malinowskiego," *Teki archiwalne* 4 (1978): 23–57. In 1859, extracts of Malinovskii's report were read to the London Peace Society and subsequently published in the *Herald of Peace,* the publication of the American Peace Society: see William E. Butler, "Law and Peace in Prerevolutionary Russia: The Case of V. F. Malinovskii," in *The Weightier Matters of the Law: Essays on Law and Religion,* ed. John Witte Jr. and Frank S. Alexander (Atlanta: Scholars Press, 1988), 167.

eral system in which a union of the linguistically defined "Slavo-Russian nation" would emerge alongside new Italian and German federations, all participating in a collaborative colonial mission. Malinovskii's model for such a union was the incorporation of Scotland and (most recently, with the union of 1801) Ireland into Great Britain, though he also noted that this was a model that "can and should be corrected."[74] Unlike Czartoryski, however, Malinovskii was critical of Vattel's attenuated account of justice, which he rejected in favor of a new "general law of nations" that reasserted a conception of a *civitas maxima*.[75] Malinovskii defined Europe in mystical terms as a Christian community, a union grounded in a "holy pledge of truth."[76] On this basis, the new European constitution described by Malinovskii provided for the creation of a central federal authority: a council that would serve as the final arbiter of disputes among the pan-national federations while safeguarding their autonomy.

Unlike Malinovskii's report, the elaborate 1805 manuscript by Piattoli did not appeal to a *civitas maxima*. Unlike Czartoryski's 1803 draft, however, Piattoli's draft explicitly called for the Russian mediator to act directly in the service of collective security: it would be playing the "most beautiful role" in politics by acting as the head of a general coalition, intervening as a mediator in exceptional circumstances.[77] Russia would play this role in three stages: these recall Pufendorf's procedure while also showing how liberals could later experience the proclamation of the Holy Alliance as resuming a recognizable process that had begun with Alexander's march across Europe toward Paris and continued with the Congress of Vienna before being interrupted by Napoleon's escape from exile. First, Piattoli explained, Russia would organize "The Grand Alliance of Mediation for the Pacification of Europe" that would be assembled through bilateral treaties. The alliance would then be proclaimed through manifestos addressed to the Russian nation, in every allied capital, and before

---

74. Skowronek, "Rozważania o pokoju i wojnie," 38–39. Revealingly, perhaps, Malinovskii also worked on a translation of Alexander Hamilton's 1791 "Report on the Subject of Manufactures"—a blueprint for consolidation as opposed to federation from Jefferson's perspective—though it was not published until 1807. See Ferretti, *A Russian Advocate of Peace*, 173. On the significant resonance of Ireland's relationship to England in European political thought, see Whatmore, *Terrorists, Anarchists, and Republicans*; James Stafford, *The Case of Ireland: Commerce, Empire and the European Order, 1750–1848* (Cambridge: Cambridge University Press, 2022).

75. Malinovskii, "Rassuzhdenie o mire i voine," 74; Skowronek, "Rozważania o pokoju i wojnie," 44–48.

76. Malinovskii, "Rassuzhdenie o mire i voine," 79.

77. Piattoli, "Memoire," 221–22.

the allied armies.[78] Though it might seem like a metaphysical subtlety to distinguish between an impartial alliance of mediation and a coalition against Napoleon, Piattoli claimed, establishing confidence in the impartiality of the mediators was crucial in order to avoid antagonizing "French national *amour-propre*": rather than provoking a struggle between rival nationalisms, the goal was to delegitimize the "ambitious and insatiable" French cabinet in the eyes of "its own nation."[79]

The second stage of Piattoli's process would be to convene a postwar congress that would settle all territorial disputes, after which the mediating allies would guarantee the security and territorial integrity of all European states and create a collaborative framework for colonial expansion (including deciding which deposed French dynasty would rule a colonized Egypt). The congress would also create independent German and Italian federal states alongside an expanded Switzerland and possibly an Iberian federation as well. These federal states, whose constitutions and fundamental laws would be fixed by the congress, would follow the American and Swiss examples in providing for collective security through a common foreign policy, but otherwise prioritizing local autonomy. The contours and constitution of the Italian state would depend on the course of the mediation, but it was clear that a form of the practice of "general mediation" would remain a permanent and recurring part of Piattoli's "new federal system." In Germany and Italy, federal bodies would serve as guarantors of smaller principalities and republics; these would rely in turn on the "great federal system of Europe" as the ultimate guarantor of their internal constitutions.[80] Finally, after the conclusion of the congress, which was to be kept short and focused, the last stage of the process envisioned by Piattoli involved the codification of a new law of nations. Piattoli suggested that Alexander invite the most celebrated jurists of Europe (or even all writers "without distinction") to submit proposed codes of international and maritime law in tune with "the philanthropy of our age" in their provisions for disarmament, the protection of trade, and the limits of international intervention and mediation. All individual European states would then be invited to ratify the new codes.[81]

Some of the key elements of Czartoryski's and Piattoli's drafts were reflected in the diplomatic instructions prepared for Count Nikolai Nikolaevich Novosiltsev, the Russian statesman who had also participated in

78. Ibid., 242.
79. Ibid., 262–63, 266.
80. Ibid., 259.
81. Ibid., 261.

the "unofficial committee" and who was sent to negotiate an alliance with the British government in 1804. The instructions specified that the alliance would have to be premised on reclaiming the moral high ground from France, on persuading Europe that the allies were not fighting against France or to restore the old regime but rather to "secure liberty founded on its true principles."[82] This meant that peoples had to be protected from the passions and ambitions of their governors. It also meant that relations between European governments had to be regulated by "a new code of the law of nations," ratified by a majority of states, which would address the right to free trade and the limits of international intervention. Most governments, the instructions predicted, especially those of smaller states, would be eager to join "a league that would guarantee their peace and security to the highest degree."[83] This new system, in which Russia and Great Britain would exercise "a certain degree of preponderance" as "the two protective powers" best positioned to identify their interests with the collective security, would finally achieve the general peace that the Treaty of Westphalia had been intended to create.[84] The British response acknowledged that the ultimate goal of the alliance would be "to form at the restoration of the peace, a general agreement and guarantee for the mutual protection and security of different Powers, and for re-establishing a general system of public law in Europe."[85] In the twentieth century, this response became the subject of much controversy among British diplomatic historians, who debated whether or not it amounted to a precedent for the eclipse of national sovereignty under the League of Nations as the successor to the Holy Alliance.[86] By contrast, Czartoryski

82. Alexander I to N. N. Novosiltsev, September 11/23, 1804, in *Vneshniaia politika Rossii XIX i nachala XX veka: Dokumenty rossiiskogo Ministerstva inostrannykh del*, vol. 2, ser. 1 (Moskva: Gosudarstvennoe Izdatel'stvo Politicheskoi Literatury, 1961), 141.

83. *Vneshniaia politika Rossii*, 2:142.

84. Ibid., 2:141, 2:144.

85. "Official Communication made to the Russian Ambassador at London, on the 19th January, 1805, explanatory of the views which His Majesty and the Emperor of Russia formed for the deliverance and security of Europe," in Charles K. Webster, *British Diplomacy, 1813–1815: Select Documents Dealing with the Reconstruction of Europe* (London: G. Bell and Sons, 1921), 390.

86. J.A.R. Marriott, *The European Commonwealth: Problems Historical and Diplomatic* (Oxford: Clarendon Press, 1918), 339–43; Walter Alison Phillips, *The Confederation of Europe: A Study of the European Alliance, 1813-1823, as an Experiment in the International Organization of Peace*, 2nd ed. (London: Longmans, Green and Co., 1920), 41–42; H.W.V. Temperley and Charles K. Webster, *The Congress of Vienna 1814-15, and the Conference of Paris, 1919*, Papers Read at the Fifth International Congress of Historical Sciences, Brussels, 1923, Historical Association Leaflet no. 56 (London, 1923).

later complained in his memoirs that Novosiltsev had failed to make the alliance conditional on Britain's acceptance of maritime equality (though this assessment was surely colored by Czartoryski's bitter battles with Novosiltsev in Russian-ruled Poland after 1815).[87]

The mediation plans associated with Czartoryski were shelved after the coalition's disastrous defeat to Napoleon at Austerlitz in 1805, which was followed by Prussia's military collapse in 1806. In 1807, it was Napoleon, not Alexander, who presided over the reestablishment of a Polish state under a new constitution, in the form of the Duchy of Warsaw. Though Piattoli promised Czartoryski that he would continue working on a new code of maritime law from Courland, the peace treaties signed that year at Tilsit also marked the defeat of another ambition: namely, Piattoli's efforts to arrange Czartoryski's marriage to his other favorite pupil, Dorothea von Biron, Princess of Courland.[88] After Alexander as well as Czartoryski had appeared in Courland on the way to Tilsit, it became clear that the match did not suit Alexander's new pro-French foreign policy. The princess was not easily dissuaded, and it was only after she had pursued Piattoli to a nearby village, where he lay dying, that she acquiesced to the match Alexander had arranged with her mother, to the nephew of the French statesman Charles-Maurice de Talleyrand.[89] Like her half sister Wilhelmina, Dorothea went on to become a prominent and influential participant in the diplomatic negotiations at the Congress of Vienna. In 1814, Wilhelmina confided her hatred of "all liberal ideas" to her lover, the Austrian statesman Clemens von Metternich; by contrast, Dorothea went on to become the lifelong companion and collaborator of the elder Talleyrand.[90] In March 1814, as his army entered Paris, Alexander issued a proclamation declaring that the allies "will recognize and guarantee the Constitution that the French nation gives itself"; Talleyrand, as president of the French Senate, set about drafting one.[91] A year later, despite

87. Czartoryski, *Mémoires*, 1:377.

88. Many of Piattoli's papers dealing with the law of nations and maritime law are now held in the Polish Academy in Rome: http://piattoli-archive.eu. Some of them were collected by Piattoli's biographer Alessandro d'Ancona: *Scipione Piattoli e la Polonia: Con un'appendice di documenti* (Firenze: Barbèra, 1915).

89. Dorothée de Courlande, *Souvenirs et chronique de la duchesse de Dino, nièce aimée de Talleyrand*, ed. Anne Theis and Laurent Theis (Paris: Robert Laffont, 2016), 35–60.

90. Wilhelmina von Sagan to Clemens von Metternich, April 14, 1814, cited in Glenda Sluga, *The Invention of International Order: Remaking Europe after Napoleon* (Princeton: Princeton University Press, 2021), 63.

91. Pierre Rosanvallon, *La monarchie impossible: Les Chartes de 1814 et de 1830* (Paris: Fayard, 1994), 16.

the challenges resulting from Napoleon's return from exile, Talleyrand sought to reassert a European consensus that the postwar settlement would have to involve international guarantees for liberal constitutions elsewhere in Europe too, not a restoration of the old regime: "I have not seen any Sovereign or minister, who, frightened by the potential consequences for Spain of the system of government followed by Ferdinand VII, did not bitterly regret that he was restored to his throne without Europe imposing on him the condition of giving his states institutions in harmony with the ideas of the times."[92]

Though Czartoryski's collaborations with Piattoli had come to an end in 1805, after 1814 he would again attempt to orchestrate a liberal constitution for a reunified Poland under Russian rule, through an international process like the one described by Talleyrand. At the Congress of Vienna, Czartoryski again sought to position Alexander as the defender of nationalities (particularly Slavic ones) who could count on international (particularly British) public opinion to help corral the cabinets of Europe; and he held out the prospect of Poland serving as both a model for Russia's future and an engine of its transformation into a federal constitutional state. Negotiations over Poland's future became particularly fraught as Alexander struggled to reconcile Polish expectations of a reversal of the eighteenth-century partitions with Russian hostility to such concessions and his wartime allies' fears of any further Russian expansion. Napoleon's return from exile in March 1815 forced a speedy resolution to the negotiations. In May 1815, Alexander was named king of Poland—the former Napoleonic Duchy of Warsaw was now linked by treaty to the Russian Empire—but vague references to Polish interests and free trade took the place of international guarantees of its constitution and reunification of its territory. The "Foundations of the Constitution of the Kingdom of Poland" that Alexander announced in May and the constitution that he promulgated that November still drew on Czartoryski's blueprints, and in an 1818 address to the Polish diet widely cited in Germany, Alexander still described it as a model for Russia's future. At the same time, even Czartoryski's hope of an international Polish customs union (resembling the international arrangements made in 1815 for governing the Rhine) proved beyond reach; and most ominously, the military (the destination of

92. Charles-Maurice de Talleyrand, "Rapport fait au Roi pendant son voyage de Gand à Paris (June 1815)," cited in Markus J. Prutsch, "'Monarchical Constitutionalism' in Post-Napoleonic Europe: Concept and Practice," in *Constitutionalism, Legitimacy, and Power: Nineteenth-Century Experiences*, ed. Kelly Grotke and Markus J. Prutsch (Oxford: Oxford University Press, 2014), 69.

half the state's revenue) wound up entirely outside constitutional control, under the command of Alexander's brother Constantine. Nonetheless, Czartoryski would continue to pursue his goals within the constitutional framework that emerged in 1815 until the revolution of 1830.

Why Not Mr. Bentham?

In 1806, the Prussian writer and civil servant Friedrich Gentz drew an emphatic contrast between two kinds of federalism. According to Gentz, who later entered the Austrian service and was secretary-general of the Congress of Vienna, talk of legislating a new federal constitution for Europe represented the demise of federative politics at the hands of Napoleon.

> Shall that which in the corrupted dialect of the present time, and in the disgusting gibberish of the press, is called "THE NEW FEDERAL SYSTEM," take the place of the remains of that glorious edifice which our fathers reared, the old magnificent constitution of Europe, THE TRUE FEDERAL SYSTEM? Shall all, which with so much art divided, and with so much skill united the nations, be confounded by a decree of general servitude, and sink into a common grave, where its spirit will never revive?[93]

Gentz's concerns were widely shared in Britain; they were also shared in New England, where Massachusetts congressman Fisher Ames charged in 1805 that the "Virginian nobles" were imposing "a new Roman yoke" on the smaller states of America—if not, like the ancient Thebans, weakening the Amphictyonic League they would soon need to defend them from a new Philip of Macedon.[94] Gentz's contrast between confederation and consolidation fit into a broader British rehabilitation of Vattel. In the 1790s, Edmund Burke (whom Gentz had translated into German) was among those who had become critical of Vattel: he had found Vattel's conception of international community too attenuated to justify continued intervention aiming at regime change in France.[95] A few years later,

93. Friedrich von Gentz, *Fragments upon the Balance of Power in Europe* (London: M. Peltier, 1806), xiii. Gentz's work was published in German in Saint Petersburg and in English in London.

94. Fisher Ames, "The Dangers of American Liberty" (1805) in *Works of Fisher Ames* (Boston: T. B. Wait, 1809), 385–87, 410, 406. On Ames and Bostonian perspectives on federalism, see Mark A. Peterson, *The City-State of Boston: The Rise and Fall of an Atlantic Power, 1630–1865* (Princeton: Princeton University Press, 2019), 379–443.

95. David Armitage, "Edmund Burke and Reason of State," *Journal of the History of Ideas* 61, no. 4 (2000): 617–34; Iain Hampsher-Monk, "Edmund Burke's Changing Justification for Intervention," *The Historical Journal* 48, no. 1 (2005): 65–100.

in the face of the threat now posed by French interventions and French-imposed regime change, Vattel's reputation had revived. In Gentz's hands, Vattel's ideal for the future of Europe was transposed into an elegy for its destroyed "ancient constitution."[96] In the 1820s, Gentz's polemic against Napoleon was redeployed against the Holy Alliance by several prominent British and American writers. Among them was John Quincy Adams, who had met Gentz while stationed in Berlin between 1797 and 1801, and who had admiringly reviewed another of his books attacking French views of international relations.[97] However, this enduringly influential Anglo-American rendering of the Holy Alliance cannot account for the claims about sovereignty, the balance of power, and constitutional change developed in Czartoryski's draft memorandum of 1803: claims that also derived from Vattel's approach to the law of nations and that Czartoryski later reasserted in systematic form (and applied to the Holy Alliance) in his *Essay on Diplomacy*.

Alongside the categorical declarations of federalism's demise produced by Gentz and Ames in 1805–6, a variety of other views continued to accompany changing perceptions of the political landscape in the early nineteenth century. In Germany, the initial ambiguity of Napoleon's intentions produced a wide range of claims about the future of federative politics.[98] For a time, Napoleon's concerted appeals to imperial tradition led some German patriots to claim that French intervention might help restore the Imperial Constitution: as the historian Niklas Vogt wrote in 1805, "As guarantor of the Peace of Westphalia and the Peace of Lunéville, he will maintain the balance of power in the German Empire, which alone

96. The rehabilitation of Vattel was particularly striking in the case of the English lawyer Robert Ward: see Nakhimovsky, "Carl Schmitt's Vattel and the 'Law of Nations' between Enlightenment and Revolution," 161–62. On the evolution of Vattel's treatise into an Anglophile perspective on the law of nations, and its association with Britain's claim to serve as the protector of small states, see Koen Stapelbroek, "The Foundations of Vattel's 'System' of Politics and the Context of the Seven Years' War: Moral Philosophy, Luxury and the Constitutional Commercial State," in *The Legacy of Vattel's Droit Des Gens: Contexts, Concepts, Reception, Translation and Diffusion*, ed. Koen Stapelbroek and Antonio Trampus (Cham: Palgrave Macmillan, 2019), 95–133.

97. On Gentz and Adams, see Alexander von Hase, "John Quincy Adams als Kritiker von Hauterive und Gentz (1801): Ein amerikanischer Beitrag zu einem europäischen Gespräch," *Historische Zeitschrift* 215, no. 1 (1972): 33–48.

98. Matthias Pape, "Revolution und Reichsverfassung: Die Verfassungsdiskussion zwischen Fürstenbund und Rheinbund," in *Verfassung und Revolution: Hegels Verfassungskonzeption und die Revolutionen der Neuzeit*, ed. Elisabeth Weisser-Lohmann and Dietmar Köhler (Hamburg: Felix Meiner, 2000), 40; Whaley, *Germany and the Holy Roman Empire, Volume 2*, 617.

can save its ruined Constitution."[99] In a similar spirit, Duke Carl August of Weimer looked to Russian influence, hoping that Alexander's dynastic connections in Germany might impel him to champion a new *Fürstenbund* that would save the constitution from Austria, Prussia, and France.[100] For others, however, the role Napoleon seemed poised to play in shaping the federal future of Germany was not savior of the Imperial Constitution but the catalyst for radical constitutional change—the position that so alarmed Gentz. One remarkable statement of this last position took the form of a learned study of Thucydides and ancient federalism, published in 1809 by the German professor August Ernst Zinserling.[101] Zinserling, who took his epigraph from Condorcet's *Sketch for a Historical Picture of the Progress of the Human Mind*, drew a distinction between "federative government" (*gouvernement fédératif*) and the form of government produced by "federative politics" (*politique fédérative*). The former was a democracy of states, a collective security arrangement that (like all democracies) invariably degenerated into a competitive struggle for supremacy among its members, some of whom would eventually enlist outside powers as allies. This had been the fate of ancient federations like the Achaean or Amphictyonic League, and Zinserling did not expect the United States of America to escape the same fate. "Federative politics," by contrast, was a strategy for securing the allegiance of dependent smaller states: rather than incorporating them by extending sovereignty over them, it involved granting them generous terms of alliance and taking responsibility for collective security while respecting their internal autonomy. Invented out of necessity by city-states in the ancient Mediterranean, it was long neglected by European regimes more inclined to pursue expansion through incorporation; revived by the French Revolution, it had been modernized and systematized by Napoleon, as his magnanimous treatment of his southern German and northern Italian allies showed. From this perspective, the

99. Niklas Vogt, "Künftige Reise des Pabstes zu Napoleon nach Paris den 20. Brumaire d.J.," *Europäische Staats-Relationen* 3 (1805): 75, cited in Pape, "Revolution und Reichsverfassung," 63.

100. Pape, "Revolution und Reichsverfassung," 75; Whaley, *Germany and the Holy Roman Empire, Volume 2*, 617.

101. August Ernst Zinserling, *Le système fédératif des anciens mis en parallèle avec celui des modernes* (Heidelberg: Engelmann, 1809). Other contemporary discussions of a new federal constitutional order in Europe from a Napoleonic perspective include Joseph Jean Baptiste Gondon, *Du droit public et du droit des gens, ou, Principes d'association civile et politique; suivis d'un projet de paix générale et perpétuelle*, 3 vols. (Paris: Brasseur, 1808); Johann Christoph Aretin, *Ueber die gegner der grossen Plane Napoleon's: Besonders in Teutschland und Oesterreich* (Strassburg, 1809).

constitutional future of small states depended on the will of the federating agent, and the Rhineland was fortunate, Zinserling concluded, that its future would be shaped by such a virtuoso of "federative politics."

Unlike Zinserling, but also unlike Gentz, Czartoryski continued to identify the more expansive exercise of federative power as a strategy for realizing a constitutional order that was neither reductively voluntaristic nor bounded by historic rights and privileges. Czartoryski saw the legislation of principles of representative government, in the spirit of the American and French Revolutions (and the Polish Constitution of 1791), as the indispensable foundation for the progress of "civilization." After Piattoli, Czartoryski's most important ally and guide in charting this strategy was Bentham. In the British context, the contrasting approaches to federative politics articulated by Gentz and Czartoryski (to whom, in fact, Gentz personally appealed for support in the wake of Prussia's military collapse in 1806) were associated with very different positions on the political spectrum.[102] Gentz, in addition to having translated Burke, was supported financially by the government of William Pitt; Bentham, who became Czartoryski's ally in his long-running efforts to secure the constitutional future of Poland, was a particularly fierce critic of Pitt. In the 1820s, Bentham offered his expertise in codifying laws to "all Nations Professing Liberal Opinions" and came to acquire a global reputation as "legislator of the world"—a title famously bestowed on him by the statesman José del Valle.[103] Bentham was well positioned to become a prominent advocate for the propagation of liberal constitutions and representative institutions: he was more skeptical of justifications of colonialism based on claims of European superiority than his follower James Mill, while also remaining more committed to a universal standard for international law than his follower John Austin.[104] Bentham's efforts to serve as "legislator

102. Friedrich Gentz to Adam Jerzy Czartoryski, December 29, 1806, Czartoryski Library 5534 III, 73–79, http://gentz-digital.ub.uni-koeln.de/portal/databases/id/gentzdigital/titles/id/3115.html?l=de.

103. José Cecilio del Valle to Jeremy Bentham, May 21, 1826, in *The Correspondence of Jeremy Bentham, Vol. 12: July 1824 to June 1828*, ed. Luke O'Sullivan and Catherine Fuller, Collected Works of Jeremy Bentham (London: Athlone Press, 1968), 217–18, http://dx.doi.org/10.1093/actrade/9780199278305.book.1. The letter was subsequently published by Bentham in a supplement to his *Codification Proposal Addressed to All Nations Professing Liberal Opinions*: see Jeremy Bentham, *"Legislator of the World": Writings on Codification, Law, and Education*, ed. Philip Schofield and Jonathan Harris (Oxford: Clarendon, 1998), 370, http://dx.doi.org/10.1093/actrade/9780198207474.book.1.

104. Jennifer Pitts, "Legislator of the World? A Rereading of Bentham on Colonies," *Political Theory* 31, no. 2 (2003): 200–234; David Armitage, "Globalizing Jeremy Bentham," *History of Political Thought* 32, no. 1 (2011): 63–82.

of the world" became most closely associated with liberal reforms in Spain and Portugal, the causes of Greek and Spanish American independence, and a "Liberal International" of southern European exiles in London that defined itself against the Holy Alliance.[105] However, it is also important to recognize the continuities linking these better-known efforts to Bentham's earlier attempts to legislate for Russia and Poland. From this perspective, Bentham, alongside Czartoryski, emerges as a key figure in the history of another "Liberal International" associated with the Holy Alliance.

Bentham first met Czartoryski in London in 1791, where the young prince was being hosted by Lord Lansdowne (formerly Shelburne), who had long encouraged Bentham's legal projects and whose Polish connections included the Poniatowski and Czartoryski families (Lansdowne had sent his own son to Poland in 1786).[106] In February 1791—just months before the promulgation of the new Polish constitution—Lansdowne passed along to Bentham a set of queries conveyed by Czartoryski from his father with the suggestion that Bentham open a correspondence with King Stanisław August and send him a copy of *Political Tactics* (the analysis of parliamentary procedure that Bentham had composed prior to the meeting of the Estates General of France): "why should not Mr. Bentham as well as Rousseau give a constitution to Poland?"[107] Bentham addressed the queries but politely declined the invitation, explaining that despite his esteem for the Polish monarch, the experience of his old friend John Lind (who had long served Stanisław August, and whose letters to the king Bentham claimed to have occasionally ghostwritten) had persuaded him of the futility of such a correspondence.[108] In fact, however, Bentham's work on developing a new approach to legislation had long been pinned to his hope

105. Philip Schofield, "Jeremy Bentham: Legislator of the World," *Current Legal Problems* 51, no. 1 (1998): 115–47; Maurizio Isabella, "Mazzini's Internationalism in Context: From the Cosmopolitan Patriotism of the Italian Carbonari to Mazzini's Europe of the Nations," in *Giuseppe Mazzini and the Globalisation of Democratic Nationalism, 1830–1920*, ed. C. A. Bayly and Eugenio F. Biagini (Oxford: Oxford University Press, 2008), 37–58; Maurizio Isabella, *Risorgimento in Exile: Italian Émigrés and the Liberal International in the Post-Napoleonic Era* (Oxford: Oxford University Press, 2009).

106. Edmond Dziembowski, "Lord Shelburne's Constitutional Views in 1782–3," in *An Enlightenment Statesman in Whig Britain: Lord Shelburne in Context, 1737–1805*, ed. Nigel Aston and Clarissa Campbell Orr (Woodbridge: Boydell Press, 2011), 231.

107. Lord Lansdowne to Jeremy Bentham, February 23, 1791, *The Correspondence of Jeremy Bentham, Vol. 4: October 1788 to December 1793*, ed. Alexander Taylor Milne, Collected Works of Jeremy Bentham (London: Athlone Press, 1981), 242, http://dx.doi.org/10.1093/actrade/9780485132045.book.1.

108. Jeremy Bentham to Lord Lansdowne, February 24, 1791, Bentham, *Correspondence of Jeremy Bentham, Vol. 4*, 244.

that it would be put into practice by the empress of Russia: a process for introducing constitutional change that was linked in turn to the remarkable career of his charismatic younger brother, Samuel Bentham.

Samuel was a naval engineer whose deficit of patronage and lack of prospects in Britain led him to entertain the idea of entering the Russian service; Jeremy was an admirer of Catherine's *Grand Instructions to the Commissioners Appointed to Frame a New Code of Laws for the Russian Empire* (translated into English in 1768), which he later listed among the factors that had prompted his turn from chemistry and botany to law.[109] Both brothers were drawn to the greater opportunities for innovation that seemed available in a country with many fewer entrenched institutions and where, Jeremy imagined, "merit as far at least as depends upon the empress is sure to be encouraged."[110] Like their predecessor John Brown, the Anglican cleric whose brief career as Catherine's advisor in the 1760s was discussed in chapter 2, they were also attracted to the prospect that the "improvements" they introduced in Russia could translate into progress (and opportunity) in Britain. Their initial Russian contact was the minister to the Russian church in London, Andrei Afanas'evich Samborskii, who happened to be Malinovskii's father-in-law and was later Alexander's religious tutor: he was nonetheless judged by Jeremy to be "altogether one of us"—a code, Philip Schofield has explained, that the brothers used with each other to refer to those "whom they conceived to be sympathetic to their own political and religious views, or to what Bentham on one occasion referred to as 'the cause.'"[111] However, the strategy pursued by the Benthams did not share Brown's or Samborskii's prioritization of agriculture and religion as the natural foundations for the progress of "civilization." Instead, the Benthams were committed to a view of Russian development much more like that of Voltaire (whom Jeremy greatly admired): it would be driven by industry and legislation, the former advanced by Samuel, and the latter by Jeremy.

109. Jeremy Bentham to John Foster, April/May 1778, *The Correspondence of Jeremy Bentham, Volume 2: 1777–80*, ed. T.L.S. Sprigge, Collected Works of Jeremy Bentham (London: Athlone Press, 2015), 99, http://dx.doi.org/10.1093/actrade/9780485132021 .book.1.

110. Ibid., 111.

111. Jeremy Bentham to Samuel Bentham, May 15, 1780, Bentham, *The Correspondence of Jeremy Bentham, Volume 2*, 450; Philip Schofield, *Utility and Democracy: The Political Thought of Jeremy Bentham* (Oxford: Oxford University Press, 2006), 174. On Samborskii, see Anthony Glenn Cross, *"By the Banks of the Thames": Russians in Eighteenth Century Britain* (Newtonville, MA: Oriental Research Partners, 1980), 39–43, 60–64, 87–88.

Samuel delivered on his side of the plan. After arriving in Russia in 1780, he navigated his way through court politics, toured the empire, and wound up working for Prince Grigorii Potemkin, Catherine's former lover and the governor of Russia's vast new territories in the Black Sea region. Besides shipbuilding (including a special commission for Catherine's famous southern tour with her Austrian ally, Emperor Joseph II), Samuel applied his technical expertise to managing and mechanizing an industrial conglomerate on Potemkin's estate in Krichev (now in Belarus).[112] After many delays, Jeremy finally joined his brother in Krichev in 1786, where his endeavors included extending one of Samuel's managerial innovations into his famous idea of a "panopticon," as well as drafting a new approach to the law of nations that he began to call "international law." However, he never published the legislative code that he had been planning to present to Catherine since the late 1770s, and even stayed sequestered in a village three miles away when the empress's tour made its way past the estate in 1787 (Bentham had a recurring "tendency to take fright when long-coveted opportunities appeared to be near realization").[113] The same tendency reappeared at the beginning of Alexander's reign, when Dumont visited Saint Petersburg and reported back to London about the enthusiastic Russian reception of his recently published compendium of Bentham's theory of legislation, whose translation into Russian was ordered by Alexander's mother, the Dowager Empress Maria Fedorovna.[114] Dumont reported that among the greatest Russian enthusiasts for Bentham's work was the civil servant Mikhail Mikhailovich Speranskii, who had been charged by the "unofficial committee" to prepare a report on the judiciary (decades later, after many trials and tribulations, and under Alexander's successor, Speranskii did finally complete a codification of Russian law).[115] Dumont was less enthusiastic about Gustav Rosenkampf, head of the commission Alexander had appointed to compile the laws of

112. On Samuel Bentham's career in Russia, see Ian R. Christie, *The Benthams in Russia, 1780–1791* (Oxford: Berg, 1993); Roger Morriss, *Science, Utility and Maritime Power: Samuel Bentham in Russia, 1779–91* (Farnham: Ashgate, 2015); Roger P. Bartlett, *The Bentham Brothers and Russia: The Imperial Russian Constitution and the St Petersburg Panopticon* (London: UCL Press, 2022).

113. Stephen Conway, "Bentham versus Pitt: Jeremy Bentham and British Foreign Policy 1789," *The Historical Journal* 30, no. 4 (1987): 796.

114. The translation appeared in 1805–11. See Aleksandr Nikolaevich Pypin, "Russkie otnosheniia Bentama," in *Ocherki literatury i obshchestvennosti pri Aleksandre 1* (Petrograd: Ogni, 1917), 32–39.

115. See Marc Raeff, *Michael Speransky: Statesman of Imperial Russia, 1772–1839* (The Hague: Martinus Nijhoff, 1957).

the empire—but even Rosenkampf claimed to have spent two weeks in seclusion studying Bentham's ideas.[116] Bentham's prevarications about his potential role in Russian legislation intensified when Samuel returned to Saint Petersburg in 1805, this time on behalf of the Royal Navy ("Peter I should come out of his tomb to greet your brother," enthused Dumont, "had he foreseen that in less than a century the premier naval power would go to buy ships in the port whose foundations he laid").[117] Nonetheless, even promising reports of Samuel's efforts to build a "Panopticon School of the Arts" in Saint Petersburg failed to entice Jeremy to rejoin him in Russia.[118]

In 1814, by contrast, Bentham did take further action. After fantasizing about moving to Mexico, or perhaps Venezuela, to write constitutions, he did actually write to President James Madison in 1811, offering his services to the United States of America; in 1814, with the help of Albert Gallatin, another Genevan exile who had become secretary of the treasury, Bentham wrote again to the governor of New Hampshire.[119] That June, Bentham also met with Czartoryski, who was visiting London with Alexander, where (as discussed in chapter 3) the emperor's public diplomacy was targeting leading British reformers. Bentham and Czartoryski discussed legislation, in the expectation that Alexander was going to appoint Czartoryski to govern Poland.[120] Bentham gave Czartoryski a letter formally offering his services to Alexander, which was finally delivered in April 1815. Alexander's reply, promising to direct his legislative commission to contact

116. Étienne Dumont to Samuel Romilly, June 10, 1803, in *The Works of Jeremy Bentham*, 10:406–7. See also Jeremy Bentham to Samuel Parr, September 16, 1803, *The Correspondence of Jeremy Bentham, Vol. 7*, 244.

117. Étienne Dumont to Jeremy Bentham, July 22, 1805, *The Correspondence of Jeremy Bentham, Vol. 7*, 312.

118. Mary and Samuel Bentham to Jeremy Bentham, August 19, 1806, Bentham, *The Correspondence of Jeremy Bentham, Vol. 7*, 360.

119. Theodora L. McKennan, "Jeremy Bentham and the Colombian Liberators," *The Americas* 34, no. 4 (1978): 460–75; Annie L. Cot, "Jeremy Bentham's Spanish American Utopia," *Revue d'études Benthamiennes*, no. 17 (2020), https://doi.org/10.4000/etudes -benthamiennes.7427; H.L.A. Hart, "Bentham and the United States of America," *Journal of Law & Economics* 19, no. 3 (1976): 547–67; Schofield, "Jeremy Bentham: Legislator of the World," 137–38.

120. Henry Brougham to Jeremy Bentham, June 27, 1814, and Jeremy Bentham to Albert Gallatin, January 28, 1815, in *The Correspondence of Jeremy Bentham, Vol. 8: January 1809 to December 1816*, ed. Stephen Conway, Collected Works of Jeremy Bentham (Oxford: Clarendon Press, 1988), 382, 446, http://dx.doi.org/10.1093/actrade /9780198226154.book.1; Adam Jerzy Czartoryski, *Dziennik ks. Adama Jerzego Czartoryskiego, 1813–1817*, ed. Małgorzata Karpińska and Janusz Pezda (Warszawa: Wydawnictwo DiG, 2016), 342.

Bentham for guidance, and including a ring as a gift, provoked an extensive response that Bentham sent in June 1815, together with the unopened gift.[121] As Bentham explained to Czartoryski, his candid letter would serve as a "test," since the whole process of legislation as he understood it was predicated on the intention of the sovereign as manifested through the invitation to the legislator.[122] In combination with Bentham's initial overture to Alexander, the letter also amounted to an introduction to the theory of legislation that he had been developing since the 1770s: a theory that, in the 1780s, took the form of an extensive but unfinished draft (in French) of a *"Project for a Complete Body of Laws,"* subtitled *"An Offer from an Englishman to the Sovereigns of Europe."*[123] In 1817, he published his reply to Alexander in the supplement to his landmark *Papers Relative to Codification and Public Instruction,* alongside his letters to Czartoryski and his similarly didactic reply to Madison (who finally penned an evasive reply to Bentham's offer in 1816).

The purpose of a truly comprehensive and systematic codification of laws, Bentham explained to Alexander, was to eliminate all the obscurity and uncertainty that created so many opportunities for abuse of power within the legal establishment. A code based on Roman law (like the Napoleonic Code) might be better than "that wretched substitute to law, which is called unwritten law, and which, in plain truth, is no law at all," but such an ancient and haphazard edifice, further encumbered by a preamble of abstract principles that could only be applied arbitrarily, was no substitute for the real thing: "a body of law produced, supported, and elucidated, from beginning to end, by a perpetual Commentary of Reasons: all deduced from the one true and only defensible principle—the principle of general utility—under which they will, all of them, be shewn to be included."[124] Without such an apparatus, laws were "but manifestations of will,—of the will of the mighty, exacting obedience from the helpless"; through such an apparatus, acts of "command" could become acts of

121. Jeremy Bentham to Alexander I, January 1814, *The Correspondence of Jeremy Bentham, Vol. 8,* 369–71; Alexander I to Jeremy Bentham, April 22, 1815, ibid., 454–55; Jeremy Bentham to Adam Jerzy Czartoryski, April 25, 1815, ibid., 455–56; Jeremy Bentham to Alexander I, June 1815, ibid., 464–87.

122. Jeremy Bentham to Adam Jerzy Czartoryski, June 21, 1815, *The Correspondence of Jeremy Bentham. Vol. 8,* 459.

123. Bentham Papers, University College London, 99, fol. 156, cited in Emmanuelle de Champs, *Enlightenment and Utility: Bentham in French, Bentham in France* (Cambridge: Cambridge University Press, 2015), 87.

124. Jeremy Bentham to Alexander I, June 1815, *The Correspondence of Jeremy Bentham, Vol. 8,* 484.

"instruction," or instances of "that mutually honourable influence, which is exercised by understanding on understanding."[125] In short, necessity would become obligation, and legal reform would become a pathway to progress in manners and morals: a position that aligned Bentham with Montesquieu and against the republican reversal of this sequence by Rousseau and his revolutionary admirers, like Bentham's friend Jacques Pierre Brissot, for whom legal change presupposed new political institutions and the collective agency to construct them.[126] Bentham's position also led him to prioritize the completion of a penal code before all other areas of law because, as he had originally explained to Shelburne in 1781, the reasons for such laws were the most universal as well as the most immediately connected to individual pleasure and pain.[127] To Czartoryski, Bentham added the consideration that codes of penal and civil law, and even a good deal of judicial procedure, were applicable under any form of government, whereas a codification of constitutional law, given Bentham's definition of law as originating in command, raised a series of unanswerable questions about the extent of the concession that granted the constitution and the balance of power that would result from it:

> What is the monarch willing to leave or to concede to you nobles and the great body of the people, taken together? What are the monarch and you nobles, taken together, willing to leave or to concede to the great body of the people? What are the people at present in a condition to receive, if the powers, on which it depends, were willing to concede it to them? What more, within a moderate space of time, may they be expected to come of themselves to be in, or to be capable of being put into a condition to receive,—and by what means? All this, if known to anybody, is known to you:—not a particle of it to me.[128]

Nonetheless, Bentham informed Alexander that he was certainly prepared to tackle constitutional law for Poland, which would serve as a model for

125. Ibid., 483, 478; Jeremy Bentham to Alexander I, June 1814, ibid., 371.

126. Champs, *Enlightenment and Utility*, 82–87. Cf. Istvan Hont, *Politics in Commercial Society*, ed. Béla Kapossy and Michael Sonenscher (Cambridge, MA: Harvard University Press, 2015), chap. 3.

127. Jeremy Bentham to the Earl of Shelburne, July 18, 1781, Jeremy Bentham, *The Correspondence of Jeremy Bentham, Vol. 3: January 1781 to October 1788*, ed. Ian R. Christie (London: Athlone Press, 1971), 29, http://dx.doi.org/10.1093/actrade/9780485132038 .book.1. See Mary Peter Mack, *Jeremy Bentham: An Odyssey of Ideas* (New York: Columbia University Press, 1963), 375–76.

128. Jeremy Bentham to Alexander I, June 1815, *The Correspondence of Jeremy Bentham, Vol. 8*, 460.

Russia, or even for Russia itself; and that in this case he would be willing to follow the procedure of supplying answers to queries (much as he had for Czartoryski's father in 1791). However, Bentham further explained to Alexander, the full benefits of a general codification of laws could not be realized under the auspices of a commission like the one headed by Rosenkampf (whom Bentham regarded as a hostile influence in any case). Salaried officials had little incentive to complete a code, nor to expose it to public criticism before it emerged *"armed with the force of law."*[129] This was why Bentham insisted on risking offense by returning Alexander's gift. It was also, he explained, why neither Catherine's nor Alexander's commissions had ever produced any tangible results; in any case, a code produced piecemeal "by a variety of hands" would not be truly systematic or comprehensive.[130] While even the bare threat of outside competition would doubtless improve the performance of "the official hand," the best strategy would be to issue an open invitation to single unsalaried authors to submit universal outlines of legislation, to be printed by a new *"School of Legislation*, built on the *Tribunal of free criticism"* in Saint Petersburg.[131] Eventually, a Russian selected by the School would apply the chosen model code to varied local circumstances in the empire. The advantage of a foreign author like himself, Bentham added, was that his proposal for a universal code would be subjected to international criticism as well, since "an Englishman being the workman, critics can never be altogether wanting in England": Bentham had long considered the "tribunal" of public opinion to be an indispensable restraint on power, and in his view what distinguished England from other countries was not its fabled constitution but rather its unparalleled commitment to the liberty of the press, which enabled Britons "to shed light among the nations."[132]

Bentham had sent his proposal to Alexander over the objections of his friend Pavel Vasil'evich Chichagov, the exiled Russian general who had been blamed for allowing Napoleon to escape Russia in 1812, and who as head of the Admiralty had previously enlisted Samuel Bentham to build the panopticon school of the arts in Saint Petersburg. Since 1814, Chichagov had been warning Bentham not only that Alexander was "fickle as a weathercock" but also that "the best arguments of a member of a free government should find no application at all to an individual of the most arbitrary and

129. Ibid., 467.
130. Ibid., 469.
131. Ibid., 480.
132. Ibid., 478. Bentham Papers, University College London, 17, fol. 4, cited in Champs, *Enlightenment and Utility*, 88.

the most hateful one," and that "an Englishman can have no language or expressions fit to apply to despotism and Slavery."[133] Nonetheless, when Bentham learned from the newspapers that Czartoryski had been passed over for the "Vice Royalty" of Poland in favor of "a man that nobody had ever heard of," he still blamed Alexander's failure to recognize and pursue his own interests rather than accepting Chichagov's more far-reaching claim that his theory of legislation was fundamentally inapplicable to Russia. In early 1816, Bentham recounted the whole episode, including Chichagov's judgment of Alexander, to Aaron Burr (the former American vice president whom Bentham had also imagined as a potential collaborator on various projects). In doing so he also made his first allusion to the Holy Alliance, which he associated with the influence that the religious mystic Juliane von Krüdener allegedly exercised over Alexander:

> A man [Chichagov] with whom I am intimate and whom I will not name for fear of accidents knowing the person [Alexander] most perfectly and knowing the whole matter said he was not at all surprised. Every man who had ever placed any confidence in him was deceived by him: that his head and heart were upon a par: no—but the fault lay most in the head: that the state of that country was most deplorable: that the man who happened at the time to be at his elbow (he might have added or the woman especially if an impostor, pretending to be a bigot) [Krüdener] was at all times inventor of his resolutions. And to tell the truth I had been furiously blamed before hand for taking any sort of trouble on the supposition that any possible good could come out of him. But Cz. [Czartoryski] I understood was always at his elbow, and it was in him I put my trust.[134]

By 1822, when Bentham drafted a preface for a new edition of his 1776 *A Fragment on Government*, he was prepared to go well beyond such allegations of epistemic deficiency and to indict "Sinister interests"—particularly

---

133. Jeremy Bentham to Samuel Bentham, July 4, 1814, Bentham, *The Correspondence of Jeremy Bentham*, Vol. 8, 385; Chichagov to Bentham, October 12, 1815, ibid., 498–99. On Chichagov and the panopticon, see Jeremy Bentham to José Joaquín de Mora, November 19–21, 1820, Jeremy Bentham, *The Correspondence of Jeremy Bentham, Vol. 10: July 1820 to December 1821*, ed. Stephen Conway, Collected Works of Jeremy Bentham (Oxford: Clarendon, 1994), 160, http://dx.doi.org/10.1093/actrade/9780198226178.book.1 . Chichagov and his wife had also been close to Roxandra and Alexander Stourdza, as well as Joseph de Maistre: an indication of how easily categories like liberalism and reaction can mislead.

134. Jeremy Bentham to Aaron Burr, February 23, 1816, *The Correspondence of Jeremy Bentham*, Vol. 8, 512–13.

"lawyer's interest and ruling statesman's interest"—for conspiring to stifle or deflect the legislative process he had theorized: this had also become Bentham's explanation for why the governments of the United States, dominated by lawyers accustomed to interpreting English common law to justify whatever they wanted to do, had roundly rejected his codification proposals.[135] The result of this reconsideration was a major adjustment to Bentham's theory of legislation: a reversal of the sequence of his earlier approach. In *Constitutional Code*, an unfinished work begun in 1822 and addressed to "All Nations and All Governments professing Liberal Opinions," Bentham no longer prioritized the codification of penal law—applicable under all forms of government—over constitutional legislation. Instead, legal reform was now predicated on prior constitutional change that rendered legal authority dependent on public opinion.[136]

Bentham's revision of his approach to legislation parallels the emerging arguments against the Holy Alliance leveled by its most prominent Anglophone critics in the 1820s. These arguments constructed an enduring set of contrasts between the liberal constitutionalism of western nation-states and the reactionary absolutism of the Holy Alliance. The former came to be associated with the principle of national independence, and the latter with the supranational authority arrogated by the Congress of Laibach in 1821: members of the Holy Alliance had intervened to reverse constitutional change in Naples, and threatened to do the same to the independence of the new Spanish American republics, while declining to intervene in support of the Greek uprising against Ottoman rule. From this perspective, whether Alexander was deemed sinister himself or merely ignorant or deceived by the Austrians or other interests, the Holy Alliance was defined by the principle that constitutional rights could only be concessions granted by constituted legal authorities—together with an assertion of a broad right to intervene against threats to this constitutional principle. This argument made a significant appearance in the 1821 address delivered on the Fourth of July by John Quincy Adams (Bentham's for-

135. On "sinister interests," see Jeremy Bentham, *A Fragment on Government*, ed. J. H. Burns and H.L.A. Hart (Cambridge: Cambridge University Press, 1988), 120. According to David Lieberman, despite the novelty of the term and its much wider application in the 1820s, the concept was already part of Bentham's approach to the common law in the 1770s: David Lieberman, "Bentham's Democracy," *Oxford Journal of Legal Studies* 28, no. 3 (2008): 613–14. On the influence of lawyers in the governments of the United States, see Jeremy Bentham to José Joaquín de Mora, September 26, 1820, *The Correspondence of Jeremy Bentham*, Vol. 10, 97–98.

136. David Lieberman, "Bentham on Codification," in *Selected Writings*, by Jeremy Bentham, ed. Stephen G. Engelmann (New Haven: Yale University Press, 2011), 471.

mer walking companion in London before he became secretary of state): an address famous for its description of the United States of America as founder and champion of a new liberal order based on popular sovereignty and national independence. "The whole address," Adams explained to the Philadelphia journalist Robert Walsh, "is a contrasted view of liberties founded on *grant*, and liberties founded on *acknowledgment*": the former illustrated by the Magna Charta, now a relic of the distant past, and the latter by the Declaration of Independence, representing the providential progress of liberty. The intended audience, Adams told Walsh, was not only domestic but extended to "the Holy allies of Laybach and their subjects": it aimed to establish that it was in fact the Declaration of Independence of 1776—or as Adams referred to it in his speech, "the genuine Holy Alliance of its principles"—that represented the will of divine providence, not the decrees of European despots.[137]

Adams's argument against the Holy Alliance was further extended by Massachusetts congressman Daniel Webster in a speech supporting the Greek Revolution, delivered in the House of Representatives in response to President James Monroe's 1823 message to Congress (a message largely crafted by Adams announcing what later became known as the Monroe Doctrine, which declared the Americas closed to further European colonization—and to interventions by the Holy Alliance). "The great political question of the age," Webster claimed, was "whether society shall have any part in its own government." Against "the spirit of the times," the Holy Alliance was reasserting the antiquated principle that society would have to be "satisfied with having kind masters."[138] In further asserting its right to enforce its regressive constitutional principle, the Holy Alliance stood in "open violation of the public law of the world."[139] The rejection of the principle of national independence threatened to replace civic friendship between society and government with a horizontal union of sovereigns against their subjects: "The end and scope of this amalgamated policy," Webster warned, was "to interfere, *by force*, for any government, against any people who may resist it."[140] As the "leading republic of

137. John Quincy Adams to Robert Walsh, Jr., July 27, 1821, in *Writings of John Quincy Adams*, ed. Worthington Chauncey Ford, vol. 7 (New York: Macmillan, 1917), 131, 136; John Quincy Adams, *An Address Delivered at the Request of a Committee of the Citizens of Washington; On the Occasion of Reading the Declaration of Independence, on the Fourth of July, 1821* (Washington, DC: Davis and Force, 1821), 22.

138. Daniel Webster, *Mr. Webster's Speech on the Greek Revolution* (Boston: Cummings, Hilliard & Co., 1824), 8.

139. Ibid., 18.

140. Ibid., 17.

the world," the United States could not rest content with dividing up the world with the Holy Alliance but had to denounce its violations of the law of nations, precisely because the progress of society since the days of the Magna Charta meant that "the public opinion of the civilized world" had acquired real political efficacy.[141]

The classification of the Holy Alliance as a rejection of the premise of national independence was given a fuller legal formulation by Frederick Eden, a British lawyer who published a history of the law of nations in 1823. Eden's arguments paralleled Webster's in many respects: they both cited the same passage in Pufendorf to explain why a positive convention affirming universal moral principles (such as the treaty of the Holy Alliance) was superfluous at best.[142] Eden's history culminated in an account of the Holy Alliance as the latest incarnation of a recurring fantasy: "the brilliant illusion of a great Commonwealth, where injustice and violence were entirely prevented or immediately repressed," made concrete through "the establishment of a general superintending council, which, like the Amphictyonic Assembly in Greece, should regulate, in solemn deliberation, the affairs of the European commonwealth, and enforce the observance of its Public Law, by the joint authority of the whole confederacy." Like other previous and subsequent critics of the ideal of a *civitas maxima*, Eden claimed that such an institution either would lack the capacity to contain endemic political conflicts among its members or would acquire it through "such a sacrifice of national independence as no degree of security would adequately compensate."[143] By contrast, Eden identified Vattel (despite his shortcomings) as a good guide to the principle of individual responsibility for collective security and expressed confidence that these "ancient federal maxims of the European Commonwealth" would prevail over "this inauspicious innovation of the new Amphictyons, and consign it to the contempt and execration of mankind with the armed neutrality of Catharine, and the continental system of Buonaparte."[144]

The "ancient federal maxims of the European Commonwealth" that Eden opposed to the Holy Alliance still left ample scope for Britain to perform the "delicate office" of upholding the federal system by maintaining

141. Ibid., 20.

142. Frederick Eden, *An Historical Sketch of the International Policy of Modern Europe: As Connected with the Principles of the Law of Nature and of Nations, Concluding with Some Remarks on the Holy Alliance* (London: J. Murray, 1823), 7; Webster, *Mr. Webster's Speech*, 11.

143. Eden, *An Historical Sketch of the International Policy of Modern Europe*, 34.

144. Ibid., 9, 110, 112.

the balance of power among its member states.[145] Britain's capacity to do so against the Holy Alliance was elaborated in a consequential 1824 speech to the House of Commons by James Mackintosh (the Scottish jurist and Whig politician whose lectures on the law of nations had served as Eden's starting point).[146] Mackintosh spoke in support of a petition from the City of London (whose signatories included the banker Alexander Baring and the political economist David Ricardo) to recognize the independence of the Spanish American republics. Mackintosh claimed that the act of recognition in question did not amount to an affirmation or denial of Spanish sovereignty, which remained a matter between Spain and its former colonies. However, the law of nations entitled Britain to exercise its federative power according to its own judgment. In the aftermath of the Congress of Verona in 1822 (which had authorized French intervention in Spain over British objections, resulting in the suspension of the liberal Spanish constitution), Mackintosh argued that recognition would be in Britain's interest, while also maximizing general utility or international justice. In Britain, recognition would help forge a stronger bond between society and government by aligning the public interest with private commercial interests in South America—and, Mackintosh claimed, also teaching private interests to regard the public interest as their own: the vast loans extended to the new South American governments on the London bond market would help stabilize them (much as Baring's 1817 loans to finance French reparations payments had done in France, and as Bentham hoped the 1824 loan to the Greeks would also do) while fueling what was widely expected to be explosive economic growth. In this way, Britain's society and government could act in concert, within the constraints of the law of nations, to

> prevent the dictators of Europe from becoming the masters of the New World; to re-establish some balance of opinions and force, by placing the Republics of America, with the wealth and maritime power of the world, in the scale opposite to that of the European Allies; to establish beyond the Atlantic an asylum which may preserve, till happier times, the remains of the Spanish name; to save nations, who have proved their generous spirit by their pursuit of liberty, from becoming the slaves of the Holy Alliance.[147]

145. Ibid., 45.

146. Ibid., 1.

147. *Substance of the Speech of Sir James Mackintosh in the House of Commons, June 15, 1824, on Presenting a Petition from the Merchants of London for the Recogni-*

The categories defining the opposition between liberalism and the Holy Alliance that were developed by Adams, Webster, Eden, and Mackintosh in the 1820s cannot accommodate either Czartoryski's collaboration with Bentham or his most fully developed statement of his approach to the politics of federation: *Essay on Diplomacy*, the treatise he completed in 1826 and published in 1830. In some respects, Czartoryski's *Essay on Diplomacy* was very much a product of the 1820s. Czartoryski wrote it in France and Geneva, where he had traveled in 1823 after Russian authorities (led by Czartoryski's former colleague Novosiltsev) suppressed a student conspiracy at the University of Vilna and seized control of the institution over which he had long presided. In Geneva, Czartoryski involved himself in the Greek cause together with Ioannis Kapodistrias, his former colleague in the Russian service who would soon go on to become the first president of independent Greece: Czartoryski had earlier condemned Alexander for failing to exercise Russia's responsibilities as guarantor of Christians in the Ottoman Empire on behalf of the Greeks, thereby making a mockery of the principles of the Holy Alliance, and *Essay on Diplomacy* was published under the pseudonym *un Philhellène*.[148] At its core, however, *Essay on Diplomacy* remained a work of the 1780s rather than the 1820s. (Tellingly, the manuscript was entrusted to an associate of Rochefoucauld-Liancourt, who had belonged to the circle around Condorcet and Jefferson in the 1780s.)[149] In *Essay on Diplomacy*, Czartoryski reasserted the theory of federative power that he had encountered as a teenager in Paris and London and that had informed his plans for Russian intervention in Europe before 1805. *Essay on Diplomacy* represents a liberalism that did not fashion itself in opposition to principles attributed to the Holy Alliance, because it remained oriented

---

tion of the Independent States Established in the Countries of America Formerly Subject to Spain . . . (R. Taylor, 1824), 74. For the context of Mackintosh's arguments, see Gabriel Paquette, "The Intellectual Context of British Diplomatic Recognition of the South American Republics, c. 1800–1830," *Journal of Transatlantic Studies* 2, no. 1 (2004): 75–95; Simeon Andonov Simeonov, "Consular Recognition, Partial Neutrality, and the Making of Atlantic Diplomacy, 1778–1825," *Diplomatic History* 46, no. 1 (January 2022): 144–72. On Baring's 1817 loan (implicitly guaranteed by the allied armies occupying France, under the command of the Duke of Wellington, who helped arrange the loan), see Beatrice de Graaf, *Fighting Terror after Napoleon: How Europe Became Secure after 1815* (Cambridge: Cambridge University Press, 2020), 333–42. On Bentham and the Greek loan of 1824, see F. Rosen, "Theory and Practice II: Bentham and the First Greek Loan," in *Bentham, Byron, and Greece* (Oxford: Oxford University Press, 1992), 103–22.

148. Zawadzki, *A Man of Honour*, 285; Czartoryski, *Mémoires*, 2:379–86.

149. *Essai sur la diplomatie: Manuscrit d'un philhellène publié par M. Toulouzan* (Paris: Firmin Didot Frères, 1830), v–vii, https://gallica.bnf.fr/ark:/12148/bpt6k5473925r.

primarily around the experiences and ideals of the 1780s: a standpoint from which it remained possible to see the Holy Alliance as an emancipatory exercise of federative power gone wrong.

The main claim of *Essay on Diplomacy* was that diplomacy (which Czartoryski defined capaciously as the science of the external conduct of the state) had failed to keep pace with the progress of civilization. Internally, the interests of nations—increasingly expressed through representative institutions—had decisively superseded the interests of princes as the principle of government, and the "opinion of the Christian world" would not permit a regression to the obsolete doctrine of Louis XIV.[150] Extending this transformation meant exposing the external conduct of the state to publicity and reorienting it around the needs of nations. A science of diplomacy would rule out any external interventions by states that were incompatible with general utility as determined by international public opinion. However, Czartoryski claimed, this standard of justice still allowed for a state or concert of states to assume responsibility for collective security by intervening as guarantors of federal treaties. The result would be the legislation of a new treaty system. "Europe has a right to demand" that states too small to act as viable members of the international system on their own should enter into federal unions on the Swiss or American model: such unions could adopt a variety of institutional arrangements designed to reconcile internal autonomy with external security. Likewise, "the guarantee of Europe" would ensure that personal unions of national governments under a single sovereign did not violate "the fundamental character of the federal pact": external intervention in such a case—and Czartoryski hardly had to name Poland—would not represent an unjust intervention in domestic affairs but a defense of national autonomy.[151]

Czartoryski's *Essay on Diplomacy* remained committed to Bentham's original approach to legislation and continued to envisage its application through federative power. The historical horizons of Czartoryski's science of diplomacy also remained those of the eighteenth century. Like the Abbé de Saint-Pierre, but also like several Americans in the 1780s, Czartoryski invoked the fabled "Grand Design" of King Henri IV of France as the archetype of a modern federal politics—not as a deviation from the ancient federal constitution of Europe (as Eden had).[152] Both Napoleon

150. Adam Jerzy Czartoryski, *Essai sur la diplomatie*, ed. Marek Kornat (Lausanne: Éditions Noir sur blanc, 2011), 193.

151. Ibid., 213.

152. Eden, *An Historical Sketch of the International Policy of Modern Europe*, 33; Czartoryski, *Essai sur la diplomatie*, 2011, 219–75. American invocations of Henri IV

and Alexander had ultimately failed to realize this ideal; in Alexander's case, Czartoryski faulted the Holy Alliance for misidentifying the general utility of nations with a fixed political order rather than a harmonization of their respective strivings.[153] Nonetheless, Czartoryski still identified Alexander (who died in 1825) as the true heir of King Henri IV: "the intentions of the creator of the Holy Alliance cannot be doubted," Czartoryski declared. Its principles had "emerged pure from his mind," only to be "sullied and profaned by diplomats."[154] *Essay on Diplomacy* conceded that the future of liberalism was now easier to envisage in the Americas; in the absence of better leadership from Russia, a reform of the 1815 treaties led by an Anglo-French alliance remained the best prospect for ensuring that the global expansion of European state relations took a collaborative form and resulted in a proliferation of independent nations (including the eventual federalization of the Russian Empire).[155] Czartoryski's *Essay on Diplomacy*, then, does not represent the flip side of the antimony between liberalism and the Holy Alliance that was developed in the 1820s by Adams, Webster, Eden, and others. Rather, it represents the continuation of Bentham's efforts to extend his approach to legislation to what he had long ago begun to call "international law," or the law of nations reformatted to focus

include Stiles, *The United States Elevated to Glory and Honor*, 20, 50. Especially striking is the lengthy discussion of Henri IV, comparable in many respects to Czartoryski's in his *Essai*, that appears in the lectures delivered in Philadelphia in 1790–91 by the Scottish-born lawyer James Wilson. Wilson, who had been one of the principal architects of the United States Constitution of 1787, described it as realizing Henri IV's idea: "Here the sublime system of Henry the Great has been effectually realized, and completely carried into execution." *Collected Works of James Wilson*, ed. Kermit L. Hall and Mark David Hall (Indianapolis: Liberty Fund, 2007), 1:662. Similarly, Roxandra Edling-Stourdza—Alexander Stourdza's sister and an influential member of Alexander's close circle—later described the Holy Alliance as "the magnificent dream of Henri IV and the Abbé de Saint-Pierre," rendered "in a more religious and therefore more positive form." Roxandra Edling-Stourdza, *Mémoires de la comtesse Edling (née Stourdza): Demoiselle d'honneur de Sa Majesté l'impératrice Élisabeth Alexéevna* (Moscow: Imprimerie du St.-Synod, 1888), 242, cited in Stella Ghervas, *Conquering Peace: From the Enlightenment to the European Union* (Cambridge, MA: Harvard University Press, 2021), 111.

153. Czartoryski, *Essai sur la diplomatie*, 2011, 196.

154. Ibid., 274.

155. The federalization of the Russian Empire was a possibility explored in the 1818–20 draft of a constitutional charter prepared for Alexander by Novosiltsev. See George Vernadsky, *La charte constitutionnelle de l'Empire russe de l'an 1820*, trans. Sergei Oldenburg (Paris: Librairie du Recueil Sirey, 1933); Marc Raeff, *Plans for Political Reform in Imperial Russia, 1730–1905* (Englewood Cliffs, NJ: Prentice-Hall, 1966), 110–20. For broader context, see Mark von Hagen, "Federalisms and Pan-Movements: Re-Imagining Empire," in *Russian Empire: Space, People, Power, 1700–1930*, ed. Jane Burbank, Mark von Hagen, and Anatolyi Remnev (Bloomington: Indiana University Press, 2007), 494–510.

exclusively on the external relations among states.[156] The significance of that approach, and its application to the Holy Alliance, extends beyond the emerging field of "international law" narrowly defined and points to an important strand of nineteenth-century constitutionalism.

Bentham's initial investigations of international law in the 1780s, and the economic and political arguments against colonial empire which they had begun to develop, were closely tied to a vision of an Anglo-French federal system associated with the Earl of Shelburne (later Lord Lansdowne). Shelburne had hoped to use his tenure as prime minister (which began in 1782) not only to end the War of American Independence but, more ambitiously, to orchestrate a definitive resolution to the Anglo-French rivalry over trade and empire. Shelburne had imagined a genuine reconciliation, cemented by a free trade agreement that would enable both Britain and France to escape impending financial catastrophe and become the core of a new system of transatlantic free trade. As British and French interest in maintaining rival colonial empires weakened, smaller and poorer European states like Poland would be able to flourish under their protection, while Austria, Prussia, and Russia would be compelled to redirect their energies from conquest to commerce.[157] Intending to attack mercantile interests that were well represented in the House of Commons, where he lacked a majority, Shelburne had aimed to implement his ambitious program through an expansive reassertion of executive authority (royal prerogative).[158] After his rapid fall from power in 1783, Shelburne next tried to involve Bentham in plans for a new journal to be called *The Neutralist*, dedicated to expounding principles of free trade and a new law of nations.[159] Though this project never materialized, Bentham's work on the manuscripts that later became known (in the hands of his posthumous

---

156. M. W. Janis, "Jeremy Bentham and the Fashioning of 'International Law,'" *American Journal of International Law* 78, no. 2 (April 1, 1984): 405–18.

157. Andrew Stockley, "Shelburne, the European Powers, and the Peace of 1783," in *An Enlightenment Statesman in Whig Britain: Lord Shelburne in Context, 1737–1805*, ed. Nigel Aston and Clarissa Campbell Orr (Woodbridge: Boydell Press, 2011), 183–84; Dziembowski, "Lord Shelburne's Constitutional Views in 1782–3," 220–23; Richard Whatmore, "Shelburne and Perpetual Peace: Small States, Commerce, and International Relations within the Bowood Circle," in *An Enlightenment Statesman in Whig Britain: Lord Shelburne in Context, 1737–1805*, ed. Nigel Aston and Clarissa Campbell Orr (Woodbridge: Boydell Press, 2011), 249–73.

158. Dziembowski, "Lord Shelburne's Constitutional Views in 1782–3," 230–31.

159. The project was also supposed to involve Richard Price, whose *Observations on the Importance of the American Revolution* (1784) described a reformed American Congress as a model of a new European federal system.

editors) as *A Plan for an Universal and Perpetual Peace* grew directly out of his subsequent collaboration with Shelburne: an attack on the British government's pro-Prussian and anti-Russian interventions in European politics. In his *Letters of Anti-Machiavel* of 1789, and in a private letter to William Pitt himself (both of which were supposed to contribute to a parliamentary campaign orchestrated by Shelburne), Bentham criticized what he described as a narrow-minded conception of national interest that ran directly counter to the kind of federal system for collective security advocated by Shelburne.[160]

The approach to international law that Bentham began to develop in the 1780s represents a distinctive variation on other contemporary discussions of Vattel. Bentham followed Vattel relatively closely in seeking to guide judgments of utility by individual states, bringing the laws made by states to govern their external conduct into alignment with international justice, or "the common and equal utility of all nations."[161] While there could be no question of punishment for violations of international law, Bentham did not conclude (as John Austin later would) that international law was not really law because it could only be enforced through "moral" or "religious" rather than "political" sanction: despite the suspicion of guarantees of foreign constitutions that he expressed elsewhere, Bentham did cite the guarantee mechanism in a 1782 manuscript as an example of a moral sanction with real efficacy.[162] By codifying international law, and introducing international institutions to adjudicate their disputes as well as expose their external conduct to the scrutiny of public opinion, Bentham maintained, states could learn to take responsibility for collective security and prosperity, without asserting authority over other states or opening up a dangerously broad scope for intervention. In 1786, Bentham illustrated his claim that judgments of national interest could converge with a reference to Empress Catherine's Armed Neutrality of 1780: its appeal to other

160. Conway, "Bentham versus Pitt." On the many problems arising from the editing of Bentham's 1780s manuscripts on international relations and international law, see Gunhild Hoogensen, *International Relations, Security, and Jeremy Bentham* (London: Routledge, 2005), 40–54.

161. "Projet matière—Entregens" (1786), Bentham Papers, University College London, 25, fol. 1; Jeremy Bentham, "Principles of International Law," in *The Works of Jeremy Bentham*, ed. John Bowring, vol. 2 (Edinburgh: W. Tait, 1843), 537.

162. Jeremy Bentham, *Of Laws in General*, ed. H.L.A. Hart, Collected Works of Jeremy Bentham (London: University of London, Athlone Press, 1970), 70; Janis, "Jeremy Bentham and the Fashioning of 'International Law,'" 412. Bentham's suspicion of guarantees appears in "Inter-National Principles and Measures" (1789), Bentham Papers, University College London, 25, fol. 134.

states could not be reduced to fear of Russian power because it reflected the appreciation of its "common utility" by other nations.[163]

In later years, Bentham aspired to replace Vattel's treatise with a new one that would dispense with Vattel's obfuscating efforts to ground the law of nations in natural law: "He builds upon a cloud," Bentham once complained. "When he means anything, it is from a vague perception of the principle of utility; but more frequently no meaning can be found."[164] In 1806, Bentham sent Dumont a copy of Vattel's treatise, only to complain that he could not get his collaborator to prioritize a new work on international law.[165] Much later, in 1827, Bentham again sent notes on international law to another potential collaborator—the lawyer Jabez Henry—whom he exhorted to "undertake a new edition of Vattel or rather a new book upon a similar principle": a work, "grounded on the greatest happiness principle," that would, Bentham promised, "if the plan and execution be more moral and intellectual than Vattel's, possess a probability of superseding it, and being referred to in preference."[166] The notes that Bentham sent to Henry reveal how, despite their divergent evaluations of the Holy Alliance, Bentham also continued to develop and refine his approach to international law in parallel with Czartoryski. As in his manuscripts of the 1780s, Bentham still envisaged the creation of an international congress that would function as a "proper legislative authority" and appoint a judiciary. It would also serve as an organ of publicity extending to "all civilized nations, which at present is as much to say, all nations professing the christian religion."[167] In the 1780s, Bentham had ruled out any power of punishment over states beyond the moral or religious sanction, but he had also suggested that states might secure the efficacy of the international

163. "Projet matière—Entregens" (1786), Bentham Papers, University College London, 25, fol. 1; Bentham, "Principles of International Law," 537. "The confusion of *moral approbation* with the *moral qualities* which are its objects, common to Mr Bentham with many other philosophers, is much more uniform and prominent in him than in most others." James Mackintosh, *Dissertation on the Progress of Ethical Philosophy, Chiefly during the Seventeenth and Eighteenth Centuries* (Edinburgh: Adam and Charles Black, 1836), 292.

164. *The Works of Jeremy Bentham*, 10:584. Bowring dates the remark to 1827–28.

165. Jeremy Bentham to Samuel Bentham, May 10–16, 1806, *The Correspondence of Jeremy Bentham. Vol. 7*, 342. See Stephen Conway, "Bentham on Peace and War," *Utilitas* 1, no. 1 (1989): 86.

166. Jeremy Bentham, "International Law" (June 11, 1827), British Library Add Ms. 30151, fol. 22, fol. 15. On Bentham and Henry, see Ernest Nys, "Notes Inedites de Bentham sur le Droit International," *Law Quarterly Review* 1 (1885): 225–31; Armitage, "Globalizing Jeremy Bentham"; Lorenzo Cello, "Jeremy Bentham's Vision of International Order," *Cambridge Review of International Affairs* 34, no. 1 (2021): 46–64.

167. Bentham, "International Law" (June 11, 1827), fol. 15.

"public opinion tribunal" by introducing legislation "guaranteeing the liberty of press in each state" and even hinted at the provision of some sort of enforcement mechanism "as a last resource."[168] Bentham now affirmed categorically that such an institution could not exercise any powers of enforcement, which would amount to "an attempt to establish an universal republic, inconsistent with the sovereignty of the several sovereigns."[169] As before, the creation of an international congress and the legislation of a new body of international law would have to result from the exercise of federative power by states assuming individual responsibility for collective utility. For Britain to assume the role of initiating this process, it would have to begin by affirming its commitment to the legal equality of other states by abandoning its claim to "assume the superiority over other nations on sea, by exacting tokens of submission."[170]

In the end, Bentham's idea of rewriting Vattel's treatise was realized not by Dumont or Henry but by the Luso-Brazilian philosopher and statesman Silvestre Pinheiro Ferreira, who produced a widely recirculated critical commentary on Vattel's *Law of Nations* in 1838: Pinheiro Ferreira labeled Bentham "the head of the modern philosophical school, in morals as in jurisprudence," and identified his greatest happiness principle as "the fundamental moral basis for all men and the politics of all nations."[171] Like Czartoryski, Pinheiro Ferreira also remained committed to Bentham's original approach to legislation even after repeated disappointments in attempting to apply it in Portugal.[172] Remarkably, Pinheiro Ferreira (who had studied philosophy in Germany before 1809 and settled into exile in France after 1825) also diverged from other southern Europeans in his characterization of the Holy Alliance. In his commentary on another work on the law of nations by Georg Friedrich Martens, Pinheiro Ferreira attacked the Göttingen professor turned diplomat for his criticisms of the "Declaration of the Rights of Nations" originally proposed in 1793 and 1795 by the revolutionary Bishop Henri Grégoire (which had anticipated the 1799 proposal by Barlow discussed above). Martens, according to Pinheiro Ferreira,

168. Jeremy Bentham, "Pacific. & Emancip." (1786), Bentham Papers, University College London, 25, fol. 35; cf. Bentham, "Principles of International Law," 554.

169. Bentham, "International Law" (June 11, 1827), fol. 15.

170. Ibid., fol. 18.

171. Emer de Vattel, *Le droit des gens, ou, Principes de la loi naturelle appliqués à la conduite et aux affaires des nations et des souverains* (Paris: J. P. Aillaud, 1838), 3:27; Silvestre Pinheiro Ferreira, *Cours de droit public interne et externe*, vol. 1 (Paris: Rey et Gravier, 1830), 8.

172. Oscar Ferreira, "Un Sieyès 'rouge'? Regards sur le système politique de Silvestre Pinheiro Ferreira," *Revue de la recherche juridique, droit prospectif* 38, no. 146 (2013): 105.

had failed to distinguish between laws and principles of legislation (in Bentham's terms, between commands and reasons). Grégoire's proposed Declaration was no more a code of international law than the Declaration of the Rights of Man and Citizen was a code of civil law. Where Burke had praised the Polish Constitution of 1791 in order to attack the French Revolution, Pinheiro Ferreira now defended the French Revolution by praising the Holy Alliance, which he likened to Grégoire's proposed Declaration. "Nothing is better known, or more generally avowed, than the principles contained in the famous *Act of the Holy Alliance*," Pinheiro Ferreira pointed out, "yet M. de Martens does not dare to call it a diplomatic superfluity. The intention of the sovereigns in signing it was to nullify all the diplomatic acts that could come from their cabinets in the future, in contradiction with its principles."[173]

Out of a Russian Head

In November 1830 a Polish uprising broke out, prompted in part by the decision of Alexander's successor, Nicholas, to mobilize the Polish army (as was his constitutional prerogative) to intervene in Belgium, against its bid for independence from the Netherlands. Czartoryski hoped that the uprising would create an opportunity to renegotiate Poland's relationship with Russia and amend the Polish Constitution within the framework of the Vienna Treaties. However, his attempts to solicit British and French mediation in Poland (on the model of their interventions in Belgium and Greece) were unsuccessful. As the uprising escalated, Nicholas was deposed by the Polish diet and Czartoryski was elected the reluctant president of the National Government in January 1831. Later that year, as the uprising collapsed, Czartoryski narrowly escaped capture by the Russian army (thanks to a false Austrian passport supplied by Metternich!) and returned to London, where Talleyrand and Dorothea von Biron (Piattoli's former pupil, now the Duchess of Dino) watched the British government reject his final appeals for intervention.[174] The history of Czartoryski's strategy for securing Poland's constitutional future via Russian federative

173. G. F. de Martens, *Précis du droit des gens moderne de l'Europe, fondé sur les traités et l'usage*, vol. 1 (Paris: J. P. Aillaud, 1831), 11, https://catalog.hathitrust.org/Record /009724707.

174. Zawadzki, *A Man of Honour*, 304–18; Adam Jerzy Czartoryski, *Memoirs of Prince Adam Czartoryski and His Correspondence with Alexander I: With Documents Relative to the Prince's Negotiation with Pitt, Fox, and Brougham, and an Account of His Conversations with Lord Palmerston and Other English Statesmen in London in 1832*, ed. Adam Gielgud (London: Remington, 1888), 2:316–36.

power had come to an end. Beyond Poland, however, the history of Czarto-ryski's strategy helps explain why some contemporary liberals in Germany and France initially hailed the proclamation of the Holy Alliance as the establishment of a federal guarantor of constitutional change: as part of a process for introducing representative government throughout Europe. As chapter 5 will show, a range of liberals, including prominent British and American abolitionists and reformers, were able to integrate the procla-mation of the Holy Alliance into their understandings of the progress of civilization and the triumph of liberalism. From this perspective, the Holy Alliance represented the dawning of a future age, not the dead weight of the past.

The history of Czartoryski's strategy also opens up a broader perspec-tive on the history of federalism. The Polish uprising of 1863, like the one of 1830, did not result in British or French intervention, but it did prompt the French emperor Napoleon III to declare, in support of the Poles, that the treaties of 1815 "no longer existed." The French philosopher Pierre-Joseph Proudhon responded with a defense of the treaties of 1815 that compre-hensively dismantled the premises of the emperor's statement—and in doing so, identified the idea of the Holy Alliance as the basis for a future federal constitution of Europe. The treaties of 1815, Proudhon claimed, had introduced a new legal principle into the public law of Europe, which had originally been established in 1648 by the treaties of Westpha-lia. The public law of 1648 had enshrined the "essentially federalist idea" that Europe would remain a plurality of states never to be consolidated under a single authority.[175] The treaties of 1815 had added constitutional-ism to this pluralism. The popular mobilization required to defeat Napo-leon's armies had appropriated the ideals of the French Revolution (as Piattoli had hoped). It had established a link between the restoration of an external equilibrium among independent states and the reform of their internal constitutions. The age of constitutions had therefore truly begun not with the initial "antagonism" of 1789 but with the "synthetic reason" of 1814: not with a revolutionary assertion of national sovereignty but with the postwar achievement of a consensus that admitted no "extra-constitutional . . . mystical element" and reduced all powers to functions defined by and responsible to the constitution.[176] "The real constitutional

---

175. Proudhon, *Si les traités de 1815 ont cessé d'exister?* 19. On Proudhon's approach to federalism and his international thought more broadly, see Alex Prichard, *Justice, Order and Anarchy: The International Political Theory of Pierre-Joseph Proudhon* (New York: Routledge, 2013).

176. Proudhon, *Si les traités de 1815 ont cessé d'exister?* 30, 45.

moment," Proudhon claimed, "is the one when peoples and sovereigns, conquerors and conquered . . . unite in the double thought of guaranteeing each state's independence, with the aim of giving it a constitution."[177] It was a "singular thing," Proudhon continued, referring to Alexander's role in the restoration of the Bourbon monarchy in France under the Constitutional Charter of 1814,

> that it was the emperor of all the Russias who betrayed the secret of the age, who—no doubt as a disinterested sovereign whose subjects were not mature—sounded the death knell of despotism, proved himself the most inflexible regarding principles, and who imposed the revolutionary dogma on the most Christian king.[178]

The aim of the Holy Alliance, in Proudhon's view, had been "to create a mutual guarantee" among sovereigns that would "inaugurate *the age of principles* in international politics." Alexander's treaty was "nothing less than an oath to the Revolution, in the presence of the Holy Trinity." The idea of an "*age of principles*" may have "come out of a Russian head" in 1814, Proudhon concluded, but "it would have done honor to Lafayette. I have no hesitation in claiming it as French; it is the application to international affairs of the Declaration of the Rights of Man."[179] Though the subsequent development of the post-Napoleonic order had been marred by bad faith on both sides, the principles that Alexander had proclaimed "in the candor of his mysticism" had endured. They amounted to "the first draft of the future constitution of Europe," which would be complete once a third principle, equality, had been enshrined alongside the pluralism of 1648 and the constitutionalism of 1815.[180]

Proudhon's account of the development of European public law produced a strikingly contrarian analysis of nineteenth-century politics. According to Proudhon, the constitutions that proliferated in Europe after 1814 were certainly not "models of liberalism," but they had remained "instruments of progress" despite their abuse by both monarchists and nationalists.[181] In the 1820s, it was the leaders of the Holy Alliance themselves who had violated the principles of 1815 by suppressing constitutions. Appealing to the threat of terror, they had tried to turn the Congress of Verona into a kind of supreme court exercising judicial review (*une espèce*

177. Ibid., 32.
178. Ibid., 33.
179. Ibid., 44.
180. Ibid.
181. Ibid., 34–35.

de jugement de cassation) over national constitutions.[182] It had become impossible for sovereigns to simply reject the federal principle that had emerged in 1648; likewise, they were now incapable of fully suppressing the constitutional principle which they themselves had proclaimed "joined and correlative" to it in 1815. The revolutionaries of 1830 had reasserted this linkage by amending their constitutions without disrupting the European balance of power: "the July revolution was the consecration of the *principles* proclaimed by the Holy Alliance, not at all the rebuttal of the thought of Vienna."[183] In fact, the external relations between European states had been further stabilized through constitutional change in 1830, as the expensive system of fortifications built on the French frontier after 1815 had instantly become obsolete with the internationally negotiated independence and neutralization of Belgium.[184] Similarly, in Proudhon's analysis of the revolutions of 1848, it was the Hungarians demanding constitutional reform who were reaffirming the principles of 1815, which had been violated by Metternich with his systematic opposition to constitutionalism.[185]

Over the course of the nineteenth century, Proudhon claimed, the linkage between the federalism of 1648 and the constitutionalism of 1815 had become so strong that it was no longer possible to distinguish insurrections and civil wars from foreign wars, or public law from the law of nations. From this perspective, both the Polish uprising of 1863 and Napoleon III's declaration that the treaties of 1815 "no longer exist" were profoundly regressive developments. The emperor (whose unconstitutional seizure of power and expansionism had already violated the principles of 1815) might have been doing no more than giving the Poles false hope with empty words. Or he might have been signaling a return to the 1820s with a new conspiracy of sovereigns. But the treaties of 1815 were now so tightly woven into the legal fabric of Europe that the emperor might as well have declared that the civil and penal codes of France no longer existed. If the treaties of 1815 no longer existed, there was little reason to suppose that a new law of nations would be more "favorable to civilization"; there were plenty of reasons to expect the "annihilation of civilized Europe" or a regression to its condition before 1648.[186] Proudhon was equally scathing

182. Ibid., 49.

183. Ibid., 48.

184. Ibid., 51. On the earlier significance of these fortifications and their financing for the post-1815 settlement, see de Graaf, *Fighting Terror after Napoleon*, 357–426.

185. Proudhon, *Si les traités de 1815 ont cessé d'exister*, 63.

186. Ibid., 11–12, 55.

in his criticism of Polish demands for national independence. In demanding the abrogation of the 1815 treaties, they were asking the rest of Europe to sacrifice its entire legal system for the interests of a single nationality. In fact, Proudhon claimed, the eighteenth-century partitions of Poland had advanced the progress of law in Europe: they represented a perfectly legal response to the threat posed to collective security by the endemic weakness and instability of the Polish state, which had become a recurring cause of conflict. The Polish state had been betrayed repeatedly by its retrograde aristocracy masquerading as a nation. Their resistance to the long over-due reform efforts led by the Czartoryskis, culminating in the demise of the Constitution of 1791, showed that much of the Polish aristocracy continued to prefer the destruction of the Polish state to the emancipation of the Polish people. After 1815, rather than taking the treaties as a constitutional starting point for "the rehabilitation of Poland," they continued to oppose their interests to those of "democratic, egalitarian and constitutional Europe."[187]

Underlying Proudhon's political analysis was the argument of his 1861 work *War and Peace: On the Principle and Constitution of the Law of Nations* (the title evidently impressed Tolstoy, who visited Proudhon in Brussels that year).[188] In *War and Peace*, Proudhon had set out to show why generations of European international lawyers had failed to set moral limits on war and fulfill humanity's yearning for peace. Vattel had claimed to supersede his natural law predecessors, just as his successors, from Kant to Pinheiro Ferreira, had all claimed to correct his errors. Nonetheless, according to Proudhon, they had all continued to replicate the fundamental error of treating war as a legal fiction rather than a real and therefore law-governed phenomenon: an error that had appeared in its purest form in the writings of Thomas Hobbes. In Proudhon's estimation, Hobbes had anticipated Hegel's dialectics by attempting to derive justice from an abstract definition of the state of war as a condition without justice.[189] In fact, Proudhon's "phenomenology of war" affirmed what humanity had always demonstrated in practice: force generated authority, and justice was "not simply an idea, but a power," an innate human power that "brings about and conditions all the others."[190] Hobbes's followers

---

187. Ibid., 87, 74.

188. On Proudhon and Tolstoy, and debates about the extent of the former's influence on the latter, see Feuer, *Tolstoy and the Genesis of "War and Peace,"* 169–70, 181–82, 272.

189. Pierre-Joseph Proudhon, *La guerre et la paix: Recherches sur le principe et la constitution du droit des gens* (Paris: E. Dentu, 1861), 1:176.

190. Ibid., 2:389.

had qualified his account of justice in various ways, but since they all continued to treat war as a legal fiction rather than a generative phenomenon, they could not supply guidance on the proper scope of federative power, which would determine when collective security might justify the consolidation or disaggregation of states. Instead, they had resorted to a further abstraction, an ideal of a higher legal authority over states. But this ideal of perpetual peace (which Proudhon associated with the Anglo-American peace movement together with the Holy Alliance) was merely the negation of the Hobbesian theory of the state—the negation of a negation of a negation—which could only issue in Europe's regression to the illiberal unity of the Middle Ages. Proudhon's point, in Kant's terms, was that Hobbes, Vattel, Kant, and the rest were all "sorry comforters."[191]

For Proudhon, the key to Europe's progress beyond the constitutionalism of 1814 was the further development of federalism, understood as a nested system of mutual guarantees among autonomous units. As Proudhon elaborated in *The Federative Principle and the Necessity of Reconstituting the Party of Revolution* (1863), this concept of federalism was "liberal *par excellence*": it represented the culmination of a historical process that had to begin (temporally as well as logically) with force becoming authority but could end with authority becoming "the instrument or servant of liberty itself."[192] However, neither the concept of liberty (which strived to judge, limit, and divide power) nor the concept of authority (which aimed to amass it) could comprehend the totality of this process. This was why, despite their respective principles, democrats wound up reasserting authority while monarchists were "led to republicanize themselves."[193] "Always the flag of liberty has served to disguise despotism," Proudhon observed, "always the privileged classes have surrounded themselves with liberal and egalitarian institutions in order to protect their privileges."[194] Since the French Revolution, successive efforts to establish the principle of liberty had failed. Neither appeals to the fiction of a sovereign people nor the construction of institutional checks and

191. Cf. Kant, "Perpetual Peace," 103. This point is made in Edward Castleton, "Pierre-Joseph Proudhon's *War and Peace*: The Right of Force Revisited," in *Commerce and Peace in the Enlightenment*, ed. Béla Kapossy, Isaac Nakhimovsky, and Richard Whatmore (Cambridge: Cambridge University Press, 2017), 272–97.

192. Pierre-Joseph Proudhon, *Du principe fédératif et de la nécessité de reconstituer le parti de la révolution* (Paris: E. Dentu, 1863), 114, 62. Where possible I have quoted from the partial English translation: Pierre-Joseph Proudhon, *The Principle of Federation*, trans. Richard Vernon (Toronto: University of Toronto Press, 1979), 72, 33.

193. Proudhon, *The Principle of Federation*, 20.

194. Ibid., 32.

balances ("word against word, fiction against fiction") could change "the reality of the nation state" or restrain the relentless growth and consolidation of "the active powers of a great people."[195] The principle of liberty risked dissolving into a "confusion of language and thought": "anyone may describe himself at will as a republican, monarchist, democrat, bourgeois, conservative, distributivist, liberal—and as all of these at once, without fear of being accused of deception or error."[196]

Proudhon claimed that only a decentralized system of mutual guarantees could advance the principle of liberty while achieving a stable resolution of its contradictions with authority. As the case of Switzerland showed, the federal agency of such a system could be limited to exercising the functions delegated to it by a "plenitude of autonomies."[197] (By contrast, the civil war raging in the United States of America confirmed that the flaws highlighted by the eighteenth-century French critics of its 1787 Constitution—slavery and an excessive concentration of power in the federal government—had set it on the unstable path of regressive consolidation.)[198] To secure the future of liberty, the development of the federative principle had to extend to the reorganization of social and economic life, through the proliferation of associations to "guarantee mutually the conditions of common prosperity." Only the genuine subordination of state power to the federative principle could resolve the contradictions in human economic life and foster the emergence of a federal Europe: not the "United States of Europe" imagined by contemporary French democrats, which would amount to "a new Holy Alliance," but a "confederation of confederations."[199] Otherwise, class conflict would cause the contradictions between liberty and authority to continue intensifying; where the latter predominated, elites in each state would combine internationally "to guarantee from state to state the exploiting classes against the exploited classes, consequently to form a coalition of capital against wages, whatever

195. Ibid., 60–61.
196. Ibid., 33.
197. Ibid., 40.
198. Ibid., 42, 66. Proudhon went so far as to claim that what "little true liberalism" had appeared in the United States of America was reflected from the French Revolution, and that under Jefferson's presidency, "if it had not been for that negative liberty which resulted from a small population and land of amazing fertility, it would have been better to live under the despotism of Louis XIV or Napoleon than in the American republic" (55–56).
199. Ibid., 53. On the evolution of Proudhon's thinking about associations, see Edward Castleton, "Association, Mutualism, and Corporate Form in the Published and Unpublished Writing of Pierre-Joseph Proudhon," *History of Economic Ideas* 25, no. 1 (2017): 143–72.

language and nationality they all may be."[200] In short, the dream of the Italian nationalist Giuseppe Mazzini—that a system of democratic nation-states would emerge once a "holy alliance of the peoples" had superseded the Holy Alliance of princes—was Proudhon's nightmare.[201] "The twentieth century will open the age of federations," Proudhon declared, "or else humanity will undergo another purgatory of a thousand years."[202]

200. Proudhon, *Du principe fédératif et de la nécessité de reconstituer le parti de la révolution*, 198–99.
201. On Proudhon's criticisms of Mazzini, see Prichard, *Justice, Order and Anarchy*, 54.
202. Proudhon, *The Principle of Federation*, 68.

CHAPTER FIVE

Narrating Progress

It is already a beginning of the dominion of the good principle and a sign
"that the Kingdom of God is at hand," even if only the principles of its
constitution begin to become public; for in the world of the understanding
something is already there when the causes, which alone can bring it to
pass, have taken root generally, even though the complete development of its
appearance in the world of the senses is postponed to an unseen distance.

—KANT, *RELIGION WITHIN THE BOUNDARIES OF MERE REASON*[1]

IN EARLY 1816, German newspapers began reporting a news item from
Saint Petersburg: Emperor Alexander I of Russia had published a Christmas manifesto publicly proclaiming the Holy Alliance, which had been
signed in Paris by two of his wartime allies (the king of Prussia and the
Austrian emperor) in September 1815, and subsequently by the restored
king of France. In response, the philosopher Wilhelm Traugott Krug
rushed into print a pamphlet offering the complete text and translation
of the treaty, together with his analysis. From a "cosmopolitan" perspective, Krug wrote, the enduring world-historical significance of Europe's
postwar settlement in 1815 was not to be found in the diplomatic negotiations at the Congress of Vienna (which so clearly recalled the peace of
Westphalia in 1648) but in the proclamation of the Holy Alliance.[2] The
Holy Alliance represented a progression from a military coalition, which had
formed at a particular moment to resist an unjust aggressor, to a federation

1. Immanuel Kant, *Religion and Rational Theology*, ed. Allen W. Wood and George Di
Giovanni, Cambridge Edition of the Works of Immanuel Kant (Cambridge: Cambridge
University Press, 1996), 175; *Kant's gesammelte Schriften* (Berlin: G. Reimer, 1902), 6:151.

2. Wilhelm Traugott Krug, *La sainte alliance: Oder Denkmal des von Oestreich,
Preußen und Rußland geschloßnen heiligen Bundes* (Leipzig: H. A. Koechly, 1816), 23.

of states, founded on universal and timeless principles of justice. The text of its "founding document" declared the compatibility of these principles with the moral teaching of Christianity. It categorically rejected the view, which had reached its apotheosis with Napoleon, that morality had no place in politics and that religion was merely a tool of social control. Instead, it invited all states which recognized its "fundamental law" to consider their peoples as forming "one and the same Christian nation."[3] Krug noted that a recent history of the Congress of Vienna by the French writer Dominique de Pradt had attributed to Napoleon the remark that "it was not the coalition that dethroned me, but liberal ideas." However, Krug continued, Pradt had been wrong to despair of the subsequent fate of those ideas, because the advent of the Holy Alliance demonstrated not the "power of princes" but "the power of liberal ideas": it was, in fact, "the most liberal of all ideas."[4]

In Krug's analysis, the treaty of the Holy Alliance was an invitation to "public opinion in all of civilized Europe" to apply the Christian principles of "justice, love and peace" as a standard for judging the internal and external conduct of states.[5] Internally, Krug claimed, these principles required the promulgation of "liberal constitutions" and toleration of all forms of religion that were compatible with them.[6] Externally, they required a new codification of international law that would guarantee collective security and definitively exclude wars of conquest. Like many earlier writers on "perpetual peace," Krug went on to claim that these principles were compatible with collective military action against the Ottoman Empire—in this case, to emancipate the Greeks. They were also compatible with a coordinated effort to dismantle Britain's maritime hegemony and monopolistic approach to international trade through a corrected version of Napoleon's continental system that would be organized according to "the principle of national equality of rights."[7] Finally, Napoleon's conquest of the pope's territories would not be repeated, but the "Holy Father" would also be excluded until he had renounced his "unchristian politics" and become a "worthy son and genuine member of the universal Christian Church" by embracing the principles of the Holy Alliance.[8]

3. Ibid., 28, 31, 37.
4. Ibid., 30, 42–43.
5. Ibid., 34, 28.
6. Ibid., 39.
7. Ibid., 46.
8. Ibid., 48. In fact, it was the pope who refused to join the Holy Alliance, not the other way around: Nikolai Mikhailovich, *L'Empereur Alexandre Ier: Essai d'étude historique*,

Krug's pamphlet contributed to a wider literature that turned the Holy Alliance into an idea of progress by incorporating it into a philosophy of history. Some of this literature, as chapter 1 discussed, was compiled in the *Archive of the Holy Alliance* of 1818–19—and it continued to develop during the early 1820s. Krug's initial endorsement of the Holy Alliance ultimately developed into the first history of liberalism. Published in 1823, *A Historical Description of Liberalism in Ancient and Modern Times* narrated the progress of "liberal ideas," starting with the ancient Greek philosophers who had first begun examining and seeking to improve the civil and religious establishments of their day. The modern development of these liberal ideas, in the form of Christianity, had culminated in the emergence of the Holy Alliance, which Krug once again identified as "the most liberal of all ideas."[9] For Krug, and others like him, the Holy Alliance supplied the ideal political framework for ensuring that progress could continue indefinitely, at a sustainable pace, without relapsing into the volatile dynamics of revolution and reaction. Krug further claimed that the religious consensus represented by the Holy Alliance—a consensus signaled by the ecumenical language of the treaty and by the fact that the original signatories each belonged to a different confession (Orthodox, Protestant, and Catholic)—was capable of transcending all the divisions of humanity without stifling the individuality of diverse communities and their respective strivings for progress.

The idea of progress that Krug called "the most liberal of all ideas" derived from an emphatically Protestant perspective on the history of religion that was also embraced by other early liberals like Benjamin Constant.[10] It diverged significantly from the view of the Holy Alliance defended by Alexander Stourdza, the diplomat who had been entrusted

---

vol. 2 (St. Petersburg: Manufacture des papiers de l'État, 1912), 210–14, https://catalog .hathitrust.org/Record/100154739.

9. "die dem heiligen Bunde zum Grunde liegende Idee in der That die *allerliberalste* ist." Wilhelm Traugott Krug, *Geschichtliche Darstellung des Liberalismus alter und neuer Zeit: Ein historischer Versuch* (Leipzig: F. A. Brockhaus, 1823), 149. Krug asserted the priority of his history of liberalism on p. vi, and it has not been questioned.

10. Helena Rosenblatt, *Liberal Values: Benjamin Constant and the Politics of Religion* (Cambridge: Cambridge University Press, 2008); Laurence Dickey, "Constant and Religion: 'Theism Descends from Heaven to Earth,'" in *The Cambridge Companion to Constant*, ed. Helena Rosenblatt, Cambridge Companions to Philosophy (Cambridge: Cambridge University Press, 2009), 313–48; Bryan Garsten, "Constant on the Religious Spirit of Liberalism," in *The Cambridge Companion to Constant*, ed. Helena Rosenblatt, Cambridge Companions to Philosophy (Cambridge: Cambridge University Press, 2009), 286–312; Bryan Garsten, "Religion and the Case against Ancient Liberty: Benjamin Constant's Other Lectures," *Political Theory* 38, no. 1 (2010): 4–33.

with Alexander's first draft of the treaty. For Stourdza, who had become notorious in Germany for an 1818 pamphlet attacking its universities, the unifying potential of the Holy Alliance was dependent on the renewal of the Orthodox Church as the true inheritor of the original unity of Christianity.[11] In his response, Krug condemned Stourdza for playing into the hands of liberal skeptics of the Holy Alliance while himself violating the true spirit of its principles; and he refused to accept that Stourdza had accurately represented the views of a Russian emperor who had recently added to his emancipatory legacy by giving "the unfortunate Poles a constitution more liberal than the Germanic peoples can hope to obtain any time soon."[12] At the same time, however, Krug shared with Stourdza not only a commitment to the cause of Greek emancipation but also a complex blend of attraction to and critical distance from the form of spirituality that was closely associated with Emperor Alexander and had become essential to his charismatic authority. Such "mysticism," as we have seen, was far from monolithic or inherently reactionary; nor was it simply apolitical or even distinctively eastern. As Paul Werth has observed, it is "probably better described as a particular kind of Evangelical Protestantism, substantially inflected by pietist tendencies," to which a wide variety of other Christians were more or less receptive.[13]

Krug's idea of progress reconnects the Holy Alliance to the much more familiar history of contemporary Anglo-American efforts to abolish slavery and war. The Anglo-American reformers who initially recognized the Holy Alliance as an instrument of providence were relying in part on the testimony of personal encounters with Alexander's spirituality, which they also found manifested in the Russian Bible Society, founded by Alexander's childhood friend Alexander Golitsyn shortly after the British and Foreign Bible Society had established itself in Saint Petersburg in 1812. Among British Evangelicals, according to Boyd Hilton's classic study, views of providence ranged from "extreme" millenarian expectations of extraordinary divine interventions to more "moderate" accounts

11. Stella Ghervas, *Réinventer la tradition: Alexandre Stourdza et l'Europe de la sainte-alliance* (Paris: Champion, 2008), 194–98, 332. See also Alexander M. Martin, *Romantics, Reformers, Reactionaries: Russian Conservative Thought and Politics in the Reign of Alexander I* (DeKalb: Northern Illinois University Press, 1997), 169–98.

12. Wilhelm Traugott Krug, *État actuel de l'Allemagne: Ou examen et réponse au Mémoire de M. de Stourdza* (Leipzig: Brockhaus, 1819), 25.

13. Paul W. Werth, "The French Connection and the Holy Alliance: Two Sources of Imperial Russia's Multiconfessional Establishment," in *Die Heilige Allianz: Entstehung, Wirkung, Rezeption*, ed. Anselm Schubert and Wolfram Pyta (Stuttgart: Verlag W. Kohlhammer, 2018), 133–34.

of its workings through predictable natural causes; from the "masochistic chiliasm" of those who resigned themselves to suffering as a "mark of grace" to more "respectable" exhortations to "improvement."[14] The dynamics among these positions also played out in Krug's remarkable meeting with the Livonian religious eccentric Juliane von Krüdener, which he documented in an 1818 pamphlet. As chapter 2 discussed, Krüdener's acolytes had ranged from Germaine de Staël and Benjamin Constant to Emperor Alexander; her fortunes had since fallen. Krug, for his part, was mainly interested in finding out what she could reveal about the origins of the Holy Alliance. Listening to her discourse from her sickbed about suffering and repentance, and about the ruinous influence of contemporary "rationalism" and "philosophism," he steered their conversation back to whether there was any truth to rumors that she had authored the treaty (it was "a direct work of God," Krüdener replied, and she had merely been the instrument through which the idea had been communicated to the emperor).[15] In his reflections on the meeting, Krug admitted that his head and heart had responded differently. He registered his disapproval of her extreme enthusiasm, but also his compassion for her suffering; they parted with mutual respect, and with a shared conviction that Europe desperately needed the Holy Alliance to succeed in its aims, in spite of the machinations of diplomats and the insouciance of the British. In his memoirs, Krug later recounted how powerfully the burning of Moscow in 1812 had affected him as a spectacular instance of divine retribution against the French invaders, just as it had galvanized Alexander and so many others in his religious circle.[16] However, Krug did not join them in proceeding to the conclusion that the Holy Alliance was the handiwork of a "second

14. Boyd Hilton, *The Age of Atonement: The Influence of Evangelicalism on Social and Economic Thought, 1785–1865* (Oxford: Oxford University Press, 1992), 10, 13–15.

15. Wilhelm Traugott Krug, *Gespräch unter vier Augen mit Frau von Krüdener gehalten und als Neujahrsgeschenk für gläubige und ungläubige Seelen* (W. Rein und Komp., 1818), 6–7, 9–10.

16. Wilhelm Traugott Krug, *Meine Lebensreise: In sechs Stazionen zur Belehrung der Jugend und zur Unterhaltung des Alters beschrieben von Urceus* (Leipzig: Baumgärtner, 1825), 177–78, https://hdl.handle.net/2027/chi.088244701. In fact, Krug admitted, the doctor and Kantian philosopher Johann Benjamin Erhard had told him "to his face" that he "must have a real Cossack soul"; he hastened to affirm that he was a genuine cosmopolitan who did not hate the French. Compare Benjamin Constant's opening declaration in the preface to the first edition of his *The Spirit of Conquest and Usurpation and Their Relation to European Civilization*, published in Hanover in January 1814: "the flames of Moscow were the dawn of liberty for the entire world." Benjamin Constant, *Political Writings*, ed. Biancamaria Fontana (Cambridge: Cambridge University Press, 1988), 45.

savior."[17] On the contrary, his judgment of the Holy Alliance was framed within a philosophy of history that confined knowledge of providence to arguments in the abstract about the historical unfolding of humanity's moral potential.

Krug's history of liberalism closely followed the approach to the history of religion that had been developed by Immanuel Kant: Krug was Kant's immediate successor as professor of logic and metaphysics at the University of Königsberg, and he spent much of his career elaborating on Kant's ideas about religion and politics. Krug associated the Holy Alliance with the Kantian idea of an ethical community whose universality transcended the ineluctable divisions locking humanity into particular states. As this chapter will show, however, others writing in the early 1820s—most notably the Danish German philosophical banker Conrad von Schmidt-Phiseldek, as well as the exiled Danish geographer Conrad Malte-Brun and the French philosopher Henri de Saint-Simon—identified the Holy Alliance with a stage in a historical process leading to the more concrete reunification of humanity. From their perspective, the reference in the treaty of the Holy Alliance to "one and the same Christian nation" under the sovereignty of God pointed to the emergence of a pan-European civic culture and the institutional development of a European federal state with a collective imperial mission. The contrasting conceptions of the historical process generating this unity were connected in turn to further sets of arguments—on aesthetics and imagined communities of taste, on public finance and monetary union, on industry and the division of labor, and on law and legitimacy—that collectively represent a further elaboration of eighteenth-century debates about the moral and material progress of civilization discussed in chapter 2. Viewed in this way, the appearance of the Holy Alliance was one of a series of moments that prompted the reactivation of an older set of expectations concerning the development of Russia, its increasing involvement in European politics, and the potential consequences for the progress of European "civilization." In the 1820s, some of the claims underlying these expectations were incisively challenged by the prominent Catholic writers Joseph de Maistre and Félicité de Lamennais, followed by the philosopher August Comte.

The notion of a pan-European "Christian nation" projected the liberal idea of the Holy Alliance onto broader imperial horizons that included the

17. Philipp Menger, "Die Heilige Allianz: 'La garantie du nouveau système Européen'?" in *Das europäische Mächtekonzert: Friedens- und Sicherheitspolitik vom Wiener Kongress 1815 bis zum Krimkrieg 1853*, ed. Wolfram Pyta and Philipp Menger (Köln: Böhlau Verlag, 2009), 209.

Atlantic world.[18] As chapter 3 discussed, leading British reformers had proven highly receptive to Alexander's public diplomacy during his visit to London in 1814. This chapter further shows how the Holy Alliance was initially perceived as a providential instrument for redeeming the sins of slavery and war by the prominent British abolitionist James Stephen as well as the founder of the Massachusetts Peace Society, Noah Worcester. These expectations of the Holy Alliance were systematically challenged by a learned American diplomat stationed in Europe, Alexander Hill Everett, who was also a perceptive reader and critic of Schmidt-Phiseldek. Drawing in part on his reading of the political economist Thomas Malthus, Everett produced a different account of the Holy Alliance, its imperial civilizing mission, and the providential future of liberalism. Everett's efforts to convey his analysis of European politics to an American audience, together with the responses of his European critics and his own observations on developments across the Atlantic in the 1820s, open up a broad new comparative perspective: a transatlantic consideration of the liberal idea of the Holy Alliance as a pan-European federal empire.

The Most Liberal of All Ideas

Krug was appointed as Kant's successor in Königsberg in 1804 thanks to the intervention of the Prussian minister Julius Eberhard von Massow, who was attracted to Krug's reputation as a prominent Kantian critic of the overly "exuberant" direction that Kantian philosophy had taken at the University of Jena.[19] For Krug, the task of philosophy was not to connect knowledge to existence by deducing the unity of subject and object in consciousness: rather, philosophical reasoning had to proceed from the fact that this unity was already present in the mind (an approach Krug called "transcendental synthesism").[20] Krug had turned his back on Kant's metaphysics—much like many late twentieth-century Kantians such as

18. This imperial context has remained absent from discussions of the Holy Alliance that recognize its connection to liberalism by presenting it as an important stage in the development of an ideal conception of European unity and as a precursor to the European Union. See, most recently, Stella Ghervas, *Conquering Peace: From the Enlightenment to the European Union* (Cambridge, MA: Harvard University Press, 2021), 106–16.

19. Steffen Dietzsch, "Von Kant zu Krug: Die Königsberger Philosophische Fakultät 1804–1809," in *Königsberger Beiträge*, ed. Joseph Kohnen (Frankfurt am Mein: Lang, 2002), 242.

20. On Krug's "transcendental synthesism," see Adolf Kemper, *Gesunder Menschenverstand und transzendentaler Synthetismus: W. T. Krug, Philosoph zwischen Aufklärung und Idealismus* (Münster: Lit, 1988).

John Rawls and his followers, who, like Krug, were most attracted to Kant's practical philosophy. In fact, with the government's support, Krug added the chair in practical philosophy to his portfolio shortly upon his arrival in Königsberg; in 1809, he left for the University of Leipzig, in his native Saxony, where he spent the rest of his career, known primarily as a spirited polemicist and advocate for liberal causes like Greek independence and Jewish emancipation. However, Krug did genuinely follow Kant in the sense that he aligned himself with Kant's own valedictory denunciation of his self-proclaimed successors. In 1799, Kant had denounced the distinction between the spirit and letter of his philosophy that had been introduced by his interpreters in Jena, and declared in an open letter that his philosophy "is to be understood exclusively from the point of view of common sense, which only needs to be sufficiently cultivated for such abstract investigations."[21] Krug opposed the view, famously proclaimed in 1801 by the philosophers Friedrich Wilhelm Joseph Schelling and Georg Wilhelm Friedrich Hegel, that philosophy was only philosophy when it constructed "an inverted world" in relation to the "common sense" rationality of a particular time and place.[22] As Krug put it in a later work, such skepticism manifested an "anarchic" spirit in opposition to the "despotic" spirit of dogmatism. Both extremes precluded what Krug described as the "genuinely republican spirit" of a "citizen of the philosophical community":

> everyone who knows how to put forward reasonable reasons [*vernünftige Gründe vorzubringen*], as a citizen of the philosophical community, has the right to represent general human reason in his person and to assert his conviction not as a mere private opinion, but as a law for all thinking fellow citizens.[23]

21. Manfred Kuehn, "The Early Reception of Reid, Oswald and Beattie in Germany: 1768–1800," *Journal of the History of Philosophy* 21, no. 4 (1983): 487. On Kant and "common sense," see also Karl Ameriks, "A Commonsense Kant?" *Proceedings and Addresses of the American Philosophical Association* 79, no. 2 (2005): 19–45. More generally, see Sophia Rosenfeld, *Common Sense: A Political History* (Cambridge, MA: Harvard University Press, 2011).

22. Friedrich Wilhelm Joseph Schelling and Georg Wilhelm Friedrich Hegel, "The Critical Journal, Introduction: On the Essence of Philosophical Criticism Generally, and its Relationship to the Present State of Philosophy," in *Between Kant and Hegel: Texts in the Development of Post-Kantian Idealism*, ed. George Di Giovanni and H. S. Harris, trans. H. S. Harris, rev. ed. (Indianapolis: Hackett Publishing Company, 2000), 283.

23. Wilhelm Traugott Krug, *Fundamentalphilosophie oder urwissenschaftliche Grundlehre*, 2nd ed. (Züllichau und Freistadt: In der Darnmann'schen Buchhandlung, 1819), 276, https://catalog.hathitrust.org/Record/008402948. As the passage suggests, a twentieth-century Krug might have found much to admire in the "Kantian constructivism"

In a ruthlessly incisive 1801 review, Hegel observed that Krug had indeed been able to reproduce the content of Kant's key doctrines, though in cloaking "common sense" in scientific jargon he had merely robbed it of its natural "popularity and easiness."[24] However, Hegel charged, Krug's approach had imprisoned itself in the rationality of the moment. At its root it had allied itself to a "dogmatic skepticism" that "lacks the noblest side of skepticism"—namely, "its orientation against the dogmatism of ordinary consciousness"—because it "places its truth and certainty in the most blatant limitedness both of empirical intuition, and of empirical knowledge."[25] For Hegel, this was to eliminate the vantage point from which the rationality of a whole series of past moments could come to be recognized as cumulative. But Hegel's 1801 analysis also serves as a discerning guide to the character of Krug's future endorsement of the Holy Alliance. The knowledge that Krug's sort of philosophy could generate, Hegel observed, was limited to an endless and fruitless oscillation between the two poles that had already been defined by Kant's philosophy. It could, with "indubitable certainty," identify the particular with the universal; and it could, with equally "indubitable certainty," identify the non-universality of the particular.[26] It could, in other words, identify the Holy Alliance as the universal ethical community of humanity; and it could also reassert the unbridgeable gulf separating any particular moment in history from the genuine realization of that idea.

Krug delivered his inaugural lecture in Königsberg in the fall of 1805. It was given less than a week after the Russian emperor had signed a treaty in Potsdam, creating the alliance that was defeated by Napoleon shortly afterward at Austerlitz, which put an end to many of the plans for remaking European politics that were discussed in chapters 3 and 4. The topic of Krug's lecture was neither logic nor metaphysics but rather Kant's theory of the state, which supplied the basis for the liberal constitutionalism that

elaborated by Rawls: John Rawls, "Kantian Constructivism in Moral Theory," *Journal of Philosophy* 77, no. 9 (1980): 515–72.

24. Georg Wilhelm Friedrich Hegel, "How the Ordinary Human Understanding Takes Philosophy (as Displayed in the Works of Mr. Krug)," in *Between Kant and Hegel: Texts in the Development of Post-Kantian Idealism*, ed. George Di Giovanni and H. S. Harris, trans. H. S. Harris, rev. ed. (Indianapolis: Hackett Publishing Company, 2000), 306.

25. Georg Wilhelm Friedrich Hegel, "On the Relationship of Skepticism to Philosophy, Exposition of Its Different Modifications and Comparison of the Latest Form with the Ancient One," in *Between Kant and Hegel: Texts in the Development of Post-Kantian Idealism*, ed. George Di Giovanni and H. S. Harris, trans. H. S. Harris, rev. ed. (Indianapolis: Hackett Publishing Company, 2000), 339. On Hegel and skepticism, see Michael N. Forster, *Hegel and Skepticism* (Cambridge, MA: Harvard University Press, 1989).

26. Hegel, "On the Relationship of Skepticism to Philosophy, Exposition of Its Different Modifications and Comparison of the Latest Form with the Ancient One," 330, 339–40.

Krug would later attribute to the Holy Alliance. In the 1790s, Krug had sketched a constitution that replaced the Holy Roman Empire with a German republic independent from both Prussia and Austria and allied with revolutionary France in the creation of a peaceful new European order.[27] In his inaugural lecture, Krug detached the idea of representative government from revolutionary republicanism and associated it with a theory of constitutional monarchy instead. In developing this approach, Krug was not only following Kant but also building on a critique of Aristotle that had been the topic of another lecture he had given in the summer of 1805 (the two lectures were published together in 1806, and Krug went on to reproduce their joint content in several of his publications after 1815).[28] Krug objected to the Aristotelian classification of regimes according to the number of rulers and whether or not they ruled in the public interest: a scheme that distinguished monarchy from aristocracy and polity, and each of these in turn from their respective deviant forms of tyranny, oligarchy, and democracy. Krug's main problem with this traditional scheme was that it conflated the representation of public power (a question of constitutional structure) with the manner in which it was exercised. As Josiah Ober has now also claimed, Krug argued that such a distinction between sovereignty (*Herrschaftsform*) and government (*Regierungsform*) had already been present in the ancient Greek distinction between *archein* (equivalent to *herrschen* in German) and *kratein* (equivalent to *regieren* in German or *gubernare* in Latin).[29] According to Krug, then, the Aristotelian

27. Wilhelm Traugott Krug, "Grundlinien zu einer allgemeinen deutschen Republik, gezeichnet von einem Märtyrer der Wahrheit," in *Die Anfänge des Konstitutionalismus in Deutschland: Texte deutscher Verfassungsentwürfe am Ende des 18. Jahrhunderts*, ed. Horst Dippel (Frankfurt am Main: Keip, 1991), 114–46.

28. Wilhelm Traugott Krug, *Über Staatsverfassung und Staatsverwaltung: Ein politischer Versuch* (Königsberg: Göbbels und Unzer, 1806), https://opacplus.bsb-muenchen.de /title/BV001455321. Cf. Wilhelm Traugott Krug, *Das Repräsentativsystem: Oder Ursprung und Geist der stellvertretenden Verfassungen; mit besondrer Hinsicht auf Deutschland und Sachsen* (Leipzig: Köhler, 1816), https://mdz-nbn-resolving.de/urn:nbn:de:bvb:12 -bsb10636428-6; Wilhelm Traugott Krug, *Wilhelm Traugott Krug's Dikäologie oder philosophische Rechtslehre* (Königsberg: Unzer, 1817), https://books.google.com/books ?id=9sgGAAAAcAAJ; Wilhelm Traugott Krug, *Dikäopolitik oder neue Restaurazion der Staatswissenschaft mittels des Rechtsgesetzes* (Leipzig: Hartmann, 1824), http://mdz-nbn -resolving.de/urn:nbn:de:bvb:12-bsb10769612-2.

29. Krug, *Über Staatsverfassung und Staatsverwaltung*, 48–51. Cf. Josiah Ober, "The Original Meaning of 'Democracy': Capacity to Do Things, Not Majority Rule," *Constellations* 15, no. 1 (2008): 3–9. The argument that Aristotle had failed to distinguish sovereignty from government dates to Jean Bodin's 1566 *Method for the Easy Comprehension of History*: see Richard Tuck, *The Sleeping Sovereign: The Invention of Modern Democracy* (Cambridge: Cambridge University Press, 2016), 9–12. For a contrasting analysis of

scheme had mixed together forms of sovereignty ending in *-archy* with forms of government ending in *-cracy*. As a result, it had fostered the mistaken view that the form of government was entirely determined by the form of constitution, which was to mistake the state for a machine and its functionaries for automata.[30] It had helped fuel recurring controversies, inflamed once again by the French Revolution, over the nature of the best regime, the relative advantages of republics and monarchies, and the relationship between civil and political liberty.

Krug's account of constitutional monarchy was designed to supersede these controversies while also reclaiming the emancipatory promise of the French Revolution. If a republic was a "public thing" (*res publica*) then it could assume many forms, including a monarchical one (as Emmanuel Joseph Sieyès had claimed in his debate with Tom Paine in 1791).[31] Electing the sovereign representative, as the citizens of a *Freistaat* or "free state" did, was only one method for protecting individuals from the exercise of public power, and not necessarily the most effective. It would be better to speak of "means of protecting liberty," Krug suggested, than to oppose "political" to "civil" liberty (because citizenship in a *polis* did not differ from citizenship in a *civitas*); and it would be best to avoid the confusing term "republic" entirely.[32] More fundamentally, superseding these controversies required recognizing that the representation of public power could only be either singular (in which case it was "monarchy") or plural (in which case it was "polyarchy," a term also appropriated from Sieyès); whereas the exercise of public power could be either "autocratic" or "syncratic" according to whether it denied or allowed "certain representatives of the people" (*gewissen Volksvertretern*) a say in how they were governed.[33] This new scheme revealed that in an astonishingly short period of time, and with only a few scattered exceptions, European states had all become "syncratic monarchies." Provocatively, Krug even included

Aristotle as a theorist of sovereignty, see Melissa Lane, "Popular Sovereignty as Control of Office-Holders: Aristotle on Greek Democracy," in *Popular Sovereignty in Historical Perspective*, ed. Richard Bourke and Quentin Skinner (Cambridge: Cambridge University Press, 2016), 52–72.

30. Krug, *Über Staatsverfassung und Staatsverwaltung*, 83–84.

31. Ibid., 32, 38–39; Emmanuel Joseph Sieyès, "The Debate between Sieyès and Tom Paine," in *Political Writings*, ed. Michael Sonenscher (Indianapolis: Hackett, 2003), 163–73. The debate was quickly translated into German.

32. Krug, *Über Staatsverfassung und Staatsverwaltung*, 92–94, 41.

33. Ibid., 25. Krug's usage of "polyarchy" differs from Sieyès's in that Sieyès had defined monarchy and polyarchy as forms of government, because his whole argument against Paine's republicanism was predicated on the shared premise of popular sovereignty.

archetypically republican Switzerland in this assessment.[34] His main point was that the great French experiment with polyarchical sovereignty in the 1790s had collapsed due to insufficient consensus among its representatives, and monarchical sovereignty had now been restored under Napoleon. The restraints on the exercise of state power in France were less effective in practice than those in Great Britain, but for Krug this was a difference in degree rather than kind. Though most European states still lacked representative institutions, they had at least inherited feudal restraints on the sovereign's exercise of state power. Above all, they were all increasingly subject to the court of public opinion, whose intensifying power over governments had spread across Europe and beyond through the medium of print: it was public opinion that now formed "the palladium of civil liberty."[35]

Krug's inaugural lecture inscribed this account of constitutional monarchy within the parameters of Kant's theory of the state. Following Kant, Krug defined the concept of the state in relation to the limitless development of human capacities: the distinctive human characteristic that Jean-Jacques Rousseau had called "perfectibility."[36] The best regime, in this context, became an ideal of maximizing both the scope of individual liberty and the efficacy of public power in securing justice. Significantly, on this occasion Krug did not rehearse Kant's unflinching insistence on the role of antagonism as the engine of historical progress toward this ideal of the legal state, though he did warn that revolution was the natural consequence of the failure of political institutions to keep pace with "the inexorably progressing spirit of the age and social relations that are always further developing and spreading."[37] However, for Krug as for Kant, perfectibility also meant that particular states were never more capable of attaining an ideal legality than particular individuals were capable of

34. Ibid., 58.What he presumably meant was that under the 1803 constitution mediated by Napoleon (discussed in chapter 3), the Swiss federal government was headed by an individual, who was the chief magistrate of one of the six cities where the federal Diet met. Krug was happy to label this *Landammann der Schweiz* a "monarch" in order to underline his broader point about the irrelevance of merely nominal distinctions between regimes: neither renaming the king of Great Britain a "president" nor changing Napoleon's title back to first consul would amount to a regime change.

35. Ibid., 96.

36. Ibid., 66–67, 88; Jean-Jacques Rousseau, "Discourse on the Origin and Foundations of Inequality among Men," in *The Discourses and Other Early Political Writings*, ed. Victor Gourevitch (Cambridge: Cambridge University Press, 1997), 141. On perfectibility, see Michael Sonenscher, "Sociability, Perfectibility and the Intellectual Legacy of Jean-Jacques Rousseau," *History of European Ideas* 41, no. 5 (2015): 683–98.

37. Krug, *Über Staatsverfassung und Staatsverwaltung*, 90.

realizing the totality of humanity's potential. No particular constitution could be eternal, Krug explained, and the collective perfection of states, as instruments of the collective perfection of the human species, would manifest as the proliferation of a diversity of particular forms.[38] Krug ultimately relied on his historical account of European state development to explain why this Kantian picture of an unattainable ideal need not be grounds for despair but could be grounds for hope in progress. The reform of European governments through the introduction and improvement of representative institutions was not predicated on revolutionary constitutional change. On the contrary, constitutional change would follow from the reform of government. In short, European states were well positioned to proceed as Kant had described. Kant had claimed that states could introduce representative institutions under the guidance of a public opinion that was enlightening itself: a process that presupposed mutual trust, such that the sovereign was exercising state power in the public interest, and that public opinion remained committed to a legal process for recalibrating positive limits on individual liberty. Kant had further claimed that monarchs were much more likely than aristocracies or democracies to introduce and develop the distinction between sovereignty and government.[39] The message of Krug's inaugural lecture was that in the wake of the French Revolution, and with the development of European public opinion, European monarchies were capable of following such a path of "gradual reform . . . from the top down"—a path that Krug would later term "true liberalism"—and avoiding the destructive anarchy that would follow another "sudden revolution . . . from the bottom up."[40]

The kind of arrangement between monarchical sovereignty and representative government invoked by Krug's inaugural lecture has been described as a transitional form of constitutionalism that was especially pronounced in Germany, where the popular sovereignty of the modern

38. Ibid., 78–82, 90.

39. Immanuel Kant, "An Answer to the Question: 'What Is Enlightenment,'" in *Political Writings*, ed. Hans Reiss, trans. H. B. Nisbet (Cambridge: Cambridge University Press, 1991), 58–60; Immanuel Kant, "On the Common Saying: 'This May Be True in Theory, but Does Not Apply in Practice,'" in *Political Writings*, ed. Hans Reiss, trans. H. B. Nisbet (Cambridge: Cambridge University Press, 1991), 84–87; Immanuel Kant, "Perpetual Peace: A Philosophical Sketch," in *Political Writings*, ed. Hans Reiss, trans. H. B. Nisbet (Cambridge: Cambridge University Press, 1991), 100–102.

40. Krug, *Über Staatsverfassung und Staatsverwaltung*, 89. On "true liberalism," see Wilhelm Traugott Krug, *Der falsche Liberalismus unsrer Zeit: Ein Beitrag zur Geschichte des Liberalismus und eine Mahnung für künftige Volksvertreter* (Leipzig: Kollmann, 1832), 45.

state was especially slow to supersede the "absolutism" of *ancien régime* monarchy. However, it is better understood as a rival conception of the modern constitutional state: as an alternative vision of Europe's constitutional future.[41] Krug went on to define this future in opposition to a different one also articulated in 1805 by the Prussian writer Friedrich Buchholz in his *New Leviathan*, a radical reinterpretation of the political thought of Thomas Hobbes. Krug's lecture celebrated the promising future of "syncratic monarchy" that could succeed where the "polyarchy" of the revolutionary French Republic had failed; by contrast, Buchholz's book denounced existing European monarchies like Prussia and England as "polyarchies." According to Buchholz, the failure of these monarchies to consolidate sovereignty had generated conflict among rival elites (from the feudal aristocracy to the Jewish *Geldaristokratie*) jockeying for political power—a conflict that, in the English case, had produced a quest for commercial empire.[42] By contrast, Napoleon had demonstrated that a consti-

---

41. See the trenchant criticism of Ernst-Wolfgang Böckenförde's influential account of constitutional development in Horst Dreitzel, *Absolutismus und ständische Verfassung in Deutschland: Ein Beitrag zu Kontinuität und Diskontinuität der politischen Theorie in der frühen Neuzeit* (Mainz: Verlag Philipp von Zabern, 1992), 128–29. Krug, as Dreitzel pointed out, was one of the first to note (in his political dictionary that began to appear in 1827) that the term *Absolutismus* had recently extended its reach beyond philosophical debates about identity and had begun to acquire a political meaning that Krug equated with *Autokratismus* (in opposition to *Synkratismus*) as well as *Hobbesianismus*. In the second, 1832 edition, Krug further linked the term to *Imperialismus*. For Krug, then, "absolutism" did not denote the standard European political form between 1648 and 1789, as it came to do in the 1830s for the Hegelian jurist Eduard Gans, but rather a deviation from the development of the modern state that had always been defined not only by sovereignty but also by the limits on sovereignty. See Wilhelm Traugott Krug, "Absolutismus" and "Hobbes" in *Allgemeines Handwörterbuch der philosophischen Wissenschaften, nebst ihrer Literatur und Geschichte: Nach dem heutigen Standpuncte der Wissenschaft*, vol. 2 (Leipzig: F. A. Brockhaus, 1827), 24, 386, https://catalog.hathitrust.org/Record /008692114; "Imperialismus," in *Allgemeines Handwörterbuch der philosophischen Wissenschaften, nebst ihrer Literatur und Geschichte: Nach dem heutigen Standpuncte der Wissenschaft*, 2nd ed., vol. 2 (Leipzig: F. A. Brockhaus, 1832), 515, https://hdl.handle.net /2027/pst.000022917935, cited in Dreitzel, *Absolutismus und ständische Verfassung in Deutschland*, 128. See, too, the growing new literature on the proliferation of "granted" constitutions in the first decades of the nineteenth century: Luigi Lacchè, "Granted Constitutions: The Theory of Octroi and Constitutional Experiments in Europe in the Aftermath of the French Revolution," *European Constitutional Law Review* 9, no. 2 (2013): 285–314; Oscar Ferreira, *Le constitutionnalisme octroyé: Itinéraire d'un interconstitutionnalisme au XIXe siècle (France, Portugal, Brésil)* (Paris: Éditions Eska, 2019); Richard Albert, Xenophon Contiades, and Alkmene Fotiadou, eds., *The Law and Legitimacy of Imposed Constitutions* (New York: Routledge, 2019).

42. I have learned about Buchholz through the work of Thomas Clausen, "Reason of State in Early 19th-Century German Political Thought" (M.Phil diss., University of Cam-

tution presupposed a unitary sovereign will, not the other way around.[43] Krug also elaborated his vision of Europe's constitutional future in opposition to contemporary defenses of the *ancien régime*. In his 1806 *Fragments upon the Balance of Power in Europe* (also discussed in chapter 4), the diplomat Friedrich Gentz highlighted the limits on power generated in every European monarchy by jurisdictional pluralism and the privileged classes as well as public opinion. After 1815, Gentz and others developed this view of monarchy into a different theory of representation: one that distinguished the representation of the social interests of the estates (which could effectively limit the power of a monarchical sovereign) from the specter of popular or national representation (behind which loomed the specter of unlimited popular sovereignty).[44] By contrast, Krug pointedly included both types of representation under the label of "syncratic" government. In his 1816 book *The Representative System*, Krug endorsed estate-based constitutions where they were already in place (such as in Saxony): not by opposing them to national representation, like Gentz or his ally Adam Müller, but by incorporating them into an expanded history of state development. This was an account of progress that was not yet called the "history of liberalism" but contained some of its key elements—including a climactic endorsement of the Holy Alliance.

According to Krug's new history of the state, the regimes of classical antiquity (whatever their constitutional structure) had invariably been autocratic. The origin of syncratic government was Germanic and initially took the form of feudalism. The history of medieval Europe was the history of battles between Roman "autocratism" and Germanic "syncratism," and modern history was the continuation of those battles, but in a less destructive form, because the "idea of right" had been enriched and developed by Christianity and the philosophy that it had inspired.[45] Syncratic government had extended its reach beyond its aristocratic origins and was gradually encompassing all of society, as peoples progressively shed

bridge, 2014). See also Dreitzel, *Absolutismus und ständische Verfassung in Deutschland*, 122; Iwan-Michelangelo D'Aprile, "Prussian Republicanism? Friedrich Buchholz's Reception of James Harrington," in *European Contexts for English Republicanism*, ed. Gaby Mahlberg and Dirk Wiemann (Farnham: Ashgate, 2013), 225–36.

43. Friedrich Buchholz, *Der Neue Leviathan* (Tübingen: J. G. Cotta, 1805), 95.

44. Friedrich von Gentz, *Fragments upon the Balance of Power in Europe* (London: M. Peliter, 1806), 117–25; Dreitzel, *Absolutismus und ständische Verfassung in Deutschland*, 122–23. On nineteenth-century debates about these different approaches to representation, see Gregory Conti, *Parliament the Mirror of the Nation: Representation, Deliberation, and Democracy in Victorian Britain* (New York: Cambridge University Press, 2019).

45. Krug, *Das Repräsentativsystem*, 20–21.

their immaturity and public opinion swung decisively in its favor.[46] The founding of the Holy Alliance was a major landmark in this process, Krug claimed, because it signaled the development of the originally crude Germanic "idea of right" into a full-fledged "Christian-philosophical art and science of politics": one that had formally theorized the "reciprocal rights and duties of people in general and of princes and peoples in particular."[47] Krug went on to become one of the most determined defenders of this science of the modern constitutional state against one of its most ferocious critics: the Swiss jurist Karl Ludwig von Haller.[48] In the first volume of his *The Restoration of Political Science*, which appeared in 1816, Haller had singled out Kant and his followers as the latest and most dangerous kind of revolutionaries:

> With Kant emerged a new school, a variation of the same revolutionary sect, that does not speak of known, original facts, of hypotheses, but of ideals or postulates of reason, of continuous reforms, of the gradual realization of a legal [*rechtlich*] state, and so on, but which basically strives for the same goals, and which, because of its disguise and apparent moderation, is even far more dangerous and enchanting than all French revolutionary ideas put together.[49]

46. Ibid., 26–27. On the history of liberalism as aristocratic, see Annelien de Dijn, *French Political Thought from Montesquieu to Tocqueville: Liberty in a Levelled Society?* (Cambridge: Cambridge University Press, 2008).

47. Krug, *Das Repräsentativsystem*, 25. In another 1816 publication, titled *Princes and Peoples with Regard to Their Reciprocal Demands*, Krug had described the difference between revolution and reform as a difference between blindly violent natural force and human "intention, deliberation, and prudence." Wilhelm Traugott Krug, *Die Fürsten und die Völker in ihren gegenseitigen Forderungen dargestellt* (Leipzig: A. H. Köchly, 1816), 136, http://mdz-nbn-resolving.de/urn:nbn:de:bvb:12-bsb10559267-0.

48. Wilhelm Traugott Krug, *Die Staatswissenschaft im Restaurazionsprozesse der Herren von Haller, Adam Müller und Konsorten* (Leipzig: Fleischer, 1817); Wilhelm Traugott Krug, *Sendschreiben des Herrn von Haller an seine Familie, betreffend seinen Uebertritt zur katholischen Kirche* (Leipzig: Rein, 1821); Krug, *Dikäopolitik*. See Béla Kapossy, "Karl Ludwig von Haller's Critique of Liberal Peace," in *Commerce and Peace in the Enlightenment*, ed. Béla Kapossy, Isaac Nakhimovsky, and Richard Whatmore (Cambridge: Cambridge University Press, 2017), 244–71; Béla Kapossy, "Words and Things: Languages of Reform in Wilhelm Traugott Krug and Karl Ludwig von Haller," in *Languages of Reform in the Eighteenth Century: When Europe Lost Its Fear of Change*, ed. Susan Richter, Thomas Maissen, and Manuela Albertone (New York: Routledge, 2020), 384–404.

49. Karl Ludwig von Haller, *Restauration der Staats-Wissenschaft: Oder Theorie des natürlich-geselligen Zustands, der Chimäre des künstlich-bürgerlichen entgegengesetzt*, vol. 1 (Winterthur: In der Steinerischen Buchhandlung, 1816), 71–72, cited in Kapossy, "Words and Things," 391. I have used Kapossy's translations of Haller here.

Haller—anticipating in this respect a great deal of more recent scholarship—traced these ideas back to Hobbes and the other natural jurists of the seventeenth century. Krug, like Kant, had followed Hobbes in starting from a theory of representative sovereignty: sovereigns ruled on behalf of the community. Haller condemned this entire legal edifice, which was based on abstract concepts and terms taken from Roman law, as dangerously detached from social reality—and also as the ultimate enabler of the massive expansion of the fiscal capacity of European states (it was easier to tax people to pay for a national war than for a ruler's personal war).[50] Restoring political science meant recognizing that law could only develop as a private relation among princes (singular or plural—Krug was well aware that Haller was a patrician Bernese republican) who governed in their own right and within their own means. Haller's ideal of the "natural politics" of the patrimonial state was famously singled out for attack by Hegel, who accused Haller of lapsing into a dogmatic arbitrariness that entirely destroyed the basis for a science of law.[51] Krug took a different approach, claiming that Haller had misunderstood the relationship between knowledge and existence: "Mr. Haller thinks that science constitutes life, whereas on the contrary life constitutes science."[52] Earlier, Krug had tried to indicate the limits of reason by challenging Hegel to "deduce" the existence of the particular pen with which he wrote—the provocation that had prompted Hegel's devastating review. But Krug's point now was that if philosophers could not deduce a pen, then they certainly could not cause a revolution.

The history of liberalism within which Krug located the Holy Alliance was not just a history of political progress. For Krug, it also had to be a history of moral progress that encompassed all of humanity and unfolded through the history of religion. In fact, Krug identified the Holy Alliance as "the most liberal of all ideas" precisely because it combined the political with the ethical and religious principles of liberalism.[53] Krug had followed Kant in describing the construction of a legal order as the product of a rationality of a particular time and place which did not presuppose morality. This was why the history of political progress had to culminate in a proliferation of diverse state forms, and why the political side

50. Kapossy, "Words and Things," 393.

51. Georg Wilhelm Friedrich Hegel, *Elements of the Philosophy of Right*, ed. Allen Wood, trans. Hans Nisbet (Cambridge: Cambridge University Press, 1991), 278–81.

52. Krug, *Die Staatswissenschaft im Restaurazionsprozesse der Herren von Haller, Adam Müller und Konsorten*, 17–18, cited in Kapossy, "Words and Things," 395.

53. Krug, *Geschichtliche Darstellung des Liberalismus*, 148–49.

of Krug's liberalism ultimately took the shape of a pluralistic federalism. Any attempt to unify humanity in the form of a state—Krug referred in one of his essays to the legal concept of a *civitas maxima*, discussed in chapter 4—would not represent the progress of legality but a regression into arbitrary relations of force.[54] However, the same historical process that could progressively legalize states internally could also legalize their external relations. The arbitrariness and instability of a "balance of power" among states could give way to the legality of a "federation of states" or "general society of nations."[55] Krug's model for such "unity in diversity" was the Holy Roman Empire and its successor, the German Federation created at the Congress of Vienna in 1815.[56] The great task facing Germany's political elites, Krug wrote in 1816, was to ensure that German aspirations to national unity were harnessed to the form of a federation (*"Bundes-Einheit"*) rather than state (*"Staates-Einheit"*). The political diversity of Germany was such that any attempt to consolidate it into a single state would be as calamitous and violent as an attempt to realize the ideal of perpetual peace through the construction of a European state or "universal monarchy": the consequences for German character and culture would be devastating. Instead, Krug called for more robust federal institutions—including an executive modeled on the president of the United States or the Landammann of Switzerland, as well as a federal court—that would help stabilize and legalize the balance of power between Prussia and Austria.[57] However, the precarity of Germany's present federation reflected the more general problem that the legality of external relations between states would always have to rely on a "guarantee" that could only be furnished through the "general improvement" of humanity's

---

54. Wilhelm Traugott Krug, "Ueber politisches Gleichgewicht und Uebergewicht, Universalmonarchien und Völkervereine, als Mittel, die Völker zum ewigen Frieden zu führen," in *Kreutz- und Queerzüge eines Deutschen auf den Steppen der Staats-Kunst und Wissenschaft* (Leipzig: Rein, 1818), 100, http://mdz-nbn-resolving.de/urn:nbn:de:bvb:12 -bsb10769616-3. For the same reasons, Krug dismissed any hopes of preventing the eventual independence of India or other colonies, even if future technological developments, such as air travel, were to shrink the distance between continents. The core of this essay was originally published in 1812: see Andreas Volkmer, "Kriegsverhütung und Friedenssicherung durch Internationale Organisation: Deutsche Ideen und Pläne 1815–1871" (PhD diss., Philipps-Universität Marburg, 2012), 89. The version published in 1818 contains appendices discussing the Holy Alliance that were omitted from the version republished in Krug's collected works.

55. "ein allgemeiner Völkerverein oder Staatenbund (*feodus civitatum universal— société générale des nations*)." Krug, "Ueber politisches Gleichgewicht," 1818, 103.

56. Krug, *Die Fürsten und die Völker*, 61.

57. Ibid., 63–68.

religious and moral as well as political and material condition.[58] On the political side, the process of state development would continue to generate resources and institutions that could help eliminate many prior causes of international conflict. On the moral side, Krug appealed to the sociability and religious tolerance that accompanied economic development. But he also insisted on the deeper need for the moral transformation of public opinion through religion, which could redirect the political machinery of each state to building peace. Writing in 1818, Krug claimed that those striving to bring about this transformation now had solid grounds for their hope that could not be dismissed as mere enthusiasm: the founding of the Holy Alliance.[59] The founding document of the Holy Alliance, with its denunciation of existing forms of politics and diplomacy, was written neither by nor for professional diplomats: Krug likened their scorn for the Holy Alliance to the rejection of Christianity itself by the ancient Jews and pagans. The proclamation of the principles of "Christian politics" by the founders of the Holy Alliance represented a rare and precious opportunity to transform public opinion. It amounted to "a new political gospel," and it was the duty of all to spread its message.[60] Failing to do so, Krug warned, would lead to the appearance of "a second Napoleon": like Rehoboam, the son of Solomon who was the last king of Israel, this one would respond to the people's plea for moderation by offering only a heavier yoke than his predecessor, thereby inciting the revolution that would permanently divide the Kingdom of Israel.[61]

The history of liberalism that Krug published in 1823 grew out of a distinctively Kantian approach to the history of religion. Krug had attained some notoriety in the 1790s as an expositor of this rationalist approach.[62] More broadly, Krug belonged to a long-standing tradition of biblical interpretation known as "accommodationism," which had been embraced by many eighteenth-century German Protestants and which

58. Krug, "Ueber politisches Gleichgewicht," 1818, 105.

59. Ibid., 110–11.

60. Ibid., 115–16.

61. Ibid., 117. Krug quoted from 1 Kings 12:10–11. "My finger is thicker than my father's waist. . . . My father scourged you with whips; I will scourge you with scorpions."

62. Wilhelm Traugott Krug, *Briefe über die Perfektibilität der geoffenbahrten Religion: Als Prolegomena zu einer jeden positiven Religionslehre, die künftig den sichern Gang einer vestgegründeten Wissenschaft wird gehen können* (Jena: Im Akademischen Lese-Institut, 1795), https://catalog.hathitrust.org/Record/100867387. Krug's initially anonymous work inspired several polemical responses, caused a minor scandal, and prompted an official inquiry that resulted in his exclusion from consideration for professorships in theology. Krug, *Meine Lebensreise*, 96.

Krug had also written about in the 1790s: it sought to understand how eternal truths were expressed in ways that accommodated the limited conceptual horizons of particular moments in human history.[63] From this perspective, the Christian doctrine of sacrifice and atonement had been the historical form that the moral teaching of Jesus had to take in order to be introduced into a culture still fixated on fear of divine punishment. As we have seen, Krug's approach to constitutionalism has been described as a transitional form between absolute monarchy and modern popular sovereignty; similarly, accommodationism has been characterized in terms of a transition between "religious (i.e. world-denying) and secular (i.e., world-affirming) ways of explaining moral purpose in the world."[64] However, Krug's accommodationism is better described as a distinct approach to what would later come to be called political theology, one that located the moral foundations of politics in a relationship between the human and divine that was defined by the concept of "perfectibility." The "perfectibility" of humanity presupposed a divine motivation for moral progress, internalized as "striving for freedom," and Krug defined "liberalism" as the expression of this striving.[65] Much as Benjamin Constant had indicated at the conclusion of his now canonical 1818 lecture on ancient and modern liberty, Krug explained that the concept of liberty in question was not just a negative absence of interference because the "developmental drive" to realize humanity's moral potential would always transcend the limits defined by the legal order of any particular time or place. Liberty therefore had to mean political liberty as well: it had to encompass a political "guarantee" (*Bürgschaft*) against subjection to arbitrary human authority. Where social relations were sufficiently developed, this guarantee would take the form of a representative constitution whose ulti-

63. On Krug and accommodationism, see Hoon J. Lee, *The Biblical Accommodation Debate in Germany: Interpretation and the Enlightenment* (Cham: Palgrave Macmillan, 2017), 149–51, http://dx.doi.org/10.1007/978-3-319-61497-7. On the longer hermeneutical tradition and its relation to conceptions of providential history, see Amos Funkenstein, *Theology and the Scientific Imagination from the Middle Ages to the Seventeenth Century* (Princeton: Princeton University Press, 1986), 209–71.

64. Dickey, "Constant and Religion," 320. Dickey refers to critics of the "compromise" theology elaborated by the liberal Protestant theologian Ernst Troeltsch (a close colleague of Max Weber's) in his *Social Teaching of the Christian Churches* (1912).

65. Krug, *Geschichtliche Darstellung des Liberalismus*, 102, 93–94. Krug's emphasis on moral motivation here recalls the approach to the idea of religion precociously elaborated by Kant's follower Johann Gottlieb Fichte in his *Attempt at a Critique of All Revelation* (1792).

mate function was to guard against the imposition of arbitrary limits on human perfectibility.[66]

Krug's history of liberalism was actually a history of the struggle between liberalism and the "anti-liberalism" that always sought to defend the civil and ecclesiastical order of the day from the challenge posed by "liberal ideas." The purpose of telling this history, Krug explained, was to show how this struggle could be conducted with moderation: its aim was to supply the grounds for reconciliation in an "age of extremes."[67] Liberalism erred when it failed to recognize the need for positive limits on liberty that would necessarily be instituted according to the rationality of a particular time and place, in which case it degenerated into revolutionary "Ultraliberalism": "Jacobinism, Sansculottism, Radicalism, Carbonarism, or however else one wishes to name it according to the period and circumstances." Anti-liberalism was correct to resist revolutionary liberalism but degenerated into extremism when it became so intransigent as to "fetter humanity in unalterable chains with respect to religion, politics, or both, and thus to make the servitude of blind faith and deed eternal": this was to violate "not only human nature, but God's will." The result was another set of labels for extremism such as "Ultraroyalism" or, Krug proposed, "Imperfectibilism." At the extremes, Krug concluded, revolutionary liberalism and counter-revolutionary anti-liberalism became indistinguishable as futile attempts to compensate for "inner weakness" with physical force. Both sides were trying to build the foundations of society out of sand rather than eternal laws.[68]

Krug's history of this struggle was a defense of moral progress that unfolded within Kant's parameters. According to Kant, humanity was defined by the irreducible capacity of individuals to make moral choices

66. Krug, *Geschichtliche Darstellung des Liberalismus*, 99, 101. Cf. Benjamin Constant, "The Liberty of the Ancients Compared with That of the Moderns," in *Political Writings*, ed. Biancamaria Fontana (Cambridge: Cambridge University Press, 1988), 327. "I bear witness to the better part of our nature, that noble disquiet which pursues and torments us, that desire to broaden our knowledge and develop our faculties. It is not to happiness alone, it is to self-development that our destiny calls us; and political liberty is the most powerful, the most effective means of self-development that heaven has given us."

67. Krug, *Geschichtliche Darstellung des Liberalismus*, vii. On moderation and extremism in the period, see Aurelian Craiutu, *A Virtue for Courageous Minds: Moderation in French Political Thought, 1748–1830* (Princeton: Princeton University Press, 2012). On Krug's typology in a broader context, see Uwe Backes, *Political Extremes: A Conceptual History from Antiquity to the Present* (London: Routledge, 2010), 86–90. More generally see Aurelian Craiutu, *Faces of Moderation: The Art of Balance in an Age of Extremes* (Philadelphia: University of Pennsylvania Press, 2017).

68. Krug, *Geschichtliche Darstellung des Liberalismus*, 102–5.

for themselves, but the realization of this moral freedom was necessarily a social endeavor whose outcome could only be considered from the vantage point of the entire course of human history. From this perspective, as Kant explained in his *Religion within the Boundaries of Mere Reason*, the history of moral progress was a history of "enduring conflict" between the eternal principles of "moral religion" (which had thus far only appeared with Christianity) and the various forms that particular communities gave to their collective ethical striving over time.[69] The moral progress of humanity could be measured by the extent to which such communities had succeeded in approximating the ideal of a truly universal "ethical community" encompassing the totality of humanity: a concept of community whose universality presupposed that "God himself is in the last instance the author of its constitution as founder."[70] However, Kant allowed, it was already an indication of moral progress—"a sign 'that the Kingdom of God is at hand,' even if only the principles of its constitution begin to become public": for Kant, moral progress had to begin with "a revolution" in thought before "a gradual reformation" of conduct could ensue.[71] Krug's history and his endorsement of the Holy Alliance were an elaboration of this outline.

In Krug's telling, the struggle between liberalism and anti-liberalism had not begun with the French Revolution, or even with the Protestant Reformation, but in ancient Greece. The idea of the social contract was originally Plato's, not Rousseau's, and it had not been a call to revolution but an attempt to articulate an ethical basis for political obligation. The progress of liberal ideas had continued with the introduction of Christianity: a new vessel for Greek philosophy whose aim had not been to overthrow the laws of the Jewish national religion but to give them a more liberal form. The "liberal spirit" had dimmed under the tyranny that began with transformation of Christianity into a state religion, but it had reawakened after the fall of Constantinople and the discovery of America; with Martin Luther, "the liberal spirit of classical antiquity called the liberal spirit of original Christianity back into life." Conflict between liberalism and anti-liberalism then intensified over the values of liberty and equal-

69. Kant, *Religion and Rational Theology*, 154; *Kant's gesammelte Schriften*, 6:124.

70. Kant, *Religion and Rational Theology*, 176; *Kant's gesammelte Schriften*, 6:152. On Kant's ideal, see Samuel A. Stoner and Paul T. Wilford, "Realizing the Ethical Community: Kant's Religion and the Reformation of Culture," in *Kant and the Possibility of Progress: From Modern Hopes to Postmodern Anxieties* (Philadelphia: University of Pennsylvania Press, 2021), 94–114.

71. Kant, *Religion and Rational Theology*, 92, 175; *Kant's gesammelte Schriften*, 6:47–48, 6:151.

ity, which were grounded in the Christian ideal of the "community of all believers."[72] After the horrors of the seventeenth century, more moderate forms of the conflict emerged with German pluralism and English constitutionalism. Internationally England's behavior had remained illiberal in spite of English liberalism, but its former American colonies now had an opportunity to flourish because of liberalism. In France, however—apart from the Archbishop Fénelon, whom Krug identified as an exemplary liberal Catholic for his commitment to economic and political as well as religious liberty—liberalism had taken a degenerate form that had unleashed revolutionary extremism when financial troubles beset the French monarchy.[73] Since the restoration, the moderate liberalism guaranteed by France's new constitution had been undermined by ultraroyalists; southern Europe remained in the grip of both forms of extremism, with liberalism increasingly becoming radicalized under obdurate repression. Nonetheless, Krug concluded his history with the judgment that liberalism was on the ascendant. Though antagonism was necessarily a feature of all life, liberalism had decisively and durably achieved predominance in the balance of power over anti-liberalism. Krug's confidence in this predominance rested less on his rather cursory sociological survey of Europe than on his claim that "the Holy Alliance guarantees it to us."[74]

Krug's prognosis of liberalism's future and the endorsement of the Holy Alliance that supported it were grounded in his philosophy of history. "The historian has been called a backward-facing prophet," Krug observed (quoting an aphorism published in 1798 by the philosopher Friedrich Schlegel): "so an actual prophet would be a forward-facing historian."[75] The latter orientation captured the indefinite future implied by the concept of "perfectibility," which remained ever beyond the reach of any particular moment in history. Rather than trespassing into actual prophecy, Krug hastened to explain, his prognosis of liberalism's future remained within the limits of logical conclusions drawn from the past. The result was a kind of historical

---

72. Krug, *Geschichtliche Darstellung des Liberalismus*, 64–65.

73. Ibid., 134, 77–82. Krug expanded on his remarks about Fénelon in a separate journal article: Wilhelm Traugott Krug, "Fenelon's Liberalismus," *Literarisches Conversations-Blatt für das Jahr 1823*, no. 53 (March 4, 1823): 209–10.

74. Krug, *Geschichtliche Darstellung des Liberalismus*, 147.

75. Ibid., 141. See August Wilhelm Schlegel and Friedrich Schlegel, eds., *Athenaeum 1798–1800* (Stuttgart: J. G. Cotta, 1960), 196, https://hdl.handle.net/2027/pst.000 005706549. I am grateful to Michael Sonenscher both for the source of this aphorism and for his insights into its significance, which will appear in his forthcoming book, *After Kant: The Romans, the Germans, and the Moderns in the History of Political Thought* (Princeton: Princeton University Press, 2023).

narrative whose nationalist English counterpart came to be called "Whig history."[76] It also produced the kind of oscillation between faith and skepticism that Hegel had identified as characteristic of Krug's version of Kantianism. In describing the Holy Alliance as a "victory" for liberalism, Krug rehearsed key attributes of the Kantian ideal of an "ethical community": its universality, its expression of eternal principles of moral religion, its recognition of God as founder and legislator.[77] The formal recognition of these moral principles by the many diverse states that had acceded to the alliance represented the moral transformation of the entire legal structure of European politics. Krug was even prepared to accept the Austrian intervention in Naples and the impending French invasion of Spain as, in principle, potentially legitimate measures to secure the future of liberalism itself (though he also published an article later in 1823 expounding an expansive theory of the right to intervention that managed to condemn both as illegal while also justifying a Russian invasion of the Ottoman Empire to liberate the Greeks).[78] The path of liberal moderation, Krug reminded skeptical readers, rested on the presupposition of the sovereign's goodwill, and more deeply, on firm faith in the workings of providence. At the very end, however, Krug's defense of the Holy Alliance concluded with a skeptical retreat to the unbridgeable gulf between any particular moment in history and an ideal expressed in terms of the entire future of human history:

> Always distinguish the idea from its appearance, the matter from the people, the alliance from the allies, as well as what individuals do from the great course of world history! Eras of humanity end; they rise and fall, only for their successors to ascend anew and still further. Whatever may happen here or there certainly brings no shame on our faith in the general progress of humanity in all that is true, beautiful and good.[79]

Krug's judgment of the Holy Alliance finally settled at this skeptical pole after the revolutions of 1830: "the idea was too great for this age."[80] Instead of

76. Herbert Butterfield, *The Whig Interpretation of History* (London: G. Bell and Sons, 1931).

77. Krug, *Geschichtliche Darstellung des Liberalismus*, 152.

78. Krug, *Dikäopolitik*, 322–64. In an 1821 pamphlet, Krug had expressed his disappointment that the founding members of the Holy Alliance had refused to intervene in support of the Greek uprising—without, however, joining those who had concluded that the Holy Alliance was either "extinct" or "degenerated": it was, in his estimation, a seed that had not yet begun to germinate. Wilhelm Traugott Krug, *Griechenlands Wiedergeburt: Ein Programm zum Auferstehungsfeste* (Leipzig: Brockhaus, 1821).

79. Krug, *Geschichtliche Darstellung des Liberalismus*, 158–59.

80. Wilhelm Traugott Krug, "Porträt von Europa," in *Politische und juridische Schriften*, vol. 3, Krug's Gesammelte Schriften 5 (Braunschweig: Friedrich Vieweg, 1835), 220.

the Holy Alliance marking the moral transformation of European politics, Krug wrote in 1831, the misapprehension and perversion of the ideal it represented had produced a reprise of Napoleonic domination, now exercised jointly by five great powers over everybody else. In Hegel's terms, Krug's enactment of the "unhappy consciousness" of the Holy Alliance had ended up unwilling to accept the present but also incapable of fulfilling its longing for an alternative.[81]

Krug's idea of the Holy Alliance was constructed out of arguments that are also integral to more familiar versions of liberalism: an overlap that poses a challenge to canonizing accounts of the history of liberalism. Krug's liberalism bears many affinities to the liberalism of Benjamin Constant, whose profound engagement with German thought is well established, and whose writings on both politics and religion Krug later praised as "truly philosophical."[82] Yet, as Krug also noted, Constant's philosophy had not prevented him from endorsing Napoleon upon his return from his initial exile on Elba in 1814; had Constant's overtures to the Russian emperor in 1814–15 not been blocked by Alexander's former Swiss tutor, Frédéric-César de la Harpe, perhaps he might also have gone on to become a liberal enthusiast of the Holy Alliance.[83] A more explicit acknowledgment of the affinities between the liberal idea of Napoleon

81. Georg Wilhelm Friedrich Hegel, *Phenomenology of Spirit*, trans. A. V. Miller (Oxford: Oxford University Press, 1977), 119–38. For an application of the concept of "unhappy consciousness" to the history of liberalism, see Judith N. Shklar, *After Utopia: The Decline of Political Faith* (Princeton: Princeton University Press, 1957).

82. Wilhelm Traugott Krug, *Allgemeines Handwörterbuch der philosophischen Wissenschaften, nebst ihrer Literatur und Geschichte: Nach dem heutigen Standpuncte der Wissenschaft*, 2nd ed., vol. 1 (Leipzig: F. A. Brockhaus, 1832), 522, https://hdl.handle.net /2027/pst.000022917928. A further indication of Krug's alignment with Constant comes from his role in posthumously publishing an unfinished epistolary work on religion and politics by his close colleague in Leipzig, the theologian Heinrich Gottlieb Tzschirner. Tzschirner had written half of his planned letters (critical of several prominent French Catholics) before he died. As Krug explained in his preface, the work was supposed to have culminated with "letters to Constant on the necessity of fighting for truth and liberty against their opponents": "on Constant's glorious efforts to counter the errors of the age in his most recent writing *De la religion*"; "Ideas for an apology for the eighteenth century"; and "Ideas for an apology for the Reformation with special regard for France." Heinrich Gottlieb Tzschirner, *Briefe eines Deutschen an die Herren Chateaubriand, de LaMennais und Montlosier über Gegenstände der Religion und Politik* (Leipzig: Barth, 1828), 6–8, http://mdz-nbn-resolving.de/urn:nbn:de:bvb:12-bsb10776927-8. On Constant and German thought, see especially Rosenblatt, *Liberal Values*.

83. On La Harpe and Constant, see chapter 2. The copy of Krug's *History of Liberalism* digitized by Google Books happens to be La Harpe's annotated copy, now held by the library of the Canton de Vaud: https://books.google.com/books?id=vecTAAAAQAAJ. The annotations include emphatic question marks in the margins of the concluding remarks on the Holy Alliance.

(which developed into a potent legend over the course of the nineteenth century) and the liberal idea of the Holy Alliance is supplied by another principal architect of the former: Emmanuel, comte de Las Cases. According to Las Cases, who had accompanied his "prince of liberal ideas" on his final exile to Saint Helena in the South Atlantic, Napoleon himself had claimed the Holy Alliance as his own: "I too should have had my congress and my holy alliance. These are plans which were stolen from me."[84]

At the same time, arguments about the religious basis of moral and political progress that were closely related to Krug's, but without the term "liberalism," also appeared in other contemporary writings that were collected, excerpted, or reviewed in the *Archive of the Holy Alliance*. Keeping them in the picture poses a further challenge to canonizing histories of liberalism. One of the most striking works excerpted in the *Archive*—an essay published in Hamburg in 1817—took the form of an elaborate analogy with the confessions of faith that appeared during the Protestant Reformation.[85] The treaty of the Holy Alliance had to be read as a comparable strategy arising in comparable circumstances: such documents arose out of struggles between public opinion and arbitrary power, in moments when established institutions could no longer meet the needs of the times. A statement of principles condemning the past articulated a new standard of judgment for public opinion going forward. In pursuing this strategy, the Holy Alliance was the descendant not only of the confessions of faith of the Protestant Reformation but also of the Declaration of Rights of the French Revolution.[86] Though the French Revolution had faltered (and Napoleon had failed to

---

84. Emmanuel-Auguste-Dieudonné comte de Las Cases, *Mémorial de Sainte Hélène: Journal of the Private Life and Conversations of the Emperor Napoleon at Saint Helena*, vol. 3 (London: H. Colburn and Company, 1823), 265. Buttressing Napoleon's claim: an 1806 article declaring that Napoleon had been "chosen by Providence to establish the foundations of civilization and to found the peace of the world" and lamenting that after "the Emperor founded Europe," so many princes remained reluctant "to enter into that holy alliance whose only object is the peace and welfare of humanity." *Gazette nationale ou le moniteur universel*, no. 132, May 12, 1806, 664, https://www.retronews.fr/journal/gazette-nationale-ou-le-moniteur-universel/12-mai-1806/149/1304453/2. The remark was later repeated by Napoleon's nephew, the future president and emperor of France: Louis-Napoléon Bonaparte, *Des idées napoléoniennes* (Paris: Imprimerie de Félix Malteste et Cie, 1839), 176. On the reinterpretation of Napoleon's political legacy that became a potent ingredient of nineteenth-century French liberalism, see Sudhir Hazareesingh, *The Legend of Napoleon* (London: Granta, 2004).

85. Friedrich Gottfried Cramer, *Betrachtungen über das heilige Bündniss besonders in Vergleich mit ähnlichen Ereignissen des sechszehnten Jahrhunderts* (Hamburg: Hoffmann und Campe, 1817).

86. Ibid., 51.

fulfill the role of its savior), the principles of 1789 had proliferated. Though the Reformation too had initially lapsed into re-creating past abuses, over the long run its principles had helped develop public opinion into the engine of progress, impelling authorities to conform to their ideals. The Holy Alliance was "fundamentally a political Protestantism": its reference to the sovereignty of God, like the principle of *sola scriptura*, established the illegitimacy of any human power incompatible with divine authority.[87] The principles of the Holy Alliance expressed a commitment to a constitutional politics that included the introduction of representative institutions (*Volksrepräsentation*).[88] Whichever path the Holy Alliance ended up taking in the short run, its principles would also continue to spread.

Finally, one of the most ambitious contributions to the *Archive of the Holy Alliance* that paralleled many of Krug's arguments was a lengthy letter to its editor by the Archdeacon of Kottbus, Ludwig August Kähler. Like Krug, Kähler inserted the Holy Alliance into an account of world history as the realization of human moral potential. His 1819 "Ideas on the Reality of the Holy Alliance" was structured by an opposition between natural and moral freedom: between the history of force becoming law, which was the history of Rome, and the history of law becoming morality, which was the history of Christianity or "a second history of humanity."[89] The history of Christianity, in turn, was characterized by the conflict between rival conceptions of human unity in terms of existence and development, or (Catholic) being and (Protestant) becoming. European history had been characterized by the resulting gap between the development of its ideals and its material reality. After the French Revolution finally dissolved the materialistic balance of power system, the degeneracy of Napoleon's regressive attempt to reunify Europe by force had aroused resistance united by shared moral outrage. It was to rescue this moral spirit from a postwar relapse into egoism that the Holy Alliance had appeared:

> for the first time the Confessions flowed together in a true unity encompassing all classes and interests; and the focal point of this unity revealed itself in the world as a holy alliance. Christian love is the highest summit of human perfection, and the idea of the Holy Alliance,

87. Ibid., 58.
88. Ibid., 102.
89. "Ideen über die Realität des heiligen Bundes, von Ludwig August Kähler, Archidiakonus zu Kottbus," in *Archiv des Heiligen Bundes: Enthaltend die denselben betreffenden Aktenstücke, Literatur, Nachrichten und Urtheile*, vol. 2 (München: Thienemann, 1819), 316, http://mdz-nbn-resolving.de/urn:nbn:de:bvb:12-bsb10555184-1.

to the extent it can have a real effect on life, the summit of political perfection.[90]

The Holy Alliance, then, was not an expression of the individuality of its founder: "the idea expressed in the Holy Alliance resides, more or less clearly and vividly, in millions of heads and hearts."[91] Alexander's role could not be reduced to fear (for Russia had nothing left to fear after its triumph over Napoleon in 1812) or interest (for Russia's power would continue to grow even without the Holy Alliance). On the contrary, Alexander's treaty expressed "the progress that European humanity has made over the past age"; he had "caught in the mirror of a great soul the image of Europe, and his age; and so the Holy Alliance came to life as the most beautiful promise of religion and political wisdom."[92] In doing so, Alexander had followed in the footsteps of the previous "creators of a new condition for Christian humanity": Constantine, Gregory VII, and Martin Luther.[93] However, Kähler concluded by leavening his faith with the same sort of skepticism as Krug: the political future of the actually existing Holy Alliance remained to be seen, and was as unknowable as the next form of Christianity or humanity itself.

Though the declared aim of the *Archive* had been to compile the full range of contemporary responses to the Holy Alliance, voices like Krug's and Kähler's were given a more receptive hearing than voices like Krüdener's. The 1816 pamphlet by Robert Hindmarsh, the leader of the Swedenborgian Church in Manchester, was criticized as a "theologico-polemical" violation of the ecumenical moral spirit of the Holy Alliance for its claim that a close reading of the treaty revealed its endorsement of Swedenborgian antitrinitarian doctrine.[94] By contrast, Krug's 1816 pamphlet was warmly praised as the definitive and most historically significant contribution to the literature on the Holy Alliance, with only one reservation, namely Krug's inevitably doomed attempt to co-opt the term "liberal": "it

90. Ibid., 308.
91. Ibid., 328.
92. Ibid., 321, 329.
93. Ibid., 325–26.
94. Robert Hindmarsh, *Remarks on the Holy League Lately Entered into by Their Majesties the Emperor of Austria, the King of Prussia, and the Emperor of Russia: Wherein They Openly Proclaim and Recommend to Their Own Subjects, and to the Christian World at Large, the Two Essential and Distinguishing Articles of the New Church, Called the New Jerusalem* (Manchester: F. Davis, 1816); *Archiv des Heiligen Bundes: Enthaltend die denselben betreffenden Aktenstücke, Literatur, Nachrichten und Urtheile,* vol. 1 (München: Thienemann, 1818), 94, http://mdz-nbn-resolving.de/urn:nbn:de:bvb:12-bsb10555183-6.

would have been better that a word whose first usage was a misuse, which came out of the most illiberal mouth that ever spoke a human language, Bonaparte's—it would have been better to have given this word back to the French language, or to have sent it to its creator on St. Helena!"[95]

One Christian Nation under God

At the end of his history of liberalism, Krug instructed readers skeptical of his endorsement of the Holy Alliance to consult *Politics According to the Principles of the Holy Alliance*, published in 1822 by the German Danish writer Conrad Friedrich von Schmidt-Phiseldek.[96] Schmidt-Phiseldek was the most prolific of the liberal commentators who sought to specify the historical process leading to the political unification of the "Christian nation" named in the treaty of the Holy Alliance. *Politics According to the Principles of the Holy Alliance* was the final installment of a sprawling trilogy that had appeared in quick succession starting in 1820. It was the sequel to *The European Federation*, which had appeared in 1821, and had integrated the Holy Alliance into a Kantian philosophy of history similar to Krug's: one that expected antagonism to assume increasingly legalized forms, ensuring the continuation of progress while increasingly excluding the violence of war and revolution from European politics.[97] *Politics According to the Principles of the Holy Alliance* further connected the proclamation of the Holy Alliance to the development of a new form of cosmopolitan politics: one that was no longer limited to expressing a utopian alternative to self-interest (which, as the philosopher Gotthold Ephraim Lessing had once suggested, too often served as an excuse not to do good).[98] Earlier cosmopolitans had asserted abstract principles of universality in opposition to the individuality of the nationalities whose resurgence had, in fact, rescued Europe from Napoleon's regressive bid for domination. By contrast, the tolerant and ecumenical religiosity invoked by the Holy Alliance reflected the entrance into European politics of a conception of human unity that embraced national diversity. Much like the Polish statesman Adam Jerzy Czartoryski, Schmidt-Phiseldek saw

95. *Archiv des Heiligen Bundes*, 2:231–32.

96. Krug, *Geschichtliche Darstellung des Liberalismus*, 152; Conrad Friedrich von Schmidt-Phiseldek, *Die Politik nach den Grundsätzen der heiligen Allianz* (Kopenhagen: Friedrich Brummer, 1822), https://mdz-nbn-resolving.de/urn:nbn:de:bvb:12-bsb10725782-6.

97. Conrad Friedrich von Schmidt-Phiseldek, *Der Europäische Bund* (Kopenhagen: Friedrich Brummer, 1821), http://mdz-nbn-resolving.de/urn:nbn:de:bvb:12-bsb10557621-9.

98. Schmidt-Phiseldek, *Die Politik nach den Grundsätzen der heiligen Allianz*, 2.

the Holy Alliance not as a device for suppressing aspirations to national autonomy but as an overarching legal framework for realizing them. He too proceeded to define politics as "the art of training and educating the individual state for interaction with other states": if states could learn how to conduct their external relations in ways that remained compatible with collective security and prosperity, the unity of humanity could be realized within the confines of a fundamentally divided and diverse world.[99] Unlike Czartoryski or Krug or Constant, but like others in the 1820s, Schmidt-Phiseldek endowed this aspiration to unity with a concrete institutional form and associated it with the emergence of a new pan-European civic identity. The Holy Alliance was "the federal act [*Bundesakt*] constituting the Christian nation," he wrote; "there lies undeniably in the Holy Alliance the idea of a European federation [*eines Europäischen Staatenbundes*] which now has to be realized."[100] Thanks to his emphatic commitment to Europe's federal future (including monetary union), Schmidt-Phiseldek has occasionally been enlisted as a precursor of the twentieth-century founding of a European Union.[101] However, this perspective leaves out the imperial side of Schmidt-Phiseldek's federalism. This was the main theme of the first and most widely read installment in Schmidt-Phiseldek's trilogy, which appeared in 1820 in German, English, French, Danish, and Dutch, and was also translated into Swedish the following year.[102] In *Europe and America, or, The Relative State of the Civilized World at a Future Period*, Schmidt-Phiseldek warned that the still unfolding independence of the Americas would ultimately precipitate the decline and fall of European civilization—unless Europe, like the United States of America, could reconstitute itself as a federal state with a collective imperial mission.

99. Ibid., 18.

100. Ibid., 27, 31. Earlier he had suggested that the Holy Alliance was in fact a preliminary to a European *Bundesstaat* or "federal state": Schmidt-Phiseldek, *Der Europäische Bund*, 167.

101. Claude Conter, *Jenseits der Nation, das vergessene Europa des 19. Jahrhunderts: Die Geschichte der Inszenierungen und Visionen Europas in Literatur, Geschichte und Politik* (Bielefeld: Aisthesis, 2004), 218–38; Thomas Brendel, *Zukunft Europa?: Das Europabild und die Idee der internationalen Solidarität bei den deutschen Liberalen und Demokraten im Vormärz (1815–1848)* (Bochum: Winkler, 2005), 114–24; Georg Cavallar, *Die Europäische Union—von der Utopie zur Friedens- und Wertegemeinschaft* (Wien: Lit, 2006). See also Heinz Gollwitzer, *Europabild und Europagedanke: Beiträge zur deutschen Geistesgeschichte des 18. und 19. Jahrhunderts* (München: Beck, 1951), 197–99.

102. Thorkild Kjaergaard, "Postscript," in *Europe and America, or, The Relative State of the Civilized World at a Future Period,* by Conrad Georg Friedrich Elias von Schmidt-Phiseldek, trans. Joseph Owen, facsimile ed. (Copenhagen: RHODOS, 1976), 275–76.

In considering the Holy Alliance as a framework for peaceful and gradual political progress, Schmidt-Phiseldek appealed to inherited expectations of Russia's involvement in European politics. He also relied on a Kantian understanding of the kind of civic culture that could sustain liberal political institutions. Born in 1770, Schmidt-Phiseldek was the son of a professor in Braunschweig who had written extensively about Russian history, and his connection to Denmark began when he became a private tutor in an influential German Danish household: Constantin Brun had been the Danish consul to Russia since 1783, while Friederike Brun was an internationally known writer who shared Germaine de Staël's views on the Protestant foundations of political liberty.[103] In the 1790s, Schmidt-Phiseldek earned his doctorate, became a Danish subject, and obtained three years of funding from the Danish finance minister Ernst Heinrich Schimmelmann to study political economy and Kantian philosophy. In 1797, Schmidt-Phiseldek published his *Letters on Aesthetic Matters, with Particular Reference to the Kantian Theory*, and went on to a long career in government, including an important stint directing and reorganizing the Danish national bank between 1813 and 1818. Schmidt-Phiseldek, who later dedicated his 1822 book on the Holy Alliance to Schimmelmann, was not the first beneficiary of the Danish minister's taste for Kantian philosophy. Previously, in 1791, Schimmelmann had helped arrange another three-year stipend for the ailing Jena professor, renowned playwright, and newly proclaimed honorary citizen of revolutionary France, Friedrich Schiller. The intensive study of Kant that Schiller was then able to undertake informed a series of letters to the Danish prince Friedrich Christian of Schleswig-Holstein-Augustenberg, and these letters in turn developed into Schiller's rather more successful *On the Aesthetic Education of Man, in a Series of Letters* (1795).

For Schiller, as for Schmidt-Phiseldek, aesthetic education supplied an indispensable corrective to the alienation produced by an expanding division of labor. The collective cultivation of a taste for beauty offered a way of bridging the divide, within the self as well as in society, between sense and reason: a way of transforming labor into an activity that produced harmony rather than conflict between the despotism of physical needs and the barbarous asceticism of abstract moral principles. With an

103. Winfried Schulze and Gerd Helm, "Conrad Georg Friedrich Elias von Schmidt-Phiseldek (1770–1832)," in *Europa-Historiker: Ein biographisches Handbuch*, ed. Heinz Duchhardt et al., vol. 1 (Göttingen: Vandenhoeck & Ruprecht, 2006), 108. On Federike Brun, see Glenda Sluga, *The Invention of International Order: Remaking Europe after Napoleon* (Princeton: Princeton University Press, 2021), 179.

eye on developments in France, Schiller had argued that political progress could not begin with the imposition of a new legal order, with or without the violent overthrow of the old one. Instead, political progress was predicated on the emergence of a unifying civic culture through the collective construction of a shared standard or common sense of beauty. "Though it may be his needs which drive man into society, and reason which implants within him the principles of social behaviour, beauty alone can confer upon him a *social character*," Schiller wrote: "only the aesthetic mode of communication unites society, because it relates to that which is common to all."[104] Like Schiller's, though less originally, Schmidt-Phiseldek's idea of a morally sound civic culture took its cue from Kant's 1790 *Critique of the Power of Judgment* (Schmidt-Phiseldek's *Letters on Aesthetic Matters* was summarily dismissed by one reviewer as "merely a diluted recapitulation of phrases" taken from Kant's work).[105] In *Europe and America*, Schmidt-Phiseldek quoted a lengthy passage from Kant that linked the cultivation of aesthetic judgment to the acquisition of the humanistic attributes needed to construct a social contract and constitute "a lasting community": namely, the "general feeling of participation" and the capacity for "an intimate and universal communication." Kant had gone on to emphasize that this communication would have to effect a synthesis of high and popular culture, and that such a synthesis would become increasingly difficult to achieve as popular culture lost its "natural simplicity and originality." In the rendering by Joseph Owen, the Copenhagen-based English merchant who translated Schmidt-Phiseldek's book into English in 1820,

> That age as well as people, in which the active propensity evinced itself, of forming a social compact, which transforms a nation into a lasting community, and which impulse had to contend with the considerable difficulties, that embrace the weighty problem of uniting freedom, consequently equality, with constraint (more from veneration and submission to laws voluntarily enacted, than from a sense of fear): it would be necessary for such an age and such a people first to invent the art of a reciprocal communication of ideas, between the most polished and the most unrefined portion of the nation; to pay attention to the several gradations, which exist

104. Friedrich Schiller, *On the Aesthetic Education of Man: In a Series of Letters*, ed. Elizabeth M. Wilkinson and L. A. Willoughby (Oxford: Clarendon Press, 1982), 215. See, helpfully, Alexander Schmidt, "The Liberty of the Ancients? Friedrich Schiller and Aesthetic Republicanism," *History of Political Thought* 30, no. 2 (2009): 286–314.

105. *Allgemeine Literatur-Zeitung* 2, no. 174 (1798): 555–58, at 555, https://zs.thulb.uni-jena.de/receive/jportal_jparticle_00016484.

between the enlightened and cultivated state of the former, and the natural simplicity and originality of the latter; and thus to discover the medium between the highest possible cultivation, and man in a contented state of nature, which alone constitutes the true scale for taste, as an inherent human feeling, not to be governed by any general rules.

A more advanced age will hardly render this model superfluous, as it will be continually departing more and more from nature, and not being in possession of any of her extant impressions, will at last be incapable of forming an idea of the happy union, in one and the same people, of the legal constraint of the highest culture, with the power and correctness of nature, uncontrouled and sensible of her own dignity.[106]

Schmidt-Phiseldek's idea of a federal Europe and his interpretation of the Holy Alliance as a stage in its emergence were based on a projection of this Kantian account of civic culture onto the transatlantic imperial stage of the early 1820s. Kant himself had already extended this account into a colonial context in his final publication before his death in 1804: a "Postscript" to a bilingual German-Lithuanian dictionary composed by some of Kant's former classmates and students in Königsberg. The dictionary was a response to the significant expansion of the Lithuanian population in East Prussia following the third partition of Poland. Kant warmly endorsed its claim that there was civic as well as scientific value to preserving the Lithuanian language, which the dictionary's editors described as a precious window to the archaic past (and perhaps even a living link to ancient Greek). As Susan Shell has suggested, Kant's fulsome praise of Lithuanian character in his postscript raised the prospect not just of turning Lithuanians into obedient Prussian soldiers but also of forging a morally sound civic culture: in the terms of the *Critique of the Power of Judgment*, Lithuanians were well equipped to supply the kind of "natural simplicity and originality" that (in Kant's estimation) had become harder to find in German culture, with its propensity for ranking and classifying as well as abstracting and systematizing.[107] Schmidt-Phiseldek's fundamental point was that, in light of the recent history of the Atlantic world,

106. Conrad Friedrich von Schmidt-Phiseldek, *Europe and America, or, The Relative State of the Civilized World at a Future Period*, trans. Joseph Owen, facsimile ed. (Copenhagen: RHODOS, 1976), 230–31. Cf. Immanuel Kant, *Critique of the Power of Judgment*, ed. Paul Guyer, trans. Paul Guyer and Eric Matthews, Cambridge Edition of the Works of Immanuel Kant (Cambridge: Cambridge University Press, 2000), 229–30; *Kant's gesammelte Schriften*, 5:355–56.

107. Susan Shell, "'Nachschrift Eines Freundes': Kant on Language, Friendship and the Concept of a People," *Kantian Review* 15, no. 1 (2010): 88–117. See also J. D. Miniger,

individual European states were no longer capable of attaining Kant's ideal: of "producing an universal national character" through a harmonious synthesis of high and popular culture.[108] These states could no longer generate the material conditions for steady political progress, driven by enlightened public opinion, whose efficacy depended in turn on aesthetic education. Without the construction of a federal Europe along the lines promoted by the Holy Alliance, Schmidt-Phiseldek warned, "It is reserved perhaps for America at some future time, to realize this idea."[109]

The opening sentence of *Europe and America* proclaimed that "the fourth of July, in the Year 1776 points out the commencement of a new period in the history of the world."[110] In Schmidt-Phiseldek's estimation (which had prompted Owen to make his book available to an American audience), this new period would be shaped above all by the unprecedented growth of the Americas—and the resulting decline and fall of Europe. The American population was already growing at a rate far higher than anticipated, thanks to the availability of land and the absence of entrenched institutional impediments to growth. This trend would continue as a result of the promulgation of the 1787 United States Constitution, which ensured that territorial expansion would proceed through the accession of new states on the basis of political equality. As generations of Enlightenment economists had theorized, the development of agriculture under such conditions would naturally expand into manufacturing for a growing domestic market and eventually lead to a homegrown flourishing of the sciences and fine arts. It was only a matter of time, Schmidt-Phiseldek claimed in 1820, before the entire hemisphere followed this path to economic as well as political independence; in the short run, Britain might find ways to profit from American independence, but it was also only a matter of time before the rise of American manufacturing and maritime power ended Britain's monopoly over global trade. In fact, Schmidt-Phiseldek claimed, South America was even better positioned for this emerging historical period than North America. This was partly because trade with North America would enable it to end its dependence on European industry sooner, and partly because more of its indigenous population seemed likely to survive the onslaught of European settlers: the

---

"'Nachschrift Eines Freundes': Kant, Lithuania, and the Praxis of Enlightenment," *Studies in East European Thought* 57, no. 1 (2005): 1–32.

108. Schmidt-Phiseldek, *Europe and America*, 11.

109. Ibid., 231.

110. Ibid., 1.

resulting "mixture of European culture and Indian originality" promised to yield a civic culture far more vital and dynamic than what European settlers could reproduce on their own.[111]

According to Schmidt-Phiseldek, this attractive American future was mirrored by the dismal specter of European decline. American development would give rise to an integrated common market no longer dependent on European manufactures, but Europe would remain dependent on American products and markets. Europe's feudal past had long ago contorted agricultural production around the demands of warfare. Its economy was further warped by the influx of Spanish American silver, which had supplied a powerful monetary stimulus to industry and enabled the expansion of trade with Asia: the idea that had come to govern European social relations was not the idea of beauty but the idea of money.[112] The conditions created by American independence would eventually make it impossible for Europe's prosperity to be secured by rival states locked into military competition with one another and burdened with astronomical levels of debt. Competitive industrialization, driven by this rivalry between European states, had exacerbated economic imbalances, leading to crises of overproduction and underconsumption: a vicious cycle that threatened to continue immiserating an increasingly urbanized population and to spur further mass migration to the Americas. No European state, not even Britain, was equipped to single-handedly withstand the monetary instability that would follow from the eventual and inevitable loss of colonial markets. Echoing many eighteenth-century jeremiads about public debt, Schmidt-Phiseldek warned that the consequences of such a financial crisis would be socially and politically catastrophic.[113]

111. Ibid., 248. Cf. Conrad Friedrich von Schmidt-Phiseldek, *Das Menschengeschlecht auf seinem gegenwärtigen Standpunkte: Ein Versuch* (Kopenhagen: Friedrich Brummer, 1827), 91, http://mdz-nbn-resolving.de/urn:nbn:de:bvb:12-bsb10445832-0. Comparable arguments circulated in the United States: for example, William Ellery Channing's 1815 article on "American Language and its Literature" envisaged a culture that had unshackled itself from its "colonial existence" and achieved "genuine originality" by drawing from indigenous language. William Ellery Channing, "Essay on American Language and Literature," *North-American Review and Miscellaneous Journal* 1, no. 3 (1815): 307–14, cited in Gretchen Murphy, *Hemispheric Imaginings: The Monroe Doctrine and Narratives of U.S. Empire* (Durham: Duke University Press, 2005), 46.

112. Schmidt-Phiseldek, *Europe and America*, 76–79, 94–95, vi.

113. On Schmidt-Phiseldek in the context of eighteenth-century fears about public debt, see Michael Sonenscher, *Before the Deluge: Public Debt, Inequality, and the Intellectual Origins of the French Revolution* (Princeton: Princeton University Press, 2007), 357–65.

Schmidt-Phiseldek's claim that American independence would instigate Europe's decline and fall was one of a variety of such warnings that appeared at the turn of the 1820s; such predictions had already been around since at least the early 1780s.[114] Schmidt-Phiseldek may have been provoked by Dominique de Pradt, whose analysis of the 1815 settlement had earlier prompted Krug to label the Holy Alliance "the most liberal of all ideas." In 1819, Pradt had claimed that the independence of Spanish America was "made for the seafaring peoples of the north."[115] Denmark, in particular, was likely to prosper as the hub of growing trade between Russia and America: the two parts of the world, Pradt noted, where population was growing most rapidly as it expanded over

114. In an 1818 essay, Krug complained that such fears had become an "epidemic," when in fact they were "groundless": America's economic self-sufficiency meant that it would not someday mirror European domination back across the Atlantic. Nor was American republicanism a threat to Europe. Indeed, Krug—like Schmidt-Phiseldek and indeed many Americans themselves—expected its constitutions to become more monarchical in nature as it became wealthier. Only a "visionary," Krug claimed, could imagine "that Americans could someday land in Europe, with the sword in one hand and republican proclamations in the other, to revolutionize in the French style." Wilhelm Traugott Krug, "Die Furcht vor Amerika," in *Kreutz- und Queerzüge eines Deutschen auf den Steppen der Staats-Kunst und Wissenschaft* (Leipzig: Rein, 1818), 228, 230, http://mdz-nbn-resolving .de/urn:nbn:de:bvb:12-bsb10769616-3. An early expression of such fears occurs in a 1782 French pamphlet: *Causes politiques secrètes, ou pensées philosophiques sur divers événemens qui se sont passés depuis 1763 jusqu én 1772: Suivies d'un projet de Haut Pouvoir Conservateur dirigé par les quatre grandes puissances de l'Europe* (Londres: aux dépens du Lord North, 1782), 48–55, 98–100, https://books.google.com/books?id=kVVaAAAAcAAJ. Comparable fears also appear in a 1795 text, discussed in chapter 4, which predicted that only a unified Europe would be able to defend the continent from future American and African fleets: Scipione Piattoli, *Épitre du vieux cosmopolite Syrach à la convention nationale de France* (Sarmatie, 1795), 133–34, https://mdz-nbn-resolving.de/urn:nbn:de:bvb:12 -bsb10421716-6. By the 1820s it had become much more common to warn that, as François-René de Chateaubriand put it in 1822, "if the New World is ever entirely republican, the monarchies of the old world will perish." *Correspondance générale de Chateaubriand*, ed. Louis Thomas, vol. 3 (Paris: Champion, 1912), 97. See also William Spence Robertson, "The Monroe Doctrine Abroad in 1823–24," *American Political Science Review* 6, no. 4 (1912): 546–63, https://doi.org/10.2307/1944651.

115. Dominique Georges Frederic de Pradt, *L'Europe après le Congrès d'Aix-la-Chapelle, faisant suite au Congrès de Vienne* (Paris: F. Béchet ainé, 1819), 47–48. On diplomatic and commercial concerns around the Baltic regarding the outcome of the Spanish American wars of independence, see Manfred Kossok, *Im Schatten der Heiligen Allianz: Deutschland und Lateinamerika, 1815–1830. Zur Politik der deutschen Staaten gegenüber der Unabhängigkeitsbewegung Mittel- und Südamerikas* (Berlin: Akademie-Verlag, 1964); Manfred Kossok and Michael Zeuske, *Legitimität gegen Revolution: Die Politik der Heiligen Allianz gegenüber der Unabhängigkeitsrevolution Mittel- und Südamerikas 1810–1830: Kommentare und Quellen* (Berlin: Akademie-Verlag, 1987).

immense inland spaces.[116] According to the diplomat Friedrich Gentz, Pradt's analysis amounted to an attempt to revive French power: in heralding a commercial alliance between a united Europe and the newly independent states of Spanish America, Pradt was describing how France could compensate itself for the loss of its former colony in Haiti and find a new way to counter British supremacy over the Atlantic that did not involve conquering continental Europe.[117] From one perspective, Pradt's plan looks like an attempt to re-create the League of Armed Neutrality of 1780, discussed in chapter 4: an initiative to impose free trade on Britain, originally organized by Catherine II of Russia and briefly revived once again in 1800 by Paul I (when it was heralded by writers like Tom Paine and Joel Barlow as the seed of a new trading system). At the same time, Pradt's vision points ahead to later French conceptions of empire: most obviously, the 1861 invasion of Mexico, promoted by the liberal political economist Michel Chevalier, who hoped to make France the hub of a new "Latin" American economic bloc.[118] In 1816, Krug had associated the Holy Alliance with a corrected version of Napoleon's continental system organized according to "the principle of national equality of rights"; in the early 1820s, Schmidt-Phiseldek linked the Holy Alliance to a vision of how to secure Europe's prosperity that was related to Pradt's but less closely tied to the revival of French power—and more closely tied to the rise of Russian power.

According to Schmidt-Phiseldek, the Holy Alliance marked an important step in the process of rehabilitating Europe by emulating the American model of an expansionary federal state and common market. The constitutional basis of this new European federalism would not be popular sovereignty, whose application to Europe Schmidt-Phiseldek associated with the "intoxication of republicanism" that had led to Napoleon's

---

116. Pradt, L'Europe après le Congrès d'Aix-la-Chapelle, faisant suite au Congrès de Vienne, 54–55, 36.

117. Friedrich von Gentz, "L'Europe après le Congrès d'Aix-la-Chapelle etc. par M. de Pradt," in Jahrbücher der Literatur, vol. 5 (Wien: Carl Gerold, 1819), 279–318, https://books.google.com/books?id=VOFMAAAAcAAJ.

118. John Leddy Phelan, "Pan-Latinism, French Intervention in Mexico (1861–1867) and the Genesis of the Idea of Latin America," in Conciencia y autenticidad históricas: Escritos en homenaje a Edmundo O'Gorman, ed. Juan Antonio Ortega y Medina (México: UNAM, 1968), 279–98. For Chevalier, inspired by Saint-Simonian ideas, the invasion was an opportunity for France to become the unifying source of capital and technology for a new international association. For one of its other defenders, the invasion (originally a joint project with Britain and Spain) was a way to forestall a future in which "there will remain only two great powers in the world: Russia and the United States."

"military autocracy."[119] Instead, like many other liberals in the 1820s, Schmidt-Phiseldek imagined that the collective struggle against Napoleon had created the conditions for a successful synthesis of the stability of monarchical sovereignty (which was insulated from fluctuations of popular will) with the dynamism of representative government (which was responsive to the "spirit of the times").[120] Like Krug, Schmidt-Phiseldek associated the Holy Alliance with this view of Europe's postwar constitutional settlement, which had been modeled by Emperor Alexander in his promulgation of a constitution for Poland. Schmidt-Phiseldek interpreted the treaty of the Holy Alliance as a *Willenserklärung*, or preliminary "declaration of intent," expressing the commitment of the signatories to a set of shared constitutional principles; it was also a "standing norm and instruction" for the ongoing reform of each member state's internal government (*Landesverfassung*).[121] In guaranteeing peace and asserting the fraternity of peoples, the signatories were committing themselves to the "establishment of a forum for arbitration" or *Austrägalforum* (a legal term adopted from the German Federation). Since the signatories had proclaimed Europe to be one Christian nation, they were committed to recognizing the legal equality of all member states and to respecting local autonomy to the extent consistent with constitutional norms: "the particularity of every existing legal order will be respected, and subjected only to the Christian nationality, that is, to the law of justice and peace." Since the signatories had identified themselves "merely as trustees and temporary administrators" of divine providence, Schmidt-Phiseldek further claimed, they had denied themselves any formally extraconstitutional power (*der ungesetzlichen Willkür keinen Spielraum geben*).[122] Finally, the signatories guaranteed accession to the treaty to all who accepted its constitutional principles: a "cosmopolitan" commitment to the interests of humanity as a whole that Schmidt-Phiseldek took to be a definitive answer to suspicions that the alliance was a mask for domination.[123] Schmidt-Phiseldek did

119. Schmidt-Phiseldek, *Europe and America*, 72. Schmidt-Phiseldek also assumed that economic development would eventually divide the United States of America into a more centralized Eastern monarchy and a democratic Western federation (234–35). On monarchy and republicanism, see also Schmidt-Phiseldek, *Das Menschengeschlecht*, 154–82.

120. Schmidt-Phiseldek, *Europe and America*, 73. Cf. Schmidt-Phiseldek, *Das Menschengeschlecht*, 179.

121. Schmidt-Phiseldek, *Die Politik nach den Grundsätzen der heiligen Allianz*, 38, cf. 46–50.

122. Ibid., 31–33.

123. Ibid., 34.

not venture to specify the institutional structure of this European federal state any further: the best procedure, he suggested, would be to give the signatories of the Holy Alliance ten years to demonstrate their commitment to their principles before the tribunal of public opinion. At that point, they could convene a general congress to produce a definitive federal constitution for Europe, one that would conclusively address all the thorny questions of representation, taxation, and debt and determine the institutional design of the federal assembly, courts, executive, and army.[124] On the American constitutional calendar, in other words, the Holy Alliance corresponded to 1776, not 1787.

Under a federal government, Schmidt-Phiseldek promised, Europe could evade the potentially calamitous consequences of American independence. Monetary union and the pooling of defense costs would open the way to fiscally sustainable government and renewed economic growth in a vast common market. Unification would also open the way to a new imperial strategy that would compensate Europe for the independence of the Americas while insulating it from the future loss of other markets through rising American competition. Schmidt-Phiseldek envisaged a new European empire, centered on the Mediterranean, that would curtail the flow of migrants across the Atlantic. Instead, the precarious (and potentially revolutionary) working classes in northern Europe's industrial centers would migrate to southern Europe and a newly liberated Greece; they would also settle newly conquered territories with great agricultural potential around the Black Sea and in North Africa (Schmidt-Phiseldek likened this prospective conquest of the Ottoman Empire to the *Reconquista*, or the Christian conquest of Iberia).[125] Schmidt-Phiseldek's imperial strategy echoed the enthusiasm of Voltaire, Diderot, Herder, and others for Russia's southward expansion, which was discussed in chapter 2; it also expressed the enthusiasm of many European liberals for Greek independence. Schmidt-Phiseldek's conception of Europe extended to the Urals, encompassing Russia; he described as prophetic Empress Catherine's unrealized project of extending her imperial reach to Greece and Constantinople.[126] Through this imperial strategy, the preponderance of European trade would be redirected from the Atlantic back to a revived Silk Road, reintegrating the European economy and correcting

---

124. Schmidt-Phiseldek, *Der Europäische Bund*, 171–72, 287–95.

125. Schmidt-Phiseldek, *Europe and America*, 147. On the mass killings that transpired during the Greek Revolution shortly afterward, see Mark Mazower, *The Greek Revolution: 1821 and the Making of Modern Europe* (New York: Penguin Press, 2021).

126. Schmidt-Phiseldek, *Europe and America*, 146.

its long-standing imbalance between agriculture and industry: "a system more suitable to the new order of things," Schmidt-Phiseldek enthused, that would furnish "novel and perhaps more secure foundations" for the "greatness" of Europe's cultural inheritance.[127] Europe was bound to lose its monopoly over global trade, but it could still make itself capable of maintaining a stable balance of power with the Americas and other continents while joining forces with them to drive the prosperity of an increasingly global civilization.[128] A healthy new European civic culture would develop, which Schmidt-Phiseldek described in 1823 in a set of imagined speeches that would provide a rhetorical model for the deliberations of a future European senate. One of these imagined speeches was a committee report to the United States Senate on whether it should accede to the treaty of the Holy Alliance: ultimately the speech recommended against doing so on constitutional grounds, because the Holy Alliance would effectively assume the Senate's constitutional functions. But this conclusion followed from a judicious discussion that recognized the universality of the Christian values underpinning the Holy Alliance and the ways in which it repudiated rather than reaffirmed the old power politics of Europe.[129] On the one hand, then, Schmidt-Phiseldek's analysis of the danger to Europe posed by American independence produced an account of the Holy Alliance that took a step beyond what Krug or Czartoryski had envisaged: a step toward the creation of a European *Bundesstaat* or *civitas maxima*. On the other hand, Schmidt-Phiseldek insisted that even United States senators should be able to recognize the universality of the values that would unify this emergent federal European state. At the same time, he insisted that this European federation remain a "free union" of individual states rather than a "government of a people"; and he insisted that it was designed to take its place within a global "national confederacy of the civilized world," an international legal order that was

127. Ibid., 126.

128. Schmidt-Phiseldek, *Der Europäische Bund*, 310–12. Schmidt-Phiseldek's vision of Europe's future is worth juxtaposing with the history of nineteenth-century competition between North American and Russian grain exports to Europe, its connection to global financial instability in the 1870s, and subsequently to intensified European migration to the Americas as well as imperial decline and political instability in the Habsburg, Ottoman, and Russian Empires in the decades leading up to World War I. See Scott Reynolds Nelson, *Oceans of Grain: How American Wheat Remade the World* (New York: Basic Books, 2022).

129. Conrad Friedrich von Schmidt-Phiseldek, *Proben politischer Redekunst: In sieben Reden* (Kopenhagen: Friedrich Brummer, 1823), 57–84, http://mdz-nbn-resolving.de /urn:nbn:de:bvb:12-bsb10119637-6.

premised on the diversity of state forms that would continue to proliferate through the development of civilization.[130]

For Schmidt-Phiseldek, the Holy Alliance pointed toward a transition
from power politics to a politics premised on consensus: a transition he
associated with the process of aesthetic education and the emergence of
a pan-European civic culture. Other writers in the first half of the 1820s
linked the Holy Alliance to different understandings of the historical
process leading to European unity. Among these was another Danish
writer, the geographer Conrad Malte-Brun, exiled to France for his outspoken republicanism and best known (if only to historians of geography)
for having named Oceania.[131] In 1825, Malte-Brun published a remarkable defense of the Holy Alliance called *Treatise on Legitimacy Considered
as the Foundation of the Public Law of Christian Europe*. The origins of
Malte-Brun's treatise lay in a series of articles proclaiming European unity
and praising the Holy Alliance, which he had published in 1816–17, and
in an 1823 article rebutting the Baron Bignon, a prominent Bonapartist
writer whose criticism of the *Archive of the Holy Alliance* was discussed
in chapter 1.[132] For Bignon, who had become a member of the French
Chamber of Deputies in 1817, the principles that German philosophers
eagerly attributed to the Holy Alliance were a deceptive mask, not even for
the old power politics but for "a new politics occupied exclusively with the
interest of the privileged classes."[133] By contrast, Malte-Brun's treatise presented the Holy Alliance as an outgrowth of centuries of European legal
and constitutional development. His treatise was dedicated to the idiosyncratic royalist writer François-René de Chateaubriand, who had previously
served as France's foreign minister. In an echo of the political aspirations

130. Schmidt-Phiseldek, *Der Europäische Bund*, 288; Schmidt-Phiseldek, *Europe and
America*, 6–7.

131. On Malte-Brun and geography, see Laura Péaud, "Relire la géographie de Conrad
Malte-Brun," *Annales de Géographie* 124, no. 701 (2015): 99–122.

132. Conrad Malte-Brun, *Traité de la legitimité, considérée comme base du droit public de l'Europe chrétienne* (Paris: Libraire de Charles Gosselin, 1825), iv–v, https://books
.google.com/books?id=PwRfAAAAcAAJ. See "De l'esprit européen, et du véritable esprit
national," *La Quotidienne*, no. 141 (May 20, 1816): 3–4; "Nouvelles de Paris, du 26 mai," *La
Quotidienne*, no. 146–47 (May 26, 1817): 3–4; Conrad Malte-Brun, "Variétés: Les Cabinets
et les Peuples, depuis 1815, jusqu'à la finde 1822; par M. Bignon," *Journal des débats politiques et littéraires*, January 26, 1823, 3–4. For attribution of the articles in *La Quotidienne*,
see Helen Maxwell King, *Les doctrines littéraires de la Quotidienne, 1814–1830: Un chap-
itre de l'histoire du mouvement romantique en France* (Northampton, MA: Smith College
Studies in Modern Languages, 1920), 220–21, 231.

133. Louis-Pierre-Edouard Bignon, *Des proscriptions*, vol. 2 (Paris: Brissot-Thivars,
1821), 215, https://catalog.hathitrust.org/Record/012295707.

and rhetorical strategy discussed in chapter 3, Chateaubriand had been approached privately by the Russian emperor at the Congress of Verona in 1822: Chateaubriand should succeed the Austrian statesman Clemens von Metternich as his chief European negotiating partner, Alexander had suggested, and France and Russia ought to jointly secure peace throughout Europe by defending their shared commitment to the "principles of the Holy Alliance" against Austria and England.[134] After 1824, Chateaubriand had aligned himself with the liberal opposition in defending the freedom of the press and advocating for Greek independence. In dedicating his defense of the Holy Alliance to Chateaubriand, Malte-Brun appealed to their shared commitment to a constitutional consensus grounded in the principle of "legitimacy." "The words liberty and legitimacy," Malte-Brun lamented, had become "the symbols of enemy factions," when in fact they were "made for a holy and eternal alliance."[135] "May liberty take the language of monarchy to make those whom it can frighten appreciate the purity of its intention," he wrote. "May the calm and majestic name of legitimacy replace all the great words of popular eloquence."[136]

The concept of legitimacy is most often associated with ultraroyalists like Maistre or Louis de Bonald. They appealed to it as the sacred and eternal basis for social and political order, impervious to the vagaries of human volition unleashed by the idea of popular sovereignty (Bonald had gone so far as to equate Rousseau's idea of the "general will" with the will of God, rather than deriving it from the "will of all" individual members of society).[137] However, the concept of legitimacy was also taken up and reinterpreted by many influential liberals, such as the French historian and later prime minister François Guizot. For Guizot, as for Chateaubriand, the reassertion of historical continuity implied by the notion of legitimacy promised to supply the basis for the reconciliation of postrevolutionary French society, by attaching liberal aspirations to its restored monarchy. This prospect of reconciliation through legitimacy had also been referenced by the statesman Charles-Maurice de Talleyrand in his successful 1814 effort to gain Alexander's support for the restoration of the Bourbon

134. *Oeuvres complètes de M. le vicomte de Chateaubriand*, vol. 8 (Paris: Parent Desbarres, 1863), 469.

135. Malte-Brun, *Traite de la legitimité*, 147.

136. Ibid., x.

137. Louis Gabriel Ambroise Bonald, "Théorie du pouvoir politique et religieux dans la société civile, démontrée par le raisonnement et par l'histoire," in *Œuvres de M. de Bonald*, vol. 1 (Paris: Le Clère, 1854), 140.

monarchy in France.[138] The object of Malte-Brun's *Treatise* was to "develop the principle of legitimacy according to the spirit of the Holy Alliance," which meant showing that this principle was "the protector of peoples as well as the guardian of thrones."[139] Legitimacy, Malte-Brun explained, was the representation of the divine principle of "universal justice" in human history. It was the historical product of the divinely implanted human capacity to sanctify the fundamental principles of collective life: to elevate them beyond the scope of normal contestation by placing them "under the guarantee of celestial thunderbolts." Malte-Brun's account was closely related to the doctrine of the "sovereignty of right" developed by Guizot (who was lecturing on the history of France and of "European civilization" in the 1820s). In Guizot's later formulation, "God alone is sovereign, and nobody here below is God, not peoples any more than kings."[140] Malte-Brun attributed the same "true principles of legitimacy" directly to the Holy Alliance. "God alone is sovereign," he opened his *Treatise*. "Who said these words? It was Europe, in signing the treaty of the holy alliance; it was Christianity, reunited around the altars of the savior."[141]

Malte-Brun's treatise on legitimacy presented another history of progress premised on human perfectibility and culminating with the Holy Alliance. The legitimacy that derived from the sovereignty of God was not just an abstract principle but a concrete "historical fact" that had persisted through the development of European legal order.[142] Malte-Brun's history of legitimacy, like Krug's history of liberalism (and indeed like many latter-day canonizing histories of liberalism), sought to detach the history of progress from the contested space of national or dynastic history. In their place it claimed to supply a deeper historical foundation for sustainable political progress: an alternative to "the principle of illegitimacy," or "political atheism" in either its revolutionary or counter-revolutionary guise.[143] Understood as a whole, Malte-Brun promised, the

---

138. *Mémoires du prince de Talleyrand*, vol. 2 (Paris: Calmann Lévy, 1891), 164–65. On Chateaubriand and Talleyrand on legitimacy, see Stephen Holmes, "Two Concepts of Legitimacy: France after the Revolution," *Political Theory* 10, no. 2 (1982): 165–83.

139. Malte-Brun, *Traité de la legitimité*, 5–6.

140. François Guizot, *Mémoires pour servir a l'histoire de mon temps*, vol. 2 (París: Michel Lévy frères, 1859), 237, https://catalog.hathitrust.org/Record/009350917. Cf. François Guizot, *The History of Civilization in Europe*, ed. Larry Siedentop, trans. William Hazlitt (Indianapolis: Liberty Fund, 2013), 173. On Guizot, see Pierre Rosanvallon, *Le moment Guizot* (Paris: Gallimard, 1985).

141. Malte-Brun, *Traité de la legitimité*, 130, 3.

142. Ibid., 12.

143. Ibid., 105, 20.

history of legitimacy could serve as "the pacifying principle of an agitated society, the arbiter between parties, the mediator between the future and the past."[144] Legitimacy in Europe was rooted in the original supranational unity of the Roman Church as well as the fundamental laws of particular European nations. In monarchies and democracies alike, the legitimacy of these laws precluded "absolute power, whether royal or popular": the "supreme power" always remained an organ of the "nation," constituted by the autonomous elements of society that mutually guaranteed their respective rights and privileges.[145] This ideal balance—excluding both revolutionary anarchy and "ministerialism" or the unmoored administrative power of the centralizing state—was best approximated in Britain, where the "gothic" legitimacy of liberty was strong enough to have survived two revolutions and a regicide. Malte-Brun characterized Britain as an "old federation of political orders": a complex society of corporations and associations extending well beyond the landed aristocracy and established church to encompass an "aristocracy of capitalists" in the City of London and "tacit confederations" in each sector of the economy.[146] The Holy Alliance had opened a new chapter in this history of legitimacy by re-creating the original supranational unity of Europe in a new form that was compatible with the principles of religious toleration and representative government: principles increasingly enshrined as fundamental laws in European states. Critics of the Holy Alliance, Malte-Brun complained, often confounded it with the Treaty of Chaumont, concluded by the military alliance against France in 1814. The latter was directed at the urgent needs of a particular moment in European history; though Malte-Brun dismissed the "lugubrious phantom" of terrorist conspiracies, he also insisted on the need for a collective security system in principle, and blamed the British for engaging in empty posturing at the Congress of Laibach rather than working to establish real legal limits on the rights and duties of international intervention.[147] By contrast, the Holy Alliance aimed not just at security but at reconciliation, and had much more expansive historical horizons: it had made "the great ideas of legitimacy and true liberty and perfectibility of society" concrete in a form applicable to all European

144. Ibid., 132.
145. Conrad Malte-Brun, "Tableau politique de l'Europe au 1er janvier 1820," in *Nouvelles Annales des Voyages, de la Géographie et de L'histoire*, ed. Conrad Malte-Brun and J. B. Eyriès, vol. 4 (Paris: Gide, 1820), 55–57.
146. Malte-Brun, *Traité de la legitimité*, 47–50.
147. Ibid., 239.

nations.[148] Unlike other European heads of state, the Russian emperor truly did exercise absolute power; but since the present emperor was "also a Christian philosopher and friend of civilization," he was uniquely well positioned to serve as a "neutral arbiter" independent of all the conflicting social interests that had divided other European states. Alexander's goal in founding the Holy Alliance, Malte-Brun concluded, was "not to consecrate the union of despotism with ignorance, nor to found a coalition of cabinets against peoples; he wanted to lay down the moral and religious foundation of all true liberty."[149]

Schmidt-Phiseldek and Malte-Brun had sought to integrate the Holy Alliance into a history of the progress of civilization leading to the peaceful prosperity of a unified Europe. Where their histories had relied on aesthetics and law, respectively, the French philosopher Henri de Saint-Simon developed a comparable evaluation of the Holy Alliance from a utilitarian starting point that relied on the concept of "industry." Saint-Simon had taken up the concept of industry from the political economist Jean-Baptiste Say: as chapters 2 and 3 discussed, Say had dedicated the 1814 edition of his *Treatise on Political Economy* to Emperor Alexander, who was also well informed about Say and his work by La Harpe. Say defined industry capaciously, as activity to develop and cultivate human capacities, including moral and intellectual ones. It was a key term in his approach to the science of political economy, and it reflected his commitment to expanding Adam Smith's narrower definition of wealth in terms of "values attached to material substances," when in fact there were also "values which, despite being immaterial, are no less real, such as all natural or acquired talents."[150] In his pivotal 1817 work *On Industry*, Saint-Simon praised Say and emphasized the link between the development of industry and moral and political progress: "morality gains as industry is perfected," Saint-Simon wrote. "It is with industry, and through it, that the need and love of being free were born; liberty can only grow with industry, and can only strengthen through it."[151] In short, Say's concept of industry served as a way of capturing human moral potential that was comparable to the idealist concept of "perfectibility": a parallel recognized by the contemporary

148. Ibid., 234.

149. Ibid., 262–63.

150. Jean-Baptiste Say, *Traité d'économie politique: Ou simple exposition de la manière dont se forment, se distribuent et se consomment les richesses*, 2nd ed., vol. 1 (Paris: Antoine-Augustin Renouard, 1814), liv–lv, https://catalog.hathitrust.org/Record/009352065.

151. Henri de Saint-Simon, "L'industrie," in *Œuvres de Saint-Simon*, vol. 2 (Paris: E. Dentu, 1868), 182–83, 187, 210, reprinted in *Oeuvres de Claude-Henri de Saint-Simon* (Paris: Éditions Anthropos, 1966), vol. 1.

Catholic critic Ferdinand Eckstein, whose comparison of Saint-Simon with Kant's follower Johann Gottlieb Fichte produced a characterization of Fichte as a "transcendental industrialist."[152]

For Saint-Simon, the progress of industry was also the force that was unifying Europe, turning it into a single nation, which Saint-Simon defined as a "great society of industry" dedicated to "the satisfaction of the needs of all."[153] Already in 1802, Saint-Simon had begun articulating a vision of peaceful progress without revolution, driven by "scientists, artists and all men who have liberal ideas."[154] Anticipating Krug's opposition of liberalism and anti-liberalism, Saint-Simon imagined that liberals, whose receptivity to new ideas enabled them to exercise "spiritual power," would do so in opposition to the "temporal power" of proprietors who lacked these ideas; and that in the context of a representative government, this opposition would be adjudicated by the remainder of society, serving as "regulators of the progress of the human spirit."[155] In 1814, Saint-Simon and his disciple, the historian Augustin Thierry, elaborated a vision of Europe's unification under a federal government in their famous essay *On the Reorganization of European Society*. Much like many of the eighteenth-century peace plans discussed in previous chapters, this unification would begin with the reconciliation of Britain and France. Now that France was adopting an English constitution, Saint-Simon and Thierry proposed, the door was open to an Anglo-French union that would secure English liberty for France in exchange for sharing Britain's debt burden. Once other states had also acquired representative government, a European government (modeled on the English constitution) could take shape and help foster a "European patriotism."[156] In 1824, toward the end of his life, Saint-Simon integrated this vision of European unification, and the morality of industry underlying it, into a religious vision that would subsequently be elaborated by his disciples. In this context, the Holy Alliance now super-

152. Ferdinand Eckstein, "De l'Industrialisme," *Le Catholique* 5 (1827): 241.

153. Saint-Simon, "L'industrie," 68–69.

154. Henri de Saint-Simon, "Lettres d'un habitant de Genève à ses contemporains," in *Œuvres de Saint-Simon*, vol. 1 (Paris: E. Dentu, 1868), 26, reprinted in *Oeuvres de Claude-Henri de Saint-Simon*, vol. 1.

155. Saint-Simon, "Lettres d'un habitant de Genève," 47, 33.

156. Henri de Saint-Simon and Augustin Thierry, "De la réorganisation de la société européenne, ou de la nécessité et des moyens de rassembler les peuples de l'europe en un seul corps politique en conservant à chacun son indépendance nationale," in *Œuvres de Saint-Simon*, vol. 1 (Paris: E. Dentu, 1868), 199, reprinted in *Oeuvres de Claude-Henri de Saint-Simon*, vol. 1. In the end, financial integration took the form of loans to fund French reparations payments.

seded the English constitution as the archetype of a European federal government best suited to promoting the progress of industry. Where the French Revolution represented an extreme regression to the anachronistic politics of classical antiquity, and Napoleon represented an only slightly less extreme regression to the imperial unity imposed by Charlemagne, the English constitution was now relegated to the status of an obsolete transitional artefact: now it was the Holy Alliance, Saint-Simon claimed, that "offers the best of all means for transitioning from the feudal to the industrial regime."[157] It was the Holy Alliance that could guarantee peace, the consolidation of royal power (which, Saint-Simon noted, had always been the most effective defender of the people's interests), and the unity of Christianity (which represented morality in its most general and universal form). This was the combination that would most effectively empower those with liberal ideas to drive the progress of society: "for the Holy Alliance, which dominates all existing institutions, and to which is reserved the exclusive power of establishing new ones, will always be dominated by public opinion, because public opinion is the queen of the world." "Thanks to the formation of the Holy Alliance," Saint-Simon concluded, "European society can be reorganized very surely, as soon as its public opinion is clearly formed regarding the institutions which correspond to the present state of civilization."[158]

Saint-Simon's effusive praise for the Holy Alliance disgusted his recently estranged disciple, the philosopher Auguste Comte. After his break with Saint-Simon in 1824, Comte sought out new intellectual contacts, including with Guizot, who provided him with German connections.[159] However, Comte's rebuttal of Saint-Simon's assessment of the Holy Alliance was primarily informed by his engagement with Maistre and the wayward priest Félicité de Lamennais: Catholic counterrevolutionary thinkers who put forward a very different view of how spiritual authority had to be exercised and institutionalized.[160] The religious idiom of the Holy Alliance did

---

157. Henri de Saint-Simon, "Quelques opinions philosophiques à l'usage du XIXe siècle," in Œuvres de Saint-Simon, vol. 10 (Paris: E. Dentu, 1868), 99, reprinted in Oeuvres de Claude-Henri de Saint-Simon, vol. 5.

158. Ibid., 101.

159. Comte was translated into German by Buchholz (author of The New Leviathan, discussed above) and reviewed (negatively) by Krug. Comte, who had been given a copy of one of Krug's books by Guizot, whom he had befriended in 1824, did not think much of Krug either. See Mary Pickering, Auguste Comte: An Intellectual Biography, Volume 1 (Cambridge: Cambridge University Press, 1993), 268–75.

160. On Lamennais, see Lucien Jaume, L'individu effacé, ou, le paradoxe du libéralisme français (Paris: Fayard, 1997), 193–210.

resonate with a variety of Catholic writers, including the Bavarian mining inspector and theologian Franz von Baader; in France, it was aligned with the newly founded interconfessional Society for Christian Morals, as well as various other mystically inclined French writers (one of whom prefaced his "Project for the reunion of the different branches of Christianity, serving as the twin and complement of the project for perpetual peace" with a quotation from Voltaire and a visitation from the ghost of the Abbé de Saint-Pierre in a romantic grotto).[161] For Maistre and Lamennais, however, this kind of universalism was to be condemned as a dangerous manifestation of "religious indifference" too attenuated to be capable of generating genuine religious sociability. From this perspective, the politics of "religious indifference" had ultimately produced the disaster of the French Revolution, and the Holy Alliance was no more effective in counteracting the centrifugal tendencies of society than the revolutionary injunction to *fraternité*. This was why, Comte charged, the Holy Alliance had devolved into coercion by a "coalition of all European bayonets."[162] This argument about religious indifference had already been applied to the Holy Alliance at the end of 1815 by Maistre in his correspondence: Maistre's diplomatic post in Saint Petersburg, where he had served since 1803, had given him a good vantage point for observing the unfolding of the Holy Alliance.[163] Comte

161. On the Society for Christian Morals, see Rosenblatt, *Liberal Values*, 186–88. On Baader, discussed above in chapter 2, see Susan A. Crane, "Holy Alliances: Creating Religious Communities after the Napoleonic Wars," in *Die Gegenwart Gottes in der modernen Gesellschaft: Transzendenz und religiöse Vergemeinschaftung in Deutschland*, ed. Michael Geyer and Lucian Hölscher (Göttingen: Wallstein, 2006), 37–59. For the preface featuring the quotation from Voltaire and visitation from Saint-Pierre's ghost, see Nicolas-Joseph de Sarrazin, *Le retour du siècle d'or, ou, Rêve véritable et surprenant, suivi des moyens de rendre infaillible son accomplissement* (Metz: C. Lamort, 1816), link.gale.com/apps/doc /U0106504641/MOME?u=29002. Cf. François Étienne Auguste de Paoli-Chagny, *Projet d'une organisation politique pour l'Europe, ayant pour objet de procurer aux souverains et aux peuples une paix générale et perpétuelle et un bonheur inaltérable* (Hambourg, 1818).

162. Auguste Comte, "Appendice général du système de politique positive, contenant tous les opuscules primitifs de l'auteur sur la philosophie sociale," in *Système de politique positive, ou Traité de sociologie, instituant la religion de l'humanité*, vol. 4 (Paris: L. Mathias, 1851), 34, cited in Tonatiuh Useche Sandoval, "Auguste Comte's Reading of Maistre's *Du Pape*: Two Theories of Spiritual Authority," in *Joseph de Maistre and His European Readers: From Friedrich von Gentz to Isaiah Berlin*, ed. Carolina Armenteros and Richard Lebrun (Leiden: Brill, 2011), 78.

163. Maistre's two initial reports on the Holy Alliance are dated October 26/November 7, 1815, and December 22, 1816/January 3, 1817. See Joseph de Maistre and Albert Blanc, *Correspondance diplomatique de Joseph de Maistre 1811–1817*, vol. 2 (Paris: Michel Lévy frères, 1860), 130–36, 310–13.

did not have access to Maistre's private judgment, but a comparable argument had been published by Lamennais in an 1822 article on the Holy Alliance:

> What is the Christianity upon which the Holy Alliance is founded? The reunion of different sects, which have neither the same faith nor the same leader, many of which do not even recognize any leader, and could not say what their faith is. Therefore, either the Holy Alliance has no foundation, or it assumes that all these sects equally profess Christianity. In the first case, there is no real alliance; in the second, it rests on religious indifference, that is to say on the very foundation of the revolution it wants to combat.[164]

For Lamennais, the true "Holy Alliance or spiritual union among peoples" lay in the pre-revolutionary past; if it were ever restored, it would be "at the foot of the cross that the hand of the supreme Pontiff will raise in the midst of a Europe submitted to his paternal authority."[165] But the ideas of social unity and harmony associated with the Holy Alliance were also attacked from a Protestant perspective—including by Hegel. Hegel was famously skeptical that aesthetic communication could counter the centrifugal effects of the division of labor, transforming the "system of needs" through the harmonious convergence that was characteristic of a healthy civic culture. It was through social conflict, not through an aesthetic escape from it, that a common civic life had to be forged. From this perspective, there could also be no such thing as a *Weltgeist* or "world spirit" that was not instantiated through *Volksgeist* or civic cultures housed within individual sovereign states. The historical individuality of these states was what made them sites of unity, and the ultimate unification of humanity could only be the product of the entirety of their historical interactions, very much including their wars. According to student notes from Hegel's lectures on the philosophy of right in the early 1820s, Hegel classified the Holy Alliance as an attempt to realize the Kantian ideal of perpetual peace: such attempts to unify humanity within an international legal framework would be "always relative only and restricted" because they would always be products of the individuality of a particular state or alliance of states.[166]

---

164. Félicité Robert de Lamennais, "De la sainte-alliance," in *Nouveaux mélanges* (Paris: Librairie classique élémentaire, 1826), 285.

165. Ibid., 289.

166. Hegel, *Elements of the Philosophy of Right*, §259, remark.

The Redemption of the Atlantic World

The appearance of the Holy Alliance was linked to the progress of civilization not only in the context of European politics, but also in relation to Africa and the wider Atlantic world. As we have seen, prominent British abolitionists were among those who identified Alexander as a "friend of mankind," an agent acting in the universal interest of humanity by defeating the *hostis humani generis*: the enemy of humanity, a legal formula for piracy applied not only to Napoleon but also to perpetrators of the slave trade. Following a well-established pattern, private meetings with prominent abolitionists (especially during Alexander's visit to London in 1814) were followed by public declarations of principle (in this case, the treaty condemning the slave trade on humanitarian grounds, signed by eight states at the Congress of Vienna, as well as the subsequent treaty proclaiming the Holy Alliance). These declarations were linked in the eyes of abolitionists as testaments of goodwill, grounding expectations that progress would ensue from the responsiveness of those wielding political authority to the judgments expressed by the arbiters of public opinion. The link was made particularly clearly by James Stephen, a key figure in the "Clapham Sect" of evangelical abolitionists who was also William Wilberforce's brother-in-law. In 1814, Stephen had dedicated the second edition of his 1803 life of Toussaint Louverture to Alexander: in defeating Napoleon, the Russian emperor had become not only "the magnanimous Liberator of Europe" but also the vindicator of the deceased Haitian revolutionary hero, now in a position to "vindicate on his oppressor the rights of suffering humanity."[167] In 1818, Stephen published a series of open letters in a London newspaper, addressed to the sovereigns of Europe: these were translated into French as *Europe Chastened and Africa Avenged, or, Reasons for Regarding the Calamities of the Age as Punishments Inflicted by Providence for the Slave Trade.*[168] As chapter 3 discussed, these letters prompted a noteworthy response from the Haitian writer Juste Chanlatte. They also made explicit the narrative of progress linking the Holy Alliance to the abolition of slavery in the Atlantic world.

167. James Stephen, *The History of Toussaint Louverture* (London: J. Butterworth and Son, 1814), iv.

168. Stephen's letters appeared in twelve installments in *The New Times* between September 16 and November 5, 1818, under the title "Foedera Africana," and in French as *L'europe chatiée, et l'Afrique vengée; ou, Raisons pour regarder les calamités du siècle comme des punitions infligées par la providence pour la traite des nègres* (London: de l'Imprimerie de Schulze et Dean, 1818).

Stephen had become an abolitionist through his own experience in the West Indies, which made him a proponent of asserting public authority over planters, by having Parliament legislate civil limits to their personal power over the enslaved.[169] His expertise in maritime law had also positioned him to become the architect of the legal strategy that led to Britain's abolition of the slave trade in 1807, by linking it to the British war effort. In *War in Disguise, or, The Frauds of Neutral Flags* (1805), Stephen charged that the French military machine was fueled by a colonial trade that was still flourishing despite Britain's naval blockade, because it was being channeled through neutral shipping (and undercutting British competition, which was burdened by higher wartime insurance rates). To address this problem, Stephen proposed a stricter interpretation of contraband that would authorize the British navy to search and seize neutral ships conducting this "war in disguise"—including ships delivering slaves to the colonies of Britain's enemies. As Ann Burton has described, Stephen's proposal led directly to the Foreign Slave Trade Act of 1806, which paved the way for the Abolition Act of 1807.[170] However, the end of the war in 1815 also put an end to Britain's ability to enforce its own laws, let alone impose an international ban on the slave trade, because it no longer had legal grounds for searching foreign-flagged ships in peacetime. Despite the declaration against the slave trade issued at the Congress of Vienna, and the innovative international commission established to monitor it, Stephen and his allies were horrified to detect its postwar resurgence. In a complex dance with the British government, they worked hard to keep abolition on the agenda at the 1818 European Congress of Aix-la-Chapelle, which was mostly dedicated to negotiating the end of the postwar occupation of France. Stephen and his allies pushed for an ambitious new system of treaties that would mutually authorize European states to search and seize each other's shipping when it was illegally engaged in the slave trade (which they further urged should be declared a form of piracy, since piracy was already universally outlawed). From their perspective, bilateral treaties granting mutual search rights (like Britain's recent treaties with Spain and Portugal) could not achieve the full abolition of the slave trade, even given British naval dominance. As Stephen's

169. Lauren Benton and Aaron Slater, "Constituting the Imperial Community: Rights, Common Good and Authority in Britain's Atlantic Empire, 1607–1815," in *Revisiting the Origins of Human Rights*, ed. Pamela Slotte and Miia Halme-Tuomisaari (Cambridge: Cambridge University Press, 2015), 140–62.

170. Ann M. Burton, "British Evangelicals, Economic Warfare and the Abolition of the Atlantic Slave Trade, 1794–1810," *Anglican and Episcopal History* 65, no. 2 (1996): 197–225.

ally Thomas Clarkson warned on the eve of the 1818 Congress, evasion under other flags of convenience would continue so long as "Abolition is left to rest upon the laws and mutual compacts of Powers relinquishing the Trade": the only definitive solution was "universal concurrence of the civilized world in the proposed plan of maritime police."[171]

In his 1818 letters addressed to "the powers about to assemble in Congress at Aix-la-Chapelle," Stephen incorporated this demand into a providential framework that identified the sin of slavery as the cause of war and abolition as the route to atonement. Such millenarian views had long circulated among abolitionists who had already begun attributing the crisis of the British Empire in the 1770s to divine punishment for slavery.[172] Similarly, Stephen had recognized the war threatening England following the French Revolution as divine punishment for slavery, which had in turn created an opportunity for redemption. In 1797, Stephen confided to Wilberforce his conviction that war with France had been "concerted in the cabinet of heaven to bring forth its long oppressed, degraded children with a mighty hand and with an outstretched arm": "it would be impossible," he claimed in an 1807 tract, "not to recognize with wonder and awe, the chastising hand of God."[173] Stephen's 1818 letters, which quoted extensively from his 1807 work, revived these arguments in order to secure the Russian emperor's support in strengthening the British government's commitment to abolition while helping to corral the more or less recalcitrant governments of the remaining European states. As Stephen explained to Wilberforce, the British minister Lord Castlereagh had told him that Alexander's support might be expected "on moral and religious principle, and as he says on no other": Castlereagh had informed him of Alexander "not only that he is seriously religious, but that he has very strong impressions as to the Government of Divine Providence in the world, ascribing all his own deliverances and triumphs to that cause."[174]

171. "Copy of a Pamphlet Distributed by Mr. Clarkson at Aix-La-Chapelle," in *Thirteenth Report of the Directors of the African Institution, Read at the Annual General Meeting Held on the Twenty-Fourth Day of March, 1819* (London: Ellerton and Henderson, 1819), 83.

172. Christopher Leslie Brown, *Moral Capital: Foundations of British Abolitionism* (Chapel Hill: Omohundro Institute of Early American History and Culture, University of North Carolina Press, 2006), 169–88.

173. James Stephen, *The Dangers of the Country* (London: J. Butterworth, 1807), 212.

174. James Stephen to William Wilberforce, box 2, Correspondence 1814, 17, William Wilberforce Papers, Rubenstein Library, Duke University, https://idn.duke.edu/ark:/87924/r4bk18j97, cited in Paul Michael Kielstra, *The Politics of Slave Trade Suppression in Britain and France, 1814–48: Diplomacy, Morality and Economics* (New York: St. Martin's Press, 2000), 88.

Stephen's invocations of providence in his 1818 letters reflected the evangelical transformation of political economy that, as Boyd Hilton observed, no longer focused on explaining how private vices resulted in justice: rather, it pursued an understanding of "blessing in disguise" that showed how suffering created the possibility of moral improvement.[175] Stephen was a co-director, alongside Wilberforce, of the African Institution, founded in 1807 to turn the new colony of Sierra Leone—established as a refuge for freed slaves—into an exemplar of the moral and material progress of civilization that would be unleashed through abolition. In his 1818 letters, Stephen allowed that direct divine intervention in human affairs could only be discerned with certainty through revelation. However, it was both morally necessary and useful to reason through "the causes of the divine displeasure" according to scriptural principles and "the ordinary course of Providence" that guided "the Divine Government" of the world— even as the impetus for moral improvement derived from regarding the effects of this divine displeasure as "special or particular Providences."[176] From this perspective, the systematic moral economy characteristic of divine justice would emerge from expanding knowledge of the "physical causes" linking punishments for the vice of some to rewards for the virtue of others.[177] The 1807 act of abolition had been "a genuine act of national contrition and repentance" after which "England was delivered from the guilt of the Slave Trade" and rewarded with a string of military victories beginning with the Peninsular War.[178] Similarly, the United States had been rewarded for its efforts to curtail the slave trade with the growth of its shipping, while other European states continued to be punished for their sins by being turned into a "second Africa" by the French Revolution (with the Portuguese court, for example, fittingly banished to Brazil).[179] Stephen's message in 1818 was that Europe as a whole had yet to atone for the sin of the slave trade. "The deliverance and renovation of Europe is accomplished" with the victory over Napoleon, but "it is a melancholy and opprobrious truth, that the liberation of Europe has been to Africa a calamity and a curse." The sovereigns of Europe, who had "publicly recognized the government of God over the world," needed to act definitively against the slave trade, for there was no sin subject to more severe divine punishment than

175. Hilton, *The Age of Atonement*, 32, 22.

176. James Stephen, "Foedera Africana, No. III," *The New Times*, September 24, 1818.

177. James Stephen, "Foedera Africana, No. VII," *The New Times*, October 10, 1818.

178. James Stephen, "Foedera Africana, No. VI," *The New Times*, October 7, 1818.

179. James Stephen, "Foedera Africana, No. V," *The New Times*, October 2, 1818; James Stephen, "Foedera Africana, No. VIII," *The New Times*, October 16, 1818.

conscious abuse of the weak and poor by those with superior power and knowledge: "let there be one grand perpetual compact for the deliverance of Africa, by which all civilised nations shall mutually pledge themselves to each other for the suppression of that execrable traffic."[180]

In the wake of the Congress of Aix-la-Chapelle, Stephen and his allies continued to associate Alexander and the Holy Alliance with the abolitionist cause. In its account of the diplomatic negotiations at Aix-la-Chapelle, the 1819 report of the directors of the African Institution detailed how the British proposal for suppressing the slave trade through mutual search rights was met by an even more ambitious Russian counterproposal that more fully answered the demands of the abolitionists: "a special Association between all States, having for its end the extinction of the traffic in Slaves," with this traffic legally defined as piracy. This proposed association, which would constitute an international court together with an international maritime police force, was identified as a "practical manifestation" of the Holy Alliance:

> The execution of the Law should be confided to an Institution, the seat of which should be in a central point on the Coast of Africa, and in the formation of which, all the Christian States should take a part. Declared forever neutral, to be estranged from all political and local interests, like the fraternal and Christian alliance, of which, it would be a practical manifestation, this Institution would follow the single object of strictly maintaining the execution of the Law.[181]

Ultimately, as Brian Vick has described, the joining of slavery with piracy (also an issue on the Barbary Coast in the Mediterranean Sea) proved fraught, thanks to suspicions of British naval dominance on one side and of Russian expansion into the Mediterranean on the other.[182] The European consensus on collective security proved even more fragile when projected beyond Europe, and it was the British system of bilateral search rights and mixed commission courts which expanded in the 1820s and extended to the independent South American republics. When a mutual

---

180. James Stephen, "Foedera Africana, Letter I," *The New Times*, September 16, 1818; James Stephen, "Foedera Africana, No. XII," *The New Times*, November 5, 1818.

181. *Thirteenth Report of the Directors of the African Institution, Read at the Annual General Meeting Held on the Twenty-Fourth Day of March, 1819* (London: Ellerton and Henderson, 1819), 22.

182. Brian Vick, "Power, Humanitarianism and the Global Liberal Order: Abolition and the Barbary Corsairs in the Vienna Congress System," *International History Review* 40, no. 4 (2018): 939–60.

search treaty between Britain, France, Austria, Russia, and Prussia was finally realized in 1841, it was hailed by the British negotiator Lord Aberdeen as "in truth a holy alliance, in which the undersigned would have rejoiced to see the United States assume their proper place among the great powers of Christendom"—but was greeted with renewed suspicion by the American lawyer and diplomat Henry Wheaton, who complained that the treaty was designed "to bring to bear upon America the moral weight of this Holy Alliance against the traffic in human beings, in order to compel her to sacrifice her maritime rights": the United States subsequently signed a separate treaty with Britain providing only for the parallel enforcement of national laws.[183] In short, the political architecture of redemption remained contested, along the lines of the debates about the Holy Alliance, the law of nations, and the federative powers of states that were discussed in chapter 4.

The Holy Alliance was also incorporated into a redemptive history by the emerging American peace movement. The Massachusetts Peace Society was founded in 1815 by Noah Worcester, a close associate and collaborator of the prominent Unitarian theologian William Ellery Channing. As we have seen, the leaders of the Massachusetts Peace Society were among those who initially embraced the Holy Alliance (whose true "ground," "spirit," and "object" they correctly discerned in Alexander's Christmas Manifesto); in 1817 they ventured an exchange of letters with the Russian emperor and his minister Golitsyn, and in 1822 they still expressed the hope that "our government will not be the last to accede" to the Holy Alliance.[184] This response to the Holy Alliance was rooted in a historical perspective informed by understandings of providence and redemption comparable to those articulated by Stephen. The January 1816 installment of the Massachusetts Peace Society's publication, *The Friend of Peace*, set out to "excite a general abhorrence" of war by recounting the history of Napoleon's invasion of Russia in 1812. The narrative of the

---

183. Henry Wheaton, *History of the Law of Nations in Europe and America: From the Earliest Times to the Treaty of Washington, 1842* (New York: Gould, Banks, & Co., 1845), 696; Henry Wheaton, *Enquiry into the Validity of the British Claim to a Right of Visitation & Search of American Vessels Suspected to Be Engaged in the African Slave-Trade* (London: J. Miller, 1842), 167.

184. Philo Pacificus, "The Friend of Peace, No. X," in *The Friend of Peace*, vol. 1 (Boston: J. T. Buckingham, n.d.), 24, 27–30, https://hdl.handle.net/2027/hvd.hxj9mf; Philo Pacificus, *The Friend of Peace, in a Series of Numbers: Together with a Solemn Review of the Custom of War, as an Introduction to Said Work* (Ballston Spa: J. Comstock, 1822), 278, https://hdl.handle.net/2027/ucl.b3138474. The correspondence with Alexander and Golitsyn was also published in London.

suffering that attended each battle was punctuated by biblical quotations and followed by a comparison of the daily, weekly, and monthly death tolls with the populations of various towns and cities in New England. "It is proper that we should reflect on the righteous retributions of Providence in the Russian Campaign," the essay explained, noting that both sides had suffered because both empires had formed through war: the British, too, would eventually face imperial ruin unless they also atoned for their wars, for "above all other nations they now possess the means of giving peace to the world."[185] Finally, the essay warned (rather presciently), unless the United States of America succeeded in disarming and demilitarizing itself, its rapid rate of population growth would produce a dreadful civil war within fifty years: "the horrors of Smolensko, Borodino, Moscow and Beresina, may be repeated in our land."[186]

The Friend of Peace welcomed the proclamation of the Holy Alliance as a genuine moral reaction to the "miseries occasioned by war."[187] The unusual form of the treaty reflected the singularity of the historical experience that had prompted its proclamation. Had Britain endured suffering and destruction on a comparable scale, constitutional technicalities would not have been cited as a pretext for declining to accede to the Holy Alliance. *The Friend of Peace* went on to publish a memorial submitted by the Massachusetts Peace Society to the United States Congress, expressing its hope, "if it be consistent with the principles of the constitution, that the solemn profession of pacific principles, lately made by several distinguished sovereigns of Europe, may be met with corresponding professions on the part of our own government." Although the aim of the peace society was to turn public opinion against war, the memorial explained, its unusual direct appeal to the government was prompted by the convergence of principles it had detected between the proclamation of the Holy Alliance and the final State of the Union Address delivered by President James Madison in 1816. Despite the risk of hypocrisy, public pronouncements like the treaty of the Holy Alliance could not only transform the content of public opinion but also enhance its "invisible sovereignty" over government by articulating a clear standard for judgment. Issuing such a proclamation would help position the United States as a "nation, espousing the cause of peace and humanity," "sincerely disposed

185. Philo Pacificus, "The Friend of Peace, No. III," in *The Friend of Peace*, vol. 1 (Boston: J. T. Buckingham, n.d.), 1, 19–20, https://hdl.handle.net/2027/hvd.hxj9mf.

186. Ibid., 31.

187. Pacificus, "The Friend of Peace, No. X," 23.

to sustain the august and sublime character" of "the pacificator of the world," taking the lead in promoting disarmament instituting a system of international arbitration.[188]

The Massachusetts Peace Society's enthusiastic reception of the Holy Alliance was immediately challenged by Alexander Hill Everett: a Boston man of letters who became editor of the influential *North American Review* and pursued a long career as a diplomat. Everett had been the protégé of John Quincy Adams, whom he had accompanied to Russia in 1809–11; he spent the 1820s stationed in The Hague and Madrid. His commentaries on European and American politics circulated widely in Europe as well as the United States. *Europe, or, A General Survey of the Present Situation of the Principal Powers, with Conjectures on Their Future Prospects* appeared in 1822 and was translated into German the following year; the sequel, *America, or, A General Survey of the Political Situation of the Several Powers of the Western Continent, with Conjectures on Their Future Prospects*, appeared in 1827 and was translated into both German and Spanish. In his 1817 review of *The Friend of Peace*, Everett praised the Massachusetts Peace Society while condemning "the solemn farce of Holy Alliances" that proclaimed peace while remaining systems of military government opposed to the interests of society. For Everett, the same criticism applied to the British imitations of the American peace societies, since Britain's government, too, was "essentially military."[189] His review prompted a particularly sharp condemnation of American admirers of the Holy Alliance by Adams (whose father had already rebuffed the Massachusetts Peace Society's overtures):

Philip of Macedon was in very active correspondence with a Peace Society at Athens, and with their cooperation baffled and overpowered all the eloquence of Demosthenes. Alexander of the Neva is not so near nor so dangerous a neighbor to us as Philip was to the Athenians, but I am afraid his love of peace is of the same character as was that of Philip of Macedon. . . . While Alexander and his Minister of Religious Worship,

---

188. Philo Pacificus, "The Friend of Peace, No. VIII," in *The Friend of Peace*, vol. 1 (Boston: J. T. Buckingham, n.d.), 28–31, https://hdl.handle.net/2027/hvd.hxj9mf.

189. Alexander Hill Everett, "The Friend of Peace, No. 1–8. By Philo Pacificus," *North-American Review and Miscellaneous Journal* 6, no. 16 (1817): 42, 26. For the attributions to Everett's articles in the *North American Review*, see Kenneth Walter Cameron, *Research Keys to the American Renaissance: Scarce Indexes of the Christian Examiner, the North American Review, and the New Jerusalem Magazine for Students of American Literature, Culture, History, and New England Transcendentalism* (Hartford, CT: Transcendental Books, 1967), 148.

Prince Galitzin, are corresponding with the Rev. Noah Worcester upon the blessedness of peace, the venerable founder of the Holy League is sending five or six ships of the line, and several thousand promoters of peace armed with bayonets to Cadiz, and thence to propagate good will to man elsewhere. Whether at Algiers, at Constantinople, or at Buenos Ayres, we shall be informed hereafter.[190]

In his writings of the 1820s, as in his 1817 review, Everett went on to castigate the Holy Alliance as a mask for Russian despotism, "a peace establishment of only 800,000 bayonets." The intervention to suppress revolution in Naples had shown that the "holy allies" were "precisely similar in their essential features" to Napoleon, only even more hypocritical.[191] By contrast, Everett presented the United States as having arrived (thanks to James Madison and Alexander Hamilton) at an ideal federal solution to the fundamental problem of keeping political institutions aligned with the progressively developing needs of society. Everett developed this claim into a theory of progress through his engagement with the population principle of the English political economist Thomas Malthus, to whom he was introduced by the Scottish Whig politician James Mackintosh: an encounter that produced Everett's *New Ideas on Population: With Remarks on the Theories of Malthus and Godwin* (first published in 1823, and translated into French in 1826).[192] Malthus's population principle had emerged out of a debate with his father about Rousseau; it developed into an attack on the accounts of progress premised on perfectibility that had been advanced by the Marquis de Condorcet and William Godwin.[193] Malthus claimed that their respective projections of an egalitarian society liberated from the burdens of poverty and the constraints of necessity rested on unwarranted extrapolations about universal effects from limited knowledge of particular causes: a flawed approach that had blinded them to the providential impossibility of productivity increasing to match an

190. *Writings of John Quincy Adams*, ed. Worthington Chauncey Ford, vol. 6 (New York: Macmillan, 1916), 280–81, https://hdl.handle.net/2027/mdp.39015011733741. For John Adams's correspondence with the Massachusetts Peace Society, see Philo Pacificus, "The Friend of Peace, No. IV," in *The Friend of Peace*, vol. 1 (Boston: J. T. Buckingham, n.d.), 25–26, 28–30, https://hdl.handle.net/2027/hvd.hxj9mf.

191. Alexander Hill Everett, *Europe, or, A General Survey of the Present Situation of the Principal Powers, with Conjectures on Their Future Prospects* (Boston: Oliver Everett, 1822), 380, 140.

192. Alexander Hill Everett, *New Ideas on Population: With Remarks on the Theories of Malthus and Godwin*, 2nd ed., Reprints of Economic Classics (New York: Augustus M. Kelley, 1970).

193. Christopher Brooke, "Robert Malthus, Rousseauist," *The Historical Journal* 63, no. 1 (2019): 15–31.

unchecked rate of population growth. At the same time, Malthus shared Godwin's commitment to the cultivation of private judgment as the driver of progress (hence his preference for the moral discipline of delayed marriage as the best check on population); and he also shared Condorcet's commitment to a property-based social order (hence his accommodationist approach that historicized the scriptural injunction to be fruitful and multiply). If Malthus remained a theorist of progress, as many of his readers at the time maintained, this progress was premised on necessity and the fear of scarcity as well as self-interest and the inducement of prosperity—the threat of divine punishment for inactivity, as well as the promise of reward.[194] However, as Alison Bashford and Joyce Chaplin have shown, Malthus was widely read not just within Europe, as a critic of schemes for eliminating poverty, but also around the world, as an investigator of the comparative demographic, economic, and political destinies of settler colonial, enslaved, and indigenous populations.[195]

Everett was one of Malthus's most prominent readers in the United States, which, as he noted, had furnished Malthus with his estimate for unchecked population growth. Everett lined up with Malthus's opponents in judging Malthus's view of population growth as a paradox reminiscent of Rousseau's account of humans as solitary by nature.[196] On the other hand, Everett joined Malthus in criticizing the principle of perfectibility, though this did not prevent him from forecasting the indefinitely sustainable growth of the American population: three hundred million by the middle of the twentieth century, and four times that a few centuries later.[197] The position Everett developed was that Malthus and his opponents alike had been misled by underestimating the influence of political institutions in maintaining or disrupting the natural equilibrium between population and productivity that characterized a democratic society.[198] This position was grounded in the premise that political power reflected

194. Donald Winch, *Riches and Poverty: An Intellectual History of Political Economy in Britain, 1750–1834* (Cambridge: Cambridge University Press, 1996), 259–60.

195. Alison Bashford and Joyce E. Chaplin, *The New Worlds of Thomas Robert Malthus: Rereading the Principle of Population* (Princeton: Princeton University Press, 2016).

196. Everett, *New Ideas on Population*, vi, 29–30; Sonenscher, *Before the Deluge*, 353–54.

197. Alexander Hill Everett, *America, or, A General Survey of the Political Situation of the Several Powers of the Western Continent, with Conjectures on Their Future Prospects* (Philadelphia: H. C. Carey & I. Lea, 1827), 348.

198. Bashford and Chaplin, *The New Worlds of Thomas Robert Malthus*, 251; Dennis Hodgson, "Malthus' Essay on Population and the American Debate over Slavery," *Comparative Studies in Society and History* 51, no. 4 (October 2009): 742–70; Joseph J. Spengler, "Alexander Hill Everett: Early American Opponent of Malthus," *New England Quarterly* 9, no. 1 (1936): 97–118.

the distribution of property: Everett claimed that in the absence of the entrenched concentrations of inherited property that were the legacy of feudalism, public credit under the aegis of representative government would fuel rapid growth by dramatically increasing not only the availability of capital but also (following the arguments of Jean-Baptiste Say) its continual circulation.[199] By contrast, the kind of predominance retained by the British landowning class would generate fiscal and commercial distortions that would eventually prove politically destabilizing and financially unsustainable. From this perspective, it was federalism, which prevented the political institutions of the United States from ever becoming a parasitic "military system," that was decisive in ensuring the long-term sustainability of its rapid population growth. For having failed to recognize the novelty of American institutions, Everett singled out for criticism the former Massachusetts congressman Fisher Ames, whose fear of the demise of American federalism at the hands of the Virginian aristocracy was mentioned in chapter 4: instead Everett implicitly echoed the contrasting view of federalism that had been articulated by Joel Barlow, a New England ally of Thomas Jefferson's: "It is in the effects of the union still more, than in those of our pure and simple forms of administration," Everett wrote, "that we immediately feel the great advantages of our political situation."[200] Federalism ensured not only that both the federal and the state governments remained representative, aligning the balance of power with the balance of property, but also that every one of these representatives of public power occupied a constitutionally defined function: they were all "subject to the control of a common superior," and this meant that rival claims to sovereignty became "questions of construction" that were "in their nature legal and not political."[201] Were it ever to lose this federal union, Everett observed, American politics would come to resemble those of Germany. Not only would its formerly "free and happy population" come to be oppressed by standing armies, despotic rulers, and "an insulting and oppressive aristocracy": foreign meddling would also make it impossible to remove these oppressors.[202] Liberal principles could not be applied to government in Germany, or any other country in Europe, because there—as it had been during the Reformation—"the political world is divided into two parties in regard to this subject."[203]

199. Sonenscher, *Before the Deluge*, 366–67.
200. Everett, *Europe*, 335.
201. Everett, *America*, 93–94.
202. Everett, *Europe*, 228.
203. Ibid., 384.

Having effectively arrogated sovereignty to itself, the Holy Alliance was distorting the balance of power between these two parties by throwing its weight behind interests opposing liberal reforms, which would otherwise be swept away by the rising tide of civilization. Should the American union fall apart, Everett concluded, American states would find themselves in a similar position: "we should find ourselves entangled in a web of various oppression, which it would be at once impossible to shake off, and torment and death to wear."[204]

On one level, Everett presented a straightforward rebuttal of the liberal hopes invested in the Holy Alliance. For Everett, unlike for Schmidt-Phiseldek, the contrast between Europe and America revealed that the Holy Alliance, far from being an instrument for the progress of civilization, was in fact empowering atavistic political forces that constrained and distorted social and economic progress. Everett criticized Schmidt-Phiseldek for overestimating how quickly the growth of American manufacturing would yield economic independence, while also underestimating the extent to which colonial expansion would continue to supply a stimulus to European industry. However, Everett also praised Schmidt-Phiseldek as an "intelligent writer" and *Europe and America* as an "eloquent and philosophical work."[205] Into the 1830s, as the English visitor Frances Trollope rolled her eyes at American credulity toward the "prophecy" of a Danish "Fiddlestick" who had never even traveled across the Atlantic, Everett continued to quote Schmidt-Phiseldek's opening line about 1776 as a world-historical turning point at his Fourth of July orations.[206] In fact, as Everett himself implied, and as a perceptive German reviewer of Schmidt-Phiseldek pointed out in 1823, Everett's views were not as opposed to those of the Danish writer as it might appear. Both Everett and Schmidt-Phiseldek had ultimately denied that American independence would necessarily lead to Europe's decline and fall, and both writers had described a historical process through which the progress of civilization would be secured. According to the German reviewer, neither had made the mistake of those enthusiasts whose political

204. Ibid., 228.

205. Ibid., 395.

206. Frances Milton Trollope, *Domestic Manners of the Americans*, vol. 2 (London: Whittaker, Treacher & Co., 1832), 140, https://catalog.hathitrust.org/Record/007675076; Alexander Hill Everett, *An Oration, Delivered at the Request of the City Government, before the Citizens of Boston, on the 5th of July, 1830* (Boston: John H. Eastburn, 1830), https://catalog.hathitrust.org/Record/008587093; Alexander Hill Everett, *A Defence of the Character and Principles of Mr. Jefferson: Being an Address Delivered at Weymouth, Mass. at the Request of the Anti-Masonic and Democratic Citizens of That Place, on the 4th of July, 1836* (Beals and Greene, 1836), 32–33.

judgment rested on unwarranted claims to understand the workings of providence. The difference between them, according to the reviewer, was that the historical process described by Schmidt-Phiseldek was premised on the availability of goodwill, whereas Everett's was driven by antagonism and natural necessity.[207] In Everett's account, the barrier to civilization erected by the Holy Alliance was actually self-undermining, because in order to maintain the military might that suppressed the advance of liberal principles in western Europe, the rulers of the comparatively undeveloped eastern empires had to rely on western creditors, and this process would accelerate the transfer of their property to the very interests they were trying to suppress. It was, Everett surmised, "one of the most singular instances perhaps that could be produced of an effect, 'counter-working its cause'"; or, as Michael Sonenscher put it, alluding to *The Communist Manifesto*, "Public debt would, in this way, dig the graves of liberty's own grave-diggers."[208]

Everett advanced a broader account of how, to extend the allusion to Marx, Europe's resurrection had already been announced by the screeching of Russian eagles.[209] The progress of European civilization could not be halted because the great stimulus from the colonization of the Americas—the real source of the revolutionary spirit in Europe, and the ultimate cause of the French Revolution—would only dissipate very gradually, as Schmidt-Phiseldek himself had observed. Nor had the global process of European colonization ended—in fact it was accelerating, across Africa, the Middle East, and Asia, "by fair means and foul."[210]

207. *Allgemeine Literatur-Zeitung* 2, no. 143 (June 1823): 273–80, http://zs.thulb.uni-jena.de/receive/jportal_jparticle_00186165; *Allgemeine Literatur-Zeitung* 2, no. 144 (June 1823): 281–84, http://zs.thulb.uni-jena.de/receive/jportal_jparticle_00186168; *Allgemeine Literatur-Zeitung* 2, no. 153 (June 1823): 353–58, http://zs.thulb.uni-jena.de/receive/jportal_jparticle_00186617.

208. Everett, *Europe*, 26; Sonenscher, *Before the Deluge*, 369. "What the bourgeoisie, therefore, produces, above all, is its own grave-diggers." Karl Marx and Friedrich Engels, *The Communist Manifesto*, ed. Gareth Stedman Jones (London: Penguin, 2002), 243.

209. "*the day of German resurrection* will be announced by the *crowing of the Gallic cock*." Karl Marx, "A Contribution to the Critique of Hegel's Philosophy of Right: Introduction," in *Marx: Early Political Writings*, ed. Joseph J. O'Malley (Cambridge: Cambridge University Press, 1994), 70.

210. Everett, *Europe*, 436, 425–26. Everett hoped that China would fare better than Peru had, if not because the Europeans had become more humane, as Schmidt-Phiseldek hoped, then because the Chinese would "prove themselves more courageous and politic than the unfortunate Americans" (431). Everett died in 1847 in China, having just arrived to assume a diplomatic post.

Europe would long remain "the central point of this great universal system of colonization" and its industry would therefore continue to flourish.[211] The more European society advanced without its liberal principles finding their natural political outlets, the more pretexts it would furnish for Russian intervention. "Suppose, for example, an explosion to occur in Prussia," Everett speculated in 1822: "a Russian army would immediately march into Berlin." The more Russia came to rule "by actual force," the more pretexts for revolution it would generate, and the process would continue "from capital to capital" until "we may see at last the two-headed eagle extend his wings triumphantly over the tower of London itself."[212] Even this scenario, in Everett's view, would advance the cause of civilization, because the vaunted old European balance of power, in Everett's estimation, had never been more than an ineffectual substitute for an actual federal government. In any case, the debate about the European balance of power had been rendered moot once the "civilization of the Russian nobility" in the eighteenth century had created a "new Macedon" on the edge of Europe.[213] The transfer of authority from one segment of what was in fact already a pan-European elite to another would not be fatal to European society; on the contrary, the expanding Russian Empire would furnish another major colonizing stimulus for all of Europe. Ultimately "the effect of the increasing influence of Russia upon the political forms must be considered as decidedly favourable," Everett concluded, because the more the Russians acted as the de facto illiberal federal government of Europe,

> the advance of civilization would immediately begin to exercise the same influence upon the new general government, that it now does upon each of the separate ones: and the final result in this case, as in the other, would be the organization of an universal European commonwealth on rational and liberal principles. Thus the ambition or fanaticism of the Russian government, like most other moral and physical evils, while it produces great immediate mischief and suffering, may tend materially towards the promotion of a very important object connected with the general good.[214]

211. Ibid., 431.

212. Ibid., 393.

213. Ibid., 348. It might have been possible to save the old European balance of power, Everett felt, by organizing a new western alliance around France and liberating Greece.

214. Ibid., 450.

In the early 1820s, then, for Everett no less than for Schmidt-Phiseldek, the Holy Alliance still marked the first stage in the formation of a federal Europe and the consolidation of a liberal core of an increasingly global civilization.

Outbreak with a Vengeance

In his efforts to communicate his diagnosis of European politics to an American audience, Everett drew a series of transatlantic analogies. According to Everett, the European "era of good feelings"—the reconciliation of peoples and princes through their shared emancipatory struggle against Napoleon—may have been fleeting, but the historical process he had outlined would position Europe as the heart of a vast empire, analogous to the fate Everett envisioned for New England. "Europe will be to the three ancient continents what New England now is to the United States," Everett promised, "the most civilized and populous, the wealthiest and the happiest portion of a civilized and populous, a wealthy and a happy world of kindred origin."[215] Everett's response to Schmidt-Phiseldek, together with his concurrent commentaries on European and American politics, places the liberal ideal of the Holy Alliance in comparative perspective with two other great federal projects of the 1820s across the Atlantic: the United States of America and Gran Colombia (the republic led by Simón Bolívar that aspired to unite the newly independent Spanish colonies of South America). Reading Everett in this way reveals not only the prospect that Schmidt-Phiseldek's Holy Alliance might make Europe look more like the Americas, but also the specter of Everett's America confronting the kinds of problems that Schmidt-Phiseldek and others had hoped the Holy Alliance would address.

The German translator of Everett's *America* was unimpressed by Everett's idealized account of American federalism. The translator objected to Everett's criticism of Ames, who had described the relationship between New England and the United States as the tragic subjugation of Boston to the imperial power of a Virginian Rome. The translator also pointedly contrasted Everett's federal ideal to what they described as the defiance of a federal ban on slavery in Missouri and the State of Georgia's unjust war against indigenous Americans in defiance of the federal government.[216]

215. Ibid., 435.

216. *Alex H. Everett's Amerika, oder Allgemeiner Ueberblick der politischen Lage der verchiedenen Staaten des westlichen Festlandes, nebst Vermuthungen über deren künftiges*

The potential for an existential clash between the federal guarantor of collective security and the principle of state sovereignty was very much in evidence. From this perspective, Missouri's admission to the union as a slave state also revealed the problem that—according to the political analysis of the Genevan writer Jacob Frédéric Lullin de Châteauvieux, discussed in chapter 2—the Greek Revolution of 1821 posed to the Holy Alliance: the problem of maintaining a constitutional balance of power among heterogeneous states while also undertaking expansion that threatens to disrupt it.[217] In the case of Missouri, its admission as a slave state was opposed and initially blocked by northern opponents of slavery in 1819, until an arrangement for further expansion was negotiated which maintained the balance of power between slave and free soil states. The potentially existential stakes of this clash also seem to have reminded Thomas Jefferson of the Holy Alliance. As he wrote to James Madison in January 1821, referring to congressional opponents of Missouri's admission as a slave state, "I think our Holy alliance will find themselves so embarrassed with the difficulties presented to them as to find their solution only in yielding to Missouri her entrance on the same footing with the other States, that is to say with the right to admit or exclude slaves at her own discretion."[218] Nine days later, Jefferson employed the analogy again in a letter to John Adams. Here he likened the federal imposition of conditions on Missouri's admission to the Holy Alliance's tyrannical pretensions to overrule the national sovereignty of European states:

> Our anxieties in this quarter are all concentrated in the question What does the Holy alliance, in and out of Congress, mean to do with us on the Missouri question? and this, by the bye, is but the name of the case. it is only the John Doe or Richard Roe of the excitement. the real question, as seen in the states. afflicted with this unfortunate population, is, Are our slaves to be presented with freedom and a dagger? for if Congress has a power to regulate the conditions of the inhabitants of the states, within

Schicksal, übersetzt und mit erläuternden anmerkungen Versehen, vol. 1 (Hamburg: Hoffmann und Campe, 1828), 110, 121–22, https://hdl.handle.net/2027/mdp.39015016777487.

217. The journalist William Duane, who had helped elect Thomas Jefferson, attributed British ambivalence over Greek emancipation to the fear that a closer alliance between Russia (whose Holy Alliance he compared to Napoleon's continental blockade) and Greece (whose maritime prowess he compared to New England's) would pose a dire threat to English naval supremacy (but no threat to the Americas, in his view). William Duane, *The Two Americas, Great Britain, and the Holy Alliance* (Washington: Edward De Krafft, 1824).

218. Thomas Jefferson to James Madison, January 13, 1821, Founders Online, National Archives, https://founders.archives.gov/documents/Jefferson/98-01-02-1764.

the states, it will be but another exercise of that power to declare that all shall be free. are we then to see again Athenian and Lacedemonian confederacies? to wage another Peloponnesian war to settle the ascendancy between them? or is this the tocsin of merely a servile war? that remains to be seen: but not I hope by you or me.[219]

Everett's own discussion of slavery, and his commentaries on related problems of American politics in the 1820s, also diverged from his ideal theory of federalism and converged with liberal discussions of the Holy Alliance. Everett's commitment to the principle of popular sovereignty later led him to support Andrew Jackson and to condemn the Federalist Party as the defunct American equivalent of the European party of legitimacy: though Boston may have embraced Emperor Alexander in 1815, he noted in 1836, by 1830 it was enthusiastically supporting the Polish uprising against Russian domination, and in fact it was the Democratic Party that had identified the best approach to reconciling the principles of law and liberty all along.[220] However, Everett's efforts to grapple with the problem of slavery took him some distance from the principle of popular sovereignty, and led him to embrace the kind of top-down approach to gradual reform advanced by European liberals, including those who embraced the Holy Alliance. Everett's approach to the history of civilization did accommodate an outspoken commitment to racial equality, but it certainly did not result in abolitionism.[221] "In this as in every other project of political improvement, we must assume and build upon the existing state of things," Everett counseled. By starting with the slow and gradual improvement of the material and moral conditions of the enslaved Black population, "emancipation will come in due time without an effort," whereas either immediate revolutionary emancipation or an "expulsion"

219. Thomas Jefferson to John Adams, January 22, 1821, Founders Online, National Archives, https://founders.archives.gov/documents/Adams/99-02-02-7457.

220. Everett, *A Defence of the Character and Principles of Mr. Jefferson*, 36.

221. "It is well known that the Europeans,—unwilling to admit that a race whom they have injured so deeply as the Africans, are naturally their equals,—have undertaken to prove that they are an inferior variety of the species," Everett explained in an 1834 address at Amherst College. "This degrading theory,—degrading, I mean, to its authors, and not to the unfortunate race whom they thus attempt to reduce below themselves in the scale of humanity, in order to have some apology for torturing and oppressing them,—this degrading theory is of course ruined by the single fact, that the Egyptians, the predecessors, and as it were the masters in civilization of the Europeans, belonged to the African family." Alexander Hill Everett, *A Discourse on the Progress and Limits of Social Improvement: Including a General Survey of the History of Civilization* (Boston: Charles Bowen, 1834), 26–27. Cf. Everett, *America*, 212–21.

akin to that of the Moors from Spain or the Protestants from France (as Everett characterized contemporary philanthropic projects of resettlement in Africa or Haiti) would lead to prolonged violence and suffering as well as significant economic damage.[222] Here, at least, Everett had arrived at a position parallel to the one taken by Krug and Schmidt-Phiseldek among many other European liberals: that inclusion in the progress of society had to come before political emancipation, not the other way around; and that such progress was premised on the exclusion of any revolutionary invocation of the principle of popular sovereignty.

Everett's uneasy commentary on the great political conflict over tariffs and the promotion of manufacturing, which he staunchly supported, reveals another convergence with Schmidt-Phiseldek. Debates about state nullification of federal law, fueled by the tariff issue, revealed, to Everett's distress, how a volatile and potentially explosive contestation over sovereignty had crept back in to a supposedly legalized federal politics.[223] As with the Missouri crisis, these debates provided another occasion for analogies to the Holy Alliance that, in this case, appeared on both sides. From one perspective, a South Carolina newspaper claimed in defense of nullification, a sovereign American state could no more be accused of rebelling against the union than England could "rebel" against the Holy Alliance.[224] From the other side, however, "the rulers of the states" who denied the representative basis of the federal government and presented themselves as guardians against "consolidated empire" were in fact rejecting the principle of popular sovereignty itself, and seeking to impose minority rule on the populations of their own states: "Are you aware that you are preaching up the same doctrines that the 'Holy Alliance' of Europe are attempting to seal with blood? To assert that the general government will prostrate the liberties of the people, is to assert that our republican experiment will fail, and that our constitution is founded upon false principles."[225] Everett himself was a great proponent of the reorientation of the New England economy toward manufacturing, which he claimed had been artificially

222. Everett, *America*, 224.

223. Alexander Hill Everett, "The Two Conventions," *North American Review* 34, no. 74 (1832): 178–98; Alexander Hill Everett, "The Union and the States," *North American Review* 37, no. 80 (1833): 190–249.

224. "Nullification," *States Rights and Free Trade Evening Post* (Charleston, SC), November 29, 1831, *Readex: America's Historical Newspapers*.

225. *Defence of a liberal construction of the powers of Congress as regards internal improvement, etc.* (Philadelphia, 1831), 6–8. (This was George McDuffie, the South Carolinian whose 1821 anti-states-rights pamphlet was reprinted in 1831 to shame him for having switched sides.)

inhibited by political causes, and therefore required exceptional remedial intervention to restore its natural rate of development, balanced with the growth of the agricultural sector. Against opponents of this policy, Everett argued that an economy based on southern commodities exported by northern shipping exposed the union to greater political risk. Even more worryingly, Everett warned, such an unbalanced economy could not in the final analysis provide the agricultural sector with a growing domestic market, but would instead support a larger European manufacturing population, in exchange for a relatively smaller American population of merchants and sailors. Only a growing domestic market would lead to broad-based consumption of "the articles of comfort and luxury which are essential to civilization." In the absence of a domestic manufacturing sector large enough to employ surplus agricultural workers locally, internal emigration to newly settled agricultural territory as well as distant manufacturing centers was very high. The former was of course easy to romanticize and had some real benefits, but the latter created a dangerously detached urban working class. Everett stressed that ultimately both forms of internal emigration had negative social and moral consequences: the constant breakup of families and disruption of social circles impoverished the natural sentiments of attachment that added up to "the whole charm and beauty of existence."[226] In Everett's eyes, in other words, the material conditions for a healthy national civic culture, of the kind evoked by Schmidt-Phiseldek, were threatened by the incapacity of the federal government to impose its tariff policy.

A final convergence arose in the context of Everett's reflections on the future prospects of the newly independent South American states. Everett's account of the relationship between America and Europe as a contest between liberty and despotism (with Britain, and to some extent France, as battleground states) retained the hemispheric aspirations of the "American system" originally invoked by Alexander Hamilton: the idea of a pan-American alternative to European power politics, grounded in federal institutions and free trade, according to which the United States recognized the independence of Spain's former American colonies from Mexico to Buenos Aires in 1822.[227] Like the post-1815 European consensus on collective security, this hemispheric "American system" came under strain

226. Everett, *America*, 156–57.

227. Joshua Simon, "From the American System to Anglo-Saxon Union: Scientific Racism and Supra-Nationalism in Nineteenth-Century North America," in *Forms of Pluralism and Democratic Constitutionalism*, ed. Andrew Arato, Jean Cohen, and Astrid von Busekist (New York: Columbia University Press, 2018), 72–94.

during the 1820s, and was significantly curtailed by divergent interests in an expanding federal empire. In convening the 1826 Panama Congress, Bolívar had invoked the idea of a new system of international law based on principles of arbitration and collective security; in the United States, even an attenuated endorsement of the Panama Congress as a starting point for concluding new commercial treaties aroused strong opposition from slaveholder interests that exercised an increasingly firm grip on federal power, especially over foreign policy. Everett's commitments to the cohesion and expansion of the federal union brought him into fraught alignment with this foreign policy. The ideal of hemispheric economic independence from Europe was increasingly challenged by fears of Bolívar's emancipatory rhetoric; the dream of absorbing Cuba into the United States (which Everett pursued) was overshadowed by fears of revolution spreading from Haiti, perhaps instigated by British "imperial abolitionism."[228] Writing in 1827, Everett still asserted his prognosis that the newly independent American republics would ultimately follow the developmental trajectory of the United States rather than that of Europe (and that Britain's intermediate position between America and Europe would prove transitional). At the same time, Everett admonished the South Americans for appearing to imitate the precedents set by the United States too closely. Instead of setting themselves up for failure by replicating its political institutions, Everett warned, they ought to have introduced less popular institutions better adapted to their own social state, and leaned more intensively on established religion in order to foster a civic culture that could sustain future liberal reforms. The separation of church and state was a Protestant fiction, Everett explained; both morality and law were properly understood as expressions of the same "sovereign power." In the United States both were democratic, whereas in Britain both were monarchical. In South America, despite lingering qualms about the compatibility of the Catholic Church with republicanism, Everett arrived at the striking conclusion that the "principle of religion" or "the will of God" was more likely to supply the sovereign will to support liberal reforms than the "principle of liberty" or "the will of the people."[229] The German translator of Everett's

228. Matthew Karp, *This Vast Southern Empire: Slaveholders at the Helm of American Foreign Policy* (Cambridge, MA: Harvard University Press, 2016), 8. In Madrid in 1825, Everett explored an unlikely scheme for purchasing Cuba from Spain; on his visit to Cuba in 1840 and subsequent role investigating fears of abolitionist activity there, see Robert L. Paquette, "The Everett-Del Monte Connection: A Study in the International Politics of Slavery," *Diplomatic History* 11, no. 1 (1987): 1–22.

229. Everett, *America*, 201–2. Previously Everett had also claimed that it was merely Protestant prejudice to prefer a balance of power among rival warlords as the de facto

America heartily approved of these remarks, interpreting them as the author's advice to his own compatriots to progress "from the free to the religious condition."[230] The author's compatriots were less enthused. It was an "outbreak with a vengeance," exclaimed Robert Walsh in his review, "from the pen of a professed republican of the nineteenth century, and a stout opponent of the *Holy* Alliance."[231]

---

federal government of Europe instead of the old Church hierarchy. Everett, *Europe,* 335–39. On James Madison's contemporary view of the relation between "religion and the Civil authority" and the limitations of the "'church-state relations' model" in the American context, see Sam Haselby, *The Origins of American Religious Nationalism* (Oxford: Oxford University Press, 2015), 22.

230. Everett, *Amerika,* 1:260–61, 263.

231. Robert Walsh, "America: Or, a General Survey of the Political Situation of the Several Powers of the Western Continent, with Conjectures on Their Future Prospects," *American Quarterly Review,* June 1, 1827, 512.

Conclusion

NEW HOLY ALLIANCES

Talk about [the League of Nations] has a grimly humorous suggestion of the talk about the Holy Alliance a hundred years ago, which had as its main purpose the perpetual maintenance of peace. The Czar Alexander, by the way, was the President Wilson of this particular movement a century ago.

—THEODORE ROOSEVELT[1]

THE IDEA OF a Holy Alliance haunted nineteenth- and twentieth-century politics. It became a potent label whose historical specificity enabled it to perform a function that has also been served by various episodes of the French Revolution of 1789, such as the Terror: the deployment of historical analogies whose moral force derives from the imputation of the exceptional character of the original case. The tension between the imputation of an exception and the deployment of analogies intensifies as the latter proliferate. In fact, what prompts such analogies in the first place is a persisting set of underlying problems: in the case of the Holy Alliance, of the economic, legal, moral, and religious problems connected to federative politics and its potential to serve as a framework for both progress and reaction. Such problems cannot be adequately addressed by selectively reasserting some of the expectations generated by the original case. Rather than engaging in a further round of what Karl Marx memorably termed "world-historical necromancy," this book has revisited the Holy Alliance in order to unpack the complexity of the

1. Theodore Roosevelt to Philander Chase Knox, December 6, 1918, cited in Henry Kissinger, *Diplomacy* (New York: Simon & Schuster, 1994), 54.

problems that originally gave rise to the liberal politics of federation.[2] From this perspective, analogies to the Holy Alliance supply a map of the historical career of these problems—a map that serves as a starting point for a more systematic assessment of the present and future possibilities of federative politics.

The term "new Holy Alliance" was already current in nineteenth-century politics, and it continued to proliferate in the twentieth century, especially in the context of debates about the League of Nations. Schemes of international arbitration proposed by the growing nineteenth-century peace movement were debated as new versions of the Holy Alliance.[3] The same happened within the increasingly institutionalized discipline of international law, most prominently in a debate that took place in the late 1870s between two eminent lawyers, James Lorimer in Edinburgh and Johann Caspar Bluntschli in Heidelberg.[4] In the case of the League

2. Karl Marx, "The Eighteenth Brumaire of Louis Bonaparte," in *Marx and Engels: 1851–1853*, Karl Marx and Friedrich Engels Collected Works 11 (London: Lawrence & Wishart, 1979), 104.

3. In a remark evidently lost on the recipient, John Quincy Adams informed William Ladd, the first president of the American Peace Society, that "the Holy Alliance itself was a tribute from the mightiest men of the European world to the purity of your principles and the practicability of your system for the general preservation of peace." Cited in William Ladd, *An Essay on a Congress of Nations: For the Adjustment of International Dispute without Resort to Arms* (Boston: Whipple and Damrell, 1840), 57. Adams had served on a panel (with James Kent and Daniel Webster) judging a competition held by the Peace Society for a Prize Essay on a Congress of Nations. Ladd had been rebuffed in a similar spirit (and with similar reference to the Holy Alliance) in an 1838 report to the Committee on Foreign Affairs of the House of Representatives prepared by Hugh Swinton Legaré, a friend of Alexander Hill Everett's: see Hugh Swinton Legaré, *Writings of Hugh Swinton Legaré, Late Attorney General and Acting Secretary of State of the United States*, vol. 1 (Charleston: Burges & James, 1846), 354–66; Elizabeth Evans, "The Friendship of Alexander Hill Everett and Hugh Swinton Legaré," *Mississippi Quarterly* 28, no. 4 (1975): 497–504. On the international peace movement and arbitration schemes more generally, see, e.g., W. H. van der Linden, *The International Peace Movement, 1815–1874* (Amsterdam: Tilleul Publications, 1987); Martin Ceadel, *The Origins of War Prevention: The British Peace Movement and International Relations, 1730–1854* (Oxford: Oxford University Press, 1996).

4. Lorimer's argument that the logic of international jurisprudence demanded a supranational political organization prompted Bluntschli to accuse him of reverting to the premodern legality of the Holy Alliance. James Lorimer, *The Institutes of the Law of Nations: A Treatise of the Jural Relations of Separate Political Communities*, vol. 2 (W. Blackwood and Sons, 1884), 181–299; Johann Caspar Bluntschli, "Die Organisation des europäischen Statenvereines," in *Gesammelte kleine Schriften: Aufsätze über Politik und Völkerrecht* (Nördlingen: Beck, 1881), 2:280. Cf. Johann Caspar Bluntschli, "Allianz, Heilige," in *Deutsches Staats-Wörterbuch*, vol. 1 (Stuttgart, 1857), 169–74. Lorimer contested the typology in his response to Bluntschli: *The Institutes of the Law of Nations*, 2:272–73. On the debate between Bluntschli and Lorimer, see Bruno Arcidiacono, "La paix par le droit international dans la vision de deux juristes du xixᵉ siècle: Le débat Lorimer-Bluntschli," *Rela-*

of Nations, analogies to the Holy Alliance distilled complex debates about
the legal structure of international institutions, and the role of public
opinion and political judgment in directing the external conduct of states,
into morally charged binaries: the possibility of progress hung in the balance.[5] From one side, the Holy Alliance stood for the threat posed by an
international "super-state" to the principle of national sovereignty. It stood
for an abstract conception of international justice serving as a mask for
various powers preferring to suppress autonomous political judgment.
From the other side, the Holy Alliance stood for the ideal of federalism
as an alternative to the balance of power: as the means for escaping from
the power politics associated with the destructive winner-take-all form of
competition generated by international anarchy.[6] One famous twentieth-
century investigation of the post-Napoleonic settlement that took this
shape was undertaken decades later by Henry Kissinger. Before he
made his mark on American foreign policy, Kissinger published *A World
Restored: Metternich, Castlereagh and the Problems of Peace, 1812–22*.[7] In
this 1957 study, Kissinger cast Alexander as the archetype of a revolutionary prophet, whose messianism posed an existential threat to political
order. Where Napoleon had attempted to impose unity on a divided
world through conquest, Alexander's Holy Alliance had attempted to
impose it by asserting and enforcing an expansive moral vision. Kissinger
himself, in a later work, approvingly cited a 1918 remark by Theodore
Roosevelt condemning the League of Nations as another Holy Alliance

---

tions internationales, no. 149 (2012): 13–26. For another challenge to Bluntschli's modern
science of international law that contested his interpretation of the Holy Alliance, see
F. Lucas, "De l'influence et du rôle du Christianisme dans la formation du droit international,"
Revue des facultés catholiques de l'Ouest 3, no. 4 (1893): 556–84.

5. On the history of debates among rival approaches to internationalism in the context of the League of Nations (as well as several instances of the "new holy alliances"
being invoked in this context), see Stephen Wertheim, "The League That Wasn't: American Designs for a Legalist-Sanctionist League of Nations and the Intellectual Origins of
International Organization, 1914–1920," *Diplomatic History* 35, no. 5 (November 2011):
797–836; Stephen Wertheim, "The League of Nations: A Retreat from International Law?"
Journal of Global History 7 (2012): 210–32.

6. See, e.g., Guglielmo Ferrero, *Problems of Peace, from the Holy Alliance to the League
of Nations* (New York: G. P. Putnam's Sons, 1919); Boris Mirkine-Guetzévitch, "L'Influence
de la révolution française sur le développement du droit international dans l'Europe ori-
entale," in *Recueil des Cours de l'Académie de droit international*, vol. 22 (Paris: Hachette,
1928), 2:295–457. See also Emil Ludwig, *A New Holy Alliance* (London: R. Hale, 1938).

7. Henry Kissinger, *A World Restored: Metternich, Castlereagh and the Problems of
Peace, 1812–22* (Boston: Houghton Mifflin, 1957). The book was based on Kissinger's 1954
doctoral dissertation at Harvard, titled "Peace, Legitimacy, and the Equilibrium: A Study
of the Statesmanship of Castlereagh and Metternich."

and identifying "the Czar Alexander" as "the President Wilson of this particular movement a century ago."[8] By contrast, in Kissinger's estimation, Metternich and Castlereagh had provided a model for the construction of a stable and enduring postwar order, as well as a reminder that the vocation of the statesman—to negotiate between the ethos particular to a national political culture and the unbending logic of power—was an inherently tragic enterprise.

Kissinger's account was partly a product of Weimar-era debates about the crisis of constitutionalism in an age of mass democracy, which remained salient in the early Cold War period and are still relatively well known today.[9] It was also a product of a British debate about federalism, the League of Nations, and the Holy Alliance. The first scholarly history of the Holy Alliance (whose "analysis" Kissinger praised as "lucid") was *The Confederation of Europe: A Study of the European Alliance, 1813–1823, as an Experiment in the International Organization of Peace*.[10] It was published in 1914 by Walter Alison Phillips, Professor of Modern History at the University of Dublin, but it had begun as a 1912 article, "The Peace Movement and the Holy Alliance," provoked in turn by a 1911 visit to the United States.[11] For Phillips, the "new Holy Alliance" described the politically obtuse legal formalism animating not only the American peace movement but also the International Peace Conferences held at The Hague beginning in 1899—which, as he pointed out, had been initiated by a Russian emperor aspiring to emulate the founder of the original Holy Alliance. Phillips traced "the ancestral tree of the Holy Alliance" back to the legendary Grand Design of Henry IV, which had later served as the basis for the perpetual peace plan of the Abbé de Saint-Pierre, before eventually making it into Alexander's head via Frédéric-César de la Harpe. Phillips's main point was that "the new Holy Alliance, of which the pacifists dream, would be faced by very much the same problems as those which confronted Alexander and his allies." It was not "extravagant

8. Kissinger, *Diplomacy*, 54.

9. See especially Udi Greenberg, *The Weimar Century: German Émigrés and the Ideological Foundations of the Cold War* (Princeton: Princeton University Press, 2014).

10. Walter Alison Phillips, *The Confederation of Europe: A Study of the European Alliance, 1813–1823, as an Experiment in the International Organization of Peace* (London: Longmans, Green, & Co., 1914); Kissinger, *A World Restored*, 343.

11. Walter Alison Phillips, *The Confederation of Europe: A Study of the European Alliance, 1813–1823, as an Experiment in the International Organization of Peace*, 2nd ed. (London: Longmans, Green and Co., 1920), vi; Walter Alison Phillips, "The Peace Movement and the Holy Alliance," *Edinburgh Review* 215, no. 440 (April 1912): 405–33.

to suppose," he warned, "that the new Holy Alliance, thus constituted, would develop, *mutatis mutandis*, very much on the lines of the old."[12]

The reason for this expectation, Phillips explained, was that federal schemes lacking a sufficiently strong shared identity had always devolved into clashes over the scope of "external" interventions into "internal" affairs. Moreover, even a cursory glance at the map of the world would reveal the arbitrariness of boundaries sure to be contested by powerful social movements: "The new Holy Alliance, then, like the old, would find itself face to face with revolutionary forces, which it would have to repress."[13] In the second edition of his book, published in 1920, Phillips was convinced that these predictions were coming to pass: "The new age has been born; the new Holy Alliance is in existence." Phillips was particularly concerned that "the surrender by Great Britain of her sovereignty" to the League of Nations would generate copious pretexts for international intervention on behalf of various interest groups—especially Irish republicans—who would use the legal structures of the League to engage in "infinitely irritating guerilla warfare."[14] Similarly, American diplomats opposed the 1924 Peace Protocol, intended to strengthen the League's system of international arbitration, as a "new Holy Alliance": one that threatened to inhibit interventions by the United States in the Americas while also (especially in light of Japanese involvement in the Protocol) threatening international legal action over the racial exclusions of its immigration policy.[15] These concerns were amplified in a 1924 article comparing the Peace Protocol to the Holy Alliance by the lawyer and journalist John Hunter Sedgwick. Sedgwick drew on a recent study of the Holy Alliance by William Penn Cresson (the former secretary of the American Embassy in Petrograd, who had taken advantage of the revolution of March 1917 to avail himself of the Imperial Archives) to explain that the Peace Protocol was the "grandchild" of the Holy Alliance. "Americans can learn and should learn from the Holy Alliance what the Peace Protocol may become," Sedgwick warned. "The Super-State shall decide what is a domestic issue. . . . No more doubt can

---

12. Phillips, "The Peace Movement and the Holy Alliance," 411, 431, 432.

13. Ibid., 434.

14. Phillips, *The Confederation of Europe*, 1920, 282, 304, 287.

15. On the politics surrounding the failure of the Peace Protocol, see David D. Burks, "The United States and the Geneva Protocol of 1924: 'A New Holy Alliance'?" *American Historical Review* 64, no. 4 (1959): 891–905; Nicholas Mulder, "The Rise and Fall of Euro-American Inter-State War," *Humanity Journal* 10, no. 1 (2019), http://humanityjournal.org /issue10-1/the-rise-and-fall-of-euro-american-inter-state-war/.

there be of the understanding by those at Geneva that 'domestic issue' means immigration."[16]

By contrast, the analogy between the League of Nations and the Holy Alliance was sharply qualified by the British historian and diplomat Charles Webster (who would later be involved in drafting the Charter of the United Nations). In a paper presented at a 1923 conference, Webster noted that the League's Covenant had often been compared to the Holy Alliance. Webster allowed that there were "superficial resemblances" between the Russian czar of 1815 and the American president of 1919, in terms of the ideals they espoused and their power to imprint them on the postwar settlement. However, Webster concluded that "the comparison is, in fact, very misleading." Webster drew on Harold Temperley's distinction between Alexander's original treaty and Metternich's interventionist "neo-Holy Alliance" to make the point that the League's Covenant had reproduced neither. Alexander's treaty had been "neither a workable instrument, nor a permanent bond," whereas the League's Covenant was "part of the treaties, and of the public law of Europe." Metternich's interventionism had led to the breakdown of the whole system of collective security established in 1815 "because some of its members tried to commit others to obligations which were not implied in the original treaty bonds," whereas the League "is, in no sense, a super-state." In short, the League of Nations was not doomed to repeat the trajectory of the Holy Alliance—a declaration of ideals that had quickly degenerated into a mask for a repressive supranational machine—because the League had anchored its ideals in a concrete political process from the outset: it was "a method, rather than an institution, for advising, conferring, recommending and discussing," which was why, Webster concluded, "historical comparisons with the only other essay in international government of similar magnitude certainly suggest that the League has a good chance of survival."[17]

The Holy Alliance was identified as the most important precursor to the League of Nations in a very different spirit by the Oxford historian J.A.R. Marriott. Marriott's *The European Commonwealth*, published in 1918, was aimed against the ideal of "the unified and consolidated Nation-State" and efforts to construct international systems premised upon it,

16. John Hunter Sedgwick, "The New Holy Alliance," *North American Review* 220, no. 825 (December 1924): 204, 208, 202; William Penn Cresson, *The Holy Alliance: The European Background of the Monroe Doctrine* (New York: Oxford University Press, 1922).

17. H.W.V. Temperley and Charles K. Webster, *The Congress of Vienna, 1814–15, and the Conference of Paris, 1919*, Papers Read at the Fifth International Congress of Historical Sciences, Brussels, 1923, Historical Association Leaflet no. 56 (London, 1923), 16–17, 21, 23.

which had invariably collapsed into rival bids for domination. Marriott lamented that eminent British historians such as John Robert Seeley had joined the Germans in "the cult of the great Nation-State" and had come to treat small states merely as atavistic sources of international instability.[18] Instead Marriott joined the historian and Liberal politician H.A.L. Fisher in defending "the value of small states" whose pluralism and autonomy were responsible (in Fisher's words) for "almost everything which is most precious in our civilization."[19] The name of the solution to the problem of the small state's survival was federalism, Marriott explained; the Holy Alliance was a landmark in the long history of its application to international relations that was especially "pregnant with instruction for the statesmen and the peoples of our own day."[20] Marriott's Quaker background may have primed him to consider Castlereagh's initial judgment of the Holy Alliance as "a piece of sublime mysticism and nonsense" much more skeptically than Phillips or Webster: for Marriott, though it had been "an irreparable failure," the Holy Alliance represented the first plan for an international federation that had reached "embodiment in a definite and accepted scheme."[21] The ultimate reason for the Holy Alliance's failure, according to Marriott, was a "not unreal" dilemma: "Where does the province of 'internal affairs' end and that of 'external affairs' begin?" The resulting problems had not been solved by the revolutionaries of 1789 (whose internal affair had

18. J.A.R. Marriott, *The European Commonwealth: Problems Historical and Diplomatic* (Oxford: Clarendon Press, 1918), 12. For context, see especially Duncan Bell, *The Idea of Greater Britain: Empire and the Future of World Order, 1860–1900* (Princeton: Princeton University Press, 2007); Duncan Bell, *Victorian Visions of Global Order: Empire and International Relations in Nineteenth-Century Political Thought* (Cambridge: Cambridge University Press, 2007); Duncan Bell, *Reordering the World: Essays on Liberalism and Empire* (Princeton: Princeton University Press, 2016).

19. H.A.L. Fisher, *The Value of Small States*, Oxford Pamphlets (London: Oxford University Press, 1914), 12; Marriott, *The European Commonwealth*, 153. A rejection of the nation-state ideal after World War I also prompted the influential investigation of "civic humanism" by Hans Baron in the 1920s, which in turn became the launching point for the flourishing literature on republicanism in the latter half of the twentieth century. See Michael Sonenscher, "Liberty, Autonomy, and Republican Historiography: Civic Humanism in Context," in *Markets, Morals, Politics: Jealousy of Trade and the History of Political Thought*, ed. Béla Kapossy et al. (Cambridge, MA: Harvard University Press, 2018), 161–210.

20. Marriott, *The European Commonwealth*, 355.

21. Ibid., 338, 14. For Marriott's profession of his Quaker background, see J.A.R. Marriott, *Commonwealth or Anarchy? A Survey of Projects of Peace from the Sixteenth to the Twentieth Century* (London: P. Allan, 1937), 5. For another study of the Holy Alliance by a twentieth-century Quaker scholar, see Arthur G. Dorland, "The Origins of the Holy Alliance of 1815," *Transactions of the Royal Society of Canada*, ser. 3, sec. 2, 33 (1939): 59–79.

quickly become an external one), nor by Castlereagh and his successors (whose principle of non-intervention was "more honoured in the breach than in the observance"), nor by anyone else. These were the problems that "penetrate to the heart of the difficulties which confronted the Holy Alliance, and which must confront any attempt to erect now or in the future any supra-national authority."[22]

In the 1940s, with the emergence of a new globalism in the United States, the Holy Alliance again entered into discussions of the possibilities for a new postwar order.[23] As the historian Ernest Knapton put it in 1941, the evident failure of more recent efforts to outlaw war meant that it was time to reconsider the legacy of Holy Alliance: "can an age which has seen impossibly great hopes attached to the signing of the Kellogg-Briand Pact in 1928 afford to be too critical of the Tsar's earlier scheme?"[24] In 1943, Oliver Frederiksen (another historian, then serving in the Foreign Nationalities Branch of the Office of Strategic Services) also wondered how "the Napoleon of 1941" (namely, Adolf Hitler) would end up rewriting the history of the Holy Alliance: "it may well be that Alexander I will go down in history not as the victor over Napoleon but as the far-sighted initiator and champion of the World Federation which was finally achieved after World War II."[25] The Holy Alliance also became available to critics of American foreign policy. In 1944, the political scientist Frederick Schuman (a target of the House Un-American Activities Committee) undertook a comparison of American and British policy with the history of the Holy Alliance: Schuman warned that "the 'Holy Alliance' conception of Anglo-American diplomacy" was redirecting the ideals of the Atlantic Charter into another effort to secure the status quo from a revolutionary threat, thereby ruining the chance of constructing a collective security arrangement with the Soviet Union, and precipitating a postwar reversion to a balance of power

22. Marriott, *The European Commonwealth*, 359. Marriott later restated his views during World War II: J.A.R. Marriott, *Federalism and the Problem of the Small State* (London: G. Allen & Unwin, 1943).

23. On the new globalism, see Or Rosenboim, *The Emergence of Globalism: Visions of World Order in Britain and the United States, 1939–1950* (Princeton: Princeton University Press, 2017); Stephen Wertheim, *Tomorrow, the World: The Birth of U.S. Global Supremacy* (Cambridge, MA: Harvard University Press, 2020).

24. Ernest John Knapton, "The Holy Alliance: A Retrospect," *Queen's Quarterly* 48 (1941): 166. On the Kellogg-Briand Pact, see Oona Hathaway and Scott Shapiro, *The Internationalists: How a Radical Plan to Outlaw War Remade the World* (New York: Simon & Schuster, 2017).

25. O. J. Frederiksen, "Alexander I and His League to End Wars," *Russian Review* 3, no. 1 (1943): 22.

system.[26] Such fears were given more concrete expression by Nathaniel Peffer, a journalist and scholar of China. In 1945, Peffer anticipated that Europe's utter dependence on American credit after the war would create a situation in which even a hint from an American diplomat that a social or economic policy pursued by a European government was "unsound" would empower local elites to suppress it. Without appearing to have intervened in another country's "internal affairs," the United States would have "imposed its own conception of social organization nonetheless" and "vetoed social change, even though desired by the inhabitants of the country." The result would be "one of the mordant ironies of history," Peffer lamented: "America, twice in a generation breaking its tradition to enter European wars in order to preserve democracy and liberty, only to come out as the last stronghold of reaction in the modern world."

> Only a century and a half ago America was in the forefront of progress in social thought, a pioneer in political experiment, a beacon lighting a future of brighter promise to the Old World, indeed in the eyes of the European upper classes a subversive, almost a revolutionary, influence. Is it now, after what is historically only a twinkle in time, to be the symbol of obscurantism, of obstruction to social change, as far behind in social and economic thought as it was advanced in political thought? Is it to be the Holy Alliance of the twentieth century, a Holy Alliance in itself, seeking to preserve economic "legitimism" as the earlier one sought to preserve political "legitimism"? Will it meet the same degree of success and for the same reason—because, like its nineteenth-century precursor, it will be seeking to fly in the face of time?[27]

During the Cold War, the Holy Alliance remained a loaded rhetorical weapon while also serving as a tool of political analysis. In 1961, the popular historian Will Durant declared himself "oppressed by the similarity" he perceived, warning that the United States was turning its treaty organizations "into a Holy Alliance for the suppression of revolutionary movements, wherever arising, as being dangerous to the present structure of Western society."[28] Meanwhile, the French political scientist Raymond Aron employed the Holy Alliance as an analytical term in the theory of

26. Frederick L. Schuman, "The Soviet Union and the Future of Europe," *Current History* 6, no. 34 (June 1944): 470. Cf. Frederick L. Schuman, "The New Holy Alliance," *Current History* 6, no. 33 (May 1944): 391–97.

27. Nathaniel Peffer, "Is America the New Holy Alliance?" *Political Science Quarterly* 60, no. 2 (1945): 166, 168.

28. "'Holy Alliance' Lesson Seen by Will Durant," *Los Angeles Times*, May 6, 1961.

international relations he presented in his 1962 book *Peace and War*: it became the archetype of a "homogenous" system of states with closely related institutional structures and organizing principles. Aron claimed that such "homogenous" systems tended be more stable than "heterogenous" ones, because in "the 'Holy Alliance' situation," the incentive for those in power "to safeguard the shared principle of legitimacy" helped moderate their internal conflicts; this in turn helped dampen "ideological conflict" over measures taken to manage external conflicts. Aron's approach to the Holy Alliance reflects his complex engagement with the political thought of the German jurist Carl Schmitt: Aron was one of several prominent liberals to wrestle with Schmitt's fraught political and intellectual legacy over the course of the twentieth century.[29] In the 1920s, Schmitt had begun invoking the Holy Alliance in order to apply his conclusions about the distinctive character of political associations to international relations, and in particular to criticize the League of Nations and the implications of American involvement in European politics. In a 1927 lecture on the League of Nations, Schmitt had explained that World War I had not been a world war in the same sense that the Napoleonic wars had been European. The earlier conflict had divided all of Europe into juridically equal opposing camps, creating the conditions for a genuinely political resolution: a comprehensive legal ordering of Europe whose "political guarantee" had been the Holy Alliance. World War I had been another European war, but it had been decided by outside intervention (of the United States) on one side, and had not resulted in a European peace like that of 1815. The League of Nations was not a European legal order but a putatively universal one, reflecting a moralization of conflict that in Schmitt's view demolished the political construction of barriers to unlimited war. This was why, Schmitt had concluded, the Holy Alliance, after the accession of France, had represented the concept of European unity "to a much higher degree" than the antipolitical League of Nations.[30] Aron's

29. On Aron and Schmitt, including in relation to Aron's *Peace and War*, see Jan-Werner Müller, *A Dangerous Mind: Carl Schmitt in Post-War European Thought* (New Haven: Yale University Press, 2003), 98–102; Daniel Steinmetz-Jenkins, "Why Did Raymond Aron Write That Carl Schmitt Was Not a Nazi? An Alternative Genealogy of French Liberalism," *Modern Intellectual History* 11, no. 3 (November 2014): 549–74. More generally, see also Samuel Moyn, "Concepts of the Political in Twentieth-Century European Thought," in *The Oxford Handbook of Carl Schmitt*, ed. Jens Meierhenrich and Oliver Simons (New York: Oxford University Press, 2016), 291–311; Iain Stewart, *Raymond Aron and Liberal Thought in the Twentieth Century* (Cambridge: Cambridge University Press, 2020).

30. Carl Schmitt, "Der Völkerbund und Europa (1928)," in *Positionen und Begriffe: Im Kampf mit Weimar-Genf-Versailles, 1923–1939* (Berlin: Duncker & Humblot, 1988), 95.

analysis of the Cold War in terms of the Holy Alliance was an elaboration on this view. According to Aron, the bifurcation of Europe between the United States and the Soviet Union had produced two separate homogeneous blocs, each of which "tends to revive, for internal use, a Holy Alliance formula": "The Holy Alliance against counterrevolution or revolution is in the end necessary to the survival of each of the two blocs."[31] However, as Aron went on to emphasize in his 1973 assessment of American foreign policy, the source of Europe's stability ("each bloc being an equivalent of a Holy Alliance") was absent in other parts of the world. This meant that the stability of international politics outside Europe rested much more precariously on shifting calculations of national interests, and it was incorrect to suppose that these interdependent calculations were still guided by the homogeneous and predictable set of shared assumptions that had been available to stabilize the European diplomacy of the past: "If Nixon and Kissinger want 'a world restored,' as the title of Kissinger's book puts it, what sort of a world do they want?"[32]

In 1957, the same year that Kissinger published his 1954 Harvard dissertation as *A World Restored*, Carl Joachim Friedrich published a series of lectures he had given in 1956 as *Constitutional Reason of State: The Survival of the Constitutional Order*. Friedrich was a German émigré who had become an influential professor of government at Harvard University, and he was one of Kissinger's most important interlocutors in the 1950s.[33]

Schmitt did not hesitate to invoke the Holy Alliance more straightforwardly as a conventional kind of rhetorical weapon on behalf of the German war effort: in his work on international law of 1939–41 he wrote that "the liberal democratic Holy Alliance of the Western powers is today clearly on the side of the past," defending the status quo against the future heralded by the German Reich. Carl Schmitt, "The Großraum Order of International Law with a Ban on Intervention for Spatially Foreign Powers: A Contribution to the Concept of Reich in International Law (1939–1941)," in *Writings on War*, ed. Timothy Nunan (Cambridge: Polity, 2011), 89.

31. Raymond Aron, *Peace and War: A Theory of International Relations*, trans. Richard Howard and Annette Baker Fox (Garden City, NY: Doubleday, 1966), 100–101. For a less sophisticated analysis of Cold War international relations that also began with the Holy Alliance, see Fernand L'Huillier, *De la Sainte-Alliance au Pacte atlantique: Histoire des relations internationales à l'époque contemporaine* (Neuchâtel: Éditions de la Baconnière, 1954).

32. Raymond Aron, *The Imperial Republic: The United States and the World, 1945–1973*, trans. Frank Jellinek (Englewood Cliffs, NJ: Prentice-Hall, 1974), 139, 133.

33. On the close relationship between Kissinger and Friedrich, see Udi Greenberg, "The Limits of Dictatorship and the Origins of Democracy: The Political Theory of Carl J. Friedrich from Weimar to the Cold War," in *The Weimar Moment: Liberalism, Political Theology, and Law*, ed. Leonard V. Kaplan and Rudy Koshar (Lanham, MD: Lexington Books, 2012), 462n45. Kissinger and Friedrich spent 1956 collaborating on a major study of East Germany.

Friedrich's book was a history of political thought organized around the problem that had been at the center of Weimar-era debates: how to equip a constitutional order to defend itself against existential threats without destroying its own normative foundation in the process.[34] According to Friedrich, every constitution presupposed an underlying moral consensus, but it was no longer possible to appeal to the democratic citizenry as the ultimate guardian of its own constitution.[35] Friedrich's argument rested on his seminal work from the early 1930s on the political thought of the early sixteenth-century Calvinist lawyer Johannes Althusius (Friedrich regarded Pierre-Joseph Proudhon as one of Althusius's successors in the history of federalism).[36] Once the Calvinist spiritualization of civic life had faded, leaving behind a residue of rationalizing discipline—in Max Weber's terms, once the Protestant ethic had become the spirit of capitalism, and in Friedrich's terms, once Puritans had become Machiavellians—it was no longer possible to assume that the citizenry or its representatives would necessarily speak with one voice to affirm the moral foundation of its communal life.[37] Federalism was one important political strategy for ensuring the survival of constitutionalism in a disenchanted world: it was a safeguard against homegrown autocrats as well as external dangers. As Friedrich had explained in a 1938 study, all federal systems presupposed "a certain measure of homogeneity." But Wilson and the League of Nations had gone badly astray precisely because they had placed far too

34. On the early twentieth-century roots of Friedrich's genealogy of "constitutional reason of state" in German conceptions of peaceful international competition, see Duncan Kelly, "From King's Prerogative to Constitutional Dictatorship as Reason of State," in *Commerce and Peace in the Enlightenment*, ed. Béla Kapossy, Isaac Nakhimovsky, and Richard Whatmore (Cambridge: Cambridge University Press, 2017), 298–34.

35. The following claims diverge from Udi Greenberg's illuminating account of Friedrich's response to Weber in dissenting from the claim that Friedrich aspired to a much more robust restoration of the "Calvinist roots" of democracy. See Greenberg, "The Limits of Dictatorship and the Origins of Democracy," 453. In fact, what Friedrich saw himself as defending, as he put it later in his life, was "the humanist core of constitutionalism in an age when the religious foundations of constitutionalism have almost vanished." Carl J. Friedrich, *Transcendent Justice: The Religious Dimension of Constitutionalism* (Durham: Duke University Press, 1964), 115.

36. Carl J. Friedrich, ed., *Politica methodice digesta of Johannes Althusius* (Cambridge, MA: Harvard University Press, 1932); Carl J. Friedrich, *Constitutional Government and Democracy: Theory and Practice in Europe and America*, 4th ed. (Waltham: Blaisdell, 1968), 190.

37. Carl J. Friedrich, introduction to *Politica methodice digesta of Johannes Althusius* (Cambridge, MA: Harvard University Press, 1932), lxxiii; Carl J. Friedrich, *Constitutional Reason of State: The Survival of the Constitutional Order* (Providence: Brown University Press, 1957), 74–75. Friedrich had studied with the sociologist Alfred Weber, Max Weber's brother.

much stock in "the ideological aspect" and paid far too little attention to "the real politics of leagues and federations." "It is rather puzzling," Friedrich wrote, "that Wilson, an American and a Southerner at that, should have overlooked the operation of balances of power within federal systems, and the possibility that at the breakdown of the balance, war, a civil war, became inevitable."[38]

The urgent question, in 1938, was how democracies could relearn "the lesson of Napoleon." Like the British in 1800, they had to overcome the temptations of isolationism and appeasement. They had to find a way to band together, hazarding the souls of their constitutions by fighting for their survival. The only alternative was "a long, dark night of fierce struggles between great empires contending for world supremacy."

> Anyone can redraw the map of the world to suit his fancy, grouping it around centers like Tokyo, Moscow, Berlin, Rome, London, and perhaps even Washington. Out of their contest, one victor may emerge supreme, fulfilling Napoleon Bonaparte's dream. Or, more likely, these empires may devour each other as mankind relapses into barbarism.[39]

In order to survive, and save what remained of their souls, the democracies had to solve the problem of a federal balance of power, which Wilson and the League of Nations had failed to address. Friedrich's intensive dialogue (and unlikely personal friendship) with Schmitt during the 1920s and 1930s had made him a sharp critic of reductively moralizing approaches to political ideas and their history, such as the ideal of federalism as an escape from the balance of power (an approach Kissinger would later reproduce by merely flipping the evaluation on its head, presenting the balance of power as the alternative to the chaos of revolution).[40] By contrast, Friedrich treated the idea of a balance of

38. Carl J. Friedrich, *Foreign Policy in the Making: The Search for a New Balance of Power* (New York: W. W. Norton, 1938), 133.

39. Ibid., 254.

40. On Friedrich's close and enduring relationship to Schmitt, see also Greenberg, "The Limits of Dictatorship and the Origins of Democracy," 445–48. In an appendix to *Constitutional Reason of State*, Friedrich reprinted his 1931 review of Friedrich Meinecke's *Die Idee der Staatsräson in der Neueren Geschichte* (1925), which had appeared in English translation in 1956 (the same year as Friedrich's lectures at Brown) as *Machiavellism: The Doctrine of Raison d'état and Its Place in Modern History*. Friedrich's review criticized Meinecke for failing to fully disentangle political concepts from legal ones, thereby creating the "dangerous possibility," as Duncan Kelly puts it, "of moralizing political ideas and flattening out their history." As Kelly points out, Friedrich's review was a close copy of an earlier review of Meinecke by Carl Schmitt. Kelly, "From King's Prerogative to Constitutional Dictatorship as Reason of State," 323. It is tempting to speculate that Friedrich reproduced

power as a political rather than a moral concept, and focused his attention on the causal mechanisms it involved. The lesson Friedrich drew, from Swiss as well as American constitutional history, was that "there has been a *balancer* behind each balance" and that "such a balancer can be found only in a sufficiently strong federal (national) authority."[41] In the absence of a supranational equivalent to a national authority maintaining a balance of power within a federal structure, Friedrich observed, a coalition of League members might have taken the task upon themselves; or the United States might have "stepped into the breach as an effective balancer, if the American people had been willing—as they evidently were not—to sacrifice the war debts for international leadership."[42] Democratic peoples were not only politically divided but "of a divided mind; they desire both peace and the things which lead to war."[43] Democratic majorities were fragile and fleeting; "The people's voice as a means of diplomatic pressure is getting dim," Friedrich wrote. The absence of this voice allowed private interests to take precedence over calculations of constitutional survival, as in the case of American "dollar diplomacy." In such tragic situations, Friedrich allowed, the claim that only an undemocratic statesman could impose coherence on the "divided mind" of a democracy was "almost unanswerable." Friedrich contemplated an intervention by a version of what Carl Schmitt had called a "commissorial dictator": perhaps "some superman, some benevolent master-intriguer, could hold the scales in balance."[44]

In his postwar *Constitutional Reason of State*, Friedrich portrayed the recourse to such a figure as a slide into absolutism. The problem of constitutional survival had not gone away. The difference in Friedrich's postwar outlook, of course, was that his conception of federalism had spread from the United States to Europe. Friedrich, who played a key role assisting the American military authorities with the drafting of the German Basic Law

his review in 1957 with Kissinger as a target, since Kissinger had nothing but praise for Meinecke's approach to "the conflict between the nationalist and the cosmopolitan values of the nineteenth century": Kissinger, *A World Restored*, 344. On Friedrich, Meinecke, and Schmitt, see also Michel Senellart, "Le problème de la raison d'Etat constitutionnelle selon C. J. Friedrich," in *Raison(s) d'etat(s) en Europe: Traditions, usages, recompositions*, ed. Brigitte Krulic (Bern: Peter Lang, 2010), 173–95.

41. Friedrich, *Foreign Policy in the Making*, 126.

42. Ibid., 221.

43. Ibid., 60.

44. Ibid., 75, 131. On Friedrich's engagement with this aspect of Schmitt's thought, see Senellart, "Le problème de la raison d'Etat constitutionnelle selon C. J. Friedrich," 180–87; Nicolas Guilhot, *After the Enlightenment: Political Realism and International Relations in the Mid-Twentieth Century* (Cambridge: Cambridge University Press, 2017), 226–27.

(making him a twentieth-century version of Frédéric-César de la Harpe), saw the United States of the 1940s as having finally assumed the federal balancing role for Europe that it had previously declined. Friedrich also dedicated himself to the cause of European integration and to buttressing the normative consensus that underlay the new federal order (including appeals to the "Judeo-Christian" tradition and shared historical experience that made Europe, as he put it in a 1969 book, "an emergent nation").[45] It was in this context that Friedrich described the United States as having fulfilled the role that the German philosopher Immanuel Kant had once scripted for revolutionary France in his famous 1795 essay on perpetual peace. Friedrich had published a study of Kant's essay in 1948, linking it to the founding of the United Nations (making him a twentieth-century version of Wilhelm Traugott Krug); in 1969, Friedrich again cited a passage from Kant's famous essay:

> If good fortune should bring it to pass that a powerful and enlightened people develops a republican form of government which by nature is inclined toward peace, then such a republic will provide the central core for the federal union of other states.[46]

It was also in this context that Friedrich described the Holy Alliance as an earlier implementation of another famous plan for perpetual peace: the early eighteenth-century proposal for a European Union by Charles Irenée de Castel, Abbé de Saint-Pierre.[47] The Holy Alliance, according to Friedrich, was "an attempt at putting the Abbé Saint-Pierre's ideas to work" through the establishment of a European federation.[48] Alexander's aim had been to institutionalize the guarantor of European constitutionalism, to create a league that would serve to maintain the balance of power in a federal Europe. However, Alexander's institution had been perverted by Metternich into an "instrument of reaction," and the federal

45. Greenberg, "The Limits of Dictatorship and the Origins of Democracy," 444–45. Friedrich specified that by nation he did not mean "that close-knit political and cultural entity which produced the modern European nation-state" but rather a "complex and vast entity," such as India: a highly heterogeneous population that could be organized into "a union of group selves, united by one or more common objectives, a community of communities." Carl J. Friedrich, *Europe: An Emergent Nation?* (New York: Harper & Row, 1969), 213–14.

46. Carl J. Friedrich, *Inevitable Peace* (Cambridge, MA: Harvard University Press, 1948); Friedrich, *Europe*, 6. I have reproduced Friedrich's translation of Kant here.

47. Charles Irenée de Castel, Abbé de Saint-Pierre, *Projet pour rendre la paix perpetuelle en Europe* (Utrecht: A. Schouten, 1713).

48. Friedrich, *Europe*, 7.

character of Europe subsequently disintegrated in the face of the nationalist reaction.[49]

Friedrich's historical juxtapositions seem less unlikely in light of the story told in this book. In fact, they were shared by many other observers of systemic change in the twentieth century, including W.E.B. Du Bois, whose 1945 book *Color and Democracy* placed the Holy Alliance in the "long and desperate line of human endeavor"—stretching from the Achaean League to the Dumbarton Oaks Conference of 1944, where the postwar international organization that became the United Nations was discussed— "seeking some modicum of unity in the government of mankind to displace the horror of the planned murder which is war."[50] Such historical juxtapositions also point toward a further insight. "From the standpoint of the student of international affairs under democratic conditions," Friedrich had written in 1938, "the decisive lesson is this: never to interpret democratic foreign policy merely by states, but always politically and with reference to parties and groups."[51] Wilson's ambition for the United States to become a "central core for the federal union of other states" had ultimately foundered on the fragility of his domestic coalition.[52] Friedrich's own invocations of Kant's essay on perpetual peace in 1948 and 1969 must be approached from a similar angle. They belong to the history of the New Deal coalition and to the career of the liberal Protestantism that sustained many of its international as well as domestic aspirations and endeavors.[53] They also belong to the history of the international monetary system: in the terms discussed in this book, the shift from the *civitas maxima* of the gold standard to a financial system guaranteed by a "central core" of institutions coordinating the policies of sovereign states and intervening in their economies; and the continuing evolution of the federal structure and federative politics of the "new

49. Ibid., 8.

50. W.E.B. Du Bois, *Color and Democracy: Colonies and Peace* (New York: Harcourt, Brace and Company, 1945), 17. On Du Bois's criticism of Dumbarton Oaks for its failure to confront the colonial roots of global conflict, see Adam Dahl, "Constructing Colonial Peoples: W.E.B. Du Bois, the United Nations, and the Politics of Space and Scale," *Modern Intellectual History* 20, no. 3 (2023): 858–82.

51. Friedrich, *Europe*, 114.

52. See Adam Tooze, *The Deluge: The Great War and the Remaking of Global Order, 1916–1931* (New York: Viking, 2014).

53. David A. Hollinger, *Protestants Abroad: How Missionaries Tried to Change the World but Changed America* (Princeton: Princeton University Press, 2017); Gene Zubovich, *Before the Religious Right: Liberal Protestants, Human Rights, and the Polarization of the United States* (Philadelphia: University of Pennsylvania Press, 2022).

international monetary constitution" once envisaged by John Maynard Keynes.[54]

The liberal idea of the Holy Alliance discussed in this book rested on manifestly fragile claims about the availability, capacities, and internal coherence of the "central core" tasked with ultimate responsibility for the collective security and prosperity of a complex federal system. It is an open question whether assessments of the federal systems of the present age will seem less implausible to the hindsight of future generations than initial liberal expectations of the Holy Alliance do today. At the same time, it would be precipitous to conclude from any particular crisis of any particular federal system that the politics of federation is always and everywhere unworkable.[55] Whatever they might turn out to look like, future federative solutions to problems of international competition and constitutional survival will not represent a world restored. The map of the world will continue to change; systems of state finance and social welfare will continue to evolve. A historical understanding of such developments is best served by systematically examining rather than selectively reasserting some of the expectations that they have generated: expectations that, as a twenty-first-century version of the economist Albert Hirschman might put it, often see only "federal shackles" or "federal blessings" without being able to account for the countervailing perspective.[56] In the absence of definitive solutions to the kinds of problems which the liberal idea of the Holy Alliance had sought to address, expectations of their disappearance will continue to diverge from historical experience.

54. See Jamie Martin, *The Meddlers: Sovereignty, Empire, and the Birth of Global Economic Governance* (Cambridge, MA: Harvard University Press, 2022). On the "new international monetary constitution," see Stefan Eich, *The Currency of Politics: The Political Theory of Money from Aristotle to Keynes* (Princeton: Princeton University Press, 2022), 175.

55. Cf. John Dunn, ed., *Contemporary Crisis of the Nation State?* (Oxford: Blackwell, 1995).

56. Albert Hirschman, "Rival Views of Market Society," in *Rival Views of Market Society and Other Recent Essays* (New York: Viking, 1986), 105–41.

A NOTE ON THE TYPE

{⸺⸻⸺}

THIS BOOK has been composed in Miller, a Scotch Roman typeface designed by Matthew Carter and first released by Font Bureau in 1997. It resembles Monticello, the typeface developed for The Papers of Thomas Jefferson in the 1940s by C. H. Griffith and P. J. Conkwright and reinterpreted in digital form by Carter in 2003.

Pleasant Jefferson ("P. J.") Conkwright (1905–1986) was Typographer at Princeton University Press from 1939 to 1970. He was an acclaimed book designer and AIGA Medalist.

The ornament used throughout this book was designed by Pierre Simon Fournier (1712–1768) and was a favorite of Conkwright's, used in his design of the *Princeton University Library Chronicle*.